THE BIRTH OF EUROPE

COLLIDING CONTINENTS

AND

THE DESTINY OF NATIONS

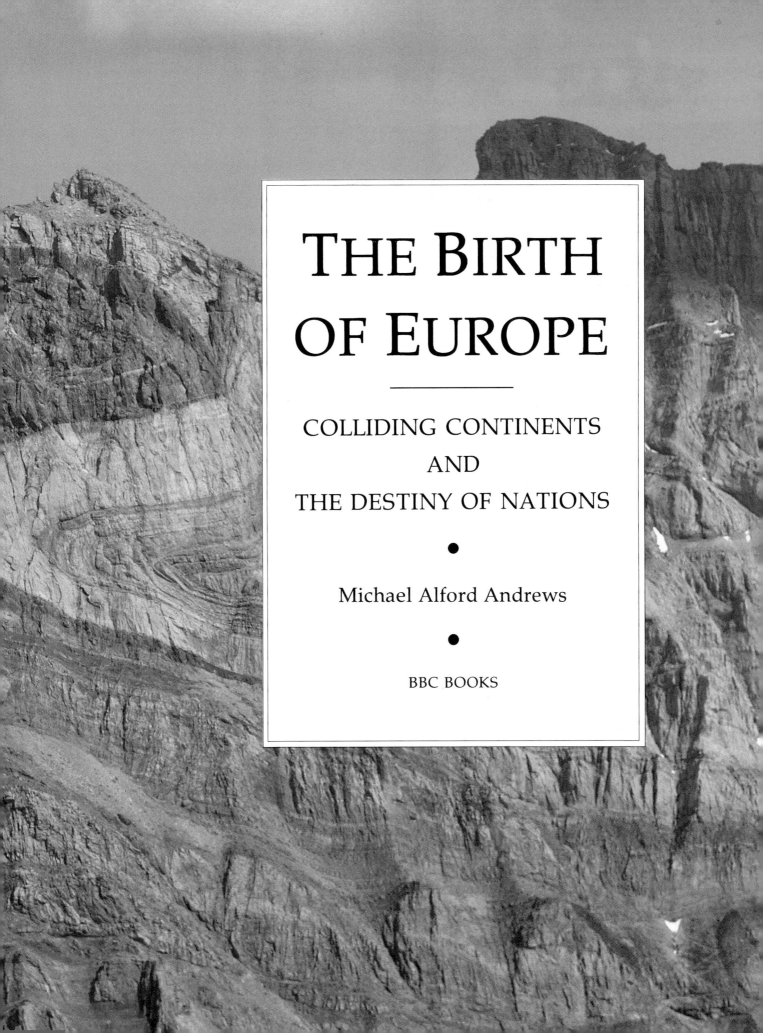

THE BIRTH
OF EUROPE

COLLIDING CONTINENTS
AND
THE DESTINY OF NATIONS

●

Michael Alford Andrews

●

BBC BOOKS

TO R.A.A.

AND

IN MEMORY OF R.S.A.

Published by BBC Books
a division of BBC Enterprises Limited,
Woodlands, 80 Wood Lane, London W12 0TT
First published 1991

Reprinted 1991

Designed by Harry Green
Maps by David Hoxley
Palaeographic maps by Gary Hinks

Set in Palatino by Ace Filmsetting Ltd, Frome
Printed and bound in Great Britain by Clays Ltd, St Ives plc
Colour separations by Technik Ltd, Berkhamsted
Jacket printed by Belmont Press Ltd, Northampton

HALF TITLE
The first signature of modern man in Europe, made some 20,000 years ago by blowing manganese pigment onto a cave wall by mouth or through a hollow bone.

TITLE PAGE
The Dent de Morcles, Switzerland. Limestones which were formed beneath the Tethys ocean that once lay between Europe and Africa have been folded and pushed on top of the European continental crust.

CONTENTS

PHOTOGRAPHIC ACKNOWLEDGEMENTS

Half-title page Ancient Art & Architecture Collection; *title page* Michael Andrews; 14–15 Bruce Coleman/ Hälle Flygare; 18–19 Bruce Coleman/Erwin & Peggy Bauer; 22 *both bottom left* Michael Holford, *all top right* British Museum; 23 BBC; 26–7 Michael Andrews; 31 Michael Holford; 32 Musée d'Aquitaine, *photo* Magnum Photos/Erich Lessing; 33 Musée des Antiquités Nationale, St Germain-en-Laye, *photo* Andrew Lawson; 34–5 GSF Picture Library; 38–9 *left* Oxford Scientific Films/T. C. Middleton; 39 *right* B. & C. Alexander; 40 Michael Andrews; 42 Magnum Photos/Erich Lessing; 48 *both* Michael Andrews; 52–3 Explorer/Plisson; 54–5 Robert Harding Picture Library; 58, 62–3 *both*, 66 *all*, 69, 70 & 74 Michael Andrews; 75 Ashmolean Museum, Oxford; 79 Michael Andrews; 82 *top left* Herakleion Museum, *photo* Michael Andrews, *bottom left* Michael Andrews; 82–3 *right* Zefa Picture Library/Konrad Helbig; 86–7 Michael Andrews; 90 *both* Herakleion Museum, *photos* Michael Andrews; 92–3 Michael Andrews; 94–5 Spectrum Colour Library; 96 Michael Andrews; 98–9 Spectrum Colour Library; 106–7 Museo Gregoriano Etrusco, Vatican, *photo* Scala; 110–11 Spectrum Colour Library; 113 Mensun Bound/Oxford University MARE; 114–15 & 117 Museo di Villa Giulia, Rome, *photos* Michael Andrews; 118–19 Explorer; 122 Musée Archéologique, Châtillon-sur-Seine, *photo* Magnum Photos/Erich Lessing; 125 British Museum; 126 Museo Archeologico, Reggio, *photo* Scala; 127, 130–1 & 135 Michael Andrews; 138 Sealand Aerial Photography; 143 Fergus Beeley; 144 Statens Historiska Museum, Stockholm, *photo* Michael Holford; 146 Musée Condé, Chantilly, *photo* Giraudon; 147 British Library *Add. MS 42,130 f171*; 151 National Trust Photographic Library/Nick Meers; 152 Sandrine Morvan; 156–7 Mansell Collection; 158 British Library *Roy. 14 E IV f28ᵛ*; 162 Victoria & Albert Museum, *photo* Michael Holford; 163 Zefa Picture Library/Shuji Kotoh; 167 Kunsthistorisches Museum, Vienna, *photo* Bridgeman Art Library; 170 Bibliothèque Nationale, Paris, *photo* Lauros/Giraudon; 171 Carnavalet, Paris, *photo* Bulloz; 174–5 *left* Giraudon, 175 *right* Explorer Archives; 178–9 City Gallery, Salford, *photo* E T Archive; 182–3 Walker Art Gallery, Liverpool; 186–7 Science Museum Library, London; 190–1 Ironbridge Gorge Museum Trust; 192 Science Museum Library, London; 194–5 Darlington Museum; 198–9 E T Archive; 202 Explorer Archives; 207 Mary Evans Picture Library; 209 Fried. Krupp GmbH; 210–11 Mary Evans Picture Library; 214 Mansell Collection; 216 Society for Cultural Relations with the USSR; 218 Mary Evans Picture Library; 221 H. Roger-Viollet/Boyer; 224 *both* Quadrant Picture Library; 226 Gosfilmofond Archive, Moscow; 227 Fiat (UK) Ltd; 230–1 *left* National Maritime Museum, London, 231 *right* Popperfoto; 233 Imperial War Museum; 237 Associated Press; 238 H. Roger-Viollet/ Lapi; 241 & 243 Imperial War Museum; 246–7 Zefa Picture Library/E. Streichan; 250–1 *left* Zefa Picture Library/Rossenbach, 251 *right* Michael Andrews; 256–7 *left* Topham Picture Source, 257 *right* Bild am Sonntag, Hamburg; 258–9 Robert Harding Picture Library; 263 Frank Spooner Pictures; 267 Robert Harding Picture Library; 270 Network/Lewis; 274–5 Science Photo Library/Peter Menzel; 276–7 Novosti Press Agency; 280–1 Zefa Picture Library/Buchner; 283 Michael Andrews.

ACKNOWLEDGEMENTS

Comme quelqu'un pourrait dire de moi que j'ai
seulement fait ici un amas de fleurs étrangères,
n'y ayant fourni du mien que le filet à les lier.

One could say that I have only gathered a bunch
of other people's flowers, my own being no more
than the string that binds them.

MONTAIGNE

The idea for the television series, 'The Birth of Europe', has a complex origin. It was developed by myself and Mary Colwell following conversations with Derek Ager who approached me after seeing 'The Making of a Continent', a series of three programmes about the geology and natural history of western America and which I had produced.

Much of the research for the television programmes has been used to write this book and I am indebted to the production team and the experts who helped both them and me to construct the series. It has taken over two years of correspondence, an extensive search of published sources, and countless discussions with scientists and scholars from a score of countries and disciplines to create *The Birth of Europe*. I am therefore grateful to have this opportunity to thank the production team and experts we consulted for their help and guidance.

In particular, I would like to thank: Mick Aston, Jilly Bond, Jill Cook, Neil Cossons, Barry Cunliffe, Christos Doumas, Rod Gayer, John Hassan, Vassileos Lambrinoudakis, Alan Milward, John Ridgway, Anthony Snodgrass, Andrew Sherratt and Tim Young. I would also like to thank Suzanne Webber from BBC Books for her encouragement and support during the writing of the book, and Harry Green for designing and successfully bringing together its various physical elements. Finally, I would like to thank Gary Hinks and David Hoxley for their excellent work on the maps and diagrams in the book.

THE BIRTH OF EUROPE PRODUCTION TEAM

Producers Michael Andrews, Martin Hughes-Games; *Assistant Producer* Karen Bass; *Researchers* Mary Colwell, Fergus Beeley; *Film Research* Lawrence Breen; *Production Assistants* Judy Copeland, Sally Cryer, Sue Storey, Anna Thomas; *Production Secretary* Elizabeth Toogood; *Production Coordinators* Constantin Antonov (USSR), Vladimir Barov (Bulgaria), Maria-Luz Escribano (Spain), Vicky Gellert (Hungary), Tom Goeler (Germany), Sandrine Morvan (France), Marijan Oresnik (Yugoslavia), Sue Pugh Tassios (Greece), Julia Stewart (Rome), Tiziana Toglia (Naples); *Principal Cameramen* Graham Frake, Richard Ganniclifft; *Film Editors* Tim Coope, Elizabeth Thoyts; *Design* Stephen Brownsey, Christine Kinder; *Graphic Design* Kathleen Reeves; *Music* Terry Oldfield; *Narrator* Nigel Anthony; *Executive Producer* Michael Andrews.
A BBC TV Production in association with Arts and Entertainment Network, Coronet/MTI Film and Video, The Seven Network.
Radio 4 Series Producer Mary Colwell.

INTRODUCTION

Thanks to television, we have recently watched from our armchairs as the continent of Europe has been convulsed by some of the greatest political and economic changes since the birth of the nation-states in the fifteenth century. As the western countries drew together into an ever tighter union based on trade, the ideologically-based communist regimes fell to a popular revolution made possible by electronics. It was television which reflected the anger and frustration of the peoples of Eastern Europe back to themselves to swell the numbers demonstrating on the streets. It allowed them to know their power, and us to participate in history when the Berlin Wall came tumbling down.

The television series which in turn inspired this book was planned long before these dramatic events took place, but its purpose, to examine the relationship between society in Europe, and the structure of the continent out of which that civilisation grew, has been given a new urgency and relevance by these sudden and profound political and economic changes. Its theme is that the long-term development and future of Europe depends not so much on the skill of statesmen and generals but on resources like metals, agricultural land, coal and, these days, oil.

As more and more people are educated, and human knowledge expands faster and faster, aided now by information technology, subjects become more and more compartmentalised. Already, a century ago, the great divide had begun to appear between the arts and sciences. But a more fundamental division reaches back two millennia to the time when Christians began to believe that man had been created in the image of God, and was separate from the animals. History and natural history are seldom taught together, and it is only as we have begun to question our very survival as a species on this planet, that we have come to understand the fragility of our industrial civilisation, and that the economy of nature and the ecology of man are inseparable.

I come from a family, not of intellectuals, but of travellers and magpies, and, growing up in a world where I could hunt for Nazi bomb-shrapnel in the garden, and play with real stone axes which my mother had bought at auction, I began to wonder about the connection between the two. It is one of the most important capacities of the human brain to be able to analyse cause and effect in the outside world, and to seek patterns behind events as an aid to survival, but the history I was taught at school seldom made the interesting connections. While I wondered why my cardboard cut-outs of Africa and South America fitted so neatly together, no one ever suggested that, had they not split apart, human history might never have begun. Geology and history were written in different books and taught by different people, while current affairs were ignored completely. I rejoice that my children are taught in a somewhat more broad-minded way, but I left university with an assortment of discrete lumps of knowledge about different subjects from geo-tectonics to Greek pottery, without any idea how they might relate to one another. But I was born curious and I wanted to make those patterns.

I still find it extraordinary that when the resources and the opportunities that the Earth provides have in so many ways shaped history, and continue to do so, that the story of these fundamental relationships has never been told before. If nobody else was going to make the connections then I would, and I had to start with those shifting continents. What I found was that Europe was a unique region, a cross-roads where the drifting continents kept on colliding, and that this turbulent tectonic past had produced not only a complex geology but also the rich endowment of the metals and minerals that a varied geology brings. The crumpling and folding that all those collisions created, coupled with the effects of the ice ages, not only left resources conveniently near the surface, but had jumbled them up so that rocks and thus resources from very different origins lay accessible side by side. This led to an early European dominance of metallurgy and craftsmanship that was to be carried around the world.

Once human technology had advanced enough to make use of a resource, Europe had another geographical advantage over the great undeformed continental land-masses like Africa, Australia and China; it had a highly indented coastline and many large rivers penetrating the interior. Even today, transport of goods by land is far more expensive than by water; two hundred years ago carting was so expensive that coal doubled in price only 15 kilometres from the pit. River- and sea-trade were then enormously important for the prosperity of a society. This topographical advantage is again unique to Europe.

As I learned that ecological catastrophe has again and again, since the days of the first farmers, been brought down by man on his own head, I also came to understand that the very complexity of the cultural and geological heritage of Europe has left Europeans uniquely equipped to develop and change in response to the natural imperatives of the Earth. We now face an environmental challenge all the greater because it is not beyond the wit of the human race to solve it, and, once again, Europe is likely to play a key role in the success or failure of that endeavour. To write this book I took courage from our present desperate need to understand our civilisation's relationship with nature.

I knew that I would infuriate many historians by shifting my focus back from the affairs of men to the greater scheme of nature, but I had already discovered, when making science documentaries, that as a science journalist I had to tread a path between the conflicting opinions of different scientific camps. There is always the danger that a non-specialist will make half-baked conclusions, but it has been gratifying to discover that more often than not my path led in the right direction, and I took comfort from Kipling who wrote:

There are nine and sixty ways of constructing tribal lays,
And every single one of them is right!

Chronology timeline chart. Columns represent world regions; rows represent time periods (B.C. / Years Ago scale at right).

THE REST OF THE WORLD	EGYPT AND N. AFRICA	SYRIA, PALESTINE AND MESOPOTAMIA	ASIA MINOR	GREECE AND AEGEAN	ITALY AND WESTERN MEDITERRANEAN	CENTRAL AND EASTERN EUROPE	WESTERN EUROPE	SCANDINAVIA	Pan-regional / Climate	B.C.	YEARS AGO
							EARLIEST CAVE ART, S.W. FRANCE		ONSET OF COLDEST PHASE OF LAST ICE AGE, SEA LEVEL 100m LOWER THAN TODAY		30000
		WILD BARLEY HARVESTED							HUNTERS ROAM TUNDRA AND STEPPE		27000
		DOMESTICATION OF ANIMALS BEGINS					SOLUTRÉ, BARBED ARROWHEADS; VENUS OF BRASSEMPOUY		MAXIMUM EXTENT OF ICE SHEETS		20000
	FIRST GRINDING STONES FOR WILD SEEDS	CLIMATE WETTER BARLEY AND WHEAT CULTIVATED				MAMMOTHS HUNTED	ANTLER HARPOONS DECORATED TOOLS	FJORDS FLOODED	CLIMATE STARTS TO IMPROVE, ICE SHEETS BEGIN TO RETREAT, SEA LEVEL RISES; NORTH SEA BASIN FLOODED; MOUNTAIN ICE CAPS MELT		14000
JAPAN, EARLIEST KNOWN POTTERY		SHEEP DOMESTICATED		BOATS USED TO CROSS AEGEAN SEA; FRANCHTHI DOMESTICATED SHEEP AND GOATS					LAACHER SEE VOLCANO ERUPTS		10000
		ÇATAL HÜYÜK FOUNDED; ÇAYONU TEPESI NATIVE COPPER IN USE					BRITAIN CUT OFF BY RISING SEA LEVEL	HUNTERS REACH ARCTIC CIRCLE			9000
		ÇATAL HÜYÜK LEAD SMELTED		FARMING VILLAGES		FARMING REACHES BALKANS, KARANOVO; KARANOVO LEVEL II, FIRST COPPER ORES FOUND; LEPENSKI VIR, PERMANENT FISHING SETTLEMENT			POTTERY MAKING IMPORTED FROM EAST; FORESTS SPREAD NORTH		8000
	IRRIGATION					TELLS IN HUNGARIAN PLAIN; POLAND ETC., FLINT MINES					7000
EURASIAN STEPPES, DOMESTICATION OF HORSE	FIRST USE OF SAIL	EARLIEST LINEN TEXTILES		SMALLER ISLANDS COLONISED	TAGUS, SHELL MOUNDS AND STONE BURIAL CHAMBERS	KARANOVO LEVEL V, COPPER SMELTED; VARNA GOLD	BARNENEZ, BRITTANY PASSAGE GRAVES	TYBRIND VIG FISHING VILLAGE			6500
						CLIMAX OF COPPER AGE	FARMING REACHES BRITAIN; CHALAIN, CLAIRVAUX ETC. LAKESIDE VILLAGES; SALZACH VALLEY AUSTRIA, COPPER MINING	DENMARK, AGRICULTURE AND CHAMBER TOMBS			6000
DRYING STEPPES START NOMADIC MIGRATIONS?		MESOPOTAMIA, FIRST URBAN CIVILISATION				KARANOVO VII, CONTACT WITH KURGAN HORSEMEN	GAVR'INNIS, NEWGRANGE, MAES HOWE ETC. PASSAGE GRAVES; WEST KENNET LONG BARROW		INTRODUCTION OF WHEELED CART, MILK AND ALCOHOL		5500
FIRST METALWORK IN CHINA	UNIFICATION OF EGYPT; HIEROGLYPHICS; FIRST EGYPTIAN PYRAMID; GREAT PYRAMID, GIZA; USE OF SAIL; END OF OLD KINGDOM; END OF MIDDLE KINGDOM; NEW KINGDOM; VALLEY OF KINGS TOMBS	TELL BRAK, FIRST PICTOGRAPHS; FIRST LOST WAX CASTING OF COPPER; EARLIEST TIN BRONZE; ROYAL GRAVES AT UR	WOOL-BEARING SHEEP, MILK, ALCOHOL	POLIOCHNI, LEMNOS FIRST EUROPEAN CITY; NAXOS, SIPHNOS LEAD AND SILVER MINING; BRONZE WORKING REACHES TROY		ARSENICAL COPPER BATTLE-AXES; BRONZE AGE; VUČEDOL HILLFORTS	FIRST STONE CIRCLES, STONEHENGE DITCH; TIN MINING IN CORNWALL; SETTLEMENT SHIFTS TO DEFENSIBLE HILLTOPS; STONEHENGE SARSEN CIRCLE	AMBER TRADE; FLINT DAGGERS (NO BRONZE); IMPORTED BRONZE SWORDS	WARRIOR PRINCES REPLACE MORE EGALITARIAN SOCIETY	2000	5000
		BABYLONIAN RULE; HEBREWS MIGRATE TO EGYPT; HITTITES SACK BABYLON	HITTITE EMPIRE FORMED	CRETE; FIRST MINOAN PALACES; SECOND PALACE PERIOD; LINEAR 'A' SCRIPT; 1627/8 B.C. ERUPTION OF THERA		TUMULI			INCREASING SOCIAL PRESSURE; MOST OF NORTHERN EUROPE DEFORESTED; MIDDLE BRONZE AGE		4000
1200 B.C. PERU, CHAVIN PYRAMIDS; 1150 B.C. ICELAND, HEKLA III ERUPTS	1337 B.C. TUTANKHAMUN'S BURIAL; 1166 LAST GREAT PHARAOH RAMESSES III DIES	1200 B.C. HEBREWS SETTLE ISRAEL, SYRIANS SYRIA; COLLAPSE OF LEVANTINE STATES; PHOENICIANS INCREASE TRADING, DEVELOP ALPHABET; 950 ASSYRIAN EMPIRE FOUNDED		1500 FALL OF KNOSSOS; MYCENAEANS; 1500 GOLD MASKS, MYCENAE; 1300 B.C. MYCENAEAN EMPIRE EXPANDS; 1250 B.C. TROJAN WAR; 1200 COLLAPSE OF HITTITE EMPIRE; 1130 FALL OF MYCENAE; CRETE, FROST KILLS OLIVES?					NORTHERN FORESTS RETREAT SOUTH, ALPINE GLACIERS ADVANCE; MOST FAVOURABLE CLIMATE	1500	3500
	750 CARTHAGE FOUNDED BY PHOENICIANS	612 FALL OF ASSYRIAN EMPIRE; 550 CYRUS FOUNDS PERSIAN EMPIRE; 521 PERSIAN RULE FROM NILE TO INDUS	650 FIRST COINS GREEK COLONIES ON COAST; 600 ATHENS CONTROLS HELLESPONT (DARDANELLES); 545 PERSIANS CONQUER LYDIA; 494 IONIAN REVOLT AGAINST PERSIANS	IRON AGE BEGINS; DARK AGES; POPULATION EXPANDS; 800 CITY STATES BEGIN; 776 FIRST GAMES AT OLYMPIA; 730 EXPANSION OF GREEK COLONIES OVERSEAS TO FORM MAGNA GRAECIA; 540 CORINTH, TEMPLE OF APOLLO; 505 ATHENS, DEMOCRACY ESTABLISHED; 490 PERSIANS DEFEATED AT MARATHON; 480 PERSIANS DEFEATED AT SALAMIS AND PLATAEA; 446 PARTHENON BEGUN; 431-404 PELOPONNESIAN WARS BETWEEN ATHENS AND SPARTA	VILLANOVAN CULTURE IN TUSCANY; 850 FIRST VILLAGE AT ROME; 770 EUBOEAN GREEKS FOUND PITHEKOUSSAI; 753 TRADITIONAL FOUNDING OF ROME; 750 ELBA, IRON SMELTING; 733 SICILY, CORINTHIANS FOUND SYRACUSE, GREEK COLONIES ON COAST OF SOUTHERN ITALY; 700 LEAGUE OF 12 ETRUSCAN CITY STATES; 550 BANDITACCIA, ETRUSCAN TOMBS, PEAK OF ETRUSCAN POWER; ETRUSCAN KINGS EXPELLED; 510 FOUNDATION OF ROMAN REPUBLIC; 480 HIMERA, CARTHAGINIANS AND ETRUSCANS DEFEATED BY GREEKS; 474 CUMAE, ETRUSCANS DEFEATED BY GREEKS FROM SYRACUSE; 470 NAPLES FOUNDED BY GREEKS		HILLFORTS; 800 CELTIC HALLSTATT CULTURE, PRESTIGE WAGON BURIALS, CADIZ FOUNDED BY PHOENICIANS; LA TÈNE CULTURE, RHONE WINE TRADE BEGINS; C.650 ETRUSCANS FOUND ST BLAISE; 600 GREEKS FOUND MARSEILLES; 520 VIX TREASURE CHARIOT BURIALS; GREEK COASTAL COLONIES		MARGINAL LANDS LOST TO AGRICULTURE	1000 / 750 / 500	3000 / 750 / 500
329 INDIA CONQUERED BY ALEXANDER; 207 ICELAND, LAKI ERUPTS, FAMINE IN CHINA, BLACK HUNS SWEEP WEST	241-146 ROMANS FIGHT THREE PUNIC WARS AGAINST CARTHAGINIANS; 149 ROMANS DESTROY CARTHAGE; 30 ROME RULES EGYPT	CONQUERED BY ALEXANDER; 4 B.C. BIRTH OF CHRIST	334 ALEXANDER THE GREAT'S CONQUESTS	146 ROMANS SACK CORINTH, RULE GREECE	390 ROME SACKED BY CELTS; 290 ROMANS CONQUER CENTRAL ITALY; 241 ROMAN CONQUEST OF SICILY; 218 HANNIBAL CROSSES ALPS AND INVADES ITALY; C.200 ROMAN CONQUEST OF ETRURIA; 49-44 CAESAR DICTATOR; 44 CAESAR MURDERED; 27 AUGUSTUS FIRST ROMAN EMPEROR; 79 COLOSSEUM COMPLETED, ERUPTION OF VESUVIUS		206 ROMAN CONQUEST OF SPAIN; 105 TEUTON INVASION DEFEATED AT AIX-EN-PROVENCE; 58 CAESAR BEGINS CONQUEST OF GAUL; 52 VERCINGETORIX DEFEATED AT ALESIA; 43 ROMAN INVASION OF BRITAIN		117 ROMAN EMPIRE REACHES GREATEST EXTENT	250 / 0 AD	250 / 0 AD

CHRONOLOGY

Movement of the continental plates

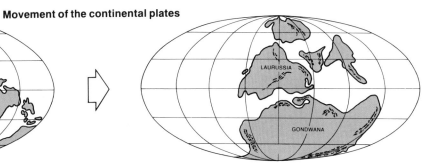

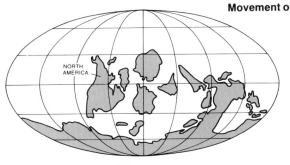

440 million years ago
Caledonian Mountains formed

320 million years ago
Hercynean Mountains and coal fields formed

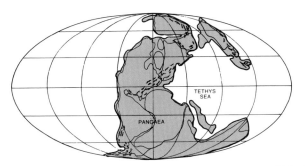

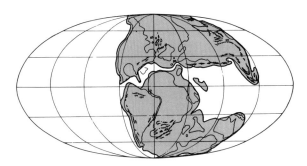

250 million years ago

160 million years ago
Limestone and chalk
seas flood continents

135 million years ago

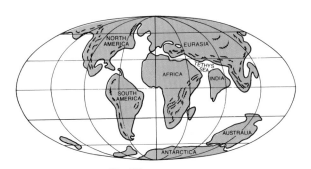

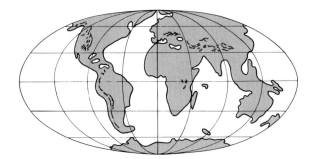

45 million years ago
Alps are formed

Present day continental plates

CHILDREN OF
THE ICE AGES

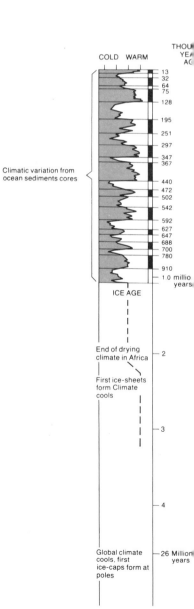

Climatic variation from
ocean sediments cores

THOU[
YE/
A[

COLD WARM

13
32
64
75
128
195
251
297
347
367
440
472
502
542
592
627
647
688
700
780
910
1.0 millio
years

ICE AGE

End of drying
climate in Africa   2

First ice-sheets
form Climate
cools

3

4

Global climate   26 Million
cools, first   years
ice-caps form at
poles

Compared with the eruptions that had happened before in the Rift Valley it
was not large, but when dawn broke there was no birdsong. And when
the family emerged from their shelter beneath the rocks they saw a land transformed, drained of all tropical colour. The ash fall had covered everything in a
deep grey mantle, its weight had torn the limbs from the trees and the low sun
could now draw sharp shadows of the trunks across the ground. This place, that
we now call Laetoli in northern Tanzania but which was their home, was hushed
with the stillness of death. Now that the volcano had ceased to roar, even the ants
were silent. They must leave. There was no water, no streams even in this grey
skeleton forest, and with their child they set off in search of other survivors and a
new life. As they walked their footsteps crunched in the newly fallen pumice ash
in the unnatural silence.

Three and a half million years later their footsteps were discovered, fossilised
in the ash. It was less than ten years after Neil Armstrong had left the imprint of
his boot in the dust of the moon. That great leap of mankind out of Africa into
space had been achieved thanks to the evolution of the human brain. But
although in his splendid isolation the astronaut could look down on the distant
planet of his birth, he could not survive without a whole technological parapher-
nalia of equipment, food and oxygen brought with him from the Earth. Though
he was an American, that scientific and mechanical technology was born in
Europe; and it was in Europe, too, that much of early man's cultural development
had taken place.

This is the story of the long journey that got us to where we are now. But each
step of the way was taken in response to opportunities provided by the resources
of the land, be they mineral, vegetable or animal. Because, for all our vanity, we
can never escape our place as fellow animals dependent on the whole life system
of the Earth. So this is the tale of the fascinating relationship between the developing civilisation of Europe and the continent that formed its cradle; of the rise
and fall of its mountains, as well as cities, industries and nations. With some
exceptions, it is not an account of kings and campaigns and human ambition. It is
told to a slower rhythm than that of human generations. Instead it explores our
profound dependence on the resources left within our grasp by the shifting con-

OVERLEAF For most of the last million and a half years northern Europe was covered by ice sheets similar to those in Eastern Greenland.

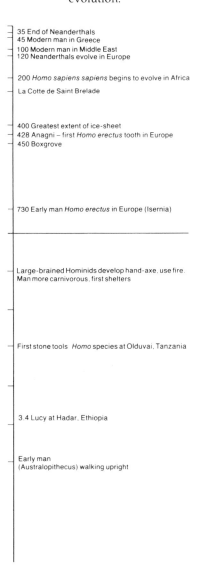

The ice ages and human evolution.

35 End of Neanderthals
45 Modern man in Middle East
100 Modern man in Middle East
120 Neanderthals evolve in Europe

200 *Homo sapiens sapiens* begins to evolve in Africa
La Cotte de Saint Brelade

400 Greatest extent of ice-sheet
428 Anagni – first *Homo erectus* tooth in Europe
450 Boxgrove

730 Early man *Homo erectus* in Europe (Isernia)

Large-brained Hominids develop hand-axe, use fire.
Man more carnivorous, first shelters

First stone tools *Homo* species at Olduvai, Tanzania

3.4 Lucy at Hadar, Ethiopia

Early man
(Australopithecus) walking upright

tinents; and how our ecological relationship with one particularly complex continent changed, as new ideas and technologies made available ever more of the riches that lay in the mountains, meadows and seas.

The changing climate

As the twentieth century comes to a close, it does so amid mounting concern at the scale of our domination of the natural world and the sustainability of our complex industrial civilisation. In particular, scientists are worried that by burning ever-increasing amounts of fossil fuels we are warming the atmosphere: conducting a gigantic experiment with the planet with no knowledge of the possible consequences, heedlessly setting off into the unknown. Yet ironically the climate never has been constant, and throughout its history the Earth has seen epochs of dramatic changes from ice age to short periods of warmer temperatures.

About two and a half million years ago wind-blown sediments were scattered over the northern Pacific Ocean, showing that the deserts of the world were spreading. More and more water was being locked up in the ice at the poles as the climate cooled towards an ice age, reducing the size of the oceans and making the atmosphere drier. Pollen analysis shows that in Africa habitats changed at about the same time from woods to more open shrub-covered savannah. The number of species adapted to life on these plains steadily increased: elephants, antelopes, horses, pigs, primates and carnivores. As the changing environment allowed some individuals to take advantage of the new opportunities, they evolved into new species, while other less adaptable creatures of the diminishing forest lost out. The classic cast of animals that now draw the tourists to the Rift Valley national parks was assembling.

The fragments of fossil evidence suggest that it was in this slowly changing world that early man evolved in different directions. By the end of this drying out, some two million years ago, as many as five different species of erect-standing, large-brained hominids (the Australopithecines) co-existed in Africa, each finely adapted to exploit a different set of natural resources. Only one of them was to survive to stand at the root of the human family tree.

Because we are used to our own climatic regime it seems scarcely credible that since then – for roughly the last million and a half years – northern Europe has been blanketed with ice nine tenths of the time. In Scotland it was up to 1500 metres thick (1800 metres over Scandinavia). In fact there has been not just one ice age but about seventeen, with the warm intervals between far shorter than the cold stages; and the last 10,000 years is but a respite in an age of ice.

The start of an ice age requires a temperature drop of only 4 degrees Celsius in European latitudes (10 degrees at the poles) and scientists now believe that the switch to a glacial epoch can occur in as little as a few hundred years. Once a sufficient thickness of ice has built up it can also spread surprisingly fast – as much as several kilometres a year for a thousand years. At its greatest extent, 400,000 years ago, the northern icecap reached as far south as the north coast of Devon, Hanover, Cracow and Kiev. To the south an arctic tundra and steppe extended to the Pyrenees, northern Italy and the Black Sea.

Nobody is sure why ice ages come and go but we do know a number of possible factors that may be causes. For example, as the Earth swings through space it does not remain at an equal distance from the sun. Over a period of about 96,000 years its orbit changes from circular to more elliptical. It also wobbles very slowly like a spinning top and rotates its axis around. This means that the poles can get warmer in summer and colder in winter. Over the same period even the tilt of the

axis changes by about three degrees, like the roll of a ship, again affecting the incidence of the sun's rays and thus slightly changing the amount of energy that warms the atmosphere and the ground beneath. The combination of these movements adds up to a temperature difference of only one or two degrees Celsius, but this can be enough to allow the polar icecaps to build up, and the combined cycle roughly correlates to the coming and going of the ice, with the coldest periods every 100,000 years.

Another factor that influences climate is that as the restless continents drift across the surface of the globe they affect the circulation patterns of major ocean currents, and a continent drifting across either of the poles can, by blocking the circulation of warm water from the tropics, encourage the development of an ice sheet. At present the configuration of the continents is most unusual, one lies squarely across the south pole, but the north pole, though an ocean, is almost completely hemmed in by land. For the last 30 million years or so this has had an important effect on the climate, as massive icecaps can build up in the south, but in the north, although the sea can freeze, the restricted ocean circulation still supplies warmth to prevent a massive build-up of ice.

When whole continents collide to build great mountain ranges such as the Himalayas these can block the passage of major weather systems like the monsoons. While less dramatic distortions of the Earth's crust can cause volcanic eruptions which may throw huge clouds of gas and ash high into the atmosphere, intercepting the radiation from the sun, and thus lowering the temperature.

The amount of radiation produced by the sun varies too on a much shorter time scale. Sunspots are areas of the surface of the sun that are cooler, and thus darker, than their surroundings. They can be several times the diameter of the Earth in size, and last from a few hours to several months. Sunspots are associated with intense solar activity and flares which produce showers of high-energy particles responsible for geomagnetic storms and the aurora borealis or northern lights. Their numbers increase and decrease over a period of about eleven years, and this sunspot cycle is known to affect the climate. For example, few sunspots were reported between 1640 and 1710, a period when the Thames froze and when glaciers advanced in the Alps. As I write this in 1990, particularly intense sunspot activity is causing damage to satellites and has induced fluctuations of current in high-voltage power-lines large enough to trigger a temporary shutdown of the Canadian electrical power system.

No doubt it is a combination of many factors that influences climatic change, and the trigger that finally causes an ice age may even be the feedback of biological cycles dependent on solar energy, such as the growth of plankton in the upper level of the oceans. These continuous complex fluctuations make it extremely difficult to gauge the effect of modern human activity on the global climate. Yet as our knowledge increases, the opposite relationship – how climate has affected humankind – is becoming clearer, and it appears that the changing climate may indeed have provided the environmental conditions that allowed the evolution of a large brain to set us apart from the other apes.

African origins

The ecological history of mankind in Europe begins with our relationship with the natural world. We still share 98 per cent of our genes with chimpanzees, and in the darkness of African prehistory the causes of the evolution of the other 2 per cent are far from clear. The story has been pieced together from stone tools and a few barrow-loads of fragments of bone into a pattern which changes almost from year to year as new discoveries are made. But some incontrovertible facts stand out, and some discoveries in the last two decades have been remarkable. For example, the fossils as well as the footprints found in the volcanic ash at Laetoli show beyond doubt that the critical evolutionary change to upright walking had already been made at least 4 million years ago.

Then the discovery of a hominid skeleton at Hadar in Ethiopia in 1974 was like an illuminating flash of lightning. Nicknamed Lucy (the shape of the pelvic bone revealed that she was a female), she was remarkable in almost every way. There was almost half a skeleton, when most other ancient hominid remains were no more than fragments. She was adult but little more than a metre tall, and her brain was similar in size to that of a chimpanzee, far too small to be human. She probably lived in trees, venturing on to the ground only when necessary, but she certainly walked upright some 3.4 million years ago. Her small skull size immediately disproved one theory: that the development of manual dexterity and a large brain had led to more tool-using and thus had forced apes into an upright stance so that they could carry more things around with them. Clearly, walking upright had come first. It may be that as hominids left the shelter of the forest for open grasslands, the ability to stand up to look around for predators improved their chances of survival.

Lucy's combination of human and ape-like traits established her as the earliest example of the man-like hominids called the Australopithecines. About 2.6 million years ago, as the African climate dried out, different populations of Lucy's Australopithecine descendants apparently evolved apart into diverse species as they became better adapted to different diets and environments. For instance, the Robust Paranthropines, which have massive jaws and a bony crest along the top of the skull with huge jaw-muscles attached, have heavily scratched and pitted teeth that suggest a diet of hard nuts and seeds and fibrous plant food. They had evolved physically and become specialised to eat foods too tough for other hominids. By contrast other populations evolved by making the crucial discovery of learning to turn a round stone into a cutting edge and thus developing the first stone tools. These were choppers with sharp edges made by striking flakes off the edge of one stone with blows from another, a process which needs skill, planning and manual dexterity. The use of these tools was an adaptation which led away from the path of specialised life that required physical adaptation to specific food resources. Instead it was a step in the direction of intelligence and adaptability, which were to become mankind's greatest assets.

Lacking sharp canine teeth it is almost impossible for a human to get through the hide of an antelope without some kind of sharp implement, and before the use of stone tools, early hominids may have had to hunt small animals they could rip apart, or else scavenge from larger carcasses already ripped open by other animals. Early man was not alone in using tools. Egyptian vultures use stones to break eggs, as do otters to crack crabs. Galapagos finches use cactus spines to pry grubs out of holes, and chimpanzees use twigs to fish termites out of logs and leaves to soak rainwater out of holes in trees. But the difference was that rather than just copying the use of sticks and stones, humans deliberately manufactured stone tools in a way that needed forethought and ingenuity.

Each time the climate dried out, the less adaptable species succumbed; and each time the climate improved again, the survivors were able to evolve to take advantage of new unused resources. It was a regime that gave an enormous evolutionary advantage to adaptability. By 1.6 million years ago our ancestors stood 1.5 metres tall and had a skeleton differing only slightly from our own. It is at this

time that hominid teeth are first found with the particular pattern of pitting characteristic of a more carnivorous diet, and becoming more carnivorous allows a species to disperse over a much wider selection of habitats. This is because one kind of meat is much like another, whereas vegetarians specialising in the plants of one kind of habitat have mortgaged their fate to its survival. Meat also provides far more nutrition or energy, weight for weight, than most plants, and a day's food is far less bulky. This allows less time to be spent actually eating, though carnivores may have to travel further for their food, encouraging them to explore further afield.

With a large brain and a hunger for meat, there was a need for improved stone tools in order to butcher large animals. In a repeatedly changing environment, early man had the advantages of being partly carnivorous and having a large brain. Comparing species, larger brains correlate with greater intelligence, and this allowed the evolution of social behaviour like group hunting (although the early humans probably could not speak); and soon the modification of his personal environment. The first remains of shelters, found in the Olduvai Gorge of Tanzania, are 1.8 million years old, and although it is still not certain when a human first snatched up a flaming brand from a bush fire and found that fire could be tamed, it was probably at least a million and a half years ago. Of course it

Musk-oxen, last survivors of the great cold-adapted animals that roamed northern Europe as the ice sheets retreated.

The greatest extent of the ice sheets, about 400,000 years ago.

had enormously important consequences. Aided by fire for warmth, defence against predators and probably for cooking meat, and able to construct shelters, the first bands of families could now range across less hospitable habitats, and move north out of Africa.

We still know next to nothing about the lives of these families, but about 1.5 million years ago a new sophisticated and often beautiful kind of stone tool began to be made – the Acheulian handaxe. These were formed by striking flakes from all round a piece of flint or other stone which fractured to a sharp edge, and were worked on both faces. They are far more than casually broken stones, and they are found in both Africa and Europe.

Man in Europe

During the ice ages, when the sea level fell dramatically, Sicily was at times joined to the toe of Italy, and Malta to Sicily, but there was still a deep strait of water between Africa and Europe both there and at Gibraltar, and so the first humans probably arrived in Europe via a land bridge at the Dardanelles. Much of the Aegean and Adriatic seas would have been fertile plains, and the mountains of Greece were surrounded by broad fertile lowlands, making the journey to the west much easier via this route.

This migration was not in itself remarkable. Early man was just another scavenger and predator, and he arrived in Europe at the same time as the lion, leopard, hyena and wolf. At this stage he would have been able to move from Africa into northern areas with a similar savannah grassland habitat, and we know from the bones found in the famous caves at Zhoukoudian in China that he was able to hunt and kill elephant, rhinoceros, horse, bison and other large animals, which must have required quite sophisticated teamwork. Even in Europe the grasslands and their animals were not so different from his ancestral habitat in Africa. But there were other big differences. The climate in Europe, though warmer than today, was much more seasonal than that of the tropics, and, unlike Africa, Europe is a comparatively young continent, with a far more complex geology and geography than that of the tropical areas left behind. So as man moved north he

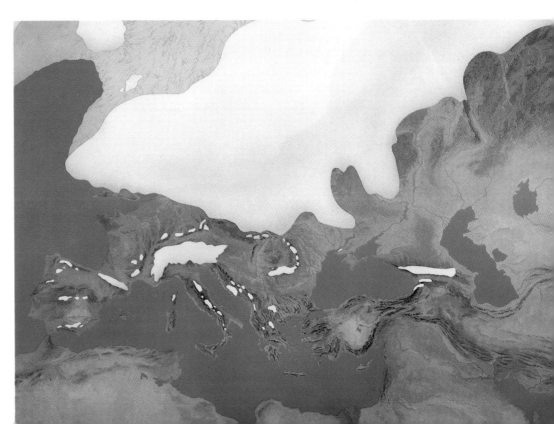

Early man sites.

was challenged by new climatic stresses and aided by new natural resources that were crucial to the social development of the species that was later to dominate the world.

Early man sites.

The task of tracking down the first movements of our ancestors in Europe is not easy. With, so far, a total lack of human fossils until the last half million years, the evidence for human occupation rests on stone artefacts. Such a collection of tools was found in 1978 at the site of La Pineta at Isernia in the Molise Mountains of central Italy by contractors digging an underpass beneath a railway for a trunk road. Five metres below the surface they uncovered a layer of massive fossil bones. La Pineta rates high on the scale of unattractive surroundings. To drive to the site means negotiating a maze of roads like aerial spaghetti and tiny streets lined by houses propped apart by timbers following the 1980 earthquake; evidence of the tectonic forces that also covered and preserved the site beneath volcanic ash. A metal shed now covers the excavation which is as hot as an oven in summer, but here lies what is probably the earliest site of human occupation found in Europe to date.

Painstaking excavation has revealed an extraordinary spectacle: a jumbled mass of huge bones of bison, rhinoceros, straight-tusked elephant (larger than the African elephant), bears, hippopotami, giant deer, warthogs and lions; an amazing inventory of the large animal life of the surrounding grassland. Scattered throughout the two levels of fossil bones, which are separated by a layer of flood debris, are thousands of stone tools: large limestone choppers and small worked flint flakes. Round areas of reddened clay, apparently baked, suggest the sites of fires, and several cobbles have even been found coloured with red and yellow ochre (although their purpose is unknown, it is very unlikely to have happened naturally). The site has been dated as 730,000 years old.

From the bones and pollen collected on the site, scientists can show that Isernia was an area of grassland savannah with sparse trees, having a dry climate and a short rainy season – very similar to East Africa today. The camp was beside a lake or swampy river, and the occupants appear to have used the large bones of the big animals: elephant tusks and femurs, bison skulls and so on, to consolidate and build up an artificial island in the marshy ground, possibly to defend themselves against predators. If this is true, it is the first defensive structure in Europe, and further evidence of the increasing complexity of human thought and behaviour. It is suggested that large lumps of travertine rock, which had been carried some distance, were placed in a rough circle to form the base of hut walls. The bones of birds, amphibians, reptiles and fish suggest that the occupants had a varied diet. Already a large section of the site has been removed and reconstructed in the safety of a new museum at Isernia.

At another central Italian site, Fontana Ranuccio at Anagni, early man fashioned tools, including one magnificent handaxe, not from stone but from the large bones of elephants (these being used because the area was covered in volcanic ash with few suitable stones on the surface). Here, too, one of the earliest human fossils in Europe was discovered, a tooth 428,000 years old (teeth are more resistant to decay than bones, so in sites less favourable to fossilisation they are often the only evidence found).

More evocative evidence of early man's residence in Europe appears at Terra Amata, Nice, where a site on the beach shows signs of repeated occupation as a seasonal camp some 400,000 years ago. Set in the earth beside a hearth, like a seal of ownership on the soil of Europe, is a footprint. Because the flint chippings show little sign of disturbance by trampling, it seems that the site was only used for short periods, and the presence of broom pollen shows that those were in early spring. Warmed by fire, early man had already taken the first step towards emancipating himself from the direct effects of climate, and, no longer fixed in one habitat, was clearly exploiting different ecosystems, but he still had to follow the available food supply. This meant that it was hard to stay in one place all the year round when larger animals migrated and vegetable foods were seasonal. At Terra Amata, as well as hunting animals as varied in size as elephants and rabbits, the community caught birds, collected shellfish, and were skilful enough with tools to have learned somehow to catch fish.

At Bilzingsleben on the River Wipper between Halle and Erfurt in East Germany, a warm spring flowing into a lake probably kept it free of ice in winter, making it an ideal site for a winter encampment of hunter-gatherers. The mixture of marsh, woodland and grassland offered a wide range of food resources, from fish, water birds and beaver for furs (with the implication of possible clothes), to wild pigs and deer, and the big game of rhinoceros, elephants and horses. And the hot spring even offered the possibility of warm baths. The travertine deposited by the hot water (like the fur on the inside of a kettle) has preserved not only stone tools but the remains of shelters, wooden tools such as rods, and even leaves, fruits and berries. There the remains of a human skull were found, some 400,000 years old, and it is possible to piece together a few more aspects of such an individual's life. Different areas were used for tool-making – with large stone and bone anvils and hammer-stones, and for butchery – with the bones of large animals like rhinoceros showing the cuts from stone tools.

Few tool remains are more informative than those found at Boxgrove in West Sussex. There a sand and gravel quarry on the edge of the South Downs has cut a section through the sediments of the last half million years to reveal ancient tool-making 'workshops'. At Boxgrove, too, several different kinds of habitat are close by: woodland and grassland on the downs, the flat coastal marshy strip which was a corridor for larger animals like deer (the butchered bones of four species have been found) and the tidal area itself. These combined, as they had at Terra Amata and Bilzingsleben, to provide a rich supply of alternative foods. A multi-disciplinary team of scientists has analysed the flora and fauna, and can show that rhinoceros, wolf, bear, horse and bison were among the large animals, while smaller ones such as badger, mink, rabbits, lemmings and birch-mice, together with beavers, demonstrate the great ecological diversity of the area some 450,000 years ago.

The ancient shoreline was at the highest level reached in the ice ages, but the sea was retreating. The hunters moved down from their camps on the wooded downland on top of a 20-metre cliff to hunt along a strip of flat brackish marshy land at its foot. The chalk cliff was eroding in places, providing an abundant supply of nodular flints which were knapped to form the classic Acheulian biface handaxes. One remarkable feature of the site is that the chippings still lie as they fell almost half a million years ago, becoming a kind of flint snapshot of an instant in the life of individual hunters. The cores and chippings can be reassembled to show not only exactly how they were made, but even whether the hunter was standing up or sitting down as he worked, and whether he was right or left handed. The archaeologists have shown by comparison with modern knapping that the tools were roughed out by impact with another flint, but that a soft hammer was used for finishing them – almost certainly a deer antler. The tools were apparently made quite casually on the spot for use in skinning and butchering, rather than being carried around as we would carry a precious knife, which

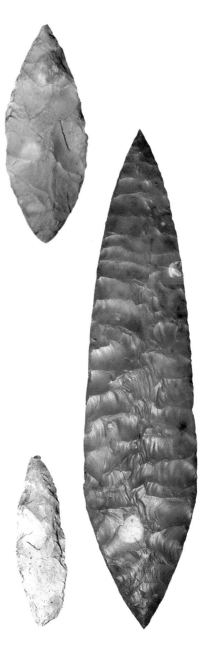

ABOVE By the last ice age modern man had learned to pressure-flake flint to make delicate points and blades like these from Solutré.

LEFT The earliest stone tools like these stone choppers from the Olduvai gorge were made by striking flakes off one end of a large pebble of lava or quartz, about 2.5 million years ago.

suggests that they were easily made, and as a result were not considered by their makers to be particularly valuable. One collection of chippings even tells a very human story: having worked away at a flint for some time, the individual came upon a fault in the stone which meant it was impossible to continue. In a fit of temper he smashed it to pieces with a blow.

But the site also demonstrates the close connection between climate and human occupation. Shortly after it was abandoned, the scattered tools were covered by coarse, flinty gravels eroded from the cliff above. These flints were shattered by frost; tell-tale evidence of the onset of another ice age which drove the hunters away to the south. At that time, Britain was joined to Europe by a chalk peninsula stretching from the Isle of Wight to the Isle of Thanet. The Rhine then flowed out to the North Sea, and as the global sea level fell the Thames became its tributary, while the Seine and the Somme flowed westwards towards the Atlantic. Then as the ice advanced south it acted as a huge dam between Britain and Scandinavia, and the North Sea turned into a lake, which filled steadily until it overflowed across the peninsula. As the overflow grew from a trickle to a torrent it rapidly cut away the chalk until a catastrophic flood carved out the Strait of Dover, to leave the famous chalk cliffs to north and south. The residents of Boxgrove had already moved on as the woods and animals retreated south before the ice, and it may have been too cold for any of them to witness the amazing spectacle of the flood.

At such times Europe presented a bleak picture. Southern Britain and also uplands like the Massif Central were treeless tundra. In the Netherlands there was a polar desert, and icecaps covered all the mountain ranges as far south as Crete. But large areas of Europe were cold steppe, allowing animals such as the saiga antelope (now at home in central Russia) to reach Britain and western France. The atmosphere was dry with bitterly cold strong winds. But a crucial factor for the future were small sheltered areas with warmer microclimates which became refuges where trees like limes and olives could keep a foothold on the continent. As the climate changed, these vegetational zones were constantly fluctuating, and the changing conditions provided both challenge and opportunity to early man.

ABOVE Animated reconstruction of Neanderthal man.

The Neanderthals

Each time the polar icecaps grew and locked up water, the falling ocean levels exposed huge areas of the continental shelf for colonisation by both animals and the men who pursued them. For example, the island of Jersey, though by accident of history British, is only 21 kilometres from the coast of France and separated by water less than 20 metres deep; so for long periods it was a part of continental Europe. The south coast of the present island is fringed by impressive cliffs; and in one of the southern promontories is a T-shaped ravine containing one of the most important archaeological sequences in Europe. Over 50 metres deep, it records the changing climate and fauna over about a quarter of a million years – a period that included several ice ages.

This dramatic cleft in the cliffs, called La Cotte de Saint Brelade, was used by people only during 'windows' of temperate climate, when it was joined to the mainland but when the climate was not too cold (at the peak of the ice ages the mean January temperature would have been −40 degrees Celsius, equivalent to the coldest part of Siberia today). At such times it lay at the tip of a largely wooded peninsula, and it was used about 250,000 years ago both as a camp and also for a more spectacular purpose. Deep in the excavated layers lie two distinct levels of the massive bones and skulls of woolly rhinoceros and at least twenty woolly mammoths. The bones that remain are probably only a fraction of what was originally a much larger accumulation since washed away by the sea. Many of the huge shoulder-blades are neatly stacked to take up less space, and the mammoth skulls have been smashed to extract the brain for food. It seems that *Homo erectus* hunters stampeded these great beasts along the natural funnel of the top of the headland until they fell some 30 metres into the natural trap, which is not visible until you are right on top of it. They then butchered the carcasses *in situ*, carrying off the bones bearing the best meat. The remaining mess of rotting flesh was probably so offensive that the site would have had to have been abandoned for some time. Eventually the bones could be cleared away and normal occupation resumed until another opportunity occurred for a drive of animals. The two levels of stacked bones were preserved because on those occasions the abandonment was much longer, and they were covered by natural debris.

Despite finding over 100,000 man-made objects, no human remains have been found in the lower layers of the excavation at La Cotte de Saint Brelade. However, during the first excavations, which took place in 1911, thirteen human teeth were discovered in the layer corresponding to the most recent ice age. They are those of Neanderthal man.

It might have been expected that when the European anthropologist had human bones to study, the task of tracing our history would have become easier. But once again there is no clear accepted version. The oldest human skull so far found in Europe is probably the Arago skull from north of the Golfe de Lion (400,000 years old), or the Petralona skull from north of the Aegean, of about the same age. Although they are fragmentary they both show the pronounced brow-ridge similar to that found on later fossils of Neanderthals. Experts still disagree as to whether they should be classified as *Homo erectus* or *Homo sapiens*, but it seems likely that the Neanderthals were their direct descendants, evolving some 100,000 years ago.

Neanderthal man was named after a cave in the Neanderthal valley in the Ruhr, where in 1856 a German science teacher Johann Fuhlrott recognised that fossil bones being dug from a quarry were human, but not those of modern man. This was one of the first fossil skeletons of an early man to be found, and it caused fierce controversy which still continues to the present day. At first the debate centred on the conflict between his existence and that of Adam and Eve as our first ancestors, but now it is concerned as to whether Neanderthal man (*Homo sapiens neanderthalensis*) was indeed a true ancestor of anatomically modern man, *Homo sapiens sapiens*, or whether he was *Homo sapiens* at all.

The definitive fossil for Neanderthal man was discovered in the cave of La Chapelle-aux-Saints in the upper Dordogne valley of France in 1908. The skull has strongly developed brow-ridges and cheek-bones and a sloping face owing to more prominent teeth than modern man. These particular bones belonged to an old man, and the long leg and arm bones had been crippled by arthritis and bowed by rickets. This led to the erroneous reconstruction of Neanderthal man as a stooped, shambling, primitive creature – the very metaphor for brutishness. In fact his posture was no different from that of modern human beings, and it has been claimed that he would attract little attention in the street in a collar and tie. The Neanderthal's brain size is in fact slightly larger than that of modern man, but when calculated in proportion to his heavier build it is slightly smaller. He had a massive skeleton and was heavier and far stronger than we are, but had short, stubby legs and a protruding broad nose. Animals exposed to low temperature habitats, like the ice-age cave bear, tend to develop these features of large size and short extremities the better to keep warm, and it is argued that Neanderthal man, whose fossils have not been found further east than the Caspian Sea or further south than the River Jordan, were a European adaptation of hominids to the onset of the cold temperatures of the ice ages.

Most Neanderthal skulls have been found in caves, and this has led to another common misconception, that of 'cave-man'. The more prosaic fact is that fossils are much better preserved in the stable environment of temperature and humidity found in caves, and this is why more fossils are discovered in them. Neanderthal people undoubtedly did live in caves at times, but they certainly built shelters and probably travelled between different hunting camps following the seasonal distribution of plants and animals. Neanderthals have often had a bad press – the original skull was at first taken to be that of a human congenital idiot! One skull found in Italy at Grotta Guatari (Hyena cave) near Monte Circeo was found upside down in a ring of stones and appeared to have been smashed on the underside as if to extract the brain. This was interpreted as ceremonial cannibalism, when in fact the damage was natural rather than man-made.

Other contrasting evidence suggests that they revered their dead, and indeed could be altruistic in their behaviour. Violence was certainly a common feature of their lives: many skulls have been found with head-wounds, but one found at Krapina in Yugoslavia had a serious fracture of the skull which would have made the victim unconscious, yet with secondary growth of bone showing that he nevertheless survived. His companions must have realised that although his eyes were closed he was not dead, and it is possible that the damaged bone was lifted to release pressure on the brain and prevent a haemorrhage – demonstrating a capacity for tender care.

Neanderthals buried their dead, and at Shanidar in Iraq the skeleton of an old man revealed that he had been severely handicapped with the loss of one arm and one eye, and had legs so deformed that walking would have been very difficult. Unable to look after himself he must have been cared for by other members of his group. Concentrations of pollen show that he was buried with flowers laid in his grave, while another Neanderthal child was buried with a cache of ibex horns, suggesting a belief in a form of after-life with all its implications of ceremony and religion. This shows the first faint glimmerings of evidence of complex social behaviour.

The Neanderthals learned to use the thin flakes struck from the core when making stone tools, retouching their edges to form scrapers and points. They also made the important discovery that the shape of a tool could be pre-formed on a core *before* it was struck off, thus giving much better control over the shape of flake-based tools. As aboriginal tool-makers say today, 'they could see the tool within the stone'. They made small spearheads and developed a knife-like blade with one edge sharp and the other blunt, and some were notched to make an efficient saw. Microscopic analysis of the wear on modern knapped tools used for a variety of tasks can be compared with archaeological specimens to reveal which of the stone tools were used for butchery, skin-working and hide preparation, and which for working wood, bone and antler. Fire-hardened spears have also been found, suggesting that the description 'stone-age' may be as much of a misnomer as 'cave-man'. It is just that the wooden tools have long since rotted away. Scraping tools – for cleaning hides – are common, suggesting that the Neanderthals used animal skins to roof shelters, or even to make clothes.

A century ago, as enthusiastic anthropologists sought to find evidence for the

OVERLEAF The first mineral to be mined was almost certainly ochre, an iron oxide, here exposed on an escarpment at Rustrel, Vaucluse, France. It was used as a pigment, and probably used to treat hides, and also as an antiseptic.

evolution of man, they sifted through the strata of caves, especially in southern France, looking for an evolutionary sequence of stone tools that would demonstrate developing intelligence through cultural evolution. They found such an apparent development and used a 'chest-of-drawers' classification to differentiate their finds. The most primitive – the Lower Palaeolithic – went in the bottom drawer; the Middle Palaeolithic was assigned for the tools used by the Neanderthals, and the Upper Palaeolithic top drawer was reserved for modern man. Unfortunately, accurate dating of newly excavated sites does not support this simple division. For example, at High Lodge in Suffolk, tools have been found which, by the old system, could not possibly be more than 200,000 years old (Middle Palaeolithic), but which have been securely dated by modern techniques to more than 450,000 years before the present day.

This is hardly surprising. Today's hunter-gatherers, like some Aborigines, use tools of different materials and varying degrees of complexity according to where they are, what they are doing and what is to hand. Even the kind of stone available locally makes a difference to what they may use. Thus in limestone it is hard to make anything better than a crude chopper, but flint and obsidian have been made into delicate blades over 35 centimetres long. It is also easy to confuse a cultural change with a change in population: it is as if we claimed that those who rode horses and bicycles and drove cars were three different species. The only really major change in the stone tool record is now recognised as appearing 35,000 years ago when *Homo sapiens sapiens*, modern man, arrived in France.

Modern man

What became of the Neanderthals? Until a few years ago it was thought that Neanderthal man had evolved into modern man. The problem was that no one had found any fossils of hybrids. The traces of Neanderthal man suddenly disappear from all over Europe and Western Asia about 35,000 years ago; and they are abruptly replaced by those of modern man, and still nobody knows how or why it happened. As one anthropologist said: 'If Neanderthal man evolved into modern man it must have happened in about three weeks.' Then in 1988 a startling article was published in *Nature* which once again overturned all the accepted theories. It demonstrated not only that modern man had been living in the Middle East about 100,000 years ago, more than twice as early as previously supposed, but that he had actually lived in the Qafzeh cave in Israel *before* Neanderthals occupied the nearby cave of Kebara around 60,000 years ago. This overlap at once made it highly unlikely that modern man could have descended from the Neanderthals. And if not, then *Homo sapiens sapiens* must have split off from the hominid lineage *before* the Neanderthals evolved.

So where did he come from? Populations of *Homo sapiens sapiens* existed in southern Africa at Klasies River Mouth and at Omo, north of Lake Rudolf in Ethiopia at the same period as at Qafzeh. It is now generally accepted by scientists that modern people developed in Africa and moved north in their fully developed form. But if *Homo sapiens sapiens* was in the Middle East 100,000 years ago, why did he take so long to get to Europe, and indeed why did he migrate at all? Once again it may well have been the effects of the climate, this time of the penultimate ice age. As the Sahara and the savannahs dried up once again, humans would have been driven towards the more humid coasts in search of food and water. At the end of the glacial period the sea level rose once more, flooding the hunting-grounds and displacing their inhabitants.

There is considerable discussion about the dating of each glacial advance, and even about how many times each area was affected. Data from different sources give a wide variety of interpretations: for example there are traces of only four glaciations in Britain, but at least seventeen in cores taken from the Pacific ocean bed. The climate had certainly begun to cool again from about 125,000 years ago; there was a further sharp drop in temperature from 75,000 to 65,000, and again at 30,000. One factor that must have had an influence was the cataclysmic explosion of the Campanian volcano which formed the caldera, or collapsed crater, around Pozzuoli on the Bay of Naples about 35,000 years ago. This eruption was far larger than any that has happened anywhere in the world in historic times. The huge ash-cloud blanketed Crete, and even reached as far as Moscow. The main effects on climate would have been from the dust and gases thrown high into the stratosphere, which would have chilled the earth's surface in the northern hemisphere for several years. If other factors were already leading to a glacial period, it would certainly have made matters even worse.

At its maximum, the last great advance of the ice covered northern Britain, the north of Ireland, Scandinavia and the Alps; while icecaps covered the Massif Central, the Jura, Corsica, the Apennines and even the mountains of Turkey. The sea level was at least 100 metres lower than today, and huge fertile plains were left by the retreating Aegean and Adriatic seas. Britain was linked to Europe again. It was probably the hard conditions of the last ice age which drove Neanderthal man out of Europe, and possibly he arrived in the Middle East *after* the arrival of modern man.

The other great question is how modern man displaced the well-adapted and more powerful Neanderthals. There are still more questions on this subject than answers, but some evidence *is* beginning to appear: stone tools were recently found at thirty-two sites on the plain of Thessaly in northern Greece dated between 45,000 and 35,000 years old. Intriguingly, the Neanderthal tools were always found alongside those developed by modern man. In Spain two caves 500 kilometres apart (L'Arbreda in Catalonia and El Castillo in Cantabria) have revealed modern tools in layers which have been dated by the new technique of accelerator mass spectroscopy to 40,000 years ago, pushing back by a good 5000 years the date of modern man's arrival. In France at Châtelperron, a Neanderthal woman's skeleton was found with both Neanderthal and the characteristic blade tools of modern man. But does this mean that the Neanderthals had learned new tricks, or that populations were coexisting, or that they were fighting each other, or even interbreeding? The stones alone cannot tell.

The Neanderthal people had moved south as their habitat began to change with each successive advance of the ice, and it is just at the last plunge in temperature that Neanderthal man disappears, never to reappear. Apparently, and rather surprisingly, the flexible social adaptability of modern people was more important in their competition with the Neanderthals for resources during the hard times of the last ice age than the more rigid physical adaptations to cold of the Neanderthals. Just as more modern societies displaced the natives in the southern hemisphere – Indians were effectively wiped out in the whole southern third of South America, in Tasmania etc., in the last two centuries – so during the last ice age modern man displaced the Neanderthals and drove them to extinction.

The first Europeans

Homo sapiens sapiens came to be known by the unfortunate name of Cro-Magnon man, from the cave in the Dordogne where the definitive fossil was found. The cave is just one of the hundreds of limestone caves and rock shelters that are among the richest repositories of early human remains. Excavation of the floors of these caves shows that as you go up the successive layers of floor debris, and closer to the present day, the basic heavy duty tools like choppers and hand-axes of Neanderthal man are suddenly absent and have been replaced by long thin blades. These were struck off a prepared flint core with an antler hammer, and could be bound to wooden, bone or antler hafts – an important technical advance which allowed more force to be applied to the tool. At the same time, bone, antler and ivory tools also appear, followed by technical improvements like spear-throwers. After so many millennia with almost no development of stone tools, this change seems startlingly rapid.

One simple physical comparison helps to make sense of this cultural revolution. The end finger bone of a Neanderthal was almost double the width of that of modern man, although it was the same length. Immensely strong? Yes. Nimble fingered? No. The post-Neanderthal blades were meant to be hafted; bound on to the end of shafts or handles. Intelligence and dexterity replaced the brute force wielding the handaxe and scraper. It is no surprise to find that the first eyed needles appear with modern man, and eyed needles meant better clothes. At Sungir, 330 kilometres northeast of Moscow, thousands of bone beads and other objects found in graves had been sewn to the fringes of clothes, and are so numerous that they even suggest the details of the clothes then worn – they seem remarkably modern: a leather cap, shirt, jacket, trousers and shoes.

It is a mistake to think that it was a technical advance like sewn clothing that enabled the new hunters to exploit the frigid steppe lands that the Neanderthals could not. Indeed clothes may not be as necessary as we are inclined to think. Charles Darwin himself observed during his voyage to Tierra del Fuego in HMS *Beagle* that the canoe Indians, who inhabited an area with possibly the worst weather in the world, were completely naked, although they always had a fire in the bows of their canoes. 'A woman,' he wrote, 'who was suckling a recently born child, came one day alongside the vessel, and remained there out of mere curiosity, whilst the sleet fell and thawed on her naked bosom and on the skin of her naked baby!'

The hunter-gatherers

Few vegetable foods would have been available in Europe during the severe winters, even as far south as the Dordogne, and with little opportunity for storage (pottery had not yet been invented), hunting became essential for survival. New tools and skills, and perhaps better communication through language (some anthropologists believe Neanderthals did not have the right anatomy for speech), would have improved hunting efficiency as the climate of Europe descended once more to arctic temperatures.

The transition to the last ice age is clearly revealed at the remarkable site of Solutré in France, where an impressive limestone outcrop towers above the vineyards of Pouilly-Fuissé. Twenty-five thousand years ago the valley was used as a natural trap where hunters could ambush tens of thousands of the wild horses that migrated across the open countryside. These were a valuable source of food. The bones still lie in a layer 1.30 metres deep spread over an area of a hectare. Ninety per cent of the bones are those of horses, which suggests the countryside was then an open grassland steppe. The bones of other animals show that lemmings and a species of small deer were also eaten, while the brown bear was also killed, presumably in self-defence. But above that layer of bones the fossils change. The horses disappear and are replaced by bones of reindeer embedded

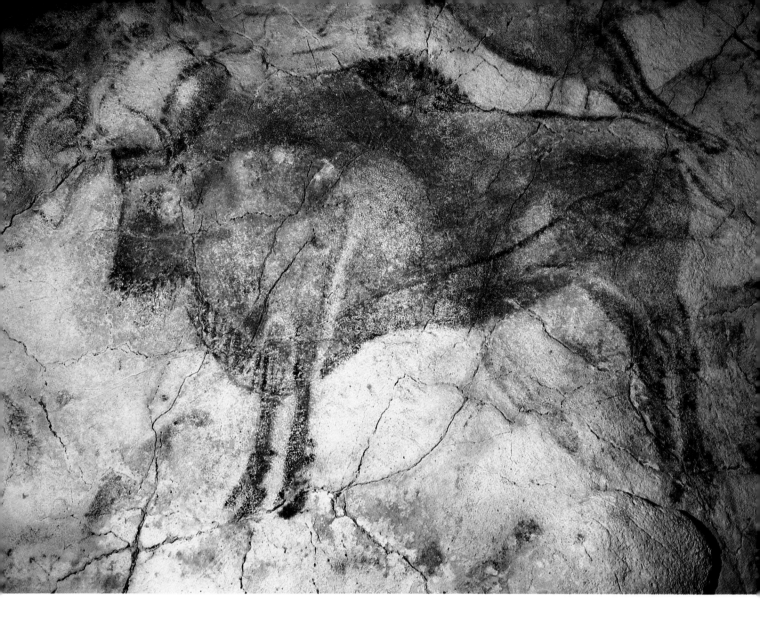

A bison painted in ochre and manganese on the roof of Altamira caves, Spain. It has been suggested that as the large food animals became scarcer, driven away by increasing cold, hunters may have invoked their spirits or used paintings to instruct their children.

in a layer of loess, a special soil blown as dust from the desiccation and debris caused by ice sheets and glaciers. Reindeer do not feed on grass, but on lichen which they can find even beneath the snow, which is evidence that the grasslands had retreated as the ice had come south. The date? Eighteen thousand years ago, the height of the last ice age.

Although on this last occasion the ice did not come as far south as when the English Channel was breached, the climate was still severe enough to drive the tree line and the forests back south of the Alps and the mouth of the Danube. Between the great Scandinavian and Alpine ice sheets lay a bleak tundra, bitterly cold in winter but, because of the southerly latitude, quite warm in summer. Some of the reindeer herds which roamed there may have numbered as many as a million animals, and both bison, woolly rhinoceros and mammoth were common too. It is clear that hunters ranged extensively over the tundra, possibly taking advantage of the remnants of forest in some of the valleys. The great animals would have kept bands of hunter families fed for weeks, especially in the cold season when meat could be preserved for months at a time. Huge numbers of them were killed. At Předmost in Czechoslovakia the remains of some 900 mammoths were discovered. Well-preserved mammoths are still found in the permafrost of Siberia and their stomach contents reveal that they fed on herbs

Venus figure apparently
holding a drinking horn,
from Laussel, France.

that still grow there. This suggests that they may not have died out from natural causes, and with a slow reproduction rate they were certainly vulnerable to extinction by man the hunter, who would have tended to kill selectively, taking the smaller, younger animals. If indeed they were one of the first species to be sacrificed to our supremacy on the Earth, their slaughter made a great difference to our own survival.

As there was little or no wood available, fires had to be made from burning bones, and across the eastern European plain, as far west as Czechoslovakia, extraordinary huts were built from mammoth bones covered with hides. At Mezhirich in the Ukraine one hut used 385 bones up to 2 metres long, and was 4–5 metres in diameter, with interlocking lower jaws below and skulls piled to complete the walls above. In the interior were found skulls decorated as if for a ceremonial purpose.

Despite, or perhaps even because of, the harshness of the times, artistic expression flourished. Hunting took up only a small portion of each day, and the few imperishable remnants of the times can still startle us with their sophistication. Solutré is famous for the beautiful stone tools in the shape of laurel leaves found there, and the craftsmen who made them became so expert that they were made as long as 35 centimetres, and so thin as to be semi-transparent. These were not objects made by miserable savages struggling to survive, but by humans with spare time, confidence and the sensitivity of hand, heart and eye to convert an everyday tool to another symbolic and mystical plane of endeavour, where craftsmanship, artistry and ceremony were ends in themselves.

But at last we have more than tools and graves by which to judge the skills of these earliest Europeans. In 1940 four young boys, who had sworn each other to secrecy, took their old schoolteacher Monsieur Laval into the cave they had discovered at Lascaux. He could not refrain from shouting out loud in astonishment and admiration. By the light of his torch was revealed, for the first time in 17,000 years, a kind of cultural explosion. While red and yellow ochre, an iron oxide, had been used to cure hides and was possibly even used as an antiseptic for wounds in Neanderthal times, the modern hunters now used it to leave the imprint of humankind quite literally on their surroundings. At first they blew ochre through a hollow bone or direct from the mouth to leave the outline of their own hands on the walls of caves, and then it was used as a pigment to paint with. Manganese provided a black colour, and the secret depths of the caves became the canvas for an incredible flowering of artistic virtuosity that stretched from the Iberian peninsula as far as the Urals.

This new artistic discovery of self and of the beasts they hunted was also expressed by carving portable objects that could travel with their owners; tools like spear-throwers with exquisite likenesses of horses, and the famous 'Venus figures' of heavily pregnant women. Their distribution across the vast distances of northern Europe suggests that trade in both ideas and information had begun. It has also given us the first portrait, a tiny ivory head of a young woman with braided hair, found at Brassempouy, to stare down twenty millennia into our clouded future.

CHAPTER TWO

FROM HUNTERS TO FARMERS

O ne of the most magnificent views in Europe is easily reached by the cable-car to Le Brévent on the Aiguilles Rouges in France. Beyond the Chamonix valley, which lies at one's feet, shines the gleaming snowy summit of Mont Blanc, and from its icecap glistening white cascades of ice tumble into the valley below. These glaciers were once tributaries that fed a greater flow of ice down the valley but they have retreated even in the last hundred years and have shrunk until now they are fenced on either side by cliffs. Further east against the sky tower the dramatic needles of Les Grandes Jorasses of the Mont Blanc massif and a little further up at Argentières the valley is joined by another glacier. A dramatic cascade of ice, half a kilometre wide, flows down a trough that it has carved in the granite heart of Europe.

At an altitude of 2000 metres, beneath the Argentières glacier, the Emosson electricity company has blasted 6 kilometres of tunnels. Water collected from beneath the glacier flows through the heart of the mountain range to fill a dam high in the Alps, and every cubic metre of water can generate 3.3 kilowatt-hours of electrical power. Where some of these tunnels emerge at the base of the glacier it is possible to stand actually beneath the ice where it slides over a low cliff. It is completely dark, and the sound of the rushing torrent drowns out any noise coming from the ice.

It is an awe-inspiring experience, not least because of the feeling that at any moment an unexpected rush of water from some unseen source might sweep one down the tunnels towards the dam. The rocky floor is strewn with jagged rocks that have been carried by the base of the glacier, held in the grip of the ice, and it is these shattered fragments of mountains embedded in the ice that are the most powerful eroding force known to Nature. The glacier flows downhill at the rate of about 1.3 metres a day in summer and 0.2 metres in winter: an irresistible force that can grind even mountains away.

The Aletsch glacier, Switzerland – the longest
in Europe. The dark stripes are pulverised rock
carried down from the sides of higher valleys,
but most of the erosion takes place
beneath the ice.

At the height of the ice age, only the peaks of the highest mountains emerged above the ice sheet, as they do today in Antarctica and Greenland. Subjected repeatedly to intense frost and thawing, the peaks are prised apart by ice to form shattered pinnacles, like Les Grandes Jorasses, but beneath the glaciers the fragments of rock embedded in the ice act like emery paper to carve away the surface of the mountains. Where there is a hollow the great weight of ice will gradually deepen it, stripping the rock from the near-vertical surfaces and using it as an abrasive to grind away the bottom. As it does so, with more snow constantly added to the highest part, the glacier cuts a deep bowl filled with ice, forming a cirque (corrie in Scotland, cwm in Wales). The effect of successive glaciations over millions of years is for the cirques to eat back ever deeper into the mountains. Then, when the ice has gone, these appear like great amphitheatres, often with a small lake at the base, like the cwms around Snowdon in north Wales.

Under the enormous weight of an ice sheet, valleys are deepened and ground into a U-shape with steep sides, and, as a mountain system is worn away, these valleys may meet to leave sharp ridges known as arêtes. When glacial erosion carves back into a mountain from several sides at once it can leave dramatic peaks like the Matterhorn. Lesser tributary glaciers do not have as great an erosive power and do not cut so deeply before they add their burden of ice and rock to the main flow, so, when the ice melts, their valleys may be left high up in the cliffs, linked to the ground by spectacular waterfalls (these are called hanging valleys). Every glacier acts as a gigantic conveyor-belt carrying rocks downhill and it can do so for enormous distances. In East Anglia there are rocks from the Scottish Highlands and from Scandinavia. Icebergs can even carry rocks hundreds of kilometres out to sea.

The ice retreats

The advance of the last ice age had driven the Neanderthals to the south of Europe, but now another climatic change was to provide an enormous opportunity for more human colonisation and social adaptation. The cold was at its worst about 18,000 years ago, but the climate had been relatively stable for 10,000 years. Then, quite quickly and dramatically, the climate began to warm. Silts in ocean cores from the Gulf of Mexico show that 14,000 years ago a massive quantity of water was pouring off the melting North American ice sheet via the Mississippi river; and the north European ice sheet, which stretched from Ireland to Siberia, began to retreat too.

With every spring, lichen and then vegetation crept further north to colonise the fertile soils left behind by the ice, which was now retreating at the rate of 30 metres a year. The cold-adapted herbivorous animals and their human hunters followed northwards, to the Baltic shores, lowland Scandinavia and Ireland. The sea level was still low, and the bed of what is now the North Sea provided huge new grasslands for the herbivores and their hunters until the rivers, which were running at up to five times their present maximum flood levels, caused the ocean level to rise sufficiently to drown the lowlands some 8500 years ago.

Continents themselves float on the fluid mantle of the Earth's core, and as the oppressive weight of ice, 1800 metres thick, was lifted from the land, northern Europe rose like an unburdened ship. The northern Baltic area has, to date, risen over 200 metres, and the land either side of the Irish Sea 100. But the total rise of sea level has been about 130 metres, and the relative movement of land and sea caused some strange effects; the Baltic became first a land-locked lake and then, as more ice melted and the oceans rose, a sea again. Britain, which the low sea level had rejoined to Europe, became an island once more around 8500 years ago, cutting its inhabitants off from the rest of the continent. The present Red Sea and Persian Gulf were inundated at the same time, causing the loss of huge hunting areas, which may even have given rise to the biblical legend of the Flood.

The Alpine glaciers were also in retreat, as were those on the Pyrenees, Apennines, Dinaric Alps, Carpathians and Caucasus. The remnants of the Scandinavian icecap are today only one-hundredth of their original greatest size. At the height of the last ice age the polar 'tree line', beyond which forest does not grow, ran from the Rhône delta to the mouth of the Danube; today it passes north of Iceland, and cuts the top of Arctic Norway, some 3000 kilometres further north. It was this massive environmental change, as the forest rapidly recolonised the continent and warmth brought back life, which was to provide enormous new opportunities, and challenges, to the first Europeans.

To the cave-dwellers of the Dordogne, the change must at first have been disquieting. Their traditional quarry, like reindeer and horses, moved north with the cold, and even salmon, which had been important for food, changed their spawning grounds to the cooler waters of Britain and Scandinavia. But many bands of hunter-gatherers chose to remain in their old territories as the habitat changed. As the glacial cycle ended and the energy of the sun reaching the ground increased, the rising oceans brought more moisture to the atmosphere and the land to the north of the Alps became far more productive.

First birch forest appeared, then pine, hazel, elm, and finally broad-leafed oak cast their shade across the land. No longer could the hunter see to the horizon across open tundra or grassland to pursue great animals that would feed whole bands of families for a month. As the tree canopy closed overhead, humans returned to the forests from which they had walked two million years before; but this time they were temperate deciduous forests, where mammals were smaller and much more scarce than in the African tropics. New techniques had to be learned to hunt these creatures: red deer, roe deer, pigs, aurochs (wild cattle) and the small fur-bearing mammals like beaver and marten.

Even before the ice began to melt, the human tool-kit had been diversified. Stone tools were smaller and more specialised, and now there were marked regional variations. Harpoons of antler and bone, bows, fish-hooks, seine nets, birch-bark containers, even boats of reed and skins were all in use, suggesting a broadly based diet. As the vegetation returned, edible leaves, roots, fruits and nuts were to hand when in season. Although archaeological evidence is scanty, annual migrations of animals like red deer and the search for different plant foods at different times of the year probably led to the use of seasonal camps, like Star Carr in Yorkshire, which was used for hunting deer, aurochs and wild boar.

It was an empty landscape of limitless possibilities and it invited great migrations by man as well. Australia was reached by boat by about 50,000 years ago, when the build-up of the ice and the falling sea level had joined together the Celebes Islands of what is now Indonesia, connecting them to the mainland and New Guinea to Australia, and had reduced the distance across the Timor or Banda seas to some 60 kilometres. By 55,000, the Bering Straits had been closed by a land bridge 1000 kilometres wide, which allowed mammoths, steppe bison and horses to migrate into the Americas down an ice-free corridor, to be followed by their human hunters perhaps as early as 45,000 years ago. So by the end of the last ice age people were distributed over most of the regions of the globe inhabited today. But as the retreating ice allowed people into new lands it also bequeathed them a European landscape that had been dramatically changed.

A virgin landscape

Many of the great land-forms that make up the topography of Europe bear the signature of the ice age. Fjords are just valleys carved into a U-shape by glaciers and flooded when the sea level rose. The Piedmont lakes of northern Italy are similar valleys dammed either by a rock sill or the masses of debris carried down by the ice which are known as moraines. Huge moraines were left by the retreating ice sheets: such as the Gooilsand, Utrecht and Eide hills of the Netherlands, and the Urstromtäler of North Germany. Because of their sandy soil made from the ground-up rock carried by the ice, many of these are now heathlands. Warsaw, Berlin and Poznan are all sited on a single moraine which provided a site for the cities elevated above the surrounding land. The sand is difficult to tunnel through, which is why Warsaw now has inadequate sewage disposal and no underground railways.

Where glaciers melted without first retreating, they dumped their debris of silt and rock in a hummocky chaos like the Valley of the Thousand Hills at Torridon

Lairig Ghru in the Cairngorms, Scotland. A U-shaped valley carved by the glaciers of successive ice ages.

North-west Greenland.
Even during the ice ages
summer warmth brought
life to the edge of the ice.

in Scotland. Sometimes large blocks of ice were embedded and they melted to leave deep pits or kettle holes in the hummocky surface. The sandy bunkers of the original golf-course at St Andrews in Scotland are kettle holes and all over the globe, from Pebble Beach to Alice Springs, the landscape-architects of golf courses have been unwittingly reproducing a glacial landscape.

The combined onslaught of successive ice sheets planed flat the ancient rocks of Finland and the heart of the old European continent which now forms Russia and the Ukraine. As the last ice sheet wasted away it left behind winding sand-deposits called eskers which had formed as the beds of streams were trapped in tunnels beneath the ice. In Finland they wind between the lakes, while in southern Ireland the country roads now follow these natural ridges across the bogs. By contrast, the low sea level during the furthest advance of the ice meant that the rivers draining the ice snout ran at a steeper angle, allowing them to cut down deep into the surrounding landscape. These formed the steep valleys of the Middle Rhine, Luxembourg, Frankfurt, Nuremberg and Stuttgart.

The new shape of the mountains did not directly affect human activities until mining for minerals began (see Chapter 3) but the changes at lower levels were crucially important for the development of human society. The rising sea level flooded many river valleys where they reached the sea to form the estuaries (called rias) of southern Britain, Brittany and the firths of Scotland. This threaded the coastlines with safe harbours that would later be a boon for fishing and the development of maritime trade. While in the Aegean it left a scattering of hilltops as islands, which were to aid the birth of the first great European civilisation. But even more important for the future Europeans was the effect that glaciation had on the fertility of the land.

During the glacial period the low temperatures caused fierce winds to blow down the glaciers which picked up the fine silt and rock-flour deposited in moraines at the edges of the glacial snouts. This was blown for long distances before falling to form fine well-drained soils called loess. In wetter areas these loess-filled valleys, like that of the Danube, became filled with dense forest, which at first was too scarce in food and impenetrable for human use. Instead, coastal and riverside habitats provided the richest opportunities and were most densely settled because, as formerly at Boxgrove and Terra Amata, they offered a variety of food all year round.

The first settlements

It is only in the last twenty-five years, as archaeological techniques have become far more thorough, that evidence has been found which begins to show how Europe was colonised as the ice retreated. But in southern Europe it is now possible to see how the first modern human families had to adapt to the changing environment as they used the same caves for shelter for tens of thousands of years. In 1967 excavations began in Franchthi cave, near Kilada on the Argolic Gulf in southern Greece. For a decade American archaeologists dug deep into the floor of the cave, going down through successive layers which had built up from debris as the cave was used as a dwelling. What is unusual about Franchthi cave is that the floor levels give an almost uninterrupted record of human occupation from the ice age to about 5000 years ago when an earthquake caused a large part of the roof to collapse. So it has become a most important site.

As the excavation went down it also went further and further back into time until, 11 metres below the present floor, it reached objects that could be radio-carbon dated as 27,000 years old – the start of the coldest phase of the last ice age.

An excavation in the floor of Franchthi cave reveals the layers of occupation debris.

RIGHT The transformation of Europe by Agriculture, which followed the loess soils.

The remains of animal bones show how, as the climate warmed, the earliest inhabitants progressed from making seasonal camps, occupied to hunt the migrating wild asses that crossed the open grasslands, to become more settled hunters of red deer and bison as the coastal plain and nearby hills were clothed with forest.

At first the cave had been some 6 or 7 kilometres away from the shore, but as the millennia passed and the sea rose and came nearer to the cave, more shellfish were brought back to supplement a diet which had also begun to include wild plants like vetch and lentil, pistachio and almond, the products of the warmer land. The first fish-bones also appear, showing that a new skill had been learned, and about 9250 years ago large fish vertebrae, probably of tuna, prove that boats were being used in order to catch bigger fish that are only found in deep water. By this time, with access to plentiful food, the cave was lived in all year round. This transformation from roaming bands of hunters to a settled existence was a profoundly important change, because it meant that possessions no longer had to be carried about, and could be much more complex, as could social ties.

It used to be thought that it was only after the invention of agriculture that permanent settlements could be made but the evidence now refutes this. One of the most remarkable of the early permanent sites was found in 1967 in a most unusual place – an inaccessible part of the Iron Gates gorge of the Danube, on the right bank, now in Yugoslavia. At Lepenski Vir a sequence of six settlements has been uncovered, each of about twenty dwellings. There, at least 7500 years ago, about a hundred inhabitants were among the first in Europe to establish a

complex social society. Not only did they develop a particular architectural style but also complex religious and economic relations.

The huts contained fireplaces, were paved with solid floors made from a kind of plaster of slaked lime, and all had the same precisely measured plan – a truncated segment of a circle (like a slice of cake with the tip cut off). Clearly it was a well-organised society, and archaeologists believe that this could happen only in a prosperous (ie well-fed) settlement and through an authority which controlled the beliefs and ritual of the inhabitants. Close to many of the hearths monumental stone sculptures were set. These were made of large boulders, carved with the outline of monstrous fish-like human heads; some also had breasts – fish goddesses. These were clearly venerated by generation after generation, and no doubt were an expression of the importance of the fish, mostly carp, which were the mainstay of their diet. These fish grow up to 50 kilos in weight and still survive even now in the polluted Danube. There is one other piece of evidence that shows how well-fed the inhabitants were. Their skeletons stood 1.88 metres tall. It was a community of giants by the standards of the time.

The rise in sea level has unfortunately hidden most of the sea-shore settlements which existed at the time of the glacial retreat, but in central Denmark the sea level change and the upward rebound of the land after the weight of ice was removed sometimes cancelled each other out, and this has recently led to the discovery of numerous sites just below the present surface of the sea. The most rewarding of these settlements, of a people known as the Ertebølle, was found by amateur divers in 1978 and has since become one of the largest underwater excavations of a stone-age site ever carried out in Denmark.

Tybrind Vig, on the western shore of the island of Fyn, was once a sheltered shallow cove fringed by reeds. Pollen analysis shows that the land was clothed with oak forest interspersed with lime, elm and pine; while hazel, elder and birch thickets lined the shore. Today, the original settlement lies about 250 metres offshore and has sunk only 2 to 3 metres since it was first occupied about 6500 years ago. The initial rather rapid rise in sea level caused an oxygen-depleted mud to cover not just the settlement but also its scattered debris in the bay and its fishing area. By inhibiting decay, wet mud preserves organic remains, and at Tybrind Vig a grave of a young mother (of 15 to 17 years old) with a newborn child has been found, along with many stone tools and also a remarkable variety of wooden goods, from dug-out canoes to arrows and even woven textiles. Unfortunately most of the settlement itself was eroded away as the sea shore rose, but the debris that accumulated in and around the lagoon can still tell us much about the way this prosperous little community thrived off the resources of the sea and the land.

The settlement, a series of scattered huts, was beside an opening to the sea, and a hard had been built from large stones along the muddy shore for beaching boats. In the bay, the most spectacular finds were the remains of two dug-out canoes, one of which was 9.5 metres long, hewn with stone axes from the straight trunks of lime trees. The bows were carved in the root end of the tree, the better to resist splitting, and the sterns were carved open, with a series of holes, presumably to lash a wooden transom in place. Near the stern was an oval layer of sandy clay and small stones with charcoal – a fireplace, probably used for eel fishing at night. Heart-shaped paddles carved from ash, fish-prongs of hazel-wood and hundreds of pointed hazel sticks placed vertically as fish traps have all survived. A wooden net-float and a kind of woven fish trap weighted with a stone, as well as several fish-hooks made from red-deer ribs, all show that fishing techniques were highly developed.

Sandstone fish-god from Lepenski Vir.

The remains of bows made from elm, and blunt-ended arrows for shooting birds, show that the families lived by hunting as well as fishing, and the bones of red deer, roe-deer, wild pig and occasionally aurochs and wild horse reveal their quarry. This also included animals hunted for fur like pine marten. One skull even shows the cuts of the flint knife used to skin it. Seals and whales were hunted along the coast, while gathered foods included hazel nuts, acorns, oysters, mussels, clams and periwinkles. The only domesticated animal at this time was the dog.

The only clues we have to the cultural life of these people are a handful of teeth of wild boar, aurochs and red deer which were drilled to make necklaces, and paddles decorated with a striking rhythmic pattern. Yet it is a sobering thought that until 150 years ago the native inhabitants of northern California were living in a very similar way.

But the picture that the evidence paints, of a skilled and thriving community living in harmony with Nature on a varied and nutritious diet is in contrast to one other piece of evidence. The scattered bones of two or three individuals which wave action had eroded from the cemetery were also found. One was part of a man's skull with two healed wounds. Such head wounds are known from other Ertebølle graveyards. They suggest that rival groups were attacking each other. Were the wounds caused by fighting brought about by competition for territory? If so, why? Was it because too many people were having to live off too few food resources? Or was the competition for status on the increase – achieved by obtaining more resources, possessions or control of society? There are no simple answers to these questions, but there is some evidence of a major increase in the population of northern Europe at this time.

There is in fact a great debate as to whether human societies, from soon after the ice age, managed to live in balance with the natural resources available to them. The disappearance of the large herbivores like the horse, camel, ground sloth, mammoth and mastodon in North America has been blamed on the unrestricted slaughter of species unused to being hunted by man – a 'Pleistocene overkill' which started when the first hunters crossed the land bridge at the Bering Straits. In some areas of Europe, too, whole species were exterminated: like the aurochs in Zealand. But when over-enthusiastic hunting led to food shortages, the hunters must have learned to avoid killing young animals and pregnant females – thus taking the first step towards herd management and actually controlling the availability of animal and plant food resources. This began one of the most important changes that humans were ever to make in their relationship with the natural world – nothing less than bringing wild animals and plants under their control.

The domestication of plants and animals

Domestication appears to have been a slow process which had started as long as 20,000 years ago, perhaps by the herding of animals such as reindeer (as shown on the rock carvings of Alta in Norway). But it was in the Middle East, not Europe, that the most important domestication had begun, when the waning of the ice age brought a climate not unlike that of today and people began to plant cereals. It would take several millennia for the knowledge of these new crops and farming techniques to spread north until they reached the shores of Denmark.

When the first evidence of domestication occurs on an archaeological site, pottery and polished stone axes are usually found too; and so these great innovations, together with a sedentary way of life, came to be called the Neolithic

Revolution. It used to be ascribed to an invasion of clever newcomers from the east, who ousted the more 'primitive' hunter-gatherers. But the slow accumulation of archaeological evidence now tells a different story, especially since radio-carbon and other more modern systems for dating have been employed to give accurate relative ages to sites. It now seems to have been the old problem of confusing a change in culture with a change in population. But the new painstaking analysis of seeds and food resources from excavations confirms that the domestication of the plants later brought to Europe – and thus the beginning of European agriculture – occurred in the Middle East.

In the mountains of the Middle East and Anatolia wild cereals grow with the winter rains. As they grow on uplands which are dry in summer they have little competition and so have a poor seed dispersal mechanism. In other words, the seeds fall to the ground near the plants and the plants grow in dense patches. The seeds must survive periods of drought, so they are large and thus of good food value. We know from roasted grain found in northern Israel that seeds of wild barley were being collected and carried back to camp 33,000 years ago, possibly even before *Homo sapiens sapiens* had colonised most of Europe.

The ears of wild cereals shatter easily to scatter their seeds but the very act of harvesting them by breaking off the heads, or cutting them with a flint sickle, means that the seed heads which shatter least will be carried home. If the seeds are then planted rather than eaten, the selection process will continue automatically, favouring the non-shattering kind and thus giving a better yield and harvest. When the plants with the biggest grain were deliberately kept for seed the process of domestication began.

Archaeologists' perceptions of the 'revolution' caused by agriculture are also being rewritten. It is now realised that at first agriculture was not of great importance. Our forebears must have been expert botanists with a profound knowledge of the location and uses of different kinds of plant, and to them there was perhaps not such a great conceptual difference in going back to the same patch of cereals each year to collect it, and the deliberate scattering of some of the seeds so that next year there would be more. Nor was it a unique discovery; agriculture began independently in at least three regions. Barley and wheat began to be cultivated in the Middle East about 12,000 years ago, millet and rice in China 8000 years ago, and maize in Central America at about the same time.

Wild cereals still abound in the Judaean Hills, and there a primitive wheat called emmer was brought down about 20 kilometres from its natural habitat to be cultivated in an oasis at Jericho in the lower Jordan valley. By 10,000 years ago domesticated (non-shattering) emmer wheat and two-row barley were being cultivated to the extent that the settlement could greatly increase in size, to about 1.6 hectares.

Wheat and barley were probably first cultivated because they had a relatively large grain, a reasonable flavour and because they could be stored. But the pressure which first brought about their cultivation is not clear. However, one cause of the domestication of animals can be deduced from the fascinating evidence from the site of Tell Abu Hureyra in what is now Iraq. Formerly on the banks of the Euphrates, the site has now been flooded by the Tabqa dam. There a record of continuous occupation was found, starting about 11,000 years ago in the hunter-gathering (Mesolithic) period. The massive remains of mud walls, and an analysis of the remains of food-plants, suggest that the settlement was occupied all year round even then. A study of tens of thousands of bone fragments found on the site shows that the wild animal diet included wild asses, cattle, deer and the forebears of sheep, goats and pigs, but gazelle bones are by far the most common, making up some 80 per cent of the total.

Bones can reveal the age of an animal when it died, and these gazelles have a yearly growth pattern which shows that the animals were only caught at one period of the year. So, apparently, the people of Tell Abu Hureyra trapped gazelles during their annual migration from what is now north Jordan to north Syria, when whole herds were caught and killed, and no doubt dried and salted for future consumption. But about 8500 years ago stone-walled structures (known from their shape as desert kites) began to be built in large numbers across the steppe of north Jordan, at the southern end of the migration route. These traps would have caught whole gazelle herds, and at Tell Abu Hureyra the proportion of gazelle bones rapidly decreases in number until they are no more than 20 per cent of the total.

It seems that the new wholesale slaughter had led to a dramatic reduction in the number of gazelles. Their place in the Tell Abu Hureyra diet was then filled by much larger quantities of sheep and goats. When wild, these are creatures of the mountains, native to the Middle East, and would never have visited a site like the Tell, so they must have been domesticated.

The domestication of animals is a slow process that must have begun a thousand or so years before. It could not have been an instant response to the shortage of gazelles. But when the gazelles were over-exploited elsewhere the people of Tell Abu Hureyra were forced to fall back on eating domesticated animals.

By this time, to the diet of wild plants from the Euphrates valley had been added a kind of primitive wheat called einkorn, which was probably cultivated, and when large-scale animal rearing joined plant cultivation the first fully farming communities were born.

The disadvantages of agriculture

Scientists have now also begun to challenge the Victorian assumption that the move from 'animal-like' foraging to planned agriculture and animal husbandry was an important social advance. Certainly agriculture allows a large quantity of food to be produced in a small area but it requires a lot of input in human labour to cultivate the soil, weed the crop, protect it from pests etc. In contrast, present-day hunter-gatherers, like the Bushmen of the Kalahari desert, only spend about twenty hours a week actually collecting food. At Tell Abu Hureyra, the hunter-gatherers had a diet of some 150 seed plants and at least seven animal species, but their farming descendants had to make do with eight kinds of food plant and only two main species of animals. Nutritionally they were probably worse off.

The nutrition value of cereals, which are grasses, does not compare favourably with that of meat, nuts, roots and fruits. So large quantities, which have to be ground to meal, are necessary to keep a family alive. The labour of milling grain on stone saddle-querns was so great that the arm bones of the farmers at Tell Abu Hureyra became deformed, backbones became arthritic, toes were bent to an angle of 90 degrees by so much kneeling, and teeth became worn down by the stone dust included in the meal. It is as if when we left the plenty of the Garden of Eden we were indeed cursed to eat bread in the sweat of our faces.

But if it was such an inferior way of life, why did it take over? The answer appears to be that agriculture allowed an increase in food production per unit area, which in turn allowed the already increasing human population to be fed off the same amount of land near a settlement. The settled stock-breeders and farmers were fruitful and multiplied, and as the population increased they had no choice but to opt for agriculture. In evolutionary terms their greater breeding success made them fitter to survive than the hunter-gatherers and they began to displace them. Now we may argue that it was only a short-term advantage but evolution only involves the survival of the next generation. Once the old generation with its knowledge of the wild plants and hunting techniques was dead, if their children had not been taught them there was no going back. In practice, both farming and feeding off the land continued side by side and do so to this day – most modern farmers have a gun for rabbiting, but the strict laws against poaching reflect the scarcity of game compared with the size of the population. With a large population, hunter-gathering is no longer an option for society.

Communities were now able to store grain against lean seasons (grain is too bulky to be carried around by hunter-gatherers), but stored products could encourage attacks by acquisitive neighbours. The people of Jericho defended their settlement with walls 3 metres thick and a tower over 9 metres high. The belief that man was now a master of his own destiny is, sadly, an illusion. Instead, families were now tied to the land in a way that they had never been before. In a bad season they could no longer simply move camp to fresh hunting grounds. A change in rainfall, a shift in the climate, the erosion of soil through overcropping or the accumulation of salt through irrigation could all spell disaster (even to those who practised shifting agriculture) and did so repeatedly with dreadful consequences in the years to come.

If agriculture was not carried into Europe by invaders, it was almost certainly brought by trading contacts. Goods had been exchanged or traded from the earliest times of European colonisation – chocolate-coloured flint found at Cracow in Poland had been carried 400 kilometres from its source; amber, fossil and recent seashells found in the Ukraine had been brought 750 kilometres from the Baltic coast; Hungarian obsidian and many other small high-value goods were traded over large distances. Other perishable valuables like salt, furs, dried and salted fish, and even cereals and legumes or animals on the hoof may well have been part of a system of exchange which would leave few archaeological traces. Exchange could have carried these commodities, and with them skills like the sowing of domesticated grain and pottery making, into the Taurus and Zagros Mountains, then Anatolia and finally into the Balkan areas of Europe by 8000 years ago.

The first European farmers

The heavy rains following the glaciation had left deep layers of eroded sediments and silt in former lakes and valleys, and many had sources of stone for tools conveniently near them. These sediments, including the bottoms of former lakes and inland seas, provided the fertile soils that were to become the first heartland of agricultural occupation, and soil or mud began to assume a central role in the life of mankind. Food was grown in it and houses were made first from dried mud and then from mud brick. Where rainfall was sufficient to allow cereals to be grown (300 millimetres a year or more), large shapeless mud mounds like Tell Abu Hureyra can still be found. Tells, as they are called in Arabic or *Hüyük* in Turkish, slowly accumulated, almost by accident, when fire or earthquake (and seismically this is a very active area) destroyed a mud village and another was built on top. The different layers are quite easy to distinguish in cross-section, with floors and burnt layers recognisable by texture and colour. Within the layers, which are of course sequential in time, the archaeologist can now find the most useful and indestructible items of his evidence – sherds of pottery. Not only

The oldest street in Europe, made about 8000 years ago from pebbles and clay, was brought to light in the second level at Karanovo in 1989. Here it stands above the level of the first agricultural village on the site which has raised hearths and stone querns to grind grain. Post holes show the outline of mud and wattle huts, while rubbish pits dug in later years break up the outline.

Karanovo Tell, its centre
carved away by
archaeologists, was
formed from the layers of
debris of successive
farming villages built one
on top of the other for
4000 years.

does pottery style help to define areas with a particular culture, it also acts as a valuable guide to the progress of civilisation as technical competence improves and the kind of object made becomes more sophisticated.

Baked clay figurines had been made during the ice age, but pottery had been invented (in India or China) before the first farming settlements spread to Europe. It is already present in the earliest layers of European tells such as those in the fertile valleys of Bulgaria. At Karanovo, the largest tell, near Nova Zagora, the excavation of the bottom layer, at ground level, yielded a curving red-deer antler set with flints on the inside to form a sickle – a clear enough proof that even this first village built on the site was sustained by agriculture, but still reliant on products from wild animals. The settlement was a cluster of small U-shaped huts, their walls made from posts and wattle daubed with clay, each with its own hearth and pottery storage jars. At the layer above ran a street of pebbles set in clay: the oldest street in Europe. At Karanovo, for no less than four thousand years, farmers harvested a living from the rich soil around this tell, and the pottery fragments scattered within its layers reflect the slowly emerging technical sophistication of this astonishingly stable community.

About 8000 years ago agricultural settlements also spread to coastlands and even to the larger islands in the Mediterranean such as Cyprus and Crete. The arrival of domesticated animals there proves that not only people, but their domestic animals too, were able to travel by boat. Farming communities in Sicily and southern Italy also probably began when pioneers arrived by boat, presumably displaced from further east by growing population pressure. But Franchthi cave provided the most remarkable evidence – that boats have been island-hopping across the Aegean for 13,000 years. Flakes of black obsidian, chippings of volcanic glass valuable for stone tools, were found there which could only have come from the volcanic outcrops on the island of Melos in the Cyclades; and the level in which they were found at Franchthi proves their antiquity.

Even though the sea level was then lower, and the longer journeys would have been made by island-hopping, the craft that carried them must have crossed one expanse of at least 20 kilometres of open sea. Almost certainly the boats were made of papyrus reeds. Similar rafts called papyrellas were in use in Corfu until a generation ago, and one was recently reconstructed by the Hellenic Institute for the Preservation of Nautical Tradition. It is capable of being paddled at about two knots by four men, so, with a favourable wind, such a crossing could have been made in a day.

Farming moves north

Throughout the history of civilisation, the vast complexity of minerals, vegetables and animals provided by the European continent only become resources when a human technology is invented to make use of them. This is the real triumph of human adaptability – the learning of new skills to exploit new opportunities. It was only when agriculture was practised that soils became important, and the availability of water and good soil was now to determine how a new settlement pattern in northern Europe was added to the old. But first the technology of farming had to be adapted. It was one thing to learn to farm the sediments surrounding the Mediterranean, where the climate was similar to that of the Middle East, but for agriculture and animal husbandry to be successfully adopted further north and west meant coming to terms with a colder and wetter central European climate. It required new strains of cereals, and as sheep and goats were not native to the area (though introduced in small numbers), the animals of the forest, cattle and pigs, were domesticated and became more important. These new skills spread up the Danube valley into the heart of Europe. Cattle bones can still be seen sticking out of the excavated sections of the tells that still rise like giant molehills above the Hungarian plain, once the bed of an inland sea.

These were fertile lands, but even they could support only a finite number of villages. Slowly the farmers spread west across the middle Danube basin until, about 7000 years ago, the plain to the west of the Danube was fully settled, carrying a population not unlike that of medieval times. Farming then moved north beyond the Carpathian mountains. Now the farmers made almost exclusive use of the glacial loess soils. Well drained and up to hundreds of metres thick, when weathered loess provides a particularly good soil which is light enough to be tilled with primitive hoes and digging sticks. This gift from the ice ages was as important to the farmers of northern Europe as the former lake beds had been to the early agriculturalists of the south. It was along the great band of loess, which follows the Danube valley north and swings round the Alps to the northern Rhine, that agriculture now reached northern Europe. This time it may have been spread by immigration since these were virgin lands, and a similar design of pottery incised with linear patterns (called the Bandkeramic) accompanied farming as it spread northwards.

This farming culture reached the Netherlands within two or three centuries. (Farming techniques, but not the pottery style, were adopted in Britain and on the Atlantic coast some 6000 years ago.) The farms were made to a similar pattern and the loess land was so fertile that at first there was no need for shifting agriculture. Fixed plots of land were cultivated and surrounded by wattle fences to protect the valuable harvest from wild animals. These were usually near a river and, instead of dwellings being made with mud walls and roofs, small groups of thatched wooden longhouses were built. These were better able to cope with the rain of northern Europe. They were also very large, up to 45 metres long by 5 wide, and were divided for use by both people and cattle, a very different kind of communal lifestyle from that of the small family mud huts of the warmer south.

However, the loess-filled valleys were covered with dense forest and before they could farm the soils, the farmers had to cut down the trees. Thus began the first major deforestation of Europe. Even in the age of the hunters, humans had burnt forest and scrub to encourage new growth which would have attracted their quarry. Now as the population expanded, forest clearance progressed with each new generation. It might seem an almost impossible task to cut down an oak tree with a stone axe but by now there were tools equal to the job. A polished (Neolithic) stone axe can be sharp enough to shave with, and they were used to fell trees as much as 1.2 metres in diameter.

As agriculture and forest clearance swept slowly but steadily across Europe, transforming a few more kilometres of countryside with every generation, very large quantities of axes were required. This need was met by digging increasingly elaborate mines which penetrated deep into chalk sediments to layers that carried suitable flints. (Flints are concretions of silica that grow into the cavities left by burrowing animals in the floor of lime-rich seas, or are deposited there in layers.) These mines can still be seen at Grimes Graves in Suffolk, Maastricht near Rijckholt in the Netherlands, Spiennes near Mons in Belgium and at Krzemionki in Poland. In this last mining area in the Opatow district there were over 3500 shafts, in use from 6500 years ago, and the attractive flint, banded with colours, was traded as far as 900 kilometres from the mines. Flint mining was a seasonal activity, carried out in the winter when there was less work to do on the land, and the shafts only extended as far as the daylight could reach – about 7 metres. This also acted as a safeguard against asphyxiation.

Only recently with the development of underwater and wetland archaeology, where wet sediments have preserved vegetable matter, has a fuller idea of the Neolithic way of life been brought to light, and it has revealed settlements little different from those of native lake-shore dwellers today. Villages at the edge of the Alps and Jura Mountains were sometimes drowned by rising lake levels. For example at Lac de Chalain, where the lake level has recently been reduced by a power-station, a 5500-year-old hamlet has been excavated from the white calcium-carbonate shore. This has brought to light not just the stone axes as found in so many other sites, but axes set in red-deer antler handles, the mortice and tenon joints in timbers cut by the axes, the trellis walls of houses, clothes, rope, a spindle complete with its linen thread, baskets, paddles, combs, bowls, wooden spoons, and even the cores of chewed crab apples and burnt bread. At another lake site at Clairvaux, some 10 kilometres to the south, superb flint daggers were found still bound to their wooden hafts. At last the shadowy clearers of the forest begin to have substance.

Flint arrowhead styles show that the hamlet at Chalain was on a cultural boundary between the agriculturalists who had come from the Danube in the east and those who came up the Rhône valley to the south west. It was poised between the two great southern routes into the heart of Europe and thus would have adopted farming comparatively late. The houses were similar to those still built on stilts at the edges of lakes in west Africa and Colombia, a style originally adopted for defence. The inhabitants certainly fished, and they also practised slash-and-burn agriculture, sowing wheat and barley, rearing pigs and weaving clothes from linen. But they were still collecting fruit and nuts from the forest. Hunter-gatherer behaviour coexisted everywhere with agriculture for as long as was practicable for the local conditions. Indeed the analysis of food remains left on some sites in Britain now suggests that cereals may have played only a minor role in feeding the population until as late as the Bronze Age (in Britain 3000 years ago).

The earliest phase of farming in northern Europe lasted about 500 years, but then the type, and location, of the communities began to change. Instead of small-scale settlements in the valley bottoms, larger villages were built on higher ground, on the edges of valleys and in the plateau areas between river systems. About 5200 years ago cups and jugs became much more common, which has been interpreted as the introduction of milk or alcohol as an important part of the diet. Perhaps the move to higher ground was to allow more grazing ground for the increasing number of cattle. But another reason was that these new sites may have been more easily defensible. Many were now fortified with stockades, and surrounded by ditches.

Agriculture is a predatory activity. Unless the soil is allowed to lie fallow or is fertilised with dung and has its organic content renewed it loses fertility and its ability to retain moisture, and moisture content has the greatest effect on harvest size. Forest clearance and intensive agriculture reduced the sandy soils of the Netherlands to barren heathland by 4000 years ago. It may well be that yields were falling elsewhere. As population expanded, the good lands had already been occupied, forcing settlement out on to poorer land which could not sustain long-term cropping. If this was the case, it was competition for food, and by extension land, which caused hostilities between communities and the need for fortifications. Over the next thousand years the people built smaller, more widely dispersed hamlets often of poor construction, which may reflect either hard times or social conflict.

The megaliths

Compared with the mud tells of the Balkans, little evidence of Neolithic buildings has survived in the wet climate of northern Europe. But those which remain beyond the belt of the loess soils are among the most impressive prehistoric monuments to be found anywhere in the world – tens of thousands of tombs constructed out of huge stones (megaliths) and stone circles. Clearly, these were first constructed on such a massive scale to provide a permanent witness to human power and prestige. Their number and complexity of styles for a long time defied logical analysis but now, with the help of carbon dating, it is possible to see at least how the custom developed.

Along the western and northern coast of Europe there are three heartlands of megalithic architecture, Portugal, Brittany and Denmark. Each had an indigenous foraging culture which appears to have resisted the adoption of farming, not least because they frequently lacked good soils. The enormous shell mounds of the Tagus estuary in Portugal are vivid reminders of the wealth of marine resources that allowed substantial communities to exist along the Atlantic coasts. The mounds, built up over centuries from the debris of shellfish eaten by the inhabitants, were later used as burial mounds, and it is possible that their scale was the inspiration for the first simple stone chambers for collective burial which were begun some 6500 years ago. Once constructed, these conspicuous tombs could become an important ritual focus for the community.

In Brittany, the sea level has risen some 10 to 20 metres since that time, with the continuing melting of polar ice. One region now covered is the broad sheltered south-facing bay of the Morbihan. It must have been an extremely rich territory for gathering marine foods (Brittany is still famous for its shellfish). With the settlements drowned, two hilltop burial grounds still survive on what are now islands off the coast south of Carnac; at Téviec, west of Quiberon, and Hoedic, on the tip of the peninsula. Stone-lined coffin-like cists were used for burial, the skeletons framed with red-deer antlers (of domesticated stock) and draped with shell bead necklaces and seashells. It was probably from this use of stone in graves that the people of Brittany were later to develop the huge megalithic monuments which attended the major settlements on higher ground. There is no doubt that the Atlantic communities were in touch with each other by sea.

As the linear pottery tradition of the farmers of the loess belt reached Normandy and the Channel Islands, trapezoidal mounds such as the spectacular example at Barnenez, Finistère (6500 years old) began to be built in Brittany. On the summit of a small promontory overlooking the north coast, eleven 'passage-graves' stood in line under an enormous cairn. It appears that the local population had adopted the concept of grave mounds from the south – from the coasts and islands of the western Mediterranean and the Tagus – and combined it with the longhouse long mound tradition coming from the east.

Independently, and about 600 years later, in Denmark, a maritime foraging people, also noted for huge mounds of discarded shells, began to construct chambered tombs out of glacially transported boulders. This also happened at about the time they were learning the techniques of agriculture from the descendants of the farmers who brought linear pottery. As these impressive chamber-tombs became the ceremonial focus of settlements (perhaps because of

Carvings in the
passage-grave of Gavr'inis.

the organised labour required to build them) the indigenous people also began to build long trapezoidal mounds of earth similar in shape to the longhouses of the farmers. In time the two styles of construction appear to have merged into a long mound *langdysse* for burial, covering several chambers built of upright stones covered with a large block. On Moen island, for example, the long mound called Groenjaegers Hoej, itself bounded by stones as high as a man, contains three stone chambers. These stone tombs mostly occur in northern Jutland, but there are many other long mounds, not containing megaliths but which once had wooden interiors, in groups either side of the lower Elbe river.

More influences came together across the continent to produce, on the tiny island of Gavr'inis, near Auray, Morbihan, the most lavishly decorated megalithic tomb in Europe (about 5800 years old). The longest passage-grave in Brittany, it is lined with massive stones of which twenty-three are carved. The geometric decoration is very similar to that of the other great passage-grave of Newgrange, County Meath, in Ireland, which is 93 metres in diameter and almost 12 metres high. Newgrange, like Gavr'inis, and Maes Howe in the Orkney Islands, is so aligned that at the midwinter solstice the sun shines through a special opening down the long passage to reach the tomb-chamber floor.

West Kennet in Wiltshire is the largest of the Severn-Cotswold barrows and among the best known ancient monuments of Britain. It is 101 metres long and contained several burial chambers which have given up at least 46 skeletons, including, in the south eastern chamber, the bones of one man, one woman, five children and four babies. It began to be used as a monument about 5600 years ago, a thousand years before the Egyptians of the Old Kingdom began to immortalise their dead in pyramids. But these are just the most famous of thousands of massive constructions made around this time.

Such enormous works needed the organised labour of literally thousands of men over very long periods, and they reflect the centralisation of religious and temporal power that must have commanded their construction. It is not hard to see how ancestor worship and the glorification of the dead can be vested with supreme importance. But the next phase of megalithic building still defies satisfactory interpretation.

About 5200 years ago, great stone circles began to take the place of tombs. There are over 1000 stone circles in the British Isles, and 80 henges (circular ditched enclosures), while in Brittany, at the other end of what was clearly an axis of trade and ideas linked by maritime trade, there are circles and alignments and a very large number of single standing stones called menhirs (the largest of which stood over 20 metres high). These structures were of so great a scale that they must have served as social and religious centres for whole regions. The twelve rows of alignments which run between stone circles at Le Menec, near Carnac in Brittany, are associated with burial tumuli which contained rich grave goods, as is the last phase at Stonehenge, which displaced nearby Avebury as the ritual centre of Wessex. It has been estimated that to position the 26-tonne sarsen blocks at Stonehenge, brought from the Marlborough Downs 29 kilometres away, would have required two million man-hours of labour. (New geological evidence suggests that the famous bluestones were not after all brought by man from the Preseli Hills in Wales, but transported by ice.) If nothing else, these monuments indicate that it was possible to organise and feed large armies of men, which could only have been possible with a highly developed agriculture.

The stone circles' connections with astronomic prediction are undeniable, although few alignments have been satisfactorily proven. Yet they can also

appear to be an arrogant display of man's power over Nature – a self-confidence that was not well founded in reality. At Callanish stone circle, by Loch Roag, on the island of Lewis, Outer Hebrides, many of the stones had been swallowed up by peat before they were excavated. Ironically this peat is the consequence of both deteriorating climate and agriculture. The most favourable climate of the interglacial period that we are now enjoying was between 5500 and 3000 years ago, the height of the megalithic building period. Then Europeans were living even in the extreme remoteness of the Scottish Isles, as can be seen at the remarkable village of Scara Brae in the Orkneys, built almost entirely of stone because of the lack of trees, and preserved because it was overwhelmed by a sand-storm.

By this time in the story of Europe, climatic change and the over-exploitation of light soils by a growing population had undoubtedly taken their toll, by repeatedly causing harvests to fail and thus causing famine. By 3500 years ago most of Europe had already been deforested, and now even the forest on highlands like Dartmoor was cleared to make way for farming communities who built the spectacular stone walls called reaves. Once again it is possible that it was the pressure of increasing population that led people to farm this poor acid soil, and the reaves to be built to form boundaries between precious family plots and communities.

Tragically for the families concerned, the deforestation and intensive ploughing caused irreversible damage. Once the tree roots no longer drew moisture from the soil it drained downwards into the acid sub-soil forming a crust of iron or 'pan' that was impermeable. This process, called podsolisation, makes the soil sodden and too acid for earthworms, which are essential for recycling nutrients, to thrive. Accentuated perhaps by a wetter and colder climate, the sodden ground turned into a peat-bog wasteland, the villages must have starved, and were finally deserted, no doubt amid scenes of terrible human hardship. Blanket bogs may have been caused by this process across the highlands of southern Britain, Yorkshire, the Flow Country of Scotland, and Ireland. Large areas of the marginal lands of northern Europe became uninhabitable. Around the Mediterranean deforestation and a wetter climate had led to the massive erosion of soil. Far from dominating Nature, man was becoming the slave of his own mistakes.

The stone circle at Callanish.

CHAPTER THREE

THE ALPS
AND THE
FIRST METALS

Lake Geneva is a glacial lake, one of the many carved by ice and dammed by glacial moraines that the ice ages scattered around the edges of the Alps. The broad Swiss valley of Valais is now filled with sediments and has a level floor carpeted with neat rows of vines, but only 12,000 years ago it had been carved to a deep 'U' shape and lay buried under thousands of metres of ice. The river Rhône, which courses down it to fill the lake, is born even now at a glacier, a drab remnant of the huge icecap that once obscured most of the Alps from view. But the Rhône glacier has retreated some 150 kilometres to the east, shrinking even from the hotels built at the turn of the twentieth century to bring tourists and the rudiments of civilisation to its grubby glistening edge.

Of the thousands of skiers, climbers and wanderers who now venture through the gap at Martigny that the river and glacier carved between the Bernese Alps to the north and the Pennine Alps to the south, few stop to wonder why those mountains stand there, pressing in dramatically on either hand. Yet above a convenient lay-by, imprisoned in the cliffs, hangs startling evidence of the almost unimaginable forces that built Europe – the wreckage left behind by the force of continents at play.

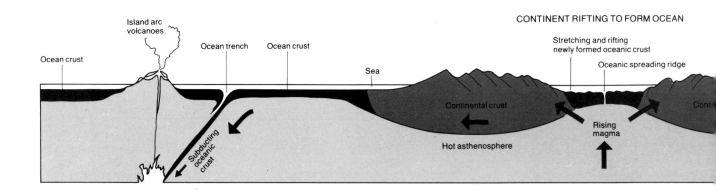

To the north, a huge cliff at the summit of the Dent de Morcles bears a pattern like the end of a flattened swiss-roll (see frontispiece). To the south, better seen from the air, the rocks of the Dent du Midi are folded to the same design. These massive curves are the edge of an immense fold of limestone that was originally formed on the floor of an ocean which lay 3000 metres deep between Europe and Africa. As the two continents collided, the limestone layer was folded up and pushed forward, like a ruck in a hearth-rug, until it lay on top of the ancient continent of Europe. It was this dramatic folding of the rocks to form the Alps that laid the foundation for the advance of European civilisation, because it brought metals within the reach of man for the first time.

It is only since 1960 that geologists have had a satisfactory hypothesis to explain *why* continents drift across the surface of the globe. Our planet Earth consists of three main parts: in the centre is the core which comprises roughly half the diameter of the globe. This is heated to a very high temperature by the radioactive decay of elements such as uranium, but which consists mostly of iron and nickel. Surrounding the core is a layer called the mantle. If you tunnel into the earth, the temperature of the rocks increases at the rate of about 30 degrees Celsius for each kilometre you descend. The deepest hole that has ever been drilled is only 12 kilometres deep (in the Kola Peninsula) but it is known from the way earthquake waves are reflected that the mantle is about 2900 kilometres thick. Being so hot and so heavily compressed, it flows very slowly like heated pitch or toffee. On top rests the third part, the Earth's crust, which is between 8 and 50 kilometres thick. Considering that all our lives and this story depend on that crust, it is worth remembering that in comparison with the Earth as a whole it is only as thick as a postage stamp stuck on a football. And our football is full of white-hot rock. What happens if that crust splits we know all too well: even minor cracks produce the spectacular fire-fountains of Iceland.

The crust is thinnest beneath the deep oceans, and along the centre line of many of them run ranges of mountains built from submarine volcanoes. The crust beneath the oceans is made up of basalt, the same dense black volcanic rock that erupts at the mid-oceanic ridges, and this led to the hypothesis that the sea-floor spreads outwards – that new oceanic crust is actually formed at a mid-ocean ridge and spreads out sideways from it, floating on the viscous mantle. The spreading occurs at the rate of several centimetres a year, so the floor of all our oceans could have been formed in some 200 million years. But the Earth is known to be about 4600 million years old, so clearly the ocean floor must be destroyed as

The processes of continental drift. As oceanic crust is formed at spreading centres, continents move apart and old sea floor has to be consumed by 'subduction' beneath other oceanic crust or beneath continents. The sideways pressure within continents forms mountain ranges.

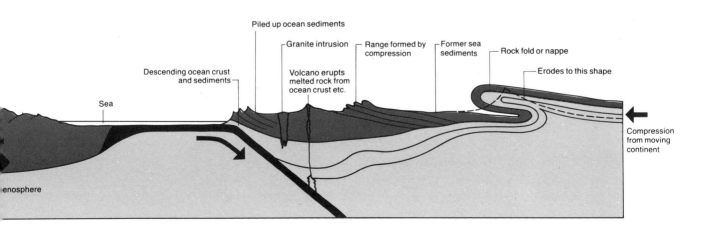

Piled up ocean sediments

Granite intrusion ─ Range formed by compression ─ Former sea sediments ─ Rock fold or nappe

Erodes to this shape

Descending ocean crust and sediments ─

Volcano erupts melted rock from ocean crust etc.

Sea

Compression from moving continent

enosphere

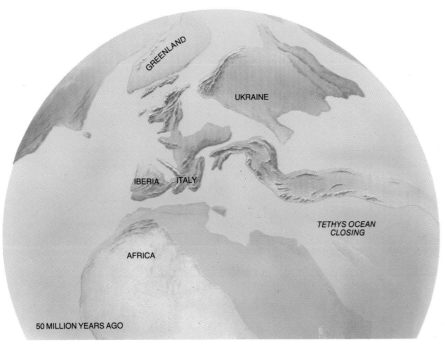

GREENLAND

UKRAINE

IBERIA   ITALY

AFRICA

TETHYS OCEAN
CLOSING

50 MILLION YEARS AGO

30 MILLION YEARS AGO

58 · THE BIRTH OF EUROPE

LEFT The summit of the
Matterhorn was carved by
glaciers descending in
three different directions.
The rocks, part of the
African continent, slid 300
kilometres on top of
Europe before the
mountain was carved to
its present shape.

well as created. What happens is that as the ocean floor spreads it pushes continents sideways. When a slab of continental crust like South America is pushed by the ocean floor from both sides, something has to give. The ocean floor basalt is heavier than the crystalline rocks which make up continents, so it is driven down beneath one of the continental edges, forming deep ocean trenches such as the Chile-Peru trench as it disappears into the Earth's core to be melted again. Meanwhile the continental slabs 'float' on top, drifting about the surface of the planet as they are pushed by plates of ocean floor. This is the basic theory of continental-plate tectonics. As the sea floor and the continent collide, the edge of the continent folds under the pressure and thickens to form major chains of mountains like the Andes. These contain volcanoes caused as rock carried down with the descending sea floor melts and boils up to the surface.

When the sea floor has all been driven down, the continents themselves collide and the edges buckle and ride over each other with few volcanoes – as in the Himalayas, formed where India is still crashing northwards into Asia. This buckling sometimes lifts up parts of the sea floor as well. The Mediterranean is one of the most complex areas for plate tectonics in the world, with several micro-plates of crust being jostled together as Africa continues to crunch remorselessly into Europe. The building of the Alpine chain began in the Pyrenees, as Africa swept westwards, ripping the Iberian peninsula away from France, and rotating it anti-clockwise to open the Bay of Biscay by about 65 million years ago. Corsica and Sardinia were then torn away from the south of Europe by the same movement of Africa, and a northward movement of that continent extended the mountain ranges eastwards to cause the Dinaric Alps, the Carpathians, and the Caucasus, where Europe's highest mountain, Mt Elbrus, is a volcano, reflecting the intense tectonic activity of the region.

Although the Alps still continue to rise, at about the same rate as your fingernails grow, under the remorseless pressure from Africa, we do not notice it. What we do notice are the lesser effects of the grand tectonic scheme of things. Volcanic

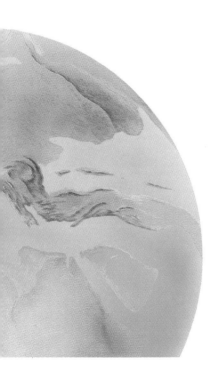

BELOW Colliding
continents. The rotation
of Africa against Europe
has turned Iberia anti-
clockwise, and piled the
floor of the Tethys ocean
on top of Europe,
crumpling the continental
crust at the same time to
form the Alps.

3 MILLION YEARS AGO

THE ALPS AND THE FIRST METALS · 59

eruptions may destroy cities and even empires but they also have incalculable effects on life on Earth through their ability to throw enormous dust clouds into the atmosphere which can block out the sun. Fortunately we have not had a serious example of this recently, although the eruption of El Chichón in Mexico in April 1982 cast a veil across the sky for several years. Among minor consequences, most of the world's airlines had to replace the glass windows in their aircraft which had been etched by the acid dust. But from Benidorm to Bukhara, cities are at risk from earthquakes. Continental compression is absorbed by the rocks sliding past each other along well-defined cracks or faults. Energy is stored up by bending the rocks on either side of a fault until the natural friction is overcome and they suddenly slide past each other with a jerk. This we call an earthquake. Local disasters caused by this release of energy will continue, and we are ill-prepared – as we saw so tragically in Armenia in 1988, and in Iran in 1990, when 40,000 people were killed.

Continents are mostly built of granite, the hard pink and grey speckled material so familiar from tombstones and the forbidding façades of banks. But granite is not as immutable as undertakers would have you believe. As Africa deformed Europe, the granite European plate was squashed and thickened, and the result can be seen clearly in the Mont Blanc massif – part of the ancient continental crust. A vertiginous cable-car climbs from Chamonix up to the Aiguille du Midi, one of a spectacular horseshoe of frost-shattered granite needle-points that stand up around the Mer de Glace ice-field in the shadow of Mont Blanc. It seems impossible that this highest peak in central Europe was once buried under three huge folds of rock, driven by the African invasion. As Africa slid on top of Europe the Earth's crust was probably shortened by about 300 kilometres, and in the process the bed of an entire ocean, called Tethys by the geologists, was folded and pushed on top of the Alps.

Several kilometres of the thickness of the upper rocks have since been eroded by ice and weathering. In fact two other immense folds used to lie on top of the one still visible at the Dent de Morcles. As they were eroded, their pebbles, which can still be identified, were washed downhill to form new sedimentary rocks, four to five kilometres thick, between the Alps and the Jura ranges. As millions of years passed, the granite heart of the Mont Blanc massif, relieved of the overlying weight, bobbed up like a cork, millimetre by millimetre, until it has risen some 10 kilometres higher on the mantle. As it rose, the top was continuously eroded down so that it stayed at about its present height. The rivers Rhône and Rhine also retained their level – carving deep valleys to maintain their course as the rocks ascended on either side.

When Edward Whymper climbed the Matterhorn for the first time in 1865 he did not realise that he stood on African rock lying on top of an ancient ocean floor, both pushed into place before the glaciers of the last ice age cut the peak to its present shape. Within sight of that peak is the Weisshorn, and halfway up a mighty cliff that leads to the summit is a clear smooth contact line where greenish oceanic rocks called ophiolites have slid hundreds of kilometres to lie above those of ancient Europe. The beautiful pyramid of the Dent Blanche is carved from African rock too, and most of the Austrian Alps are really part of Africa.

To the north-west the same compression of Europe folded the Jura Mountains out of sediments worn from the earlier Alpine summits and as far off as England and Wales, the crumpled rocks at Stair Hole in Dorset and Broadhaven in Pembrokeshire are the last ripples spreading outwards from this continental storm.

It is inconceivable that such immense changes in the topography of Europe should not have played a part in the development of its human history but it is much harder to tell just what those effects were. Clearly the mountain ranges formed a barrier separating the Mediterranean climatic region from the wetter colder region of forests to the north. In early times mountains were inhospitable obstacles between peoples, the realm of gods not mortals. But human progress has gone hand in hand with the discovery and use of different natural environments and resources. While former lake-beds and river flood-plains had aided the development of farming, it was to be the uplands that provided the mysterious elements that were to lead mankind out of the age of wood and stone.

The first use of copper

The next great step along the path of European civilisation was made when man learned to use metals, and metals only occur in certain kinds of rocks. In Europe the Alpine mountain-building lifted those ancient rocks, heating and deforming them until they appeared as mountains.

Metals are distributed throughout the Earth's crust, but can be mined only when they have been concentrated into veins. One way that this happens is during continental collision, when crustal material is pushed down into the intensely hot interior of the Earth, causing it to melt. The lighter granitic material then rises into the continental crust above to form 'plutons', huge globular masses of crystalline rock (some of these have since been exposed by erosion like the Red Cuillins of Skye). As the immense thicknesses of rock solidify extremely slowly, the materials with the lowest melting point, such as metals, solidify last. So the solutions of metals creep up through cracks in the surrounding rock and then crystallise into veins as they cool.

In Europe, most gold, silver, tin, lead and uranium is found in the granitic areas dating to the earlier Hercynian mountain-building period of 300 million years ago. But the formation of the Alps reworked these older deposits. When mountains are eroded the metals in veins are washed away too, and many will oxidise in the atmosphere, but the least reactive, like gold and tin, will remain in the river sands and gravels unchanged for millennia. As gold occurs naturally as nuggets in streams, it may indeed have been the first metal to be used – hammered into some other decorative shape; but there is, as yet, no archaeological evidence to support this.

Copper, on the other hand, was to be the first metal used for practical purposes. It usually occurs in ocean floor rocks; indeed some geologists now believe that it is concentrated in the areas where the ocean floor is actually spreading. There is also another intriguing link between the abundance of copper in Europe and Central Asia and the recent geological past. The chemistry of the copper deposits was changed by the last ice age. When mountain building and erosion leave a copper-rich zone of rocks at the surface, it is usually as a compound called chalcopyrite formed with sulphur and iron. As it is oxidised (and, astonishingly, this is done through the action of a bacterium, *Thiobacillus ferroxidans*), the iron separates into a hard oxide cap at the surface called a gossan, and the copper becomes first copper sulphate, and then, as it percolates downwards with water, forms the beautiful green and blue carbonates, malachite and azurite. Below the water-table the solutions form enriched copper sulphides.

During the last glaciation the climate became dryer around the ice sheets and the mountain icecaps of the Alps and other high ranges as far south as Anatolia and even the Zagros of Iran. This caused the water table to drop, and some of the copper compounds oxidised to form metallic copper. Pieces of native copper can

be large: one weighing 130 kilos was found in western Serbia a century ago and there is a piece a metre and a half long in the Geological Museum in London. As the rainfall increased, erosion then wore away the rock until pure native copper emerged at the surface. Greeny-blue from its associated malachite and azurite and jagged, it would be as conspicuous to a Neolithic hunter with bare feet as a broken bottle is on a beach today! To someone well versed in the characteristics of different kinds of stone for tools, it would at once be recognised as something unusual because copper is pliable.

As archaeology proceeds, more sites are excavated and the scientific analysis of the results improves, there is little doubt that evidence of the early use of metals will be found at more sites than are now known. But the earliest copper implements found so far were made from native copper over 9000 years ago. Over a hundred small copper objects like awls and hooks have been found at Çayönü Tepesí to the south of the Taurus Mountains in south-eastern Turkey. Although this is in Asia Minor, it is part of the Alpine fold-belt. The site has several layers of

LEFT South of San Vittore, Italy, the mountains of the African plate.

buildings with complex architecture, which date from about 9500 years ago, some 1500 years *before* pottery was first made in the Middle East and some 5000 years before metal work appears in China. The excavation has also revealed that the inhabitants had some unpleasant customs. Human skulls and long-bones were stacked against the walls of cellars with the horns of cattle, while carefully polished stone 'tables' and a depression contained crystals of human and cattle blood. Religion had clearly come to play an important role in their life and death.

The copper objects are little more than trinkets, but what is astonishing is that they already show evidence of having been recrystallised by heating. Copper is composed of crystals and, when a smith works it by hammering, the metal deforms as the crystals slide past one another. After a certain amount of hammer-

RIGHT Azurite, one of the copper carbonate ores first smelted into copper.

ing the metal hardens as the crystals can slide no further and less movement is possible. More hammering causes splits to occur at non-metallic inclusions which are points of weakness. By reheating it to about 500 degrees Celsius the copper recrystallises and thus can be cold-worked again. The people of Çayönü were no country rustics; one building had a decorative red terrazzo floor made of pieces of red-oxide-stained limestone bonded in a hard lime mortar and carefully polished smooth. Lime is made by burning and slaking limestone, so the builders were already skilled in the application of fire.

The craftsmen had also learned to reheat their copper to work it more. But microscopic analysis shows that the smith at Çayönü made one mistake; after finishing his hooks he reheated them, not realising that this left them in the softened state. This is hardly surprising since we are looking at the very beginnings of metallurgy, nor is it surprising that copper-smithing first occurred in an intensely active tectonic area where the sea-floor coppers from the Tethys ocean can still be found a day's walk away from the fertile valley of Çayönü, at Ergani Maden. As the mine was on the headwaters of the Tigris, the copper was almost certainly transported downstream, and much later became the major supply for the Babylonian and Assyrian civilisations. Copper is still mined there today.

The Copper Age

It is not until about 8000 years ago that the first metal actually smelted from an ore appears in the archaeological record, again in Asia Minor. Lead, the metal with the lowest melting point, can be reduced from its ore, galena, in an ordinary camp fire. Rare, and thus precious, its first appearance is as a necklace of lead beads found at the spectacular agricultural settlement of Çatal Hüyük. This is one of the earliest 'towns' so far discovered, and covers about 13 hectares. It was built on the edge of a former lake-bed – the Konya Plain of south-central Anatolia – where recent sediments provided fertile soil close to the mineral deposits of the mountains. This was a crucial juxtaposition, because only a flourishing agricultural settlement could support a work force with the free time to experiment with metals. On a mud wall of this prototype of towns another metal ore, cinnabar (mercury sulphide) was used for vermillion paint to depict the eruption of the nearby Hasan Dag volcano. Volcanic ash is rich in minerals and makes fertile soil, and volcanoes are evidence of the tectonic activity that brings metals within the reach of Man. So we must be doubly grateful for the gifts of the volcanoes that brought us metallurgy.

It was the same combination of natural resources that permitted the first smelting of copper in Europe. Stable and successful village societies had to develop on fertile soils before anyone could be spared from labour on the land to become a craftsman and be maintained by his fellow villagers. So both metalliferous mountains and fertile plains were needed before copper workers could be freed for long enough from the daily grind of gaining their bread to progress from the smithing of natural lumps to smelting and casting. The fact that these resources occurred close together in the Balkans may well be the reason why copper metallurgy was developed in Europe some 2000 years earlier than in China. This gave Europe a head start in the long march that led, ultimately, to European industrial empires dominating the whole globe.

In what is now Bulgaria the continental collision had brought copper to the surface. Here the Tethys ocean floor had been pushed beneath the Rhodope mountains, carrying copper-rich rocks deep into the crust where they melted. Copper solutions then rose to be deposited along the fault line of the more northerly range the Sredna Gorya. Fertile brown soils lying at the foot of the mountains were to attract a relatively dense population to within a few kilometres of the copper ores.

Today the valley below the mountains is covered with immensely long rows of vines belonging to the collective vineyards. But at its edge, where fresh springs emerge, stand a number of tells. At Karanovo a massive excavation has carved away the whole centre of the mound, revealing floor levels piled one on another for 4000 years. The 13-metre-high cross-section that this immense period of occupation has left behind gives a fascinating calendar of the development of this neolithic community. Its stability and prosperity were of course due to the fertility of the land from which the mud huts themselves were built.

It is still striking to see how hard peasant farmers in China and Ethiopia have to work to fill a family's stomachs from the land. There is little part of any day that is free to indulge in tasks unrelated to breadwinning – they do not even sit down to eat. But where the land is rich and harvests bountiful, the climate suitable and the society benign, the pressure may not be quite so great and time may be spent on other activities.

At Karanovo they had that rich land, they had stability and their craftsmanship developed. The bottom layer, the first village, contains simple but graceful pottery. In the higher levels the pots have handles to form mugs and some dishes have legs. Higher still, in the fourth layer, geometric patterns appear, painted with yellow and red ochre, and there are some spectacular swirling black and white designs. With time the skills of the craftsmen were improving.

Coloured pigments like manganese and ochre had already been used for tens of thousands of years, and two of the most attractive natural mineral colours, the blue of azurite and green of malachite, are copper carbonate ores. At Çayönü Tepesí a necklace of beads carved from malachite was found. So far no graveyard has been discovered at Karanovo, but at the Bulgarian island of Durankulak a necropolis with over a thousand graves yielded bracelets and necklaces also made of malachite beads. Patterned pottery 'stamps' at Stara Zagora suggest that powdered azurite was used to decorate bodies or faces; both sites are only a few days travel from Karanovo. Lumps of the ores have been found in the second level at Karanovo too (7700 years old), so copper ore had long been something rare and valued, if only for its colour.

The farmers of Karanovo must have been conservative to have survived so long in the same seasonal routine as generation was born to generation and their mud houses were built, and fell, and were rebuilt again and again in the same site, slowly to pile up the layer-cake of their tell. But when Karanovo stood at its fifth level (6500 years ago) copper objects suddenly appear. In the level below there are none. The earliest copper items, like earrings for bone figurines and awls, are very small and were probably made from native copper. When you heat copper in a fire to soften it, it burns with a strong green flame. Malachite and azurite burn with a similar green flame, and when native copper could be found in the same place as the ores it is not hard to see how accident or experiment led to the discovery of smelting.

Was it a rogue artistic eye for form and colour, youthful curiosity, or the spur of vanity that led to the release of copper from its ores? We will never know. Fire had already been used to treat flints, to make them flake more easily, and to temper native copper. At Karanovo they had already learned to fire pottery in a carbon-rich reducing atmosphere, and it was the reducing capacity of a charcoal hearth that made copper smelting possible. In 1988 the earliest smelting hearth in the Balkans was discovered at Stara Zagora. (Pottery fragments dated it to Karanovo level five.) No more than an elliptical scrape in the ground, it had a rim 6 centimetres high round one end. In it still lay charcoal and a graceless mess of melted malachite with azurite. Remarkably modern-looking ceramic nozzles for bellows were found beside it. Even in such a simple hearth blown with bellows a temperature of 1200 degrees Celsius can be reached, and the free carbon of the bed of charcoal can combine with the copper oxides to release the metal. In just such a fire the Copper Age had begun.

In 1938 a peasant was digging at the copper deposits in the Sredna Gorya mountains to collect raw copper ore to protect his vines from mildew when he found what he thought was a Roman lamp. In fact it was 4000 years older than that. He had discovered one of the earliest copper mines in the world – Ai Bunar (Bear Well), only a few hours' walk from the tells in the valley. It was evident that the copper had been mined by 'fire-setting' – building a hot fire to heat the rock and then dashing water against it to cool it. This fractures the rock, making it fairly

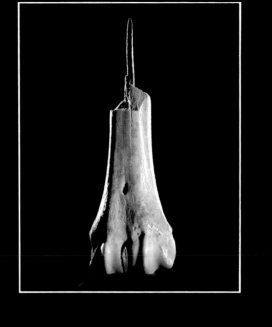

simple to pry the ore loose with red-deer antler picks. Recent radiocarbon analysis of the charcoal found at Ai Bunar dates the mine at over 7000 years old. Lead-isotope analysis has also firmly linked the seams at Ai Bunar to the copper found at Karanovo.

The first smelted and cast copper hammer-axes were copies of the fine polished stone axes of the time. Unless you have actually felt the edge on a good stone axe it is difficult to appreciate what fine tools they were. But of course they were very time-consuming to make, hard to drill using sand and bone to make a shaft-hole, and very fragile. It is often said that copper axes were only used for prestige and ceremonial purposes. But the cutting edge of a cast copper axe-head can be hammered to a hardness tougher than low-carbon steel. They would undoubtedly have been precious and sought-after tools, but there is no need to think that they were *only* used for parade or battle. Indeed chisels for woodworking were a common early form to be cast. At Ai Bunar a very battered copper hammer-axe was found which had clearly been used for mining.

At Rudna Glava in Yugoslavia, in 1968, an open-cast iron mine was dug right through ancient copper shafts, leaving some of them in cross-section, before they were recognised for what they were. There, archaeologists found not only antler pry-bars and picks, but stone mauls weighing two or three kilos – notched to take a rope or handle so that they could be swung in the confined space of the narrow shafts. The shafts were limited in depth to about 20 metres by the need for a supply of air for the small fires set against the rock. Pots to carry water for cooling the rock were also found below ground, as well as a lamp in the stylised shape of a goat which probably burned animal fat as fuel.

At Rudna Glava malachite and azurite still appear as bright coloured patches on the rock, and it is obvious that only the richest ore was considered worth mining, but, as smelting technology progressed, lower and lower grade ores could be successfully processed in most mining areas, thus cutting back the original workings. Indeed one of the problems in locating ancient mining areas is that later working has so often destroyed the evidence. Rudna Glava is not far from the large modern copper mine of Majdanpek, and many other metal deposits are known in the Dinaric Alps which have not been mined for lack of capital.

Even in the earliest days impressive quantities of copper were mined by these apparently primitive but effective methods. At Ai Bunar there are several pits that, judging by the ore content, yielded over a thousand tons of copper. Of course, all this new 'industrial' activity was to have a profound effect on the people living nearby. For the first time the craftsmen had the ability to transform a natural substance into another material, a magical accomplishment that must have seemed little short of miraculous; a cause of wonder and prestige. The heads of the settlements, possibly the smiths themselves, were soon able not only to make friends and influence people but also to get rich by trading their shining new copper. Undoubtedly, greed was to become a powerful human motive in the development of metallurgy, as copper could be traded for gold.

Copper and gold

About 180 kilometres to the north-east of Karanovo, in 1972, a tractor driver digging a trench for an electric cable in an industrial suburb of the Black Sea port of Varna noticed large squares of a bright yellow metal and bracelets of the same shining substance. He had unearthed the oldest golden treasure in the world (another has since been found in Israel of about the same date). Archaeological theories about the genesis of metallurgy were confounded when the gold, and

Pottery from the different levels at Karanovo shows a cultural progression from the crude terracotta of the first farming village (bottom right), to more complex forms fired in a reducing atmosphere in level three (bottom left), to magnificent geometric designs in black and white in level 4 (centre right), and sophisticated designs with burnished graphite coated surfaces in level 6 (centre left). Copper objects first appear in level 5, like this awl, for making holes in leather, fixed in a chicken bone, found at Stara Zagora.

numerous cast copper tools, were dated to the fifth level at Karanovo (about 6500 years old). They were far more sophisticated than any metals of that age previously found.

So far 280 graves have been excavated, revealing several thousand pieces of gold. Much of the workmanship is basic – hammered sheets, cut or punched with copper chisels – but the goldsmiths could also raise curved surfaces to form simple but graceful bracelets and a sceptre worthy of any king. As one of the earliest known examples of gold-working it leaves no doubt that gold was then used for ceremonial purposes, and had a high value. Most of the gold was found in just a handful of the richest graves: one of them held one and a half kilos. (Currently worth some $20,000!) The most valuable finds were ceremonial sceptres in the form of axe hammers in greenstone or copper with gold-covered hafts. But some of the central graves were symbolic, with no human remains, and some of these contained life-size clay masks decorated with golden eye-discs, earrings and other adornments.

This dramatic discovery shows at a glance the wealth and power that the knowledge of metallurgy had brought to the local chieftains. But it was also a total surprise that the earliest gold-work was discovered not in Mesopotamia or Egypt, but on the mainland of Europe. It appears that once copper smelting had been mastered there, gold working followed, and it is logical to assume that copper metallurgy would have been developed where the ores were to hand.

Gold is found in many of the rivers of the Balkans, in fact it is even present in the mine of Ai Bunar, but it is probable that the earliest gold was found as nuggets in the streams and rivers of the south-western Rhodope mountains, the Rila massif and the Ogosta river, a tributary of the Danube. Gold is still there today, but when nuggets and the little flakes called 'placer' gold were first collected as a curiosity it would have been much easier to find. Once its value had been realised the larger nuggets would have vanished as fast as coins left on a street corner. Many graves held copper axes and chisels, but also contained necklaces and bracelets made from dentalium and spondylus shells which could only have come by trade from the Sea of Marmara and the Aegean. It is very likely that the people of the Varna cemetery were controlling a substantial trade in copper and gold. At the time Varna was near a bay where the River Provadiya enters the Black Sea. It was a natural crossroads for the trade travelling by water from Asia Minor to the Danube and that of the Balkan metal-bearing mountains via the Provadiya and nearby Kamchiya rivers.

The fact that copper and gold was buried with the leading men of the age, in an ostentatious destruction of wealth, implies that they could afford to lose these metals for ever. Burial maintained the scarcity and price, but it also implied that new supplies must have been available. It meant that each successor to the chieftains had to earn his own status, rather than inheriting it through passed-on possessions. Effigies of sheep or cattle in the graves represented the other most valuable possessions a man could own.

Copper axes, chisels, needles and other goods were exchanged for valuable agricultural and mineral products. They were ideal for trade, being of high value, small and easily carried, and they were transported for long distances, just as amber had been in early neolithic times. Copper from the mines such as Ai Bunar and Rudna Glava has been found as far away as Denmark and two or three thousand kilometres to the north-east of the Black Sea.

In turn the copper mines became more and more important, and used more and more labour. Ten people were needed to hew wood and draw water for

Reconstruction of the Varna grave No. 43. A man aged forty to fifty was buried with a golden-hafted stone axe as a sceptre, a copper hammer-axe, spear-head and other tools, a bow bound with gold, long flint knives, and innumerable gold ornaments. The farming villages of the early Karanovo levels had shown no signs of different social status. Now the age of warrior chieftains had begun.

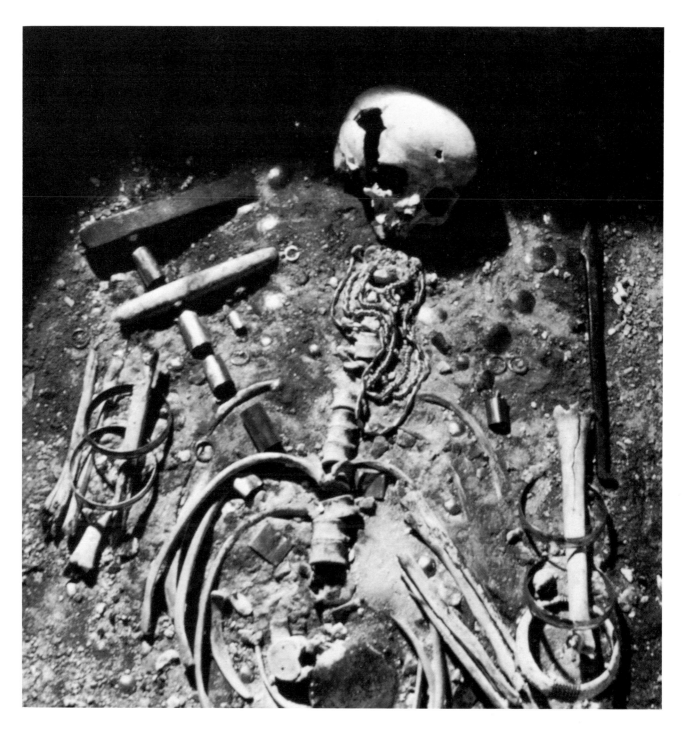

every actual miner. But mines, like people, have a limited lifespan, and by about 5500 years ago the copper carbonate ores in the Balkans were exhausted. Copper was no longer put in graves, as it was no longer replaceable, and its value must have soared. A crisis followed, and unemployed miners and smiths must have scoured the mountains of southern Europe looking for other copper sources, experimenting with different ores, desperately seeking an alternative.

It may only be coincidental, but at about this time the influence of the Balkan-Carpathian copper peoples, known for their stable tell-based agriculture, came under increasing influence from horsemen from the steppes to the north of the Black Sea, the Indo-Europeans. The seventh layer at Karanovo shows a society

undergoing a major transition. The beautiful polychrome and metallic surface pottery found in the fifth and sixth levels vanishes, replaced by plain utilitarian pots. A downward spiral of culture had begun.

The new copper ores

The way in which copper deposits had evolved had left grey sulphide ores beneath the brightly coloured carbonates. These minerals are recognisably connected with copper because they too burn with a strong green flame. But before they can be smelted they have to be roasted in an open hearth to get rid of the sulphur, an additional process that had to be discovered. However, the grey ores do have the significant advantages that they are often much richer in copper content, and that sometimes they are found naturally combined with arsenic, and arsenic is a deoxidising agent which improves the metal when added in small proportions. The copper sulphide ores are quite distinctive, as when roasted they give off a pungent smell of sulphur dioxide, and so are the arsenical compounds, which release a garlic smell even when they are hammered. With time, the smiths discovered that a garlic-smelling mixture made a superior type of metal for tools.

When copper is smelted, oxygen causes copper oxide to form round the crystal boundaries as the metal solidifies; this makes the metal less malleable, but when arsenic is added in small quantities (from 1 to 8 per cent) it combines with the oxygen and escapes from the melt as fumes. The resulting arsenical bronze is more malleable, less porous, and also melts at a lower temperature than pure copper. Its malleability means it can be hammered more and thus work-hardened to give a fine cutting-edge. But the fumes of arsenic given off when it is smelted are deadly poisonous. They cause acute dermatitis and peripheral neuritis: a disablement of the nervous system leading to weakness of the fingers, legs and feet, and finally death. It may be no coincidence that the earliest recorded metalworkers' gods – Hephaistos in Greece, Vulcan in Rome, and Weyland in Germanic countries – were often depicted as being lame.

The first arsenical copper was probably produced in the Near East and spread to the Caucasus where it was almost certainly made from copper ores containing arsenic, such as tennantite. But to get concentrations of arsenic as high as those used later, there is no doubt that it was deliberately added to the melt. Two arsenic compounds, orpiment and realgar, are both brightly coloured yellow and orange, and were later used as pigments. Guided by colour, smell and experience, even hand sorting of ores could give the right proportions for the best mixture of copper and arsenic. Another most significant improvement in metallurgy also came from the Caucasus about this time: the adoption of the two-piece mould. Until then copper tools had been made with a simple mould with an open top. By using a two-piece mould of clay, however, the finished object can be used to make a whole series of similar moulds – mass production. The first tools to be produced in this way were single-bladed battle-axes. But the technique allowed far more sophisticated and detailed shapes to be cast for the first time.

The warrior-princes

About 6000 years ago in the Steppes, a pastoralist society began to build hillforts and megalithic house-like cist graves; these were buried beneath high tumuli (called Kurgans) and ringed by upright standing stones. In them are found evidence of carts, yokes for oxen and bits for horses. The decoration and grave-goods suggest they were a hierarchical and tribal society. The cultural change visible in the seventh and highest level at Karanovo (about 5500 years ago)

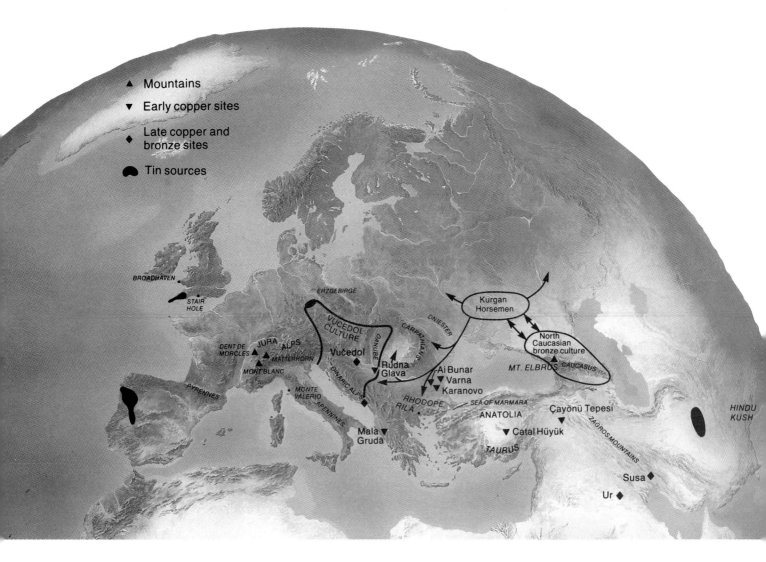

Copper Age and early Bronze Age sites.

reflects contact with these Kurgan people, but also new major trade links with Anatolia which had begun to introduce a number of important technological innovations which together were to change the whole European way of life. They included the plough, the wheel, the wool-bearing sheep and probably alcohol. Europe was suddenly catching up with the Middle East.

The climate in Europe was now at its warmest point since the ice age, but in the Carpathian Basin the dense population (called the Baden culture), although at first thriving with the new techniques, began to suffer a geologically induced crisis. The farmers had been cultivating loess soils which had been deposited by the last ice age on top of an old Eocene sea bed. When inland seas evaporate they usually produce saline soils, and over the centuries this underlying salt had come to the surface of the loess, making harvests fail. Large amounts of previously fertile farming land were now suitable only for herding cattle.

Then one of the most critical events of the whole of European pre-history occurred, a major incursion of the Kurgan horsemen deep into Europe. (Some archaeologists have suggested that this was caused by the drying out of the Steppes that were their homeland.) Karanovo was turned into a fort which became the focus of power and cultural life, and completely different half-buried houses were used by the people. A chain of hillforts was built across the plains of the lower Danube, Bulgaria and Macedonia. The old European workmanship is now found only in these hillforts and the rich tombs beneath huge tumuli, not in the ordinary villages. It was a complete transformation from a basically egalitarian society, where each man stayed in his village and grew the food that fed him, to one where mounted warriors ruled the territory of their clan or tribe.

The derelict agricultural land of the Carpathian basin began to be filled by a great influx of these horsemen, semi-nomadic pastoralists who also practised some agriculture, and who used their hillforts as a cultural focus for the tribe or clan. Some of the families were building up large herds of cattle, and in a herding and agricultural society this is one of the only ways to accumulate private capital – just as it is with the Masai in Kenya today. The old tell settlements were abandoned, and the Baden cemeteries now show evidence of both animal and human sacrifice. Dogs, horses, cattle and even ox-teams were killed and buried with their owner, as were women and children. Although they probably came from the area around the Dniester River (in the south of the modern Ukraine), the newcomers brought to Europe from the Caucasus the two-piece mould, the new arsenical copper battle-axe, and large numbers of horses. The huge quantities of battle-axes found in their graves are a good indication of the preoccupations of this new war-like mobile society, and within a few generations their Indo-European culture had taken over from that of the old-fashioned Baden people. As their influence spread north beyond the Carpathian mountains the passes were controlled by fortresses, and the graves tell the same grim story. As many as ten human skeletons are positioned according to their rank. The warrior male at one end, with family members including a female and children beside him in the same room, and other escorts within an ante-room or porch.

The Kurgan peoples spread until they had brought a common culture to a vast area, from the Caucasus to south-east Europe, and throughout Anatolia. The mass production of their battle-axes and other arsenical-bronze weapons required large copper supplies which could most easily be found in mountainous areas where the last ice age had cut away the upper layers of copper seams to leave the sulphide ores near the surface. Such areas as the Erzgebirge Mountains of western Czechoslovakia, and the Salzach valley 50 kilometres south of Salzburg, would become the foci for separate flowerings of the Bronze Age.

Copper mining began, for example, at Bischofshofen in the Salzach valley about 6000 years ago, and continued for 3000 years, producing some 20,000 tons of raw copper from this one mining area alone. The Mitterburg main vein was mined with 180 workers and yielded 20 tons of copper a year. The impact on the surrounding landscape must have been enormous as the smelters and fire-setting consumed the lumber from some 19 acres of forest every year. This implies that the forest must have been managed to produce a sustainable crop.

At a time when the first Pharaohs were centralising power in Egypt, and at Ur in Mesopotamia the rulers were being buried with their slaughtered retainers in the famous Royal Tombs, the ability to smelt sulphide ores suddenly increased the supply of copper. Beside the great trade route of the Danube at Vučedol in Yugoslavia, settled stockbreeders were introduced by the new horsemen of the Hungarian plain to the techniques of arsenical copper. These had a major value for trade, and travelling metal craftsmen were attracted by the combination of the trade routes, and the proximity of new copper mines in the Dinaric Alps. What might be considered to be the first Industrial Revolution began to transform society, to supply the insatiable demand for battle-axes (one hoard held fifty). Soon the control of this valuable resource led to power. A spreading network of rich strongholds were fortified on hilltops as centres of tribal influence. From Vučedol beside the Danube a new wealthy and increasingly warlike culture spread out into the whole of the Carpathian basin in search of metals.

It was still a society ruled by chieftains, and one grave contained one man and seven women, presumably sacrificed to die with him. Their ages, if indeed they were his wives, reflect his growing wealth and power – 45, 35, 25, 25, 19, 19 and 9. From the Vučedol hillfort of Gorika one trade-route followed the River Una down to the coast of the Adriatic at Mala Gruda. There was found a grave with a golden battle-axe and dagger, made in a fashion similar to that used in the Steppes. It was the grave of the earliest great European Prince. The age of warrior-chieftains had begun.

The Vučedol influence reached north to modern Prague, across the Hungarian plain and as far south as Albania, attaining the height of its power as Stonehenge was being built in the heart of a rich agricultural area; perhaps already connected to central Europe by another most profitable metal trade – that of tin.

Arsenical bronze is still recognised as being superior in corrosion resistance to other copper alloys and is used in steam boilers. So why, after some 400 years of use, did an alloy made with a new, rare and expensive ingredient begin to supplant it? A dark hard heavy metal was added to the copper instead of arsenic and

Reconstruction of pouring bronze into a two-piece mould.

it produced a different alloy – bronze. The metal was cassiterite or tinstone (tin dioxide). The answer is not just that the arsenical-bronze-makers were dying from their trade. When tin bronze was found to cast better, to have a greater capacity for hardening, and to keep a sharp edge longer, the smiths opted for the quality of their lives as well as the quality of their products.

Tin is a metal found in continental crust, usually in association with granite outcrops, and it is thus seldom found alongside copper. It is also far rarer than copper. The archaeological maps of Europe are strewn with theoretical sites for tin sources. As one mining geologist put it, 'most of them have one thing in common, no tin has ever been mined there'. But you can find heavy nuggets of cassiterite in clefts in the bedrock of the streams in Afghanistan today, and that may have been the original source used for the first tin-bronze. (The earliest tin-bronzes found so far are from Ur and Susa in Mesopotamia, 4600 years old.) Some archaeologists believe that tin – cassiterite in grain or pebble-sized nuggets, coloured grey, brown or almost black – was originally found while panning for gold. But it is unlikely that there would have been copper smelting near a source of gold because of the different geological origin of each metal.

Another theory is that the iron gossan or cap that occurs on top of oxidized copper deposits was frequently used in the early Bronze Age as a flux so that the copper flowed together into one molten mass when it was smelted. Tin-bearing gossans can still be found, for example at Dolcoath in Cornwall, and if they had occurred near a copper mine they might have been be used by chance. Once it was recognised that they made a superior metal it would not be difficult to distinguish the gossans that contained dense brown-black cassiterite in an otherwise earth-like substance. But such tin-rich gossans are scarce, and could not supply a sufficiently high proportion of tin to the melt to make good bronze. So how tin first come to be used with copper remains a puzzle.

Tin-bronze is about 90 per cent copper, and the copper, being of local origin, was relatively cheap. Tin, on the other hand, had to be carried from very distant areas, and we know from records in the Middle East that it was worth two thirds of the price of silver. Indeed it has been argued that the tin used in the massive central European bronze industry came all the way from Cornwall, where a piece of wood found in the Wheal Virgin tin stream-works has been dated as about 5000 years old. Pebble-sized lumps of tin can still be picked up on the beach at Pendeen near Lands End after a storm, and in those early days it would have been relatively easy to find tin lodged on the bedrock of Cornish streams.

There are also tin deposits in the Erzgebirge streams of Bohemia, and it would seem logical that they were used for the central European bronze instead, but there is absolutely no evidence of mining nor of artefacts to suggest that this tin was known in the early Bronze Age. (Just as there is no evidence to support the widespread belief that the Phoenicians later sought tin from Cornwall.) None of the classical authors refers to a central European source for tin, and it remains a highly controversial subject.

The sources of tin in antiquity have been a puzzle since the very first geographers tried to list them, but all were in agreement that it was a precious metal that came from a long way away. So one of the most important consequences of the introduction of tin into bronze-making was the stimulus it gave to long-distance trade. In fact, it is arguable that it was the need for valuable resources like tin that brought about the first great trading state in Europe. That was to be in Crete, but in the warlike north the use of tin ushered in a whole new armoury of stronger sharper weapons including the sword. A Bronze Age arms race began.

Bronze battle-axe from Hungary.

CHAPTER FOUR

SEA TRADE
AND THE
FIRST CITY-STATES

One of the great paradoxes of history is that the next hesitant advance of European civilisation – the development of the first city-states – took place not on the fertile open central European plains, but in a remote island to the south of the Aegean Sea which was completely lacking in metal resources. While the glittering mounted warrior-princes of central Europe dissipated their creative energy in warfare, a highly cultured yet peaceful society, built on trade and an agricultural surplus, emerged on Crete. The reasons for the contrast were, in essence, geological.

Greece and Turkey are intensely active seismically. Earthquakes of magnitude 6, which would be considered devastating elsewhere, are comparatively common, and catastrophic earthquakes, with earth movements of several metres, are regrettably frequent. To a trained eye the landscape is littered with the evidence: the rapid erosion of uplifted land, silted-up ports, raised shore-lines and drowned cities. At the western end of Crete at Phalasarna an entire coastline complete with its harbour was lifted 9 metres above the sea in one convulsive heave in AD 438. At the eastern end, the Minoan site of Kato Zakros is sinking beneath waters which already drown the ruins of Erimopolis, the port for Itanos, once one of the most influential Hellenistic cities of eastern Crete.

Once again it is the pressure of the African continent against Europe that is causing all these movements, but in a rather unexpected way. To the south of Crete a section of heavy ocean-floor crust is sinking beneath the continental plate that forms the Aegean sea floor. As this heavy tongue of crust moves down into the top layer of the viscous mantle, it sinks under its own weight and curves downwards at a point closer and closer towards Africa. This has had the effect of dragging Crete 300 kilometres to the south in the last five million years. In fact the Aegean is twice as long from north to south as it used to be. This stretching extends sideways into the Peloponnese mountains and Eastern Turkey.

When the Earth's crust stretches, the rocks split and rotate against each other like a row of thick books when one book-end is slowly moved away. Like the top of the row of books, the slabs of the crust are tilted. When this happens the crust also thins out, so it is lower than the other continents and thus is covered by the sea, but the highest parts of the tilted books emerge as islands. This was the cause of the islands of the Aegean. Round about them the sea is still being stretched faster than anywhere else on earth, an amazing 6 to 10 centimetres every year. The young jagged mountains of Greece and Western Turkey have been caused by the same movement and have risen so fast (in the last few million years) that they have not had time to be eroded into softer forms.

Just north of the sinking ocean-floor crust is the Hellenic arc of islands, formed by volcanic action caused by the melting of the sinking plate. It extends from Kithera through Crete and Karpathos to Rhodes. All these islands are approaching Africa. Eventually Crete will collide with Libya and the result will look something like Algeria, where an island-arc which once lay in the western Mediterranean has been thrust on top of Africa as it squeezed against Europe. These amazing contortions have produced some surprising results: the island of Evvoia (Euboea), for example, has rotated 60 degrees clockwise. But the most important consequence for the human species of this stretching was that it caused the broken mainland topography of Greece, with its fertile valleys separated by steep mountains, and the Aegean archipelago, with its complex of islands of volcanic and folded rocks which gave birth to the first city-states.

We tend to think of the sea as a barrier, a limit to a known territory and a defence against outside invaders. But in the early Bronze Age, and indeed until a century ago, it was far easier to travel around Greece and the Balkans by water than by land. Thanks to the broken coastline and the scattered islands, water was not so much a barrier as a sea-way, and with seafaring came trade.

Trade in the Aegean

The islands of the Mediterranean had been visited frequently for hunting, as the extinction of their endemic animals, like the pygmy elephants of Malta, shows. But evidence of permanent habitation on the smaller islands of the Aegean dates back only to late neolithic times (some 6000 years ago). In a semi-arid climate which made harvests unreliable, the problem was how to live off limited resources. Another disadvantage was that the sea level had risen over 100 metres since the last ice age. During the ice age the locally wet climate had washed the best soil off the mountains and this had accumulated on low-lying plains where it was now lost beneath the waves. If you fly over the islands today they really do look like the tops of mountains sticking out of the sea, and fertile cultivable land is in short supply.

With an uncertain food supply and the need to find mates from outside their own communities, if only to avoid inbreeding, the islanders could not be self-sufficient. They had to look outwards for support, and to gain it they had to trade. This not only encouraged the development of a unique culture in the Cyclades, it set the pattern for the whole future development of Greece. But the second reason the Aegean became the cradle of western civilisation was that there was one special resource that spurred on trade – a few of the smaller islands had metals.

In the Ashmolean Museum in Oxford are three model boats made of lead. They were found on the island of Naxos and are about 4800 years old. Lead is found on at least eight of the Cycladic islands and it must have been smelted from early times. But the lead ore, galena, frequently contains silver, and by that date two important sources of silver were being mined in the Aegean: at Lavrion on the mainland of Attica and at Agios Sostis on the island of Siphnos (near Naxos). There was a growing demand for silver in the already urbanised societies of Mesopotamia. Caravan trading routes had already been opened up through Asia

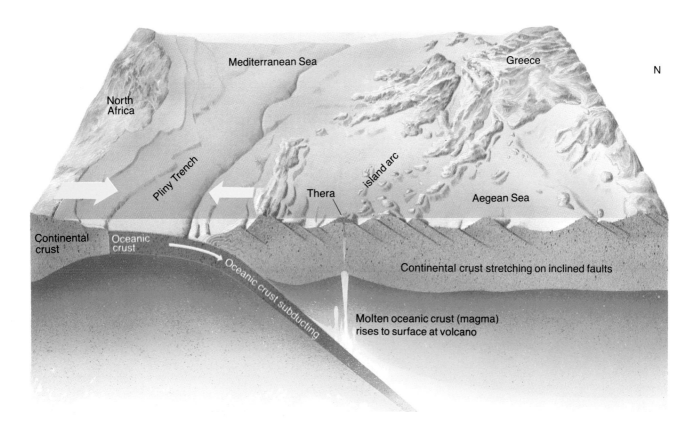

Simplified cross-section of the Aegean Sea. Crete has been dragged about 300 kilometres to the south by the rolling back of the subducting oceanic crust.

Minor and, since it was far easier and quicker to transport goods by sea than by land, the Aegean islands were soon drawn into this trade for metals. Their literal isolation from both the warring factions to the north and the incursions of invaders from the East, the ease of island-hopping voyages, their metal ores and their dependence on trade, all worked to the advantage of the islanders.

The island of Lemnos guards the entrance to the Dardanelles and the trade route to and from the Black Sea, and it was perhaps because of the metals trade that the first proto-city in Europe sprang up there at Poliochni 5000 years ago. According to the earliest of Greek writers, the poet Homer, it was also to Lemnos that Hephaistos, the god of fire and divine smith, fell, after being cast out of heaven by Zeus. This suggests that Lemnos had a strong early tradition of metal-working.

However, the main force behind the further development of maritime trade was the invention of the sail. At once ships could be larger and travel further. But the Mediterranean is notorious among modern yachtsmen for having either too little wind or too much. In summer the Etesian Winds, or Meltemi, blow strongly from the north-east, and even in calm weather, particularly in winter, white squalls of vertical winds can gust at over 40 knots near precipitous coastal areas. Despite having oars, the unwieldy ships could not sail close-hauled, and would have had to wait for a fair wind, particularly if there was a strong current against them. Just such a current made them wait at the entrance to the Dardanelles narrows, and thus a town at the entrance to the strait, Troy, now came to command and tax the valuable trade in wheat, gold, silver and tin that passed to and from the Black Sea.

One of the most famous Greek legends, which was old when Homer began to write some 2800 years ago, tells how Jason took his sailing ship, the *Argo*, manned by fifty-three men and one woman as oarsmen (the Argonauts), in a quest to

The crater of Thera with the volcanic Kaimeni Islands.

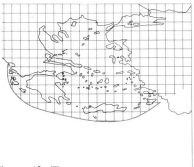

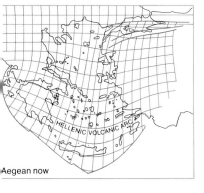

Aegean 13 million years ago

Aegean now

obtain the golden fleece from Colchis (now in southern Georgia). In the legend the fleece comes from a mythical flying ram.

> On their left hand they had the lofty Caucasus and the city of Aea, on the right the plain of Ares and the god's sacred grove, where the snake kept watch over the fleece, spread on the leafy branches of an oak.

(Apollonius Rhodius, *Argonautica*)

The reality was rather more mundane, but still gives intriguing substance to the legend. Fleeces were still in use as late as the 1930s in Georgia, pegged to boards in the bottom of washing-sluices to collect alluvial gold. They were then hung up to dry before the gold was beaten out of them. I have seen similar man-made mats in use in gold diggings in both Brazil and California.

On arrival at Colchis, Jason was set the heroic task of yoking two marvellous oxen to a plough. They had hooves of bronze and through their nostrils blew out fire and smoke. Could it be that these were furnaces? He also had to sow dragons' teeth in the ground and slay the army which grew up from them. Could that be a metaphor for the first agriculture? Even now we still speak of 'blades' of grass, and the sickle slays them. Perhaps the legend combines the separate folk memories of the earliest voyages in search of gold and the new techniques of smelting and ploughing which undoubtedly came via the Caucasus.

At a more prosaic level, archaeologists believe that the knowledge of bronze and the two-piece mould spread towards the west simultaneously along the

northern and southern edges of the Black Sea, to reach the Aegean and the early settlement at Troy at about the same time as it reached the Danube (about 4500 years ago). The second level of Troy gave up to Heinrich Schliemann the famous Troy Treasure of gold, silver and bronze vessels from this time. Many important novelties followed the trade routes westwards, including the wheel, domesticated vines and craft skills. But once the Aegean trade was well established, there was one island, poised between Asia, Africa and Europe, which was particularly well endowed to take advantage of all the new influences – Crete.

Crete and the Minoans

Crete is by far the largest of the Greek islands and had been inhabited a great deal longer than its smaller neighbours. In fact, the earliest evidence of habitation at Knossos goes back 8000 years. And with good reason: Crete had better soil and more rainfall. The Mount Ida massif reaches 2457 metres, and its neighbours, the White Mountains to the west and Dikti to the east, are well over 2000 metres tall, high enough to intercept the southerly and westerly winds which bring rain and snow. The pollen of trees and shrubs found in cores drilled from lake beds shows that during the early Bronze Age the climate was also wetter than now. Ash, alder and lime trees grew there, a combination now only found in the wettest part of Greece along the Acheron river near Albania.

Evidence was recently found that Mount Ida had even had an icecap during the ice age. Then the rapid erosion of the folded rocks, piled up by the compression of the African plate against the southern shore, left fertile sediments in the valleys. This ice-age alluvium, deposited in the gentle slopes to the north of the mountains, still provides some of most productive agricultural land in Greece, and it is capable even now of feeding the whole nation.

Although Crete does have minerals, they do not appear to have been exploited in prehistoric times. It was the agricultural wealth of the island and its situation at the edge of the Aegean – within easy sailing distance of the already advancing Egyptian civilisation of the Nile, and of the great caravan routes coming overland from the eastern cities of Mesopotamia and the Levant to the port of Ugarit (Ras Shamra) – that now allowed the unique Minoan civilisation to develop.

The topography of Crete may also have influenced what was to follow. The fertile valleys of the northern slopes are separated from each other by ranges of hills or mountains. Thus small farming areas were able to grow into relatively powerful centres of population and to coexist without feeling threatened by each other. In contrast, the open plains of central Europe were comparatively free of natural barriers, allowing free range to armies.

Crete lies in a semi-arid marginal rainfall belt where small variations of climate can create profound changes in vegetation and agriculture. So it is not surprising that the Cretans developed a religion related to the major influence on the rainfall, and thus on their lives – the mountains. Seen from the north-west, Mount Juktas, the isolated peak behind Knossos, looks remarkably like the profile of a sleeping bearded man. Both Juktas and Mount Ida were associated with Zeus, the most powerful god of the Greek pantheon. According to the myth he was hidden in a cave on Mount Ida from his father Kronos, who had devoured his other children soon after their birth. The Idaean Cave on Mount Ida is the most famous of at least twenty-five peak sanctuaries which were sacred to the worship of an earth-mother goddess and the manifestations of Nature – from springs and weather to vegetation and rocks. The mountains were the abode of gods, and the plains of men.

This concept was later adopted by the Greeks who transported the home of Zeus to Mount Olympus. Even Athene, who sprang from the head of Zeus fully armed, was a Cretan goddess, and her association with the olive tree (still to be seen growing on the Acropolis) and the snake are vestiges of ancient Cretan cults. Judged by the offerings left there, many of the early peak sanctuaries seem to have been used by shepherds, whose flocks no doubt followed the spring growth up into the mountains; but on the plains grain was cultivated.

The problem with agriculture in a variable climate is that if you grow enough acreage of grain to support you in an average year and then get a good year there is a surplus. If you are poor it is unlikely that you will have anywhere to store it, and it will be wasted. Centralised storage of surplus produce was to become the outstanding difference between the culture of Crete and other contemporary societies, and it was to be the foundation on which the Cretan civilisation could grow.

The first palaces

By about 4000 years ago, the valley settlements had drawn together into communities and had become wealthy enough in surplus produce to construct buildings on a substantial scale. The first Cretan ceremonial centres or 'palaces' began to be built. Like most ancient settlements they were subsequently rebuilt on the same site many times – beneath Knossos is a pile of ruins 7 metres thick going back a further 4000 years into the Neolithic Age. Often it is hard to appreciate the scale of structures from the foundations that remain, but here the lower courses are impressively built, and a delightful mosaic found in the ruins shows three-storey buildings painted in strikingly different colours.

These architectural complexes must have been a massive capital investment for their day. They were far too big just to be dwellings for the number of people who actually lived there, and so they must have had an important ceremonial role – and at that time no such palaces or proto-cities had appeared in central Europe.

On the north coast of Crete at Mallia there is a key piece of evidence concerning their possible function, in the form of eight large circular structures 5 metres in diameter. These were almost certainly roofed granaries. Whoever lived in the palace was probably controlling the grain surplus. The stores were far too large for the needs of the palace-dwellers alone.

Opinions are divided as to whether this was an altruistic 'social security' system to stave off hunger in the community in bad years or a store for trade with neighbouring and less fortunate valley-dwellers in times of scarcity or whether it was the local *mafiosi* cornering the crop to profiteer from artificially raised prices, as still happens in the famine areas of the African Sahel today. Whatever the reason, it is clear that a small number of people were controlling the agricultural production of the land. Once they were able to do that, they were also in a position to redistribute it according to their own rules and thus accumulate wealth of other kinds. To the eternal benefit of the rest of Europe, they chose to extend their patronage to craftsmen who were probably paid in food for their labour. In these days before the invention of money, the precious craft goods could also serve to exchange for food in times of need. The first palaces at Knossos and Phaistos were also built at this time and they too had massive storage areas. Apparently they operated independently within their own valley heartlands.

The potter's wheel had been introduced, and suddenly, brilliantly coloured, thin-walled, decorative pottery was made, designed not for function but to please the eye. Exquisite craftsmanship in metal-working was perfected, entirely on the

The beginning and the end of the Minoan civilisation?

ABOVE, the ruins of Akrotiri on the island of Thera,
overwhelmed by the eruption in 1628 BC, have been
only partially excavated.
BELOW, a clay bowl from Palaikastro in eastern Crete, modelled
with a shepherd and his flock of sheep, is older than the
earliest Minoan palaces. It suggests the importance
of the wool trade.
RIGHT, the ruins of the Minoan Palace of Phaistos stand
beneath Mount Ida, overlooking a broad fertile plain.

basis of imported bronze, silver and gold. Bronze-smiths made elaborate castings using two-piece moulds and the lost-wax process, and goldsmiths were using filigree and granulation to embellish their beautiful designs. The most famous of these is the pendant in the form of a pair of hornets clasping a honey-comb found at Khrysolakos, now in the Herakleion Museum. (The technique of granulation – making tiny beads of gold – was afterwards lost for centuries.)

In return for the metals of the Aegean and the Balkans, it is likely that Crete was exporting olive oil, wool and timber as well as the Cretan pottery which is found scattered around the shores of the eastern Mediterranean. Skills as well as luxuries were being drawn in by the magnet of agricultural wealth: cylinder seals and the technique of carving them with minute figures arrived from Syria; a seal-cutter's workshop complete with tools was found at Mallia. Hieroglyphics were written on pottery and writing may have been developed as an extension of the seal-cutter's art. One seal even provides the first record of a plank-built, masted sailing-ship – the very means by which the goods that were making the palaces rich were carried to and from the island. Scarabs attest to imports from Egypt, where society was highly advanced and the pyramids had now been built. But Crete was no Egyptian colony; it evolved in its own unique way.

So began the cultural powerhouse which was to illuminate the whole of the Eastern Mediterranean. Yet the great palaces were not on the monumental scale of the pyramids, neither do they reflect the megalomania of the palace-builders of the Near East. They were not built in defensive positions on hilltops, nor were they girt around with walls. In no way do they give the impression of the need to impose a ruthless autocracy on a subservient population. It appears that the ruling priesthood was identified with, and appropriated the power of, the earth-mother goddess Diktynna, and was revered for the power to mediate with the gods on behalf of the harvest. Since the palaces were also the administrative centres of all economic life and trade, the religious rulers had complete control over lesser mortals.

Then about 3700 years ago, at the height of their splendour, the palaces were destroyed by the very tectonic forces which contributed to the island's prosperity. A devastating earthquake struck the whole of Eastern Crete with a force which tumbled the timber-reinforced walls, scattering the masonry in ruins.

The rise of Knossos

Communities are remarkably resilient to earthquakes – throughout history we have tended to rebuild cities on the same site regardless of the threat of a recurrence. San Francisco is a good example. The Minoan palaces were rapidly rebuilt *in situ*, to an even more splendid scale and it is to this 'New Palace Period' that most of the ruins now visible on Crete belong. Knossos now seems to have become pre-eminent among the palaces, although how, nobody knows. It was Sir Arthur Evans, who actually bought the site of Knossos in 1900, who named the Cretan civilisation 'Minoan' after the legendary King Minos, the son of Zeus by Europa. Evans continued his epoch-making excavations until 1926, recording them in four massive volumes. (He was also responsible for the reconstructions, now sadly in need of repair themselves.)

The new palace at Knossos was a complex of buildings conceived on a grand scale, covering no less than 75 hectares. According to legend it was designed by the architect Daedalus, who also built the first flying machine, and one small detail can illuminate the intricacy of the planning. At the bottom of the fourth level of the domestic quarters, reached by a magnificent staircase that is itself a triumph of architectural engineering, there is a lavatory with a running-water flush system. It was not an afterthought, it was planned in from the start, just as we now start to build a house by laying the drains.

The whole purpose of the palaces was to enhance the ceremonial importance and prestige of the ruling élite. Storage of agricultural products still lay literally at the heart of the system. In Knossos hundreds of huge jars and lead-lined vats contained olive oil and grain. But major deposits of cash crops were also being stored in 'villas', mini-palaces in the countryside. This decentralisation suggests that the power of the palaces was extending further, and clay sealings with the impression of a bull relate the stores to Knossos.

Bull worship, so evident in the frescoes and treasures found in the later Minoan palaces, had evidently arrived from the Middle East, where it had been practised for thousands of years (a bull cult sanctuary found at Çatal Hüyük in Anatolia was 8500 years old). A pottery bull with tiny figures clasping its horns, now in the Archaeological Museum at Herakleion, shows that some sort of bull riding or jumping by acrobats was going on in Crete even from the earliest Bronze Age.

While there was a third less storage space in the new palaces than in the old, more and more emphasis was being put on the creation and hoarding of valuable goods crafted from metal and stone, fine woollen textiles and perfumed olive oil. The burgeoning production of the state where every detail was controlled from the centre had to be recorded, identifying seals were not enough, and writing was used for the first time in Europe – tablets written in the so-far undeciphered 'Linear A' script. Control over production had brought power within Crete and, as sea-borne exports of wool, linen, grain and perfumes prospered, the Minoan influence in the Aegean spread. The classical Greek historian Thucydides, writing in the fifth century BC, claimed:

> Minos is the first, to our knowledge, who possessed a fleet whose domination extended over the main part of the sea we call today Hellenic, and he reigned over the Cyclades. It was he who, in the majority of cases, established the first organised colonies after chasing out the Carians. He entrusted the government to his son. And in order to best safeguard the return of his revenues he did all he naturally could to rid the seas of pirates.

Many archaeologists deny that there was a Minoan empire outside Crete, but concede that trading gave the Minoans command over the seas. There was certainly a profound Minoan influence in the Cycladic islands. Kea and Melos appear to have been colonies, and Minoan burial and religious practices on Kythera suggest Cretan domination. At Akrotiri on Santorini, the religious accessories are Minoan in style, as are the famous frescoes and the architecture itself. Minoan artistic and cultural influence is also found on Rhodes and many other islands, on the coast of Asia Minor and on mainland Greece. One fresco found at Akrotiri shows a small fleet of ships, apparently carrying warriors, accompanied by a decorated 'flagship', leaving a foreign land and arriving home. The excavators believed it to have been recording the voyages of a sea-captain from Santorini, rather than a Minoan fleet, but it is a vivid depiction of the vessels of the time. Thucydides also wrote, 'The emergence of civilisation correlates to the practice of power'. Power was spreading and with it civilisation was being kindled, and, whether or not there was political domination abroad, there is no doubt that Minoan cultural influence was widespread around the eastern Mediterranean shores.

The rulers of Knossos had become the most powerful in Europe, and their craftsmen led the world in workmanship and artistry. Whether King Minos sat on the throne, as Sir Arthur Evans believed (perhaps influenced by the contemporary power of the British throne), or whether it was a priestess-goddess (as shown in the frescoes and figurines) who was attended by bull-leaping males about to be sacrificed, we may never know.

The eruption of Thera

Then the volcano of Thera exploded. It was perhaps the greatest eruption in historical times. The cataclysm began with catastrophic earthquakes and minor ash-falls; the geological evidence then suggests a lull of a few weeks or at the most two years, followed by a major eruption of pumice. Finally the central part of the old island, which had been roughly circular, collapsed into the huge void now emptied of magma, and as the edges crumbled huge blocks of rock as much as 3 metres in diameter were hurled into the air. Altogether about 27 cubic kilometres of rock were erupted (compared with one cubic kilometre during the Mount St Helens eruption in the western USA). The remnants of Thera were left as a spectacular ring of islands, covered 30 metres deep in pumice, which is now often called Santorini.

In 1939 the Greek archaeologist, Spiridon Marinatos, pointed out that the sudden collapse of the Minoan civilisation on Crete appeared to have happened at about the same time as the destruction of Thera, and drew the conclusion that it was the eruption which had destroyed the Minoan palaces. It was a seductive idea to join a great geological cataclysm with a major human catastrophe. He told of 'natural causes' being to blame, with earthquake alone quite insufficient in power to have wrought such devastation. By analogy with the somewhat similar eruption of another island volcano, Krakatau in the strait between Java and Sumatra in 1883, which cost 36,000 lives, he described how Crete must have been showered with ashes, 'some ablaze and burning', how tidal waves, or *tsunamis*, 200 metres high must have smashed whole towns to the ground, and how the oil lamps and the large quantities of oil in storage started conflagrations. He pointed out that lamps were torn from their supports and window panes shattered by the blast at Buitenzorg in Java, 150 kilometres from Krakatau, while Thera is 120 kilometres away from Crete, and the eruption of Thera was three times the size.

Archaeology is frequently an interpretative rather than an exact science, and in the face of the scepticism of his colleagues, Marinatos set out to find evidence on Santorini which would prove that the eruption and the destruction of the Minoan civilisation were contemporary. Archaeological dating was then mostly reliant on the comparison of styles of pottery sherds (this is still the basic technique for comparing dates of sites), and Marinatos needed to find pottery from a site destroyed by the eruption on Thera identical with the styles in the destruction layers on Crete.

But the archaeological evidence was against him. Before the destruction of the Cretan palaces a new style of Minoan pottery had emerged on Crete: Late Minoan 1.B, the 'Marine' style. Despite the Minoan character of the settlements on Thera, Marinatos failed to find the Marine style there: it must therefore have developed *after* the eruption. However, by way of consolation, in his quest for the elusive sherds on Thera, Marinatos unearthed the spectacular ruins of Akrotiri, a kind of Minoan Pompeii which is still only partially excavated. Apparently the preliminary earthquakes had warned the inhabitants of Akrotiri to evacuate their town. No valuables or skeletons have been found in the ruins, many of which were shaken to the ground. But other houses survived sufficiently, and were pre-

The Grand Staircase in the Palace of Knossos, a masterpiece of Minoan architecture restored by Sir Arthur Evans early this century.

served by the pumice, to give us the magnificent frescoes which can now be seen in the National Museum in Athens.

Volcanologists are now adamant that the eruption itself could not have produced earthquakes of any magnitude on Crete. They say that neither an ash flow nor an incandescent avalanche could possibly have reached so far. As for being smothered with ash and pumice, there is no evidence of burning ashes nor an ash layer on the ruins, except traces of, at the most, 5 centimetres in the most eastern part of Crete. Indeed recent discoveries of an ash layer a metre thick on Rhodes, and of 24 centimetres near Izmir, show that the ash plume was blown by the wind to the east. Cores of erupted pumice from the sea floor are thickest in the direction of Rhodes.

If the Minoan palace cities had been destroyed by *tsunami*, as Marinatos suggested, what would be left to burn, and how would wet buildings burn? How

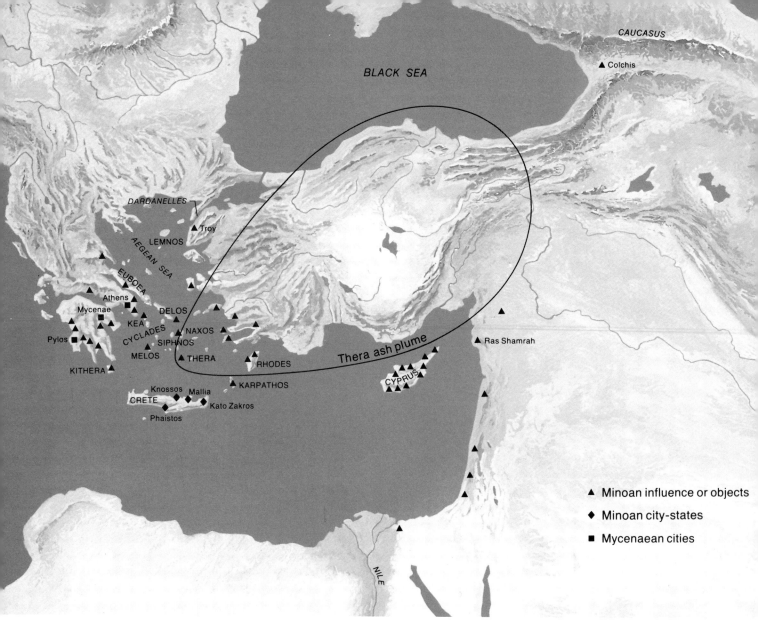

The Bronze Age in the eastern Mediterranean. Minoan and Mycenaean sites.

would Phaistos, hundreds of feet above the sea on the wrong side of a range of mountains, be destroyed? Marinatos' theory was rejected, yet there *is* a universal layer of black remains in all the Cretan ruins, above the Marine-style pots, showing that the palaces were burnt. At Gournia wooden posts and steps were burnt completely, bricks were baked bright red, the central hall of the palace was choked with timbers, charred through yet retaining their shape, bronze had been melted into shapeless lumps and plaster reconverted into slaked lime.

There are those who claim that even if a *tsunami* did not destroy the palaces then at least it must have wiped out the Minoan fleet, and thus toppled the trading empire; leading to the collapse of an overly centralised economy, too heavily dependent on luxury trade, and now too far removed from its original support – the management of the Cretan agricultural surplus. With an inadequate food reserve, civil insurrection and the looting of the Palaces could have followed in the subsequent chaos. In an interesting parallel, in AD 1650 the Cretan city of Herakleion was under siege by Turkish forces when an eruption occurred beneath the sea in the crater of Thera. A *tsunami* then swept away the Turkish ships beached on the island of Dia opposite the port, yet this was a tiny eruption compared with what had occurred in Minoan times. The Japanese word *tsunami* actually means 'harbour wave', because such long slow waves are scarcely perceptible in the open sea yet can cause catastrophic damage onshore. The Minoan port for Knossos, Amnissos, is one of the few places on Crete where there *does* appear to be evidence of *tsunami* damage, although Amnissos was also burnt.

Until 1984, archaeologists believed that the Thera eruption must have occurred in 1500 BC and the devastation on Crete about fifty years later. Then another discipline became involved which cast doubt on the actual date of the eruption – dendrochronology, the study of dating by tree-rings. At high altitude in the White Mountains of California, bristlecone pines grow extremely slowly and can live for thousands of years. The dead wood is also well preserved, and, by computer-matching the variation in size of annual growth rings, a precise sequence of rings has been extended back over 8000 years. Volcanic eruptions, like that of Krakatau and Thera, can inject huge quantities of dust into the upper atmosphere where it quickly circles the globe and can remain for years. This stratospheric layer of silicate ash, or sometimes sulphuric acid, scatters the sun's rays causing a milky cast in the daylight sky, a bluish tint to the moon and lurid sunsets. It also reduces the heat of the sun, causing a 'nuclear winter' effect. The severity of this depends on the amount of scattering, and thus the amount of material thrown into the stratosphere. A fairly minor degree of chilling of the Earth's surface can cause late frosts to damage the bristlecone trees during the growing season, and shows up in the tree-ring sequence as dark lines of frost-damaged cells. The dark lines have been found to correlate with major historical volcanic eruptions, and are accurate to a single year.

No tree-ring damage has been found around the year 1500 BC, but there was a major episode of frost damage in 1627 BC, and it was proposed that this was caused by the Thera eruption. This dated the eruption over a century earlier than previously accepted. The bristlecone rings have also been used to 'calibrate' carbon 14 dating methods. Early figures from Akrotiri gave very wide readings, possibly because volcanic gases affected the carbon 14 emissions, but recent testing of twigs and crops from Akrotiri, harvested just before the eruption, yielded a scattering of dates favouring the earlier figure. Archaeologists sometimes lose sight of the fact that even when carbon 14 figures have been calibrated against tree-ring data they still only give an approximate date, and at this period are only accurate to about half a century.

Then another independent technique of monitoring past eruptions was discovered by measuring the acidity of the annual snow layers in cores taken from icecaps. One from Greenland showed a rare peak acidity in 1644 BC. This method is not as accurate as the tree-ring scale as years can be lost if the ice melts in exceptionally hot summers. A final piece of evidence arrived in 1988 with a second tree-ring sequence from bog-oaks in Ireland which show very narrow rings following major eruptions. The Irish sequence yields a growth minimum, and thus a date for the eruption, of 1628 BC, which could quite easily have caused the chilling in California the following summer. This now seems to be the most likely date of the eruption. If this later date is accepted, it will not alter the *relative* dating of events in the Aegean, which ultimately rests on pottery styles, but it will change the chronology of the entire eastern Mediterranean Late Bronze Age relative to the historically dated culture of ancient Egypt.

The fall of Knossos

This time the tectonic forces of the Aegean appear to have been exonerated from blame, but if Thera was not the cause of the collapse of the Minoan civilisation, what was? A full-scale invasion has been ruled out by the archaeologists because there is no sudden change of cultural style in the archaeological record. After a relatively short period, Knossos continued to be the centre of power. On Thera, before the eruption, there is pottery at Akrotiri which is also found at the great Greek mainland site of Mycenae. The frescoes from the West House show warriors with long spears, long ox-hide shields and helmets made of boars' tusks which are known from Mycenaean graves. In Knossos, such weapons and Mycenaean swords are also found in the period after the destruction. So what was the role of the Mycenaeans?

The real surprise was when the clay tablets at Knossos, which minutely detailed the administration of the agricultural and craft production such as herds, wool, spinning and weaving, now written in a new language called 'Linear B', were discovered to be written in ancient Greek. There was thus the strong suggestion that Greek-speaking Mycenaeans from the mainland had supplanted the Minoans as the rulers of Crete, had taken over their trade and had learned to write their language. In several Egyptian tombs of the Ministers of Tuthmosis lll there are paintings of Cretan emissaries bearing gifts which include (c. 1470 BC) a typical Marine style collared rhyton or ceremonial libation vessel. They were depicted first wearing the Minoan costume of a cut-away kilt and codpiece, then overpainted in about 1460–1450 BC with a patterned kilt drawn into a long point at the front, the style used in Mycenae. Was this because the Mycenaeans, and not the Minoans, were now the ones who came bearing gifts? But the Egyptian dates, related to a king list, do not fit those from the tree-rings, so they remain a puzzle.

Linear 'B' tablet from Knossos, recording offerings of Olive oil to various divinities and shrines. The first two lines read:
To Dictaian Zeus
    12 litres of oil
To the shrine of Daedalus
    24 litres of oil.

The Minotaur

At Knossos, however, there is an intriguing overlap between archaeology and myth. There is no doubt at all that there was a bull-cult on Crete, but legend holds that King Minos's wife Pasiphae was cursed with a monstrous passion for a white bull sent by the god Poseidon. Enlisting the aid of Daedalus, who built a wooden cow in which she concealed herself, she conceived and gave birth to the Minotaur – half man, half bull. The Minotaur lived in the centre of the Labyrinth, the palace of Knossos, which gained its name from the *labrys*, the double axe. Its architecture was so complex that it came to be known as a maze.

King Minos's son, a famous wrestler, had been murdered by the Athenians (Athens was then a small Mycenaean city), and they obtained a promise of peace only on condition that every year Athens should send, as a tribute to Crete, seven young maidens and seven young men to be devoured by the Minotaur. These victims, who were perhaps to become acrobats in the bull-court, were selected by lot until Theseus, son of the King of Athens, volunteered to go as one of the young men. As was the custom, they were entertained on arrival for one night in the

The Bull's Head Rhyton from the Little Palace at Knossos. Magnificently carved from serpentine with eyes of rock-crystal and jasper, it was made to be filled with liquid through a hole in the crown of the head. For sacred libations this could be poured out through another hole in the mouth.

palace of the King. There his daughter, Ariadne, fell passionately in love with Theseus and gave him a spindle of wool to unwind as he threaded his way through the Labyrinth, so that he could find his way out again. She also lent him a sword with which he slew the Minotaur.

However, returning now to the real world, in a society where power was as centralised as it had been on Crete, it is not beyond the realms of possibility that an Athenian (or at least a Mycenaean Greek) expedition was able to enter the relatively undefended Palace of Knossos and kill the ruler. (Indeed, by doing precisely this, Francisco Pizarro was able to conquer the entire Inca empire of Peru with only 150 Spaniards.) Once the ruler of Knossos was dead and his power supplanted, the other palaces could easily be overcome and burnt without the need for a large invasion.

The Mycenaeans

The Mycenaeans spring out of the darkness of Greek prehistory with an astonishing wealth of gold and military might. In 1876 Heinrich Schliemann, the discoverer of ancient Troy, found graves cut as vertical shafts into the rock inside the fortifications at Mycenae, and brought to light one of the most famous hoards of gold ever found. This was looted by the Nazis during the Second World War, and subsequently disappeared, but the combination of the reunification of Germany and *glasnost* gives hope that it will now come to light again. Schliemann thought that he had found the golden face of Agamemnon, the king of Argos who had led the Greeks to besiege Troy in revenge for the abduction of his sister-in-law, Helen, the most beautiful woman in the world. But the date of the treasure does not fit that of the Trojan War, instead it is contemporary with the height of the splendour of Knossos. In the ruins of Knossos and the other palaces many Mycenaean swords have been found, which begs the question of whether the gold of the shaft graves was the booty from the sacking of Minoan Crete?

The palace at Knossos was little changed after the other palaces were destroyed. In the 'Throne Room' (more a Mycenaean concept than a Minoan one) Evans found griffins painted on the walls. The famous Lion Gate at Mycenae has two headless beasts flanking a typical Minoan downward-tapered column. They might well be griffins, not lions. Following the burning of the palaces it is clear that Knossos was closely linked to Mycenae.

But the Mycenaean empire, which grew from about 1300 BC (the date of the Lion Gate), had more in common with the warrior princes of central Europe than the cultured Minoans. Their princes and kings lived in great halls with huge hearths as if in long-houses. Their graves were filled with gilded swords, while arms had been scarce on Crete, and their treasure reveals a mixed style of intricate and coarse art, both rich and tawdry, at times intensely naturalistic and at others abstract. The goods are small, portable and apparently from foreign lands – the glittering wealth of a race of warriors. The men-at-arms whose tradition began with the battle-axe on the Steppes of Asia had now triumphed over the whole Aegean.

From this time on the history of Europe would lose the splendour of gift-bearing diplomats and echo to the tramp of marching armies. For about a century and a half the Mycenaeans extended their influence from the Tiber to the Black Sea. But it was not a time of peace. The story of 'gold-rich' Mycenae, told by Homer in the *Iliad* centuries later, is a grim record of murder, incest, fratricide and slaughter, ending in a curse. His record of the ten-year siege of Troy is now accepted as containing more than a grain of truth, though it is far more likely that the war was

fought over the control of the Dardanelles, the artery which carried the trade in grain and metals from the Black Sea, than the beauty of 'a face that launched a thousand ships'.

The start of the Greek Dark Ages

The ruins of Mycenae lower behind grim ramparts raised at the time of the Trojan War (1250 BC). But after about 1200 BC, despite the (Mycenaean) Greeks' victory (with or without the wooden horse), one by one the great Mycenaean citadels were attacked and burnt: the citadel of Pylos fell in about 1200 BC, Mycenae in 1130. The traditional explanation for this was an invasion of Dorians or the 'Sea Peoples' who were recorded as attacking Egypt at this time. But there is no archaeological evidence for a cultural change. Militarily successful, and with trading outposts stretching from Sardinia to Cyprus, why did Mycenae fall?

At about this time, throughout the eastern Mediterranean and beyond into Asia Minor, the population seems suddenly to have crashed as the result of some terrible widespread calamity. Famine drove the Hittites from the Anatolian plateau, drought caused the abandonment of north Persian towns, Libyan refugees tried to move into Egypt, disastrous floods occurred on the Hungarian plain. These are consistent with an abnormal weather pattern which has been analysed by climatologists, and which actually occurred in the winter of 1954–5. It would have brought drought to the plain of Argos and Mycenae. Greece is on the boundary between regions of inadequate and enough rainfall to grow grain, and the pattern of drought and rainfall is determined by the wind and the mountainous topography.

Did drought cause starvation and civil war? Or was the collapse caused by too large a population and an economy that had become too centralised and dependent on bureaucracy, too dependent on grain brought along extended trading networks and even from the Black Sea?

Throughout the Aegean civilisation collapsed, and there are no new settlements. But it was not only a *regional* weather change. From 1500 BC the forests of the far north in Canada and Europe began a retreat south of 200 to 400 kilometres. From 1300 BC the glaciers in the Alps began to advance (one even blocked off a gold-mine in Austria). Spruce, a cold-adapted tree, began to colonise Europe from the south-east. From 1200 BC the peat-bogs in Sweden began to grow. The lakes of the Alps rose to drown lake-side settlements. A pollen core from the Akrotiri peninsula in Crete shows a sudden decline in the pollen of olive trees which could have been caused by a frost killing off the trees.

There is a possible cause of such a weather pattern, and again plate tectonics lies at its root, with a volcano cast in the role of villain. Bog-oaks in Ireland show tree-rings which date a massive eruption of the volcano Hekla lll on Iceland to 1150 BC. It has been suggested that this high-latitude eruption (close enough to the carbon 14 dates from Greece) cast such a pall of ash over the hemisphere that it seriously worsened an already deteriorating climate, causing famine and a massive reduction in the population. The effects of the new weather pattern would have differed between areas: more rain in some, less in others. Perhaps it was this natural disaster that hastened the collapse of the Mycenaean world.

According to Herodotus (who wrote in the fifth century BC), Crete became so beset with famine and pestilence that it became virtually uninhabited. A dark age settled over the Aegean, and in the turbulent centuries that were to follow the Greeks even forgot how to write. Not for nothing did the Greeks later lament that an age of gold had been lost to one of iron.

The ruins of the great fortress city of Mycenae still dominate the entrance to the plain of Argos.

CHAPTER FIVE

GREEKS
BEARING GIFTS

The twenty-fourth of August AD 79 was a Roman holiday celebrating the birthday of the deified Emperor Augustus. The day before had been the feast of Vulcan, the Roman god of fire and furnaces, and a few residents of Pompeii had remarked how appropriate it was that a wisp of smoke was rising from a nearby mountain into the bright morning sky. Fifteen years before there had been a severe earthquake which had damaged many buildings in the prosperous little town, grown rich on the wine trade, but repairs had been made and business carried on as normal. At Herculaneum, a charming port 15 kilometres to the north-west, famed for its fertility and climate, many wealthy Romans had been attracted to build villas by the shore of the Bay of Naples. There the earthquake had brought down the dome of the bath-house. But it was now repaired, and the residents were used to earthquakes. By comparison, the repeated tremors which had rattled windows and doors for the past few days seemed merely irritating rather than dangerous.

At Misenum, the strategic Roman naval base 30 kilometres to the west, at the tip of the peninsula enclosing the Bay of Naples, the commander of the fleet was Gaius Plinius Secundus, the naturalist known as Pliny the Elder. He was working on his books when his wife excitedly called him outside to look at a strange cloud.

> The cloud was rising; watchers from our distance could not tell from which mountain, though later it was known to be Vesuvius. In appearance and shape it was like a tree – the (umbrella) pine would give the best idea of it. Like an immense tree trunk it was projected into the air, and opened out with branches . . . sometimes white, sometimes dark and mottled, depending on whether it bore ash or cinders.
>
> (*Herculaneum*, Joseph Jay Deiss, Harper & Row, 1985)

Vesuvius had been dormant for at least 300 years, and the people of Pompeii had probably not realised that it was a volcano before the rain of ash, blown by a northerly wind, began to fall on their homes. Curiosity turned to consternation as the sky progressively darkened and the first sprinkling of ash became a steady fall at the rate of about 15 centimetres an hour.

As Pliny was about to leave in a light galley to investigate, he had received a

A casualty of continental collision, the ruins of Pompeii.

note from a friend's wife begging him to rescue her from a house at the foot of the mountain, accessible only from the sea. So he now had quadriremes launched – powerful war-galleys with four tiers of oars each side – and he set off in the direction from which most others were fleeing, encouraging his pilot with the words 'fortune favours the brave'.

Great sheets of flame and extensive fires were now flashing from the summit, hot cinders were falling on the deck of the ships and the sea became choked with floating pumice. When landing was made difficult by rubble from the eruption they altered course downwind for Stabiae on the south side of the bay, where they landed and stayed the night. The next morning, overcome by sulphur gas, Pliny the Elder died.

The ash fall continued. Roofs began to collapse in Pompeii, but Herculaneum was upwind and unaffected. Pliny's nephew, who wrote down the account, described how that night at Misenum their house was not just shaken by earthquakes but turned upside down, and they spent the last part of the night in the courtyard. They loaded their possessions into carts which bucked with the violence of the earth tremors, and set off out of town.

> The shore had widened and many sea-creatures were beached on the sand. In the other direction loomed a horrible black cloud ripped by sudden bursts of fire, writhing snakelike and revealing sudden flashes larger than lightning . . . we were enveloped in night – not a moonless night, or one dimmed by cloud, but the darkness of a sealed room without lights. To be heard were only the shrill cries of women, the wailing of children, the shouting of men . . . A curious brightness revealed itself to us not as daylight but as approaching fire; but it stopped some distance from us. (Ibid.)

He was fortunate. What he had witnessed and reported so accurately was the final collapse of the erupting column of pumice and gas as the chamber of the volcano emptied. Like five other flows before, it surged down the slopes of the volcano at a speed of 110 kilometres per hour, a devastating incandescent avalanche at a temperature of over 400 degrees Celsius, sweeping away and killing everything in its path.

The first of these glowing avalanches – called *nuées ardentes* – caught the remaining population of Herculaneum in the boat-tunnels carved out of the pumice cliff facing the beach, where they had taken refuge in the hope of escaping by boat the next day. Their lungs seared by the hot gas, in agony and with no oxygen to breathe, they died within minutes. The next surges buried the whole port 20 metres deep, and drove back the sea half a kilometre. Only the last surge hit Pompeii, killing those who had failed to flee. The town itself disappeared under 7 metres of ash and pumice.

In 1709 Herculaneum was finally rediscovered by a well-digger and one of the first systematic excavations of any ancient site began. When few skeletons were found, it was thought that the population had escaped. Only in 1982 was the grim evidence from the boat-tunnels unearthed.

The volcanoes and the Mediterranean

Mount Vesuvius has erupted eighty times since AD 79, and it is still active, but it is only a small part of a volcanic system that includes the vast collapsed crater, or caldera, of the Phlegraean fields on the north-west edge of the Bay of Naples. This caldera, which erupted 36,000 years ago, is 12 kilometres wide, and 300,000 people now live within it. Yet it is active too: in 1970 repeated earthquakes forced the evacuation of the Acropolis, the old town, at Pozzuoli near the centre of the former volcano. It is one of a number of volcanic craters which pock-mark the satellite map of the central Mediterranean. They are the consequence of tectonic activity which also caused the 1980 earthquake in Irpinia, which cost 3000 lives. The behaviour of the plates beneath this part of the Mediterranean is extremely complex, with the result that there are conflicting explanations of what is happening, but an overall pattern is clear.

Twenty million years ago there was an ocean between Europe and Africa, called Tethys (so named by some classical-minded geologist after the wife of Oceanus, the Greek god of the waters that encircled the earth). It was a large body of water, 3000 metres deep. As Africa drove irresistibly northwards and the seaway was compressed more and more, part of the sea floor was pushed on top of the growing Alps. Finally, only two narrow straits at east and west linked Tethys to the Atlantic and Indian oceans. Forty-five million years ago the straits were squeezed shut, islands were pushed on top of Africa to form the Atlas Mountains, and as the Alps were slowly formed the land-locked sea began to

Dozens of victims of the eruption of Mount Vesuvius were found crowded into the boat-tunnels at Herculaneum. A mother at the right attempts to comfort her child.

The dry Mediterranean, five million years ago.

evaporate into saline lakes. Further compressed and contorted, the salt-laden lake floors were pushed up to form other ranges of mountains around a deep desert depression, much like the Dead Sea today.

Then the final drama occurred, far greater than any that was to unfold beneath Vesuvius. Five million years ago, the natural dam at Gibraltar broke, and the Atlantic flooded in. A gigantic waterfall of sea-water, 100 times the size of the Victoria falls, poured 40,000 cubic kilometres of water a year into the basin. For a hundred years this almost unimaginable flood continued, until the Mediterranean lay wine-dark beneath the desert sun. The climate changed for the wetter and colder, flowers and forest took root around the new shores, and the first of our ancestors walked in from Africa.

But the plates continued to move, and another of the consequences were the volcanoes. At present, as the African plate, which includes Malta and most of Sicily, still pushes to the north, Italy is swinging anti-clockwise about a centre near Milan. Meanwhile Sicily is rotating in the opposite direction. Italy is swinging because it is being dragged to the east by a plate of the ancient Tethys ocean floor which is descending beneath the eastern Italian coast, and (in the same way that Crete is being dragged to the south) this is expanding the Tyrrhenian Sea between Corsica and Sardinia, and Italy. This spreading began about ten million years ago and has resulted in a number of submarine volcanoes beneath the Tyrrhenian Sea which were only discovered recently, and may be linked to the ocean floor beginning to spread apart. As the ocean floor of the Adriatic descends beneath Italy it melts and some of it ascends as magma to form the line of volcanoes which stretch down the west of Italy, this is also still helping to lift the Apennine mountain range.

The volcanic activity has moved south from Latium to Vesuvius as southern

Italy has swung to the east, and now most of the downward movement of sea-floor is happening beneath Calabria where the floor of the Ionian Sea is sliding down towards the north-west, accompanied by severe earthquakes as it does so. The melting of *this* ocean floor causes the volcanoes of the Aeolian Islands. Etna is the odd man out, it appears to be associated with the intersection of different crustal movements. What it all adds up to is that tectonically this is an extremely active area, with young mountains still being lifted by frequent violent earthquakes and a recent history of major volcanic eruptions.

Ironically, the volcanic activity around the Bay of Naples was the very reason that it was settled in the first place. When it is broken down by weathering, volcanic ash forms extremely fertile soil. This is because it is well drained and full of minerals. In fact, the soils are so fertile that the fields which lie above the ruins of Pompeii still to be excavated bear four crops a year. To this day the wines of Vesuvius are famous. Volcanic activity also concentrates metals, and the metals were the most valuable trading resource at the beginning of the Iron Age.

The other key to the region's later pre-eminence was the Mediterranean Sea. Almost completely land-locked and scattered with islands like stepping stones, it is only when it reaches the south of Sardinia, Sicily and Crete that it becomes a single sea. To the north it is invaded and divided by mountain ranges forming peninsulas and islands, the shattered wreckage surviving from the collision of Africa with Europe. Indeed the shape of Europe, 'a peninsula of peninsulas', with numerous natural harbours, gave it a great advantage over other more land-locked continents at a time when sailing ships carried the bulk of trade.

The division of the Mediterranean by mountain ranges into the Aegean, Adriatic, Ionian and Tyrrhenian seas, each relatively small, with its own peculiar identity, was to influence profoundly the story of the second great civilisation in Europe; that of the Greeks, Etruscans and Romans. For these small seas allowed cities to develop through maritime trade at a time when the rest of Europe was still barbarous.

The end of the Dark Ages

Greece and the Aegean have the most extravagantly fragmented shoreline within the Mediterranean region. The sea penetrates deep into the heart of the Pindus and Peloponnese ranges, while mountains intrude across the water as a scattering of islands within the sheltering arm of the Hellenic arc that stretches from Kithera through Crete to Rhodes. It should therefore come as no surprise that since Jason first returned with the golden fleece the Greeks have been seamen, adventurers and traders. This vigorous tradition continues to the present day with the dynasties of Onassis and Niarchos. It is to the Mediterranean and its seamen and traders that Herculaneum owed its wealth, and to whom this chapter belongs.

Eight hundred years before Christ was born, the great fortresses of the Mycenaeans had lain in ruins for three centuries. The glorious palaces, golden treasures and weapons of bronze were now no more than tales for poets. The people still worshipped the gods of the Myceneans, who now dwelt on Mount Olympus, ruled by the omnipotent Zeus, but at Delphi, the centre of their known world, there was no more than a herdsman's shrine. Yet, within 300 years, the

The House of Neptune and Amphitrite, Herculaneum.
The opulence and style derived from eight centuries of
trade and cultural development by the
Greeks, Etruscans and Romans.

same sacred grove beneath the marble cliffs of Mount Parnassus was to become full of treasure-houses brought to the greatest civilisation the world had ever seen. A combination of the enterprise of the people, geography and resources had wrought an astonishing transformation.

Three-quarters of Greece is mountainous and, as on the islands of the Aegean, the rains of the glacial era stripped most of the soil from the steep young slopes. At best only a fifth of the land is cultivated, and these were not the best of times. Yet the very poverty and rugged character of the land, the narrowness of each valley, the limits of each island's resources and the proximity of the sea, set in motion a great outward quest for raw materials and land that was ultimately to bring Hellenic culture into the very heart of Europe.

At first, with peace, and perhaps an improvement in climate, the population began to expand. The villages farming olives, vines and wheat in the valley bottoms grew, and then coalesced into towns. These small vigorous communities developed facing the sea, but separated from each other by mountains or water. It was an isolation that was not complete, but which gave them protection from rivals. This was the practical geographical reason for the later development of the famous Greek city-state or *polis*, a town powerful enough to have its own laws, religion, government and even army and navy.

North of the Alps, the final phase of the Bronze Age was producing a magnificent artistic tradition which had perhaps benefited from the dispersion of the Mycenaean craftsmen. A 'Barbarian' society characterised by hillforts and rich warrior burials expanded across the centre of the continent and was to last for centuries. But in the south-east, communities had already become literate, and were beginning to make extensive use of iron. The Iron Age had begun.

In Anatolia, the Hittite Empire had collapsed at about the same time as that of the Mycenaeans. It was now succeeded by the kingdom of Urartu, centred around Lake Van, and noted for its metal craftsmanship and skill in irrigation. Meanwhile the Assyrians began an imperial expansion from their heartland to the south of the capital Nineveh in the wheatfields of the middle Tigris basin, until, within 200 years, they had not only conquered Babylon but held Syria and Palestine as far as the Mediterranean coast. By the middle of the seventh century BC they controlled the whole region to the east of the Mediterranean, from the Nile Delta to the Persian Gulf, the first of a series of great empires to dominate the Middle East. The extension of the overland trade routes from the east through the unified lands to the shore of the Mediterranean could then bring eastern technology and skills like writing within reach of the communities around the Aegean, whom we have now come to know as Greeks.

Until recently scholars knew little of what they called the Dark Ages that were now ending, not least because the Greeks were illiterate from the end of the Bronze Age to the start of the eighth century BC, so there were no records. Archaeologists had understandably dug first the spectacular sites like Troy (finally destroyed in the twelfth century BC) and those of the Classical period, which began in the fifth century BC, because they related to the more glamorous period of recorded history. But from the earliest historians, like Thucydides, and from such excavations as have taken place, it is now clear that the towns on the eastern coast of the Aegean, like the former Mycenaean colony Miletus on the River Maeander, remained occupied and retained the cultural heritage developed in Minoan and Mycenaean times. The waves of warfare and migration that had swept the Aegean had left these southern Ionian coastal and island towns a flotsam of education and ideas from many quarters of the eastern Mediterranean.

It was at Miletus that science and philosophy probably began, and it is an interesting comment on the priorities of the day that Thales, one of the first Greek philosophers, taught at Miletus (which had four harbours) that water was the one element from which all things evolved. He was also the founder of abstract geometry and discovered how to calculate the distance of ships at sea, and the use of the Pole Star for navigation. Two other Milesians, Anaximander and Hecateus, respectively drew the first map of the known world and wrote the first work of geography, *Travels round the Earth*. The city of Miletus was later to found more than sixty daughter towns on the shores of the Dardanelles, the Sea of Marmara and the Black Sea.

The Greek adventurers

As far as the development of Europe is concerned, the most important events were occurring on the other side of the Aegean. Recent excavations on the island of Euboea (Evvoia) have led to the surprising conclusion that throughout the shadowy period of the Dark Ages, trade must still have continued around the eastern Mediterranean. That Euboean traders were active in the Eastern Mediterranean at so early a date (900 BC) is also confirmed by Euboean pottery found at the earliest excavated Greek trading post overseas, in a multi-national port at Al Mina in northern Syria.

Relations between the traditional Iron-Age mounted warriors and the enterprising traders (who no doubt began to challenge the wealth and status of their rulers) were not always cordial. By the end of the eighth century the two Euboean cities of Chalcis, which was traditional and equestrian, and the outward-looking trading city of Eretria were at war with each other. Fortunately for European civilisation, the Euboean traders had already begun to look beyond the confines of the eastern Mediterranean to the promise of minerals and riches held by the next great promontory to the west of Greece, the Italian peninsula.

To a seaman sailing north along the west coast of Italy, the first well-sheltered natural harbour to offer a secure anchorage lies far to the north of the Straits of Messina in the Bay of Naples. Here a series of crescent-like bays in the Gulf of Pozzuoli lie within the embrace of the larger bay – the remaining rims of collapsed volcanoes. (They serve the same purpose to this day, often sheltering the American Mediterranean fleet.)

In about 770 BC, on a defensible promontory on the island of Ischia, sailors from Chalcis and Eretria founded a trading post. It was an ideal foothold for trade with a foreign and potentially hostile shore. They were drawn there by the lure of metals, by the copper, silver and lead of two ranges of mountains in Tuscany: the Tolfa mountains, and a range which since ancient times has been called the Colline Metallifere. Further north there was also the iron of Elba, an island which has one of the biggest iron deposits in the Mediterranean. The metal lodes had been created by the same movements of the Earth's crustal plates as had caused the eruptions of Vesuvius, the volcanic crater harbours, and indeed, built the island of Ischia itself.

When the Euboean Greeks hauled up their ships on the beach of Ischia and established themselves at Pithekoussai, they found villages on the mainland that had grown prosperous on the natural wealth of the soil, particularly in the region between the Tiber and Arno rivers which was inhabited by the Etruscans. Indeed, Victorian-minded scholars were to blame the prodigal fertility of this homeland for what they saw as Etruscan decadence. The growing Etruscan villages were in the process of coalescing into towns, just as they were on the Greek mainland.

OVERLEAF
Trade and settlement from the twelfth to sixth centuries BC.

Mainz

EIFEL
R. RHINE

R. SEINE

R. LOIRE

Vix ◆

Heuneberg ◆

Hallstatt ◆

CHAINE
DES PUYS

R. SAÔNE

R. GARONNE

R. RHÔNE

Nîmes •

St Blaise
ÉTANG DE BERRE

Antibes ▲

Massalia ●

ETRUSCAN
HOMELAND

R. ARNO

Carcasonne •

GULF OF
LYONS

Emporion

Volterra ●

COLLINE
METALLIFERE

ADRIATIC SEA

Alalia ●

Populonia ●

Tarquinia ▲

ELBA

Veii ●

CORSICA

GIGLIO

Caere ●

R. TIBER

R. TINTO

R. GUADALQUIVIR

Gades ■

▲

■

TYRRHENIAN
SEA

Pithekoussai

BAY OF
NAPLES

Cumae ▲
Poseidonia

Taranto ▲

■

■

SARDINIA ●

Metapontum ▲

Sybaris ▲

Croton ▲

AEOLIAN
ISLANDS

ION
SE

■

Motya ■

Himera ▲

Naxos ▲

■

SICILY

Utica ●

Selinus ▲

Akragas ▲

STRAITS OF MESSINA

Carthage ■

Syracuse ▲

■

MALTA ■

■

Leptis ▲

■

Nea Polis
(Naples) ●

MT. VESUVIUS

PHLEGRAEAN
FIELDS

Pozzuoli ●

Herculaneum ●

Misenum ●

Pompeii ●

BAY OF NAPLES

Stabiae ●

Pithekoussai ●

ISCHIA

Rio Tinto in Spain, ivory from Africa and pottery from Euboea, Corinth and many other ports of Greece.

We know little of the daily life of the settlers and merchants. They cremated and buried their dead in a Greek style, but the personal adornment found in the graves, like the large safety-pins (fibulae) used to clasp clothes, were all of local design. This suggests that the Greeks were marrying local women, or they would have been buried with goods that reflected their Greek preferences. One fragmented wine-cup imported from Rhodes gives a tantalising glimpse of a cheery and cultured society with a scratched inscription in Chalcidean script (written backwards, as was then the custom):

> Nestor had a most drink-worthy cup, but whoever drinks from this cup will soon be smitten with desire for fair-crowned Aphrodite.

This light-hearted verse, in excellent epic hexameters, is one of the earliest examples of Greek script to be found anywhere. It is contemporary with the final version of the two great epics of Greece the *Iliad* and the *Odyssey* that we attribute to Homer. In one brief inscription it manages to conjure up both the siege of Troy (according to Homer, Nestor, King of Pylos, voyaged with the Argonauts and travelled with the Greeks to fight at Troy), and in its lustful homage to Aphrodite the goddess of love, beauty and fertility, the Greeks' love of life.

It was in one of the Greek cities on the islands or mainland of the west coast of Asia Minor (possibly Old Smyrna) that Homer wrote, and that coast now had a profound influence on the renaissance of the Greek genius after the void of the Dark Ages. The alphabet was adopted from the Phoenicians; eventually literature, philosophy, even the use of coins began. It is likely that Odysseus' adventures as he sailed home from Troy, recorded in the *Odyssey*, reflected the contemporary stories of sailors who had ventured bearing this intellectual cargo into the unknown western Mediterranean. Tall tales, such as that of the one-eyed giant Cyclops who lived in a cave, probably derived from the presence of dwarf elephant skulls preserved in caves on islands in the Mediterranean. The rocks hurled by the blinded Cyclops at Odysseus' ship probably came from a volcanic eruption in the Aeolian Islands.

It is not surprising that this period of Etruscan culture has been called 'Orientalising' from the goods from the Near East that the Greek traders brought with them. Every trading vessel would certainly have hugged the shore, and would have sailed from port to port picking up tradeable material from different countries, in much the same way as tramp steamers used to do before the Second World War.

News of the new opportunity to trade with Etruria soon spread home. Then an important new phase began, when Greek craftsmen arrived on Ischia, first bringing the potter's wheel. The excellent local clay allowed them to make pottery of a higher standard than the Etruscans' own, and they found a ready market. As the trade in locally made goods increased, metal craftsmen arrived and workshops were set up to make *fibulae* and gold jewellery. The Greek metal-workers were more skilled than the Etruscans, especially in working gold. But the crucial knowledge the craftsmen brought from Euboea and Al Mina was their technical skill. They were expert iron-makers, and soon they were shipping iron ore from Elba to smelt at Pithekoussai.

The primitive furnaces of the day could only reduce iron ore into a kind of sponge-like mass which then had to be forged into wrought iron. It could only be produced in small quantities, and it would be centuries before it replaced bronze for general use even for such vital necessities as helmets and armour. But it was nevertheless rapidly adopted for some purposes such as horse-bits, and indeed was essential for tools for working bronze.

An industry soon developed, and it has been estimated that from 750 BC 10,000 tons of copper and iron ore were smelted every year. (In contrast, Redcar steel mill on Teesside, the largest mill in western Europe, now produces 10,000 tons of metal a day.) It is hard for us to appreciate that at the time it was industry on a scale the world had never before known. To smelt this amount on Elba huge quantities of charcoal were needed, and soon all the trees on the island had been destroyed. Production had to be shifted to the mainland at Populonia, where iron slag can still be seen piled into artificial cliffs by the shore. (Most of this slag was re-smelted in modern times, for example by Mussolini's government during the Second World War. He too was short of iron.)

The growth of the Etruscan cities

The wealth that this metal industry created is still valuable today. For centuries Etruscan tombs have been robbed, first for gold, then for bronze, and more recently for Greek pottery. The tradition continues with the *tombaroli*. They dig at night, armed with metal detectors and guns. The stakes are high. A single Archaic Greek vase can be sold for $15,000 and guards on excavations have been shot. Even the official excavations have seldom been properly written up, a recurrent fault which has made a travesty of serious archaeology throughout the Mediterranean. As one archaeologist said, 'Etruscan archaeology is worse than any other except Egyptian'. The result is that the museums of the world are full of wonderful collections of looted goods from Etruscan tombs, much of it Greek, with almost no information to speak to us about its context.

Despite this, it is not difficult to appreciate the enormous impact that the metals trade had on Etruria. Before the Greeks arrived, the Etruscans were living in wooden huts, as their child-like bronze grave-goods show. Within a century their aristocracy were building great chamber-tombs filled with golden treasure. In fact it is precisely because there is such a huge change in the wealth and culture manifested in the burials that former scholars believed these must be the relics of a new immigrant people.

The most impressive evidence was discovered to the south of the ancient city of Caere (modern Cerveteri), some 40 kilometres north-west of Rome. By the seventh century BC, Caere was the most important Etruscan town. Like most Etruscan settlements it was built on a plateau of a soft volcanic rock called tufa. With the metal-rich Tolfa mountains to the north and the sea about 5 kilometres to the west, it was protected on either side by steep escarpments dropping down to rivers. It was well placed to benefit from the fertile volcanic plateau, the heavier soils of the coastal swampy *maremma* which were then probably used for grazing, and from the metals of the mountains. It quickly grew to some 800 hectares in extent, only a tiny fraction of which has been excavated. So we know little about the daily life of its people.

In contrast, the city of the dead – the tombs of Caere – tell us a great deal about the ruling aristocracy of the area. These tombs, in the Banditaccia cemetery, were systematically raided during the eighteenth century. But the necropolis is so extensive, and the round tumuli are so huge, that it remains one of the most interesting sites of the ancient Mediterranean. The strange round tumuli, clustered together like a field of giant mushrooms, half cut down into the native rock and half built from sawn blocks, still astonish with their size and workmanship.

A gilded silver plate imported from the Near East found in the Regolini Galassi tomb at Cerveteri.

Aligned beside streets whose rock pavement has been cut deep by the passage of iron-shod wheels, they give a powerful impression of a rich and organised society. A simple agricultural economy had been transformed under the influence of the Greeks into an urban city-state.

The tomb interiors, where the bodies of the dead were laid out on rock-cut platforms that increasingly came to resemble couches, were decorated more and more elaborately – apparently to represent the grandest houses of the day. Alcoves, pillars, capitals, seats, even a relief decoration of arms, were all carved from the solid tufa in a style reflecting both Greek and oriental influences. These family vaults were each used for as long as 150 years.

In 1836 one tomb was found intact. Called the Regolini Galassi tomb, after the abbot and general who found it, like most Etruscan tombs it had been used more than once. Corbelled vaults sustained an earth tumulus, setting a pattern for future burials. In the main chamber were found the splendid offerings given to accompany a young woman, presumably a princess, beyond the grave; and written in the Greek alphabet on a silver jug was the inscription, 'I am Larthia's'. The Greeks had begun to teach the Etruscan nobility to write. The Etruscans had no *g* sound in their language, so when they transcribed their own language in Greek letters they made *gamma* a *c*. The Romans followed their example, and their usage followed their conquests north into central Europe. That is why we now say *abc* rather than *alpha beta gamma*.

There seems little doubt that Greek craftsmen and architects had followed their language ashore and were now teaching local apprentices. Greek-style temples with tiled roofs (another Greek technique) were built to the glory of their gods, and by the sixth century the Etruscans had embraced Greek ideas with such enthusiasm that they had set up their own sanctuary, or treasury, at the grove of Apollo at Delphi.

Princess Larthia's glittering treasure can now be seen in the Vatican Gregorian Museum, and it is rich with both eastern and local gold and silver. The embossed gold bracelets and pectoral are decorated with a mass of figures of animals and men, and the bronze-clad throne and funeral carriage are adorned with free variations of Assyrian and Egyptian motifs and others from Asia Minor (Ugarit) – a glittering reflection of the extent of their trade.

Gold is not found in Etruria and it may have been brought by Phoenicians from Spain, or by Greeks from Thrace, or Egypt, or the Black Sea, where other Greek trading posts had already been established. But its most likely source now appears to be the rivers which drain the Massif Central north of Carcassonne and Nîmes. It is still possible to pan alluvial gold there today. Trade in metals, especially in gold, leaves little archeological evidence, because so much is recycled, and it is hard to judge how much gold and bronze was originally placed in the Etruscan graves. But among the gold lay many magnificently painted Greek vases, demonstrating their value in Etruscan eyes, and the interesting question is: what were the Greeks getting in return for their cargoes?

Their most essential need was for raw materials, and the most important of these was tin – still in great demand for the expanding bronze industry. Traces of tin ores have been found at three locations in Tuscany, but only one has been exploited, at Monte Valerio. Small quantities were mined at the end of the eighteenth century, and this led Sir Arthur Evans to believe that it had been exported to Minoan Crete. But despite archaeologists' claims that the Etruscans exported local tin, as is so often the case, these are merely repetitions of unfounded assertions that have got into print. On hard evidence it seems unlikely that they mined enough even to satisfy their own needs. Recently discovered traces in Sardinia can be discounted, and it is much more likely that tin was brought from Rio Tinto in Spain, and across France from the Breton peninsula and Cornwall. Some was for local use and some for the Greeks.

The inhabitants of Pithekoussai may finally have been driven off Ischia by earthquakes and an associated eruption of the volcano Epomeus on the island. Before then, however, in 750 BC, a daughter colony had been set up on a defensible headland on the edge of the Bay of Naples at Cumae. Although well to the south of the Etruscan heartland between the Tiber and the Arno rivers, this was much more a colony than a trading post like Pithekoussai, and had the advantage of being surrounded by extensive level volcanic land for agriculture. The capital acquired from trade, and the excellent volcanic soils, now allowed the rapid expansion of the fiercely independent Etruscan cities of Vulci, Tarquinia, Caere, Veii, and so on, to a size never before seen on the mainland of Europe. They were themselves beginning to compete, and must have viewed this first Greek settlement on the mainland of Italy with apprehension. Since both Greek and Etruscan merchants were plying the Mediterranean in ever-increasing numbers, it is perhaps not surprising that their trading interests should begin to compete, and lead to rivalry and mistrust – especially in an age when the dividing line between piracy and competitive private enterprise often depended on the observer's point of view. Slowly this was to sour relations as Etruscan sea-power expanded.

The Greek expansion overseas

At Cumae, portions of the original defensive wall still surround the acropolis where ruins of sixth-century temples to Apollo and Jupiter still survive. Even more impressive is the tunnel called the Antrum of the Sybil, which has recently been recognised as a defensive gallery first built by the Greeks to house catapults to cover their ships hauled out on the beach below, evidence of the need to repel attacks by foreign marauders. It was remodelled by the Romans as an Oracle of Apollo, but looks astonishingly like the late Mycenaean defensive galleries of Tiryns, in the plain of Argos on mainland Greece. It might be much earlier in origin than the fourth-century date it has been given.

It is ironic that trade had a low status among the Greeks, but (as in nineteenth-century Britain) it was nevertheless a major agent for change. At Athens, much of the trade was in the hands of resident aliens who were debarred from owning land, yet Athenians had to own land to be eligible for citizenship, and even to join the heavily armed army of soldiers known as *hoplites*. Each *hoplite* had to provide his own bronze helmet, shield and greaves, a very large expense in a country short of minerals. With an unavoidable shortage of cultivable land and an expanding population crying out for its redistribution, with the age-old conflict arising between noble landed families and the newly rich merchants, many city-states began to think in terms of exporting people as well as goods to the wealthy new lands in the west. A wave of emigration began.

Corinth was situated on the isthmus, only 6.5 kilometres wide, which divided the trade of the Aegean and the Middle East from the trade with Italy. Rather than risk the voyage round the southern end of the Peloponnese mountains, which stand out like the open fingers of a hand towards the Sea of Crete, merchants preferred to tranship their cargoes at Corinth. Later, a special paved road was built along which ships could be dragged from sea to sea (now, in turn, superseded by the famous canal). Besides being a transhipment point, Corinth was an ideal collecting depot to marshal cargoes of goods for export. Benefiting from its geographical position, the city soon began to dominate western trade, as the large quantity of Corinthian perfume jars found in Etruscan graves bears witness. Corinth had no trading centre for metals in north Italy, and now began to exploit those from the north shores of the Aegean, with settlements on the Halkidiki peninsula, Mount Pangaion and Potidea. With an expanding population, a vast increase in wealth, and their knowledge of trade and opportunity overseas, the inhabitants of Corinth also began to plan satellite settlements to the west.

One of the first major Greek colonies to be set up by Corinth was Syracuse on Sicily (733 BC). The Greek geographer Strabo, who wrote 700 years later, tells us that two Corinthian entrepreneurs, Myscellus and Archias, went to Delphi to ask the oracle of Apollo where they should found settlements. The priestess asked whether they desired health or wealth. Archias chose wealth and was told to found Syracuse, while Myscellus (a hunchback) chose health and was assigned Croton on southern Italy. Syracuse was destined to become the richest colony in the west.

The colonies were designed from the outset to be independent, but, as with so much of the Mediterranean of the eighth century, only fragments of their history have come down to us. Quite why so many were set up is not clear. But in the case of the island of Thera, after a seven-year drought the population actually drew lots and compelled a tenth of their number to sail away to found a colony at Cyrene in North Africa. When expanding populations caused cities to face the grim alternatives of either reducing population by emigration or attacking their neighbours, it is likely that many cities chose to force people to leave, especially those who lacked the land qualifications for citizenship.

The eastern Ionian cities had established Naucratis on the Nile delta to exploit the valuable Egyptian trade. But by contrast, Tarentum (modern Taranto in southern Italy) was founded by the illegitimate sons of the wives of Spartan soldiers, conceived during a campaign when the Spartans had sworn not to return home until victorious, but had been so beset by the complaints of their women that they sent some young men home on leave to keep them entertained . . .

Whatever the reason for their foundation, there was a straightforward geological reason for the agricultural success of the towns like Metapontum (on the instep of the boot of Italy), which was to sport an ear of corn on its coins, and Sybaris nearby, whose name, even 2700 years later, is still a byword for luxury and the easy life. The toe of Italy, from Basilicata to Calabria, is bending northwards under pressure from the African Plate, and as the south coast stretches a series of tensile fractures, like an opening paper fan, formed wide valleys, which filled with sediments from the rapidly rising mountains. The resulting broad level plains are a completely different geological environment from that of most of Greece, and far more fertile.

As they grew in wealth to the point where they rivalled the cities from which they sprang, the colonies of what was now called Magna Graecia began to compete in the excellence of the layout of their cities, and especially in the splendour of their civic buildings such as temples. In a society which invented Democracy, where gods and their priests and priestesses presided over almost every function of life and death, it is not surprising that their temples became the richest repositories of wealth in any town.

In some regions of the Aegean the formation of the Alps had brought limestone which had been buried deep in the crust and metamorphosed into marble to the surface. In the seventh century, life-size marble sculptures began to be made on Naxos, where both marble and the hard emery needed to work it occur

OVERLEAF The much-restored Tholos, an outlying temple at Delphi. Greek trade and settlement overseas turned this herdsman's shrine into the centre of the ancient world and a prestigious international treasure house. Delphi was famous for its oracle of Apollo and the Pythian games. It has been ruined many times by earthquakes caused by the tectonic forces still raising the Greek mountains.

together. (Sculptors from Naxos are repairing the Parthenon today.) Corinth was now the greatest of the Greek cities. An outcrop of easily workable limestone is within convenient reach of the town, and the inhabitants had the wealth, the audacity and manpower in slaves to build a temple to Apollo with the traditional wooden columns replaced by stone (540 BC). The wooden pillars had been fluted for centuries as stylised impressions of the work of the carpenter's adze, as can be seen in the ruins of Nestor's palace at Pylos. The taper and bulging *entasis* of the early columns mimicked tree-trunks, and the triglyphs of the entablature represent the end of wooden beams. Thus was the Doric style born. Perhaps the huge demand – and consequent shortage – of timber for fuel, for smelting metals and ship construction during this period of great prosperity, encouraged the idea of using stone.

Little more than a few columns of most of the early temples survive, but the Temple of Hera at Paestum (poseidonia), a daughter colony of Sybaris, remains as a magnificent reminder of the wealth of the sixth century BC.

The rise of Athens

It was only in the sixth century BC that Athens began the startling development that was to carry it to the centre of the European stage in social reform, industry and art. There is a suggestion that the enterprising island of Aegina, just offshore in the Saronic Gulf, had actually blocked trade from Athens. But the city had no colonies until, in 620 BC, two were set up in the Dardanelles. These were later to give her control over the important trade in timber, grain and metals from the Black Sea.

It is important to remember that the city-state system meant that one city could be self-sufficient in a particular raw material while another went short. Athens was exceptional in having its own state silver and copper mines at Laurion (Lavrion), and had a great potential for exporting olive oil but was chronically short of grain. The extraordinary pragmatic originality of the Greeks is never better shown than in the decision, taken in 590 BC by the ruling hereditary oligarchy of Athens, to appoint a man named Solon to reform a society dominated by rich landowning families where the poor became steadily poorer.

Solon's reforms were radical, and it is hard to imagine them being applied today. They included the cancellation of all outstanding debt and the abolition of enslavement for debt. This also applied to serfs who failed to provide their annual fee of corn. At the same time the export of corn and any foodstuff other than olives was banned. This was a deliberate policy to keep local food prices down at a time of shortage. Solon also decreed that officials dining in the council house of Athens should only have wheaten bread on festival days. They must make do with barley, like the poor, for the rest. At the time wages were even paid in measures of grain and, to obtain the grain to feed its rapidly booming population, Athens had to rely more and more on overseas trade, a weakness that was in the end to bring about her downfall.

Other laws introduced by Solon to redress the balance between the poor and the rich nobility were to allow a right of appeal against sentence, and to permit a third party to plead for justice on behalf of a plaintiff. As a final proof of his wisdom, Solon then left Athens for ten years so as not to influence the working of his own laws.

In the fifth century BC, Athenian trade boomed, first in olive oil, then in wine and pottery. Wine was consumed by the rich using sets of luxury pottery cups and mixing bowls, and new skills in firing were soon established in factories to allow the remarkable black and red decoration of scenes from the Greek myths and everyday life which have made Attic pottery famous. Vast quantities of Athenian ware were shipped around the Mediterranean. Soon the beautiful black and then red-figure vases ousted Corinthian ware as the Etruscans' favourite. Fortunately, the ancient tomb-robbers of Tuscany were not interested in pottery, and over 1700 vases from Athens have been recovered from the tombs of the Etruscan city of Vulci alone. The collections of Greek pottery now distributed around the capitals of northern Europe mostly came from Etruscan tombs.

The Etruscan middle class was benefiting from the trade as much as the nobility, as the elaborate sarcophagi and exquisitely painted tombs of Tarquinia show. But the clearest view of the actual process of trade has come from an Etruscan wreck excavated by a British team from Oxford University off the island of Giglio about 60 kilometres south of Elba. Dated at about 600 BC by its Corinthian pottery, it carried a cargo of amphorae full of olives and pitch. It sank soon after picking up a consignment of granite anchor-staves. Despite looting by sport-divers it has revealed a rich variety of cargo from wooden flutes to arrowheads and a magnificent bronze helmet. But it may also answer one of the most puzzling questions about Bronze Age trade. What did they use for money to regulate trade at this date before coins had been invented? Grain would be far too bulky for such a purpose. At the site of the wreck were found large quantities of the thin iron spits, similar to those called *fasces* which became the symbol of authority in Roman times (later adopted by Mussolini to give us our word 'fascist'). There were far too many to be used only to express official power. Also discovered were large numbers of small copper nuggets, varying in size from that of a pea to a tangerine. Archaeologists are convinced that these metals were used as currency. As copper had a high value it would indicate why such nuggets are so rarely found on sites ashore. The metal was too precious to be left lying around, and once coins came into circulation any remaining pieces of copper would of course have been recycled into goods. The thin iron spits rust away very easily. In more senses than one, metals were promoting the civilisation of the Mediterranean.

Now that the shores of the Mediterranean had been linked together by extensive maritime trade routes, the valuable resources of each port of call had been parcelled out between the established trading powers: the Phoenicians, the Etruscans and the Greeks. For the first time the dominance of sea-trade became a limiting factor in the search for raw materials. All the maritime avenues of trade were already taken up, while the mountains beyond the shore, which hindered trade by land, became a constraint on looking outwards for more opportunities. But there was one route that the structure of Europe had laid bare to the heart of Northern Europe, and this was to be crucial in the centuries that lay ahead – the river Rhône.

Bronze Greek helmet from the Giglio wreck.

CHAPTER SIX

THE RICHES
OF THE RHÔNE

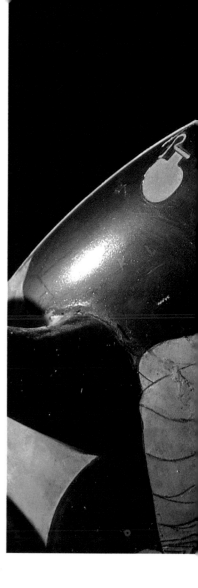

To the east of the mouth of the Rhône, the local limestone has been hollowed out by a combination of wave action and dissolving by water to form a series of lagoons. The largest of these, L'Etang de Berre, used to be connected with the sea. Near this fine natural harbour, a ridge between the two smaller lagoons of Lavalduc and Citis is flanked by vertical cliffs on three sides to make a natural fortress. In the seventh century BC the coastal people, the Ligurians, had made a settlement there, now called St Blaise. Beneath the pines and scrub, the ground even now is thickly strewn with the fragments of Etruscan wine amphorae – the heavy terracotta storage jars which were used for a thousand years to ship wine, olive oil and other products around the Mediterranean.

Throughout history, developed nations have always found it profitable to trade with those whose technology is less advanced, and alcohol has often led that trade. It is possible that the Mycenaeans had brought the domesticated vine to Italy, though it appears that the Etruscans did not know how to make wine. Certainly the Greeks did, and it was only as Etruscan society became transformed under Greek influence that wine from Italy began to be traded overseas, and they set sail with it to the north, to the coast of the Gulf of Lions. Archaeologists would maintain that wine consumption is socially desirable in a society whose structure is based on conspicuous consumption, like that of the Bronze Age warriors. Its powers to addict and to corrupt also bring obvious advantages to merchants and warriors with acquisitive interests.

A society can only make wine when its agriculture or trade is sufficiently successful to free labour from food production, but the Etruscans had already passed that stage when the Greek merchants first arrived. The tomb paintings of Tarquinia show that the rich citizens, at least, had soon adapted the Greek tradition of the drinking-party or *symposium*, where music and games accompanied conversation, into a banquet with food and wine. And while drinking parties were an all-male affair in Greece, in Etruria women took part with a freedom, equality and licentiousness which appalled the Greeks.

Dionysos, the Greek god of wine, had also been adopted by the Etruscans, and no doubt they celebrated the orgiastic rites that accompanied his festivals. In contrast to the self-discipline represented by Apollo, who stood for all that we think

A kylix or drinking cup gracefully depicting a symposium, exported from Athens to the Etruscans as part of an expensive wine-drinking kit. Etruscan tombs have yielded enormous numbers of fine Greek pots.

of as Greek civilisation, Dionysos personified the irrational side of mankind. Yet there was nothing irrational about the way in which the Etruscans, then the Greeks and later the Romans were to exploit the central Europeans' passion for wine, and the Rhône valley was to be crucial to that trade as it led into the heart of northern Europe.

Through this great natural breach in the Alps have flowed the currents that changed the destiny of Europe. Seen from the Mediterranean, the Rhône valley led to a dark secret world of forests and snow inhabited by savage warrior chieftains. But to the adventurous it was also the way to the mines of half magical metals like tin, which made copper strong, and to the fount of furs and slaves to enrich the sunnier Mediterranean world. Up the Rhône travelled the alphabet, the grape and the first coins, stimulants to culture, diet and trade, but, in the Middle Ages, it was also to be the route of entry for *Yersinia pestis*, the bacillus that caused the Black Death.

The way through the Alps

The next chapter in the human story of Europe was made possible not by the collision of continents, such as had formed the Alps, but by their splitting apart. What actually causes continents to split is poorly understood and there are conflicting theories. Some scientists maintain that circular convection currents in the molten mantle of the Earth pull parts of the surface crust along; others hold that the cold crust on the surface sinks down into the hot mantle that sustains it because it is denser, and that once an edge has dipped 100 kilometres down it pulls the rest sideways like a sheet of paper falling off the edge of a table.

About 180 million years ago, the super-continent of Pangaea started to break up and the Atlantic began to open – first as a rift valley and then, when the sea burst in, as an ocean. The North Atlantic ocean floor widened during the Cretaceous period when the great chalk deposits were laid down, and it is still spreading now – about 2 centimetres every year. The spectacular eruptions in Iceland occur because the ocean floor on which Iceland sits is pulling apart, and so is the land. As the South Atlantic opened, the African crustal plate continued to push into Europe, squeezing Italy into Europe as the Alps rose. But north Italy also moved westwards and caused the folds of the Maritime Alps that curve south at Geneva through Provence to meet the Mediterranean coast at Nice.

As Europe and North America pulled apart, the stretching of the land was not confined to just one area: all over the continent weak points gave way. At about the same time as the North Sea opened (stretching the crust 160 kilometres), Rockall and the outer Hebrides moved away from the mainland, and Ireland from Britain. The hexagonal blocks of the Giant's Causeway and Fingal's Cave are parts of a thick basaltic lava flow which erupted as the crust thinned, and then cooled very slowly and fragmented into columns as the basalt shrank. As the crust beneath stretched further, the flow split down the middle to leave half either side of the Irish Sea.

Not all the continental movement thinned the crust enough for it to dip below sea level. Wales failed to break clear of England, and in central Europe the Rhine now flows down two grabens, or rift valleys, where the continent stretched apart and the land in between sank. As this happened lines of volcanoes erupted along the edges of the rifts. The eroded cores or plugs of the old volcanoes that still line the edge of the Rhine Valley made excellent fine vantage points for feudal lords to dominate the fertile lands below and are still adorned with castles like Kaiserstuhl and Königsberg.

The two rift valleys of the upper and lower Rhine join at Mainz in Germany, and nearby in the Eifel region is a related hot-spot beneath the continental crust, where molten magma lies near the surface. This has caused eruptions in the geologically recent past: the Laacher-See crater was formed about 11,000 years ago, shortly after the last ice age had begun to retreat, and may have been seen by families of modern humans who were following the retreat of the ice in the area.

When the Alps folded up, the combined pressure from Africa and weight of the mountains caused the continental crust to sag and the Rhône valley or graben dropped down. This basic tectonic process was to be of crucial importance as far as the human history of Europe was concerned because it opened a way through the ring of mountains that surrounds the Mediterranean providing a communication link and, more importantly, a trade route.

The spectacular line of volcanoes that form the Chaîne des Puys in the Auvergne were a more distant manifestation of the same process; the granite crust of Europe is cracking there, as it is bent downwards at the Rhône. The most recent eruption in the area, at Lac Pavin, took place only 6000 years ago. The underlying faults are still active, and it would be a mistake to think that the absence of activity at the present is any guide to the future.

The lake-filled sunken volcanic craters called maars which are common in the Auvergne and Eifel regions, like Lac Pavin, the Gour de Tazenat and the Laacher-See, are the effects of explosive eruptions caused when surface streams or ground water mix with incandescent magma and flash over to steam with

OVERLEAF The volcanic
cones of the Chaîne des
Puys, Auvergne, follow a
fault line where the
continental plate of
Europe is cracking.

enormous force. Should such an eruption now occur in a populated area it would, of course, have catastrophic results.

The wine trade

By 650 BC the Etruscans had planted enough vineyards of their own (in an area now known for Chianti) to have a flourishing wine trade with the Ligurians of southern Provence and Languedoc, where fragments of Etruscan wine amphorae are still scattered across the landscape in astonishing quantities. St Blaise was the biggest depot for these imports, and most of the amphorae there can be traced back to Cerveteri where the wine must have been made. But the Etruscan wine drinking pottery found at St Blaise came from Vulci, which was the centre of the Etruscan bronze industry.

In exchange for their wine and pottery, the Etruscans appear to have been paid in metal: alluvial gold, raw metals and bronze scrap. Many hoards of worn bronze weapons and ornaments have been found in southern France, as if they were being collected for sale. At Pertuis the tomb of a 10-year-old prince contained the kind of prestige bronze metal-work from Etruria (helmet, cuirass, wine-jug and so on) that would have been given to the Ligurians to promote the export of more raw-materials (625 BC). One such valuable commodity was salt, which was much in demand for preserving food and which is produced naturally in the Etang de Lavalduc. Because of the high winds and heat of summer, the lagoon has the highest evaporation rate in Europe and is one of the sites in the Mediterranean where salt has been produced for centuries.

The Etruscans were never colonists, but they must have had a powerful influence along the length of the coast. The distribution of amphorae sherds, as well as wrecks laden with Etruscan amphorae found off Cap d'Antibes, Cavalaire and Marseilles, show that their wine was being drunk from Montpellier to Antibes and as far north as modern Orange.

The curious shape of amphorae came about from the need to stack them in the holds of ships, three or four tiers deep. The tapered bases of the upper layer fitted between the necks and bodies of the lower layer, wedging them tight against the sides of the hold so that when the ship rolled they would not crash from side to side and break. Etruscan amphorae were more rounded than the later Roman kind, but still only contained 7 to 15 litres of wine. The contents (even wine) in fact weighed less than the container, which made them impractical to transport far on land. Much of the river traffic in Europe followed the banks of the rivers rather than going by boat along them, so amphorae were decanted into lighter containers such as wineskins or barrels near the coast (which is another reason why so many fragments of amphorae are found there). To preserve the wine, amphorae were treated inside with resin – the origin of the custom of resinated wine which survives to this day in Greece.

Wine-drinking was accompanied by much ceremony, and required suitably rich containers. The Etruscans manufactured black *bucchero* pottery which imitated the thinness and style of metal, but fine Corinthian and later Athenian pottery was imported to Tuscany to satisfy the increasing demand for ever more elegant and costly wine-drinking sets.

As Greek merchants grew more confident they sought direct access to the goods, particularly tin, coming from central Europe. The Tyrrhenian Sea between Sardinia, Corsica and the Italian peninsula had been an exclusive province for Etruscan trade until the arrival of the Greeks, but now their supremacy was to be challenged. In about 600 BC, Greeks from the town of Phocaea on the

ABOVE A sixth century terracotta sarcophagus of an Etruscan nobleman and his wife, from the necropolis at Cerveteri. Sculpted reclining on a banqueting couch they give a powerful impression of serenity as they look forward to the after-life.

coast of Asia Minor established a trading post, Massalia, near the mouth of the Rhône. It was a typically Greek choice of site, with a rocky promontory for a defensible *acropolis* (upper city), and protected by the coastal range called L'Estanque from the worst effects of the violent northerly wind, the Mistral, that blows down the Rhône valley when pressure is high over the Alps. Now it is the second city of France, Marseilles.

The Massaliotes, in contrast to the Etruscans, came to stay as well as to trade. They set up daughter colonies along the coast of the Gulf of Lions and founded another trading post, Emporion (Ampurias), on the shore of metal-rich northern Spain. This gave Massalia access to resources not just from central Europe, but as far west as the River Ebro in Catalonia, where the Phoenicians' influence began. The new town became part of the extended Greek trading system which stretched right across the central and eastern Mediterranean as far as the Levant.

By drawing resources from central Europe and Spain into that extensive system the Massaliotes flourished. But in the meantime their home city of Phocaea was besieged by the Persians, half the population escaped in 544 BC and sailed to join another colony their citizens had founded on Corsica at Alalia (Aleria). This sudden increase in population provoked the Etruscans to join forces with the Phoenicians from Carthage in a naval battle against the Greeks (537 BC). The Phocaeans came off worse, in spite of winning the battle, and it enabled the Carthaginians to consolidate their hold on the settlements around the Straits of Gibraltar, effectively shutting the Greeks away from the Atlantic and the western Mediterranean and directing their trade towards the Rhône. However, Etruscan sea-power had been badly damaged and, by about 525 BC, wine produced by the Greeks near Massalia had broken the Etruscan monopoly. Instead of Etruscan pottery, amphorae from Massalia and goods from Greece predominate in the new archaeological levels. By the end of the sixth century BC, Massalia had grown rich enough to build three large Doric temples – to Artemis, Apollo and Athena – and even to establish a treasury at Delphi; but St Blaise was deserted.

The Rhône trade

Four hundred kilometres to the north of Marseilles, the wooded limestone hill of Mont Lassois stands at the edge of the fertile Paris Basin, overlooking the gentle meandering River Seine. It is situated just at the point where goods transported up the Rhône and Saône rivers, and by land across a gentle pass over the Plateau de Langres, can once again be embarked for the passage downstream. Mont Lassois had been occupied since neolithic times, and as a fortified town in the sixth century BC it could command trade in both directions, from the English Channel to the Mediterranean.

In January 1953, in a tumulus just below Mont Lassois near the village of Vix, a treasure was discovered that astonished the archaeological world. The tomb contained a skeleton, which was later confirmed to be that of a woman in her mid-thirties, and around her skull was a magnificent diadem or torc of solid gold weighing half a kilo. A masterpiece of craftsmanship, it is in the form of an arc with paws at each end standing on pear-shaped orbs enlivened with winged horses. The beauty and restraint of its design and the detailed workmanship suggest that it might have been made on the shores of the Black Sea, by Greek craftsmen influenced by the Scythians.

The tomb, clearly that of a princess or even a queen, also contained a funeral wagon richly decorated in bronze, with its wheels and shaft carefully removed, and a complete wine-drinking kit. This included a fine bronze wine-jug of a typical Etruscan form (with a beak-spout), bronze and silver bowls, and wine-cups or kylixes from Attica, one of which was decorated in the black-figure style that can be dated to about 520 BC. But the piece that continues to attract wonder and admiration is an enormous bronze wine mixing bowl, or krater. Standing 1.64 metres high, it is decorated with gorgons for handles and a frieze of *hoplite* soldiers with four-horse chariots parading round the rim.

Where had this treasure come from and what did it represent? It is not unreasonable to think that the rulers of Vix had got rich by raising tolls on the trade from river to river, and that these were prestigious gifts from rich merchants or local rulers to ease the passage of trade past Mont Lassois; what today would be the equivalent of the diplomatic presents from heads of state that still accumulate at Buckingham Palace.

The site at Mont Lassois was one of a large number of communities in a wide sweep of territory north of the Alps, roughly from Paris to Vienna, which the traders knew as Celtic. Archaeologists call them the Western Hallstatt culture after the lake and town in Austria which had achieved great prosperity through mining salt as early as the Bronze Age.

Hallstatt graves, though well provided with grave goods, are not renowned for their richness. Besides containing horse gear and weapons, and occasionally wagons, there are few luxuries more elaborate than highly decorated pots. Their bronze work was functional and plain. Yet in the sixth century BC new evidence of wealth appears in a hierarchy of very rich graves. This suggests that the power and wealth of the local chiefs increased as they controlled the flow of trade to the expanding Mediterranean cities, and in return distributed Mediterranean luxuries and wine to their henchmen. Although it was the custom to mix wine and water, the Vix krater had a capacity of 1200 litres. Even if mixed with an equal measure of water, it would still have needed 60 amphorae to fill it – a good part of a boat-load, and sufficient for a very considerable party. The lid was designed as a strainer, which does suggest that it was meant for use.

But who were the traders at Vix? The Greeks certainly had the custom of giving lavish presents, and on the krater itself, scratched behind soldiers on the rim, two Laconian Greek alphabets were found. This suggests that it was made in Sparta or a Spartan colony in southern Italy. And it can be compared with the splendour of a Laconian krater described by Herodotus, which was a gift from the Spartans to the fabulously rich King Croesus of Lydia.

The dates of the treasure all point to the last quarter of the sixth century BC, and this was just when the trading power of the Etruscans was giving way to that of the Massaliote Greeks. Was the treasure of Vix a huge bribe to persuade the Princess to forget past loyalties? We will never know.

Whoever gave it must have been very keen to get his hands on whatever was coming past Mont Lassois from northern Europe. The valuable tin trade from Britain (and possibly Finistère) probably travelled by sea to the Gironde and Garonne rivers, on a southern route across France, through a gap in the mountains at Carcassonne to the River Aude. But quite possibly it also travelled along the Seine and down the Rhône, a shorter route to Tuscany. Other traded goods were probably similar to those recorded in Roman times: hides, woollen products, salted pork, pitch, resin, honey and amber. But there was also a great need in the Mediterranean for mercenaries and slaves, and it may well have been a human cargo, the victims of power struggles between the different Celtic chiefdoms, that filled the wine ships as they sailed south from Massalia. The Greeks had a robust attitude towards their own superiority which today smacks

of fascism. The playwright Euripides has his Iphigenia say, 'It is in the order of things for the Greeks to command the Barbarians, and not the Barbarians the Greeks: they are born for slavery, we are born for liberty.'

Be that as it may, the taste for fine Greek and Etruscan craftsmanship was firmly established north of the Alps, where its influence was later to bring about the dramatic flowering of the beautiful Celtic La Tène style in the following century.

There is little doubt that the Greeks were also involved in the trade up the other great river that breaks through the Alps into central Europe, the Danube. This route from the Danube to the Rhône had been immensely important for trade since neolithic times. The Heuneberg, a hillfort mound in Baden-Württemberg, was built just at the point where the Danube becomes navigable to medium-sized boats, and where a road crossed the Black Forest for about 140 kilometres to the Rhine Valley, another useful avenue for trade. Here the usual rampart of timber and earth was replaced by a feature unique to central Europe: limestone foundations and courses of sun-dried bricks. There were also project- ing square towers – all Greek features, implying that a Greek architect had been used. The building also demonstrates that the Greeks were unused to the climate north of the Alps, which is one of the major physical differences dividing the world of the Mediterranean from that of northern Europe. Sun-dried bricks never caught on.

The threat from the East

Up to this time in the Mediterranean armed conflict had been, for the most part, on a small and fairly local scale – between the inhabitants of rival valleys, city-states and islands. Alliances had formed and dissolved, but there had been no nations. The Etruscans, like the Greeks, had never owed any loyalty to a unit larger than their home town. All was about to change, and it began with a threat that came from abroad. The East was about to challenge the West.

The Persian Empire had begun to expand towards the Mediterranean, follow- ing the trade routes to the rich towns that lay on the coast of the Levant. In about 545 BC, Cyrus the Great overthrew Croesus and won the kingdom of Lydia. Soon Sardis and the Greek cities of the coast of Asia Minor also fell. The threat from the east was growing more powerful daily. In the past the straits at the Hellespont had proved a valuable defence between Europe and Asia Minor, but now Babylon fell to Cyrus's armies, and the Persians built a floating bridge across the Hellespont, from Asia Minor to Europe, enabling them to conquer Thrace. But when they made an unsuccessful attack on the island of Naxos in 500 BC, the Ionian Greeks decided to revolt. Athens and Eretria sent help; and the provincial capital, Sardis, was burnt. Darius, now king of the Persians, bade his servant to tell him three times before he dined every evening, 'Remember the Athenians'.

Darius's first attempt to take revenge on Athens and Eretria failed when his fleet was wrecked off Mount Athos as it tried to round the peninsula. But he already had control of the timber resources of the Black Sea and Macedonia as well as of the Lebanon, and his fleet was quickly rebuilt. Two years later, in 490 BC, the new fleet carried his army directly across the Aegean to Eretria. There they sacked the city and enslaved the population before going on to land about 40 kilometres north-east of Athens at the Bay of Marathon.

The battle that followed has been sung by poets down the ages. Instead of wait- ing behind the walls of his city, the Athenian general Miltiades at once marched his heavily armoured *hoplite* army across the mountains. An Athenian messen- ger Pheidippides was despatched to the Spartans with an urgent appeal for

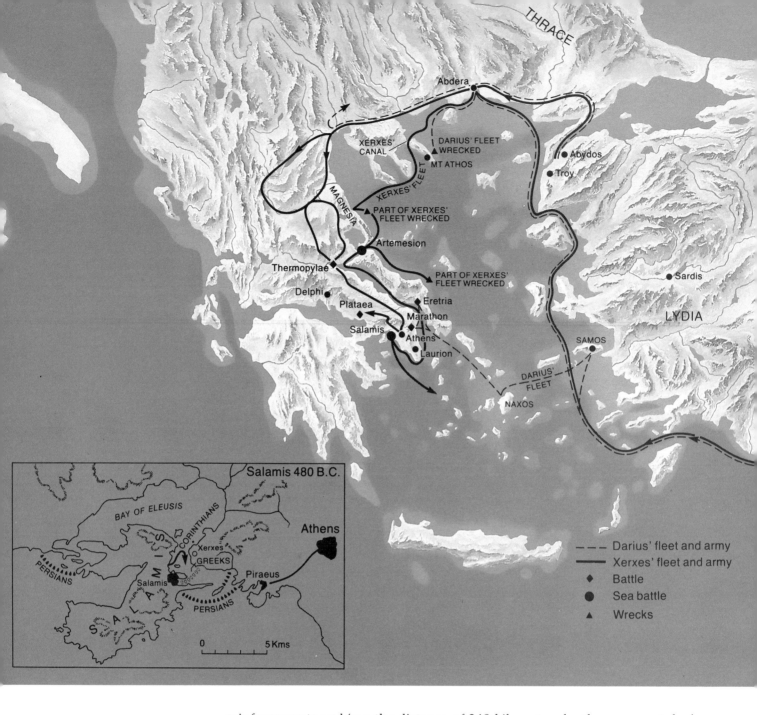

The Persian campaigns against Greece in the fifth century BC.

reinforcements and 'ran the distance of 240 kilometres by the very next day' – inspiring the modern-day marathon races. But the Spartans insisted on waiting five days until after the full moon, a holy day, before setting out, an indication of their extreme obedience to the dictates of their religion.

Miltiades meanwhile lost no time in bringing his force out on to the plain, and attacked 'running to the battle-cry'. The Persians were unable to deploy their superior strength of cavalry, and were driven back to their ships. It was indeed a famous victory: the Athenians are said to have lost only 192 men, and the Persians 6400. The Spartans arrived too late to take part.

Darius died in 486 BC, but his son Xerxes did not forget the Athenians, and in 480 BC began a new advance on Europe. The resources of the Persians were enormous, and to convey his army safely across the Hellespont, Xerxes again had a double pontoon bridge built at Abydos. About 1300 metres long, it was made with no less than 674 vessels. At the first attempt a fierce storm broke both strands, and Xerxes ordered the sea to be flogged to guarantee its submission, while the unfortunate architects of the bridge were executed.

To conquer Greece, Xerxes had gathered and coerced the tribute armies of forty-six peoples together under thirty Persian Generals. It took them a week just to march over the two parallel carriageways across the strait. The huge army, of some 250,000 men, and 75,000 beasts, 'drank the rivers dry' as they crossed through Macedonia.

Xerxes had acquired the fleets of the Phoenicians, the Egyptians, Cyprus and of many other cities to a total of about a thousand ships of war, far exceeding the numbers of the Athenian fleet. Another indication of the vast scale of the attack was that, to avoid any chance of a repeat of the loss of the Persian fleet at Mount Athos, Xerxes had a canal dug through the peninsula. By encouraging a simultaneous attack by the Carthaginians and Etruscans in Sicily, he had also ensured that the Greek cities of Gela, Syracuse and Akragas would not come to the Athenians' aid. Faced with such planning and such odds it needed little short of a miracle to save the fledgeling democracy of Athens.

The mines of Laurion

In this time of extreme peril for Athens and the whole culture of the western world, help came from an unexpected direction, and once again the turbulent tectonic history of the region was the underlying cause; just three years before, a new level of silver ore had been found in the mines of Laurion (Lavrion).

The metals of Laurion, which were being mined until 1979, occur along the eastern coast and central hills of the peninsula to the north of Cape Sounion. They have a complex geology dating back to the formation of the Tethys ocean, but the ores were concentrated when granites were intruded into a limestone mass during the late stages of the building of the Alps. There are no less than forty-five different types of ore present, but in the Classical period only argentiferous lead was mined. The lead had limited uses as weights, for cladding merchant ships, and for catapult missiles. Most of it was lost in a secondary smelting process of cupellation that oxidised the lead to litharge (lead monoxide) in a stream of air to allow silver to be recovered. (The pollution caused by this early refining can even now be picked up as lead traces in ice-cores in Antarctica.)

The hills of Laurion are composed of alternating layers of marble and limestone. The metal ores were deposited when hot solutions of metals rose towards the surface through cracks and pores in the limestone. They then settled and solidified when they reached the impermeable layers of what is locally called schist beneath the marble. This caused the ore to occur in veins, which are still visible today, in three main levels. It is possible that it was the discovery of the third level, at an unidentified site called Maroneia, that came to the rescue of Athens.

Some of the silver lodes were very rich, yielding up to 3 per cent pure silver, and, during production in ancient times, the Laurion mines yielded some 3500 tons of silver, and 1.5 million tons of lead. Most of this was mined by slaves, *andrapoda* (human cattle), working in rectangular horizontal galleries leading off vertical shafts. These were made just large enough for a man to crouch in. The slaves were forced to work in pairs for twenty-four-hour shifts by the light of olive-oil lamps, hewing the rock by hand, progressing about 8 metres a month through the rock, and carrying out the ore in baskets. There are over 3000 shafts in the area, the deepest 119 metres vertically down, and as many as 30,000 slaves worked in the Laurion mines at the same time, almost as many as the entire free population of Athens, in conditions that were notoriously appalling.

Athenian coin struck from Laurion silver.

The gulf between the rich and poor was enormous. One slave-master is recorded as owning a thousand slaves. These were often the spoils of war. As just one example, following the battle of Eurymedon (479 BC) the Athenians took 20,000 prisoners to be used as slaves. Yet by the vagaries of war the rich man and even the slave-owner himself might become a slave. Few families owning property in Attica at this time can be traced for more than three generations before their fortunes fell.

The dreadful cost in human misery of the silver of Athens is hard for us to comprehend, far less condone, as is the irony that the first democracy was founded on such servitude. But there is little doubt that the flow of metal ensured Athens' mastery of the sea, and thus her security and prosperity. The characteristic 'Owls of Laurion' – silver coins stamped with the head of Athena on one side and her symbols, the owl and the olive branch, on the other – were to become current throughout the eastern Mediterranean from the sixth century on as symbols of Athens' maritime power.

Now the whole future of Europe was to hang on the output of those wretched tunnelling slaves. But it took more than the 100 talents of silver won from the Maroneia vein to save the Athenian democracy and European civilisation. It also required the genius of one of the greatest Greek politicians and leaders in their history, Themistocles. He saw clearly that the only salvation for Athens lay in the strength of her fleet. Athenian democratic law required that the profits from the Laurion mines be distributed among the citizens, but Themistocles persuaded the Athenians to forgo personal gain and instead to build a new fleet of 200 triremes. He knew that the success of the vast Persian army depended on having command of the sea as well as the land, both for supplies and to prevent attacks from the rear.

Triremes (or triereis) were the most advanced warships of the day, propelled by three tiers of oarsmen, and designed to sink their opponents by ramming them, or by skimming the bronze ram on their prows down the side to kill the opposing crews by pinning them with their own oars. The new Athenian ships were built (Plutarch tells us) specifically for speed and quick turning (a recently reconstructed trireme can be rowed at 10 knots and sail at 13 knots, while a modern super-tanker travels at 15 knots). They were also lighter than the Persian triremes, and carried only ten armed soldiers on deck instead of the Persians' forty.

The odds were somewhat improved by delays which had held up the Persian advance until late in the summer sailing season when violent storms can lash the Aegean. In fact the Oracle at Delphi had advised the Athenians, 'Pray to the winds'. Their prayers now appeared to be answered. The Persians suffered a catastrophe when 400 ships were wrecked on the shore of Magnesia as they headed south. The Athenian fleet was sheltering at the northern end of Euboea in the hope that the Persian advance could be checked at the pass of Thermopylae.

So at Artemisium the Athenian fleet of 271 triremes drew the 600–700 strong Persian fleet into battle. The Athenians were soon surrounded, but had a strategy ready for this. At a signal, they quickly turned and back-paddled together into a rosette, their sterns in towards the centre to protect the vulnerable rear of the slower ships. At another signal they burst outwards in all directions with deadly results. The Athenians must have been extremely well trained, with the nerve to stick to orders in a threatening situation, and it paid off. They captured thirty ships before night fell. Again the winds came to the Athenians' aid, and a further 200 Persian triremes were wrecked as they tried to sail down the exposed seaward side of Euboea to catch the Athenian fleet in the rear.

ABOVE Life-size bronze of a Greek warrior, found in the sea off Riace, Calabria, where a Roman ship bearing loot from Greece was wrecked. Made in about 450 BC, perhaps by Phidias the greatest of the Classical Greek sculptors, it may once have adorned the temple of Athena Nike built on the Acropolis to celebrate the defeat of Persia.

But the Greek city-states had been unable to agree on a concerted strategy to hold back the invaders, and the Spartans' response was again delayed by a holy day. This is not the place to give a detailed account of the suicidal bravery of the battle of Thermopylae where a force of about 7000 men led by King Leonidas with a royal escort of 300 Spartiates held the pass, about 14 metres wide, between the mountain cliffs and the sea, for two days against overwhelming odds. (The topography has since totally changed because the river Spercheios has built up a broad delta which now carries the main road.) It must suffice to repeat the suitably laconic comment of one crimson-clad Spartan, Dieneces, who, when told that the Persian archers were so numerous that their arrows would darken the sun, replied, 'Good, then we shall fight in the shade'. The valiant but inadequate force was finally outflanked when the secret pass over the mountains was revealed to the Persians by a traitor.

This failure to hold Thermopylae meant that the Athenians had to give up any idea of defending Euboea and their homeland of Attica. Athens was evacuated, the Persians scaled the Acropolis by night, and a triumphant Xerxes watched as the burning and slaughter began and the temple of Athene was looted of its golden treasures. The Athenian fleet withdrew to the island of Salamis.

Xerxes also sent a detachment to plunder the treasuries at Delphi, and they had actually reached the temple of Athene Pronaia, when thunder was heard and a well-timed earthquake rolled down two huge crags on top of them. The survivors withdrew at this evident displeasure of the gods, leaving the treasuries intact – a neat but rare example of how geology can directly affect a military campaign!

BELOW Reconstruction of a Greek trireme built by the Trireme Trust and the Hellenic Navy.

The Spartans and other Peloponnesians were now intent on retreating to fortify and hold the isthmus of Corinth. But Themistocles managed to rally his allied fleet by claiming that though he had lost his city he still had 'the greatest city in all Greece, our 200 ships of war'. He then tricked Xerxes into believing that, with Athens captured, his fleet were going to run away under cover of darkness.

In response, Xerxes divided his forces, sending the Egyptian squadron round the south of the island to block the exit westwards from the Megarian channel, while the straits either side of the island of Psyttaleia were guarded all night by the remaining two squadrons of Persian triremes. The odds had now been reduced to 380 Greek ships to about 500 Persian. As dawn broke Xerxes was installed on a golden throne to watch what he expected to be an easy victory. No ships had escaped in the night, and now he saw the Corinthian vessels sailing off to the north towards the trap he had prepared with his Egyptian fleet. No trireme ever went into action with its sails set, so he thought they were fleeing. But Xerxes was tricked. As his tired oarsmen, who had been up all night, pulled their vessels into the Salamis Channel in pursuit, the Corinthians turned to attack, and the other Greek ships broke from the cover of the island now called Agios Georgios and caught the Persians by surprise.

The crushing defeat that now unfolded before Xerxes on his throne was afterwards immortalised by an eye-witness, Aeschylus, in his play *The Persians* written eight years after the battle. He has a messenger bring news to the Persian court:

> At first the great stream of the Persian fleet
> Held out; but when the ships were massed together,
> Tightly in turmoil, none could help another,
> Ship tearing sister-ship with teeth of iron,
> Shearing away the oars, while all around
> The Greek fleet circled, cool and sharp, and struck.
> Ships were capsized; the waves could not be seen,
> Smothered in shattered wrecks of human flesh. On shores
> And rocks dead men were crowded thick. From
> end to end in all the fleet of Asia
> The rowers turned to panic and retreat. But
> They with splintered oars
> And bits of plank,
> Were hacking, chopping;
> We were a catch of tunny in their net.
> So all the sea was filled with cries and groans
> Till the dark eyes of night were closed upon it.
>
> (BBC TV Series, *The Greeks* Episode 1, Tr Sir Kenneth Dover, 1980)

The silver of Laurion had saved the West.

Once the full enormity of the reversal of his fortune had sunk in, Xerxes realised that he could never defeat Greece without the command of the sea. He swiftly retreated back to Asia with an army of 60,000, fearing for his bridge. The following year the Athenians and Spartans at last managed to coordinate a joint attack against the Persian general Mardonius, who had overwintered in Thessaly with a large army. He was decisively defeated at the battle of Plataea. The power of Persia had been broken, and the Classical age of Greece began. But the very topography of Greece, which had given rise to the city-states, was to militate against any permanent alliance or nationhood, and the glory of Athens lasted little more than a century.

In Sicily, the wealthy Greek cities had been ruled by a series of tyrants, unconstitutional rulers who were not necessarily cruel despots. They had been able to unite forces to defeat the Carthaginian (Phoenician) army at Himera in 480 BC, the year of the battle of Salamis. This set the seal on the decline of the Etruscans who had joined the Carthaginians hoping to defeat the Greeks. Syracuse won a crushing victory against them at Cumae four years later, which allowed the Greeks to expand on the Campanian mainland for the first time. There Neapolis (which means new town and is now called Naples) was founded in 470 BC. Despite their love of life and revelry, the Etruscans had a morbid fascination with fate. They had long been predicting their own extinction after an allotted span of ten lifetimes.

The rise and fall of Athens

In the whole territory of Attica there were between 75,000 and 150,000 inhabitants, with possibly an equal number of slaves. It is hard to believe that it was on this tiny population that the Athenian empire, with all its political and cultural achievements, was now built.

Their dramatic recovery and ascendancy began with the League of Delos, consisting of 220 cities which had to pay tribute to Athens to build ships and raise troops to liberate the eastern Greek cities from the Persians. Again the Athenian fleet was victorious, and the Persians withdrew from the Aegean. Athens' power now reached its peak, and Pericles appropriated the money remaining in the treasury of the League, and used it to build the Parthenon, the glorious temple to Athene Parthenos the virgin goddess of wisdom and war, patroness and defender of the Athenian state. By this stage (447 BC) the Athenian fleet ruled the whole Aegean, and had control of the Hellespont and the metals and riches of the Black Sea trade. In fact their expanding population in a period of great wealth, increasing urbanism and inflation began a fatal dependency on grain from the fertile lowlands round the Danube. Soon Athens was importing two-thirds of the grain its citizens ate and was vulnerable to any attack on this supply.

An orgy of temple-building began throughout Magna Graecia, and many of the great temples that we now can see at Akragas (Agrigento), Selinus (Selinunte), Syracuse and Poseidonia (Paestum), as well as those of the mainland, date from the fifth century BC. It is impossible to stand before the vast tumbled column drums of the temples of Apollo at Selinus, or of Olympean Zeus at Akragas, and fail to be impressed not only by the immense quantities of slave labour used in their construction but also by the cost. Their construction was only possible because the temples, with their treasuries of donations, were also the state banks, and lent money to the cities even for their fortifications. There was deliberate competition between cities to build bigger and better, with all the brashness of colonials striving to outdo their mother-cities. Yet each was still dependent for its prosperity on slaves, and increasingly on booty from beyond its shores.

Civic pride was to be the midwife for a generation of destruction for the city-states. Envy, fear and greed between city and city, nurtured by a culture steeped in the honour of battle, led to a self-perpetuating struggle for wealth through conquest. Once the Persian menace had been curbed, the League of Delos had no function and began to break up. Athens seemed bent on self-destruction, squandering its wealth and energy in the futile Peloponnesian wars with Sparta. As if that were not enough they sent an expedition to capture Syracuse, and were disastrously defeated. The struggles only ended when the Athenian fleet was finally defeated in 405 BC, and, cut off from its grain supply, Athens was starved into submission.

The Carthaginians were quick to take advantage of the Greek squabbles, and advanced in Sicily. Akragas, the city that had been built by the Carthaginian slaves taken at the battle of Himera, was levelled by their kinsmen (404 BC), as were Selinunte and Himera before the end of the century. In the meantime the warfare in the Mediterranean had destroyed the Rhône trade. Mont Lassois was

abandoned about five years after the battle of Salamis. And the Celts, sensing the weakness of the northern Greek colonies and the Etruscan cities, swept south along the Danube and into the Balkans, and through the Italian peninsula. It was, tradition has it, to gratify their acquired taste for wine and fine fruits that they sacked Rome in 390 BC.

LEFT The ruins of Greek ambition. Selinus (Selinunte) in southern Sicily was sacked in 409 BC by the Carthaginians.

The rise of Rome

The weakening of the Greeks and the Etruscans now gave an opportunity to the vigorous and ambitious Romans. The villages on the hills of Palatine, Capitoline and Quirinal had coalesced to become a trading centre, situated where the major north-south road forded the navigable River Tiber. But it lacked the metals available to its great Etruscan rival Veii, about 15 kilometres to the north. There had been fourteen wars between the two cities before Veii finally fell to the Latins of Rome shortly before the Celtic invasion.

An excavation on the north side of the Palatine has recently revealed a telling

historical progression. A wall has been discovered forming the fortification which enclosed the three hills. It has been identified with the works traditionally carried out by Tarquinius Priscus, the son of a rich Corinthian Greek merchant who had been exiled from his home town. A stream which ran down a gully outside the wall was vaulted with stone blocks, and a huge sewer (the Cloaca Maxima) built before the valley was filled in. The massive engineering works that we associate with the Romans were, in fact, started by the Etruscans.

Rome was turned into a city by Etruscan merchants and engineers with the wealth earned by trading metals with the Greeks. The famous statue of the she-wolf suckling Romulus and Remus is an Etruscan bronze. The twins were added by a Renaissance sculptor, Antonio Pollaiolo.

If the Romans literally built on the foundations laid by the Etruscans and the Greeks, they were nothing if not realists. While Greek sculpture represented gods with a stylised noble beauty, the Roman statesmen, generals and merchants commissioned Greek sculptors to carve their own portraits with an almost obses-

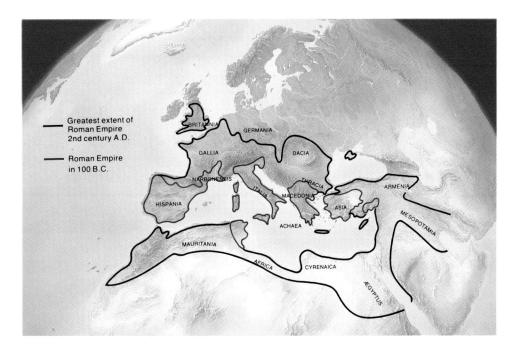

RIGHT The growth of the Roman Empire.

sive attention to realism. Stern and ugly, these faces could indeed have launched a thousand ships and conquered the Mediterranean world.

The great triumph of the Romans was to unite the whole of Italy, and then the Mediterranean, under one rule. To do so they had to secure not only the Italian peninsula, subduing the Celts, the Etruscans and the Greek cities like Taranto in the south, they also needed to control the vital Straits of Messina, in order to be able to trade with the East, and they were covetous of the agricultural wealth of Sicily. To achieve both these objectives they had to deal with the Carthaginians. The three Punic wars which followed were a struggle between the expanding Roman empire and the old Phoenician/Carthaginian trading empire of the western Mediterranean.

The Greeks had brought about the defeat of both the Etruscans and the Persians with naval battles, because maritime communications and thus fleets were still so important to the commercial survival of the countries bordering the Mediterranean. So now the Romans joined battle at sea on an even larger scale. They won the first war against Carthage with a naval victory at Aegates (241 BC), a group of small islands (Egadi) off the west coast of Sicily.

The second point of conflict with the Carthaginians was over competition for trade from another point of the compass, from Iberia, where the Carthaginians were expanding their territory to compensate for the loss of Sicily. The climax came in 218 BC when Hannibal brought a Carthaginian army from Iberia across the Pyrenees, the Rhône and the Alps, and down the whole length of Italy as far as Taranto, inflicting devastating losses on the Romans. But Rome did not fall. When Hannibal could not hold on to his conquests he took ship for Africa again.

It is possible that once again geological events took a hand in the future of Europe. Tree-ring evidence in Ireland and California, as well as ice-core samples, have shown that there was a massive eruption of the Icelandic volcano Laki in 207 BC. This cast a dust veil and climatic shadow across the whole of the northern hemisphere, just as Hekla had done at the end of the Bronze Age. In China, where records were better, the ash cloud in the stratosphere blotted out stars for three months, grain prices rose six-fold, people ate each other, and a law was passed allowing children to be sold. A third of the population starved to death.

It is hard to assess the consequences of the global deterioration of climate in Italy, but it could be that Hannibal was unable to retain his conquests in the face of this gigantic natural disaster. It was in 207 BC that this brilliant young commander withdrew from northern Italy and retreated south to Calabria. It is at least interesting to speculate that possibly, but for a volcano, I might be writing this book in Punic (Phoenician) script. For whatever cause, by 204 BC the Romans had recovered sufficiently to force Carthage to accept a humiliating peace. The third Punic War began half a century later with a Roman assault on Carthage itself. It had long been a Roman objective to destroy the Carthaginians completely, and after three years their city was razed level with the ground. A lengthy Roman campaign secured Iberia, and they then attacked the surviving Greek empire of Corinth in the eastern Mediterranean. Corinth was razed (146 BC) as an example to other Greek cities, and for the first time the whole sea finally came under the dominion of one nation-state – Rome. Now they could call it *Mare Nostrum* (our sea) which has been corrupted to Mediterranean.

The Romans in Gaul

The Romans had become interested in trading with the towns of the Gulf of Lions at the time of the Punic wars, as they supplied their forces along the road which stretches along the coast from Italy to Iberia. While merchants started to export high-quality pottery, the Roman troops had frequently to fend off the neighbouring mountain tribes, the Ligurians of the western Apennines and the Salyens from the Maritime Alps. But as the power and population of Rome grew, it was the Roman merchants' turn to look to the rich pickings available via the Rhône valley. First, however, the Barbarian tribes had to be subdued.

Diodorus Siculus, a Greek historian, gives a colourful account of the appearance and behaviour of the Barbarians at the time:

> Some shave off the beard, while others cultivate a short beard. The nobles shave the cheeks but let the moustache grow freely so that it covers the mouth. And so when they are eating the moustache becomes entangled in the food, and when they are drinking the drink passes, as it were, through a sort of strainer . . .
>
> They are exceedingly fond of wine and sate themselves with the unmixed wine imported by merchants; their desire makes them drink it greedily and when they become drunk they fall into a stupor or into a maniacal disposition . . .

He describes how they rode into battle on two-horse chariots hurling javelins before descending to fight with swords.

> Some of them so far despise death that they descend to do battle, unclothed except for a girdle . . . Trusting in the magical properties of torques about their necks. They cut off the heads of enemies slain in battle and attach them to the necks of their horses. The blood-stained spoils they hand over to their attendants and carry off as booty, while striking up a paean and singing a song of victory, and they nail up these first fruits upon their houses just as those who lay low wild animals in certain kinds of hunting . . .
> (*Greeks, Romans and Barbarians*, Barry Cunliffe, Batsford Ltd., 1988)

They also embalmed the heads of their most distinguished enemies for subsequent display, and even indulged in human sacrifice to foretell the future. Barbaric customs indeed, even compared with the Romans' excesses of cruelty.

Many of the limestone outcrops that fringe the Rhône delta north of Marseilles were used by the Barbarians as fortified settlements or *oppida*. At one of these, called Roquepertuse, there is a natural amphitheatre. This contained the broken pillars that had formed a stone portico for a religious sanctuary. The doorway had been decorated with horses and was surmounted by a monstrous stone bird, variously described as a vulture or a goose. But into the pillars were carved deep niches which served a grisly purpose. At Entremont in a similar pillar was found a skull still impaled by the long iron nail that had held it in place. Elsewhere stone figures of warriors were found holding severed heads in their laps.

The river routes to Gaul.

Embedded in most of these grim *oppida* of the second century BC are found large round stone balls – Roman catapult missiles. One by one they had been attacked and conquered by the Romans. Entremont, the capital of the Saluvians, only 40 kilometres from Massalia, fell to the Romans in 124 BC and signalled the beginning of a commitment which was to draw the centurions deeper and deeper into central Europe. The ferocity of these campaigns is brilliantly captured in the carved relief on the Amendola sarcophagus in the Capitoline Museum, Rome.

The wars as the Roman Empire expanded in the second and third centuries BC had had several important consequences. They had depopulated the Italian countryside to form the ranks of the Roman armies, and had swelled the size of Rome, which now consumed vast quantities of supplies from all around the Mediterranean shores. But more important for central Europe was that the Romans also exported colossal quantities of wine to the Barbarians. One wreck of the first century BC found at Giens had 6000 amphorae from Terecina aboard, and 29,000 were dredged from the river bottom at Chalon-sur-Saône in the nineteenth century. Huge country estates were now owned by patrician Roman families who viewed the Barbarians' love of wine, Diodorus tells us, as their treasure trove (much as the Etruscan merchants had three centuries earlier):

> They transport the wine by boat on the navigable rivers, and by wagon through the plains and receive in return for it an incredibly large price; for one amphora of wine they receive in return a slave, a servant in exchange for the drink . . . (Ibid.)

Diodorus describes the Barbarian tribesmen as 'boasters and threateners and given to bombastic self-dramatisation'. Feasting was part of the tribal ritual that maintained the loyalty of fighting retainers, but their belligerent nature and their love of wine led to quarrels and thus battles. The battles supplied prisoners to sell as slaves in return for more wine, which caused more battles. The slaves were employed on the big estates to grow yet more wine, and as the Roman merchants grew richer, conflict and wine spread hand in hand up the Rhône. Some idea of the size of the trade can be gained when 10,000 slaves could change hands in a single day at the slave market on the island of Delos.

The main beneficiaries of this trade were the tribes who held the territory between the Rhône and the northern rivers. They were literally the middle-men and controlled goods that passed in either direction, and it is not surprising that the Aedui, living in the strategically positioned Morvan massif, became allies of the Romans. But the Roman hold on the coast was continually challenged, leading ultimately to massive battles; first Fabius defeated a huge force of Allobroges and Averni at the confluence of the Rhône and Isère in 121 BC when over 100,000 Barbarians were killed. Then an invading horde of Germanic Teutons and Ambrones, travelling with their families in covered wagons, poured down the Rhône valley intent on Rome itself. In 105 BC 100,000 Roman legionaries were killed at Orange; then the most famous Roman General of the day, Gaius Marius, engaged the invaders at Aquae Sextiae (Aix-en-Provence). One hundred thousand Barbarians were slain and a similar number enslaved, a triumph still celebrated in the name of the mountain Mont Ste Victoire. The Roman arches at Orange and Carpentras are decorated with reliefs of prisoners in chains and piles of arms as trophies from these campaigns.

By now, the Romans had realised that the real danger to their cities and commerce lay in the semi-circle of easy passes at the head of the Rhône river system. These gave access to and from the Barbarian lands to the north in the Paris Basin and to the north-east across the Rhine. They lie between the upper Saône and

Hadrian's column (AD 113). Although illustrating his Dacian campaign in what is now Romania, it gives a vivid impression of Roman conquests in other parts of Europe.

Doubs rivers, and are known as the Burgundian Gate. When the Sequani, who held the area between the Saône and the Rhine, attacked and defeated the friendly Aedui (no doubt to get their hands on the tolls charged on the boat traffic), the Germanic tribes again began to stream south across this pass into Gaul.

This peril was perceived as an opportunity by an ambitious young Consul, Julius Caesar, to secure his own reputation through military conquest. First he secured the lesser passes, advancing up the Saône valley, where he headed off an invasion of Helvetii from the Alps, then up the Doubs where he seized the stronghold of the Sequani, Besontio, now called Besançon. He thus began his conquest of Gaul from a position where he controlled the whole of the Rhône corridor and its separate watersheds. In eight great annual campaigns from 58 BC he was to extend Roman rule across northern Europe.

Having come to the aid of the Aedui, Caesar overwintered at their bleak hilltop fortress of Bibracte (Mont Beuvray) behind a rampart, reinforced with timber beams, 5 kilometres long. It was here that Caesar began to write his account of his campaigns in order to maintain support in Rome. But as he pursued his conquest of Gaul which was to bring his armies even into Germany and across the channel to invade Britain with a fleet of 800 ships, the previously friendly Aedui turned against him. It was at Bibracte that Vercingetorix, the chief of the powerful Averni tribe, from the fertile volcanic heartland of the Auvergne, was elected commander of the united Gaulish forces.

His rule was short. Caesar returned and defeated him at the nearby battle of Alesia (Alise Ste Reine) in the summer of 52 BC, after a month-long siege. Within less than a decade Gaul to the west of the Rhine was under direct Roman control. Caesar proclaimed the Rhine as a frontier, and to this day it remains the limit for the German (Teutonic) language. The unfortunate Vercingetorix was to be held captive for six years before appearing in Caesar's triumphal procession in Rome, and later was strangled there in the Tullianum Prison.

The way was now open for Caesar to consolidate his power in Rome, and the Roman Empire was on the eve of its greatest expansion in Europe.

CHAPTER SEVEN

THE WEALTH FROM THE LIMESTONE SEAS

There is an astonishing contrast in northern Europe between the visible remains of imported Roman settlement – major engineering works, forts and those mosaics woken from centuries of sleep beneath green meadows and streets – and the stupendous grandeur of the medieval cathedrals, the distillation in stone of an era of faith and prosperity derived from northern Europe itself. This contrast reflects not just the passage of half a millennium, but a new influx of peoples and cultures, causing a great dislocation in the progress of European civilisation, a geographical shift away from the Mediterranean to north of the Alps. There, productive areas of fertile soil – the heritage of the age of the limestone seas – formed agricultural heartlands from which the most successful political units were to develop. But before that wealth was to flourish came a great crisis that was to plunge Europe into the Dark Ages.

Far away in central Asia a group of nomads, speaking languages from the Altai mountain region of north-east Asia, began to threaten their neighbours to the west. These mounted bands lived in tents, following the seasonal rainfall with their flocks. The children of the centre of an ancient continent, whose age was so great that few natural barriers like great mountains or rivers remained to bar their wanderings, their country was the back of a horse. Nomadic and owning nothing that could not be carried with them, they were as different from the classical civilisations as the hunters had been from the neolithic farmers. They rode to battle armed with short bows they shot from the saddle, and they were fearful warriors. By the fifth century AD, these Altaic tribes had combined with Mongolians and Iranian nomads to form huge populations of Black Huns, who swept westwards to cross the Volga, setting in motion an extraordinary series of long-distance migrations during the fifth and sixth centuries that were to sweep away the Roman world.

The collapse of the Roman Empire

For two and a half centuries Roman power, language and justice had imposed peace and prosperity across the multiplicity of lands and peoples of the European continent. But the power depended on a constant expansion of territory to supply new rewards of loot to the army, and the capture of new resources (especially slaves for manpower) to be transported back to the largely unproductive and parasitic centre of Rome. Once the expansion stopped the whole economy was unsustainable, not least because it was extremely costly to maintain a status quo. Three hundred thousand men were tied down guarding the 16,000-kilometre frontier, for the most part following natural geographical boundaries, that contained their civilised world.

It is symbolic of the change from offence to defence in the first century AD that the furthest flung legions built great walls to keep out the still unconquered barbarians. Hadrian's Wall was to stop the Picts invading England (AD 122), the fortification beyond the Rhine was built to hold back the Germanic tribes, and other walls were constructed along the Danube, in Syria and north Africa. But the extent of the empire was too great for a unified political structure at the centre to hold. The first consequence of this instability was its division, by the Emperor Diocletian in AD 285, into east and west. The Emperor Constantine turned his back on the west and deliberately set up his Christian capital at Constantinople (AD 330) in direct opposition to heathen Rome. It was at the edge of Europe, but on the axis of trade from the Black Sea to the Mediterranean where he could also control the increasingly valuable trade from the silk route. Built on the achievements of the Greeks, the eastern Roman Empire was richer, more urban and more densely populated than the west, and the great fortress city that ruled Byzantium was to withstand the onslaughts from Asia until 1453.

One very important factor that had helped the Roman expansion is less tangible than ruins and battles, and can be overlooked by historians. At the time that the Romans ruled northern Europe, building their luxurious villas even as far north as England, the climate was about 1 degree Celsius warmer than it is today. This does not sound much, but it is enough to allow vines to fruit some five degrees of latitude further north than nowadays – the equivalent of transposing Champagne to York. Besides bringing consolation to a Mediterranean people so far from home, it would have considerably improved the yields of the agriculture the Romans brought with them to the north. Although frost precluded the

The incursions of the Huns, Goths and Vandals which broke up the Roman Empire in the fifth century AD were guided by topography. The Alps proved an effective barrier.

growth of some crops like olives, Roman cultivation was transplanted, little changed from the methods they had practised in the Mediterranean, along with their astonishingly uniform architecture and society, across a huge proportion of the continent. But in the third century AD that advantage of one degree was lost as the climate grew colder again. This change may also have influenced the Germanic tribes to move south from Scandinavia in order to increase their harassment of the Roman frontier at the Rhine.

Certainly climatic variation was to have a major influence on the events of the

Hadrian's Wall, Northumberland, follows the crest of an escarpment formed by a volcanic sill. The parallel lines are the *vallum* a massive Roman defensive earthwork.

next thousand years. By the middle of the third century, Cyprian, the Bishop of Carthage, wrote of gloomy portents and economic woes:

> The world has grown old and lost its former vigour . . . Winter no longer gives rain enough to swell the seed, nor summer sun enough to ripen the harvest . . . the mountains are gutted and give less marble, the mines are exhausted and give less silver and gold . . . the fields lack farmers, the seas sailors, the encampments soldiers . . . there is no longer any justice in judgements, competence in trades, discipline in daily life . . .
>
> (Robert S. Lopez, *The Birth of Europe*, M. Evans and Co, – J.B. Lippincott Co, 1967)

It may even have been the same climatic deterioration that caused a drying of the steppes in central Asia which compelled the Altaic nomad horsemen to search for new pastures. A movement which set in motion a terrible wave of destruction as people after settled people were displaced from their homes. Almost all the progress of the last thousand years of civilisation was to be crushed beneath the thundering hooves of these migrant hordes. First the Visigoths (western Goths) were flushed out of their homelands in the Ukraine by the Black Huns and pushed across the Danube into the empire. The Emperor Valens was killed and the Roman army defeated by the horsemen. The Visigoths continued along the shores of the Mediterranean; pillaging through Macedonia, Greece and the shore of the Adriatic, before Alaric the Goth sacked Rome in AD 410. They continued their wandering depredations across the breadth of Gaul until founding a Gothic kingdom at Toulouse (AD 419). In the meantime the Vandals, a Germanic people, had been driven from the land between the Oder and Vistula rivers and crossed the barrier of the Rhine when it froze. Despite the aid of the Roman legions, which had been withdrawn from Britain in AD 410 to defend the empire, they ravaged Gaul for three years before establishing a Vandal rule in Spain. The Roman western emperors then sought to pitch barbarian against barbarian, and succeeded in having the Visigoths displace the Vandals to the North African coast. But they took Carthage, which became their base, and Rome lost one of its remaining sources of grain, while the Vandals gained a navy. In AD 455 they crossed the Mediterranean and again sacked Rome, to leave their name to stand down generations as the embodiment of mindless destruction.

It was now the turn of the Huns, led by Attila, who set off with a huge army on a path of destruction through the Ukraine and into central Europe and Gaul, where he was at last defeated near Troyes (to the north-east of Orleans) in AD 451, by a Visigoth army. The western empire of Rome had ceased to exist, and with it the whole pattern of the Mediterranean economy. The one which was to emerge from the ruins, only after an interval of 500 hundred years, was to have very different origins, with different peoples who had moved from the periphery to the centre of the European stage.

The agricultural heartland

The formation of the Alps, the Mediterranean and the Rhône valley by the collision of Africa and Europe in the Tertiary era had produced the landforms and resources on which the social development of Europe had so far been based. But now the focus of development had shifted away from the Mediterranean to be influenced by the events of another much earlier geological era, the Mesozoic – when continents were stretching apart and much of the world that we know was under the sea.

Two hundred and fifty million years ago all the continents on the globe had drifted together into one huge land-mass called Pangaea leaving a massive ocean occupying the other two-thirds of the globe. The north of Pangaea, called Eurasia, and Gondwana, to the south, were separated by the wedge of the smaller Tethys Ocean. The west of what is now Europe remained high land, with the remnants of ranges (the Hercynian mountains) forming large regions of Spain, France, the British Isles and Scandinavia, but most of the interior was a land-locked desert, intensely hot and arid, visited by rare violent storms.

Flash floods eroded away the highlands, carving wadi-like gullies in the desert choked with sand and rubble, and fierce winds blew the resulting sand into huge seas of mighty dunes. As millions of years passed and the mountains were laid low, large shallow salt lakes developed, where rivers evaporated in the scorched interior. They were too salty to support life, and there was little vegetation except conifers and scrub.

This strange congress of the continents began to break up 205 million years ago, in the Mesozoic era, in the region that was to become the Caribbean. North America began to tear away from South America and Eurasia, and gradually this Atlantic opening spread northwards, accompanied by volcanoes like those of Iceland today. Another branch rift opened between Brittany and what was to be north Spain, so that the Iberian peninsula rotated anti-clockwise towards the south. At the same time the sea level rose until it flooded across the level land of the eroded continents. This may have been because the sea floor of the oceans was raised, displacing the water, because there was so much mountain-building activity going on at the new spreading-centres in the sea-floor plates. The old Hercynian uplands were left as islands rising out of the shallow tropical seas.

The Mesozoic began after some cataclysmic event (such as the impact of a comet or meteorite) had extinguished most of the life that had evolved on earth up to that time. Never before nor since has the land been so low or the continental shelf so broad and shallow. In those vast warm seas a new complexity of life began to evolve as a microscopic flora of algal plants bloomed as plankton. Many of these tiny organisms drew calcium and magnesium salts from the sea water, and on tropical shoals the water became super-saturated in calcium carbonate from their debris. As the sea bed was stirred by wave and tidal action, spherical grains slowly built up, formed of concentric plates around a sand grain or calcium carbonate particle. As these were buried by successive layers they became lime mud and then limestone. The same process is occurring today in the Bahamas where there is a shallow bank, 2000 square kilometres in area, near the Schonner Keys to the south of Eleuthera Island.

Eighty million years ago, late in the Mesozoic era, the Atlantic had opened from Biscay to Labrador, and much of the continental land was submerged. As the oceans deepened the minute limy platelets or shells of plankton, called coccoliths, sank to the bottom to form layers which eventually became chalk. The slow rise in sea level over millions of years allowed this chalk to accumulate in layers as much as a kilometre thick, which now stretch from England to Israel, visible as the magnificent white cliffs of Dover, Beachy Head and Cap Gris Nez.

Then Europe at last began to rise from the waves as Africa began to approach, squeezing out the Tethys Ocean and compressing the continent into folds that lifted above the sea and became the Alps. As the sea advanced and retreated, layers of muds and sandstones were left in the deltas of rivers. The land was covered in steamy swamps and forests, inhabited by reptiles and the dinosaurs and birds which had developed from them, while in the seas it was the age of the spiral-shelled creatures whose fossils we know as ammonites.

Most of the crumpling and lifting of the Earth's crust as the continents collided occurred in the Alps but, like waves spreading across a lake, the crust of Europe was deformed, until the last ripples of the Alpine storm raised ranges of hills like the North and South Downs; from Champagne as far north as the Bristol Channel. Erosion could then fill the valley bottoms and limestone basins, like the valleys of the Seine and Thames, with silts full of nutrients, and the ice age winds could sift them with a layer of glacial rock-dust to form fertile loess soil.

One further factor was to make these basins the agricultural heartlands of northern Europe. The amount of moisture in the soil has a major influence on the size of a cereal harvest, and northern Europe has such a fragmented shoreline, with little high land to the west, that the depressions which build up over the Atlantic can sweep far inland, bringing with them rainfall that is distributed throughout the year.

It is hardly surprising that the limestone and chalk wealds of Britain have been scattered with monuments symbolic of the productivity of the fertile and well-watered land since the earliest days of agriculture: from the vast megalithic constructions of the Bronze Age, like Stonehenge, to the chalk-cut figures of white horses, and the Cerne Abbas giant – complete with massive phallus as an indication of fertility. These are still rich areas for growing cereals, as the towering grain-silos show. The same is true of the Paris basin; France grows more wheat than Canada.

On the soils of this Mesozoic basin settled the warriors who were to have the

Migration and invasion in the ninth and tenth centuries.

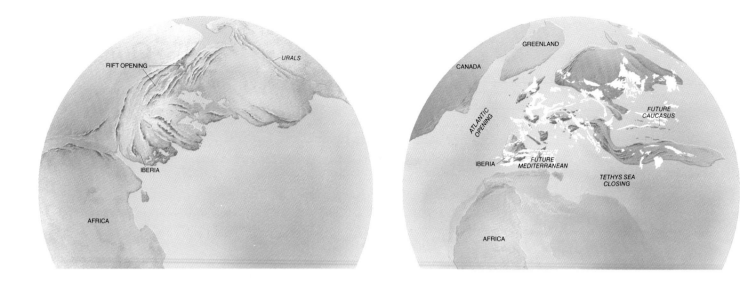

RIFT OPENING

URALS

IBERIA

AFRICA

GREENLAND

CANADA

ATLANTIC OPENING

FUTURE CAUCASUS

IBERIA

FUTURE MEDITERRANEAN

TETHYS SEA CLOSING

AFRICA

Eighty million years ago, Europe looked like the shallow subtropical seas of the Bahamas.

As the Atlantic ocean began to open, shallow seas flooded much of the level land of the continents to form widespread limestone and chalk deposits (shown in white). These would be the foundation of Europe's most fertile agricultural areas, and the reservoir for most of the world's oil supplies.

greatest impact on the future of Europe. They were Germanic tribes called the Franks, and they were more eager than other Barbarians both to farm and to take up the remaining fragments of Roman society. First established at Tournai, a great ruler, Clovis, was to assemble into a kingdom the territories which were one day to be called France. It was perhaps no accident that he moved its capital to Paris at the end of the fifth century – to the heart of the richest agricultural land. Frankish rulers managed to consolidate a Christian kingdom, later centred on Aachen (in the traditional Frankish lands), which dominated western Europe for three centuries, and reached its greatest unity under Charlemagne, who was crowned in Rome on Christmas Day 800 as the new head of the western Roman Empire. But despite his genius and success, his heirs were too weak to prevent the fragmentation of their inheritance under the repeated onslaughts of three very different kinds of peoples in the ninth and tenth centuries – the Muslims, the Magyars and the Vikings.

In 570, the birth of Mohammed provided the unifying religious inspiration which, after his death, was to ignite a powerful mixture of creed and greed that propelled the Muslim conquests of the infidel. Within a century the empire of Islam stretched from India across North Africa to Spain. This religious division between the northern and southern shores of the Mediterranean, and the Muslim indifference to trade, did much to deny the resurgence of another great empire based on its shores. The Muslim expansion was continued by the Saracens from North Africa, who, having taken Sicily and southern Italy (890), occupied Provence and the Rhône corridor, enabling them to strike deep into central Europe. Since the Saracens' main interest was in plunder, major ports such as Marseilles and Genoa, and even towns as far north as Aix-en-Provence, were pillaged and destroyed.

Then another wave of horsemen displaced from beyond the Carthapian basin, the Magyars, swept westwards into Italy, up the Danube to the Rhine and round the Alps as far as Nîmes and the Loire. The relative security of the Frankish reign had left markets and abbeys unprepared, and the Roman defences had long fallen into disrepair, leaving them highly vulnerable to the Magyars' unexpected and lightning raids.

The role of the Vikings

The third assault on the remains of Roman civilisation came from a new direction – from the northern seas. In Norway, the Caledonian Mountains had been heavily glaciated during the ice ages, and the subsequent rise in sea level had drowned the valleys to form steep-sided, bleak but sheltered fjords, leaving little cultivable land. Not surprisingly the inhabitants took to the sea. Once this Viking population had begun to expand they had little alternative but to follow the example of the Greeks before them and seek a living beyond their land of harsh winters and long nights. The chiefs' custom of polygamy, and inheritance by primogeniture, ensured a large number of younger sons eager to better themselves by the only alternative method – as warriors.

A Viking stone-carving from the eighth century.

It may have been a climatic factor that led to the surplus population and the search for new lands – the climate had started to improve again, and more children may have survived. The Vikings' first colonies were on Orkney and Shetland, environments very similar to those they had left behind, but they soon realised it was possible to get rich quicker by plundering monasteries and towns further south in the British Isles, which they began to raid in 789.

Glorying in their magnificent longships and their reckless mastery of the open sea, in an age when most craft hugged the coast, they attacked with a ruthless ferocity that terrorised countryside and town. With no interest in acquiring land, the raiders made straight for the churches and monasteries to seize their treasures, sacking towns and slaughtering men, women and infants alike. The Celts in Ireland were particularly hard hit, especially when the raids increased in scale to the point where the Vikings overwintered there. Possibly the improving climate encouraged them to stay on. They founded Dublin, Waterford and Limerick, and made settlements either side of the Irish Sea. By the end of the ninth century they too had reached the Mediterranean and their raids brought renewed terror to the coast of Provence.

The Danish Vikings in turn began to attack the English and German coastlines in 834, attacking the same towns again and again, year after year. The raids of these professional pirates spread to France and their fleets expanded until a dozen ships with 600 men would surprise the coastal settlements. Port after port was destroyed, and they moved further inland in search of richer booty. Cologne, Aachen, Rheims and Rouen were sacked, hastening the break-up of Frankish rule. They even sacked Pisa in Italy. But as the rising tide of violence spread further and further up the rivers, until a fleet of 700 ships attacked Paris in 886, these brutal barbarians underwent an important evolution from raiders and invaders to settlers. When local lords found they could buy off attacks with bribes, the Vikings soon demanded blackmail and then enormous annual taxes. By 878 they had conquered and held much of eastern and central England. In France they held the region at the mouth of the Loire and Normandy ('Norman' is a corruption of 'Northmen').

The Swedish Vikings, for their part, had pioneered river-borne trade-routes to link up with the Dnieper and Volga rivers which led to the Black Sea and the Caspian. They founded Novgorod and Kiev to trade furs, amber and the ivory of walrus tusks as far as Baghdad on the Tigris. In time becoming the rulers of their Slavic customers, they gave their own name of *Rus* to the first Russian state.

By the last decade of the ninth century much of northern Europe had been destroyed and depopulated. But for all their fearful depredations, as the Vikings became integrated with their conquered land they were to bring three great new gifts to northern Europe: their love of adventure and enterprise, their superb seamanship and their magnificent ships. With no fear of the open sea they would revitalise trade the length of Europe from the Atlantic Ocean to the Baltic Sea.

The feudal order

By the start of the tenth century, law and order, the two great monuments to Rome, were in ruins. Coinage had largely disappeared, and such trade as occurred was mostly local and by barter. Famine was endemic. Much of the countryside had become a wilderness, the Roman roads had fallen into disuse and decay, cities had shrunk to villages, and for defence against the Northmen the villagers relied on protection from their local lords. The landscape too had begun to change, taking on the medieval characteristics of mighty castle keeps and heavily fortified towns.

It was a leader of the Franks, Charles Martel, who originally learned the importance of the speed and mobility of the mounted Muslim invaders when his footsoldiers finally defeated them after a seven-day battle at Poitiers in 732. The invaders were using a strange new invention – the stirrup – which enabled them to fight on horseback. He decreed that his men must equip themselves with horse, armour and supplies, and to fight in their liege's service in return for his protection. It was indeed the spur to the development of the mounted knight, and given the constant threat from raiders, private armies were a logical outcome. Once they had recognised the need for cavalry, the Frankish kings traded offices or land for a solemn oath of loyalty for service. This became the foundation of the feudal system, which was to maintain peace and thus at last to permit the prosperity of medieval Europe to grow on the great agricultural wealds.

These royal vassals (from the Celtic word for servant), counts and lords, received a land grant or fief in return for castle-guard and battle service as armed and mounted knights. Each was in turn supported by a number of his own vassals, whom he also equipped, according to the resources of his fief. But arms and horses were very expensive, and it was more advantageous for the lords to offer fiefs in exchange for service from lesser vassals.

The manorial feudal system was a feature of these open grain-farming regions, where towns and stored harvests needed protection, and a surplus of labour could provide it. The system never spread to Scandinavia, nor to all the highlands of Britain. The majority of villeins or serfs were given a grant of land of up to fifteen hectares and the right to draw water and cut wood in exchange for a prescribed number of days of field work and labouring 'handiwork' on the lord's manor. In addition they had to pay a variety of taxes in kind. In an oath of fealty the villein surrendered his own freedom, and while the bond of the king's vassals only lasted for life, the peasant bound both himself and his family and descendants to his lord, tying them for ever to the land. It was a heavy burden, but with a secure defence, stability returned to the beleaguered villages, and the fertility of the northern lands could at last be exploited. Slowly, with the return of an agricultural surplus, a relative prosperity followed and the population started to grow.

Medieval agriculture

The preservation of hillforts and evidence of prehistoric farming such as Celtic fields and medieval strip-lynchets on the chalk uplands can make it appear that

Harrowing. From the Luttrell Psalter.

these were the centres of agriculture, but chalk itself is permeable and does not retain enough moisture to grow a good crop. It also erodes very rapidly, even dissolving in the rain which is naturally weakly acidic, so that it does not build up a depth of fertile humus. It was the limestones, silts and loess soils of the valleys that were the most fertile, while the chalk uplands, which were excellent for sheep, became the heart of the wool trade.

The medieval villages in the chalk downlands grew along the foot of the scarps, where water was available. Each had to be largely self-sufficient, and needed access to a wide range of natural environments: the ploughlands of alluvial fans and river terraces below the scarp, the wetter hay meadows of the clay vales, and the sheep pasture of the uplands, so that the parishes tended to develop in strips from the river to the crown of the scarp.

Crucial to the success of the development of these lands in early medieval times were several important inventions that increased agricultural yields. Agriculture had begun with digging sticks or primitive ard ploughs which do not turn over the soil but simply make a groove for the seed. Only light soils could thus be cultivated, and early agriculture may at first have followed the chalk uplands, using the thin soils left behind when the forests were cleared. But with the invention of the heavy iron-shod plough, with a coulter to cut the earth, a ploughshare cutting the grass at its roots, a mould-board to turn over the furrow slice, and wheels to regulate the depth, a powerful new tool was in the hands of the farmer. Drawn by teams of two to eight oxen, the heavy valley soils could now be turned. Not only was the yield better but the soils, being deeper with more nutrients, were much more resistant to heavy cropping and less prone to erosion. The uplands were only tilled as a last resort, and were usually grazed.

Another important advance was the discovery that the classical way of harnessing horses with a loop round their necks caused them to throw their heads high to avoid strangulation. Like this they could only pull a half-ton load on wheels. When a solid padded collar (originally developed for camels) rested on their shoulder blades, horses could pull far greater loads, equal to that of an ox, but half as fast again; so that a day's ploughing by a man and a team was 50 per cent more productive. When the horse-collar was introduced to Europe during

Reaping wheat and shearing sheep in July at the Château du Clain in Poitiers. Painted for the Duc de Berry by the Limbourg brothers in about 1413.

the ninth century, horses were soon bred with the strength to pull a three-ton load. A third important medieval invention was the nailed horseshoe which prevented wear on the horses' hooves.

Farming in medieval times was also improved by changing from the Roman method of cultivation in alternate years to a three-year rotation on open fields. The arable land around a manor, which might be some 350 to 1200 hectares, would be farmed by twenty to thirty families of serfs, and was divided into three great fields. Wheat or rye was grown in one; barley, oats, peas or beans in the second, and the third was allowed to lie fallow. The peas and beans fixed nitrogen from the atmosphere, helping to fertilise the land. Each field was divided into a large number of strips allocated to individual serfs, while uplands or less fertile grasslands were used for grazing. The only way that either peasant or lord of such a manor could accumulate capital was by breeding cattle, but there was a chronic shortage of winter feed for cattle and the vital power-providing oxen and horses. So many beasts were slaughtered at the end of the grass-growing season in September or October.

Oddly enough, it was the invention of hay which was to transform the productivity of the land most of all and make agriculture north of the Alps a success. The Romans did not cut grass to store for winter feed, and haymaking may even have arrived with the Norsemen. Certainly it would have been hard to keep cattle alive in the long winters of Scandinavia without it.

Other fundamental social changes were set in motion by harnessing water power to turn corn mills. It does not sound very important, but the water-mills released human energy to be used more productively elsewhere. Just as the ox and then the horse had brought more power to the ploughman's hands, so this new source of power, later to be followed by windmills, increased the productivity of the land and the village. In 1086 the Domesday survey recorded 5624 water-mills in England in 3000 communities.

By the time the Vikings became settled in northern Europe, in the tenth century, some four-fifths of the land was still covered with forest – a great hindrance to communication and trade. So returning prosperity caused a new kind of battle, this time against the woods, and the second great deforestation of Europe began. Existing agricultural areas were expanded, land-hungry settlers colonised the uninhabited higher lands, and new towns were founded by monasteries and wealthy lords: Villeneuve, Bourgneuf, Neuville, Neustadt, Newhaven and so on reflect the energy of the times.

The Norman expansion

Warfare and raiding were still commonplace between the various landowners, and this had another effect. A knight or lord could not easily divide his inheritance of a castle or land between his sons if it was to remain defensible. So the whole estate was left to the eldest, and there were large numbers of second and subsequent sons, trained soldiers with no land, who tried to gain favour from other landowners by fighting on their behalf. By 1030 the state of warfare between the landowners of Normandy had become so bad that the Bishops declared a Truce of God to which all citizens were bound. It decreed that no man might attack his neighbour between the ninth hour on Saturday and the first hour on Monday so that all men could do their duty to God on the Sabbath. Other sanctions forbade plundering a church or striking an unarmed member of the clergy or robbing a peasant, thus reducing some of the worst excesses of the bullying knights.

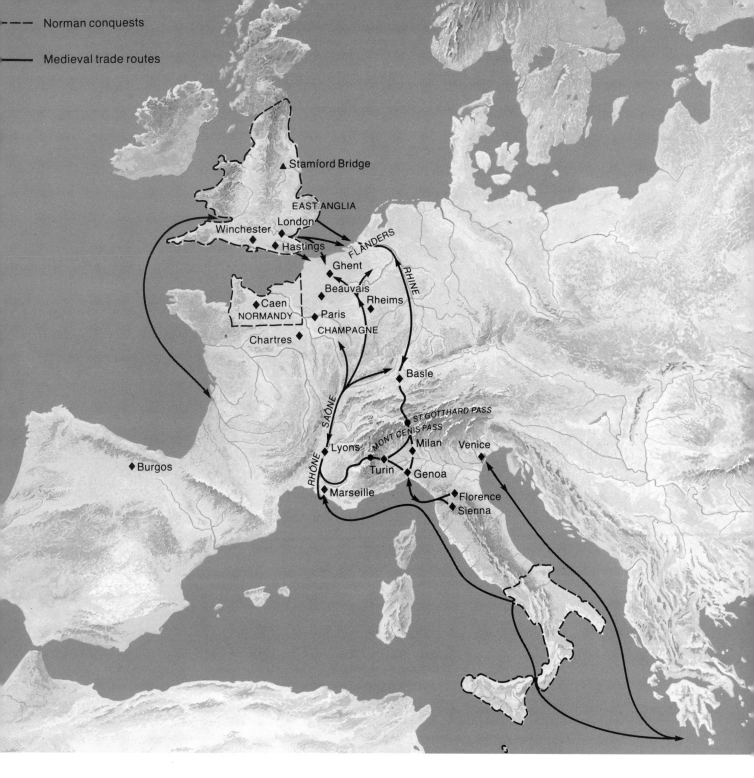

Norman conquests and medieval trade routes.

The Frankish Carolingian kings had given away so much of their land as fiefs in an attempt to buy security, that by 911 Charles the Simple ruled little beyond the lands he could personally control. This *domaine royale* was the core from which France as a kingdom was to expand once more, again founded on the wealth of the fertile soils of the Paris Basin. In an attempt to restore stability, Charles gave a huge fief of land (which was largely depopulated as a result of the Viking raids) to a Viking chieftain, Rollo the Ganger. Rollo settled in Rouen, married the king's daughter, and with his son expanded his land at the mouth of the Seine – soon to be known as Normandy. His descendants, the Normans, adopted Christianity and the French language. Normandy is another area of Mesozoic fertility famous

THE WEALTH FROM THE LIMESTONE SEAS · 149

for a particularly rich soil called marl, a limy mixture of calcium and clay, and that fertility became the power base for the Norman dukes, who soon began to expand their territories.

The fifth generation of Norman dukes saw the birth of a bastard son, William, to a tanner's daughter at Rouen, and he was only seven or eight years old when he succeeded to the Duchy in 1035. He moved to Caen, surrounded by broad grain-producing lands near the coast, but when he married his neighbouring Count's daughter, Matilda, there was some unrecorded ecclesiastical objection to the union. This the couple expiated by building two Romanesque abbeys at Caen, the Abbaye-aux-Hommes (St Etienne) and the Abbaye-aux-Dames (Ste Trinité). They were built of the local stone, a particularly fine limestone that is also a product of the great Mesozoic seas.

Aside from warfare, the only alternative employment for the nobly born was to enter the Church. Monks had to be literate in Latin, when very few nobles or knights could read or write, and the daily toil of running the monastic estates was carried out by lay brothers. The unification of the land under Christianity extended the hierarchical feudal chain even beyond the king to a perfect god-head. An ideal which was to inspire not only the chivalrous conduct of the courtly knight, but also the great upsurge of religious expression in music, painting, stained glass and architecture which followed the great spread of monasteries in the twelfth century.

Duke William's cousin was Edward the Confessor, who had promised him the throne of England, and Matilda was a direct descendant of Alfred the Great. Harold, the Earl of Wessex, had also sworn to uphold William's claim to the crown, so when he had himself made king, William was furious. It was long before the days of national identities, and England was no more than another territory inconveniently cut off by sea. The invasion that followed was only unusual for a Norman, used to a society riven by armed conflict, in that it involved a sea crossing, and to descendants of Vikings that too may have seemed commonplace. The Norman army, being mounted, defeated the English footsoldiers, although only after a long battle, and Harold (who had just successfully repelled the last invasion by the Vikings at Stamford Bridge) was killed.

William the Conqueror succeeded to the ancient kingdom of Wessex, whose material base was the fertile Mesozoic basin of the Thames Valley. He quickly established his own feudal system, giving his Norman followers lands but retaining the ultimate lordship over them. The great earls and barons and the lesser knights imposed their rule over the English landscape from the massive Norman castle baileys that began at Pevensey and still dominate strategic sites like Corfe in a gap in the Purbeck Hills. A few years later William had an enormous and minutely detailed survey made of his new lands. One of the most remarkable undertakings of the Middle Ages, not an ox, cow or pig escaped the Domesday Book (and the consequent ease of taxation). It showed that the densest population lay on the glacially modified soils of East Anglia. William must have been gratified that he had conquered a region of fertile land, relatively dense population and intensive agriculture.

Protected from attack by water, except from the north, England enjoyed an unusual stability for the times. Freedom from raiders and slowly improving agriculture meant more cattle and pigs could be raised, and thus an increase in capital. The population increased, and more than 100 new towns were founded in England and Wales between 1066 and 1190. If growing numbers threatened to overcrowd a manor there was plenty of new land to be cleared and cultivated under the protection of a new lord. Woodland covered a third of England at the end of the sixth century, but had been reduced to 15 per cent by 1086. This means that the Anglo-Saxons had cleared woodland at the rate of some 32 acres a day for 500 years, a rate unsurpassed until the twentieth century.

Across the Channel, as the areas protected by lords and their vassals increased, there was less space for the brigands who were such a threat to travel and trade. Very gradually, chaos was succeeded by order. As Norman wealth and power grew again there was a surplus of sons. So they also began to expand overseas, following their Viking forebears to Spain and then the Mediterranean. Sailing as far as the Holy Land they founded a State of Antioch in 1099, making their mark in Jerusalem. They also conquered southern Italy and, taking Palermo from the Muslims after a five-month siege, they were able to set up a Norman kingdom of Southern Italy and Sicily by 1130, helping the slow replacement of Muslim control and Saracen raids which had depopulated southern Europe.

The medieval years of plenty

The climate continued to improve, until at its optimum in the twelfth century it was some two degrees warmer than during the early part of this century. Of

Thirteenth century Cistercian tithe barn, Great Coxwell, Oxfordshire. The wealth of the Church was built on agricultural surplus.

course, as the weather improved agricultural production increased, until English vineyards were so successful that the French actually tried to have them abolished by treaty. William had established the Norman Church throughout his domains, and by bestowing huge estates, made it enormously wealthy. An annual 'Tithe', a tenth of all agricultural produce, had to be paid to the Church, and the tithes became very large. Huge tithe barns like those of Cressing Temple (Essex), Great Coxwell (Oxfordshire), Bradford-on-Avon (Wiltshire) and Vaulerent (Ile de France) demonstrate the sheer quantity of this agricultural wealth, but even more splendid are the great Romanesque and Gothic cathedrals that it built.

Having survived the popular expectation that the world would end at the millennium (AD 1000), and fired by a new sense of faith, a *morbus aedificandi*, a 'disease' of building churches, swept the land. In the preceding centuries of the Dark Ages almost the only stone constructions had been castles and walls for defence. But during the eleventh century over 1500 churches were built in France. Stone from Caen was also used in many of the massive Romanesque cathedrals built by the Normans in England, which dwarfed their Saxon antecedents, from Christchurch Priory in Hampshire to Canterbury and as far north as Durham, 900 kilometres from the quarry. This was not just because the stone was known to the Norman masons. The even grain of limestone 'freestones', such as those of Caen (which could be carved equally well in any direction), permitted fine traceries and decoration to be carved such as the remarkable rose windows, and allowed masons to conjure in stone a feeling of lightness and grace that was soon to reach its triumphant perfection in the Gothic cathedrals. A beauty born from the same Mesozoic seas that had made the region rich.

Flying buttresses, Chartres cathedral.

Where the Normans went, so did Caen stone, building monuments to the origins of their power. At the same time the adoption of the Gothic style from Burgos in Spain to Salisbury demonstrated the remarkable unity and power of the Church. Funded by their tithes and the sale of indulgences for sins (such as eating butter during Lent), the Bishops began to compete for prestige through the splendour and size of their constructions. The cathedral of Notre Dame was begun in Paris in 1163, and the vault reached 36 metres high. Chartres topped it at 39 metres (1260), Rheims reached half a metre higher, and Amiens 44 metres. Beauvais aimed for 50 metres, but they overreached themselves and the vault collapsed twice. Their funds ran out and the cathedral was never completed.

This astonishing competitive expenditure to the glory of God, so reminiscent of the grandiose temples built by the rival Greek cities, could not have taken place without the good harvests brought home by improvements in agriculture, and helped by other inventions such as the water-mill and windmill. By the time Chartres cathedral was consecrated, crafts and trade were flourishing. The towns and cities had grown on the capital built up in agriculture, and the shift away from self-sufficiency, as more goods were obtained from the towns, had begun to undermine the dependence on local production and labour which lay at the heart of the old feudal manorial system.

Many landed aristocrats endowed monasteries, some to promote a civilising influence, others for charity, or for the more worldly and understandable motives of increasing their status or expiating their sins. Their numbers expanded rapidly: for example the Cistercians built some 300 monasteries all over Europe between 1130 and 1155. Frequently these were deliberately set in remote areas or on poor land, but the skill and application of the educated monks often brought a transformation of their fortunes, making good use of what had been an under-used land resource. Oxford and Cambridge were originally monastic foundations built in malarial swamps that nobody wanted. In time many monasteries changed from the original ideal of self-sufficient isolation into being major landowners. They became an important force both in the development of agriculture and as commercial traders in wine, foodstuffs and even iron and beer. Other monastic lands were in the uplands, and the monasteries again became an important influence in the development of sheep farming and the wool trade, which allowed a valuable industry to develop from some of the poorest land. The monks defended this embrace of the world of Mammon by claiming that more land and income were needed to feed the poor and to pay for their charitable works.

Agricultural and farm products still accounted for the great majority of trade in northern Europe, and of them the wool-cloth trade was the most valuable, with the major supply of raw wool coming from England, and its manufacture into high-quality cloths like velvets centred in Flanders. The neighbouring towns of Bruges, Ypres, Ghent and Douai became great cloth centres which exported their goods to the Italian merchants, who traded their luxuries and dyestuffs from the east at the fairs of Champagne. Much of this commerce passed by river along the easy Rhône-Saône corridor. But, in addition to this, caravans of mules took the Mont Cenis pass from Turin, and the bridging of the Schöllenen gorge had opened the St Gotthard pass from Milan to the Rhine at Basle – assuring future prosperity for the Swiss.

The rapidly expanding cities of northern Italy – Venice, Genoa, Milan, Sienna and Florence – were linked by the silk and spice trade to the East. This traffic along the ancient silk route had been made possible, after a break of a thousand years, because Genghis Khan and his nomadic Mongol followers had unified Asia from the northern shores of the Black Sea to the Pacific coast in the first decades of the thirteenth century, in the greatest extent of conquests the world has ever seen.

However, in northern Europe, the fundamental relationship between the area of land available to grow food and the number of mouths to feed was becoming strained. By the thirteenth century all the best land was already being cultivated. However, with a rapidly expanding population, people were being forced to farm marginal lands, or to work existing lands more intensively. Goods became more expensive. The standard of living of the ordinary peasants began to fall, and with an abundant labour force, the lords were able to impose such low wages as to cause great hardship.

Woodland was becoming scarce as a resource for building and firewood. The Weald of north Sussex and Kent lost some 450,000 acres of forest (which had been managed successfully for the Roman iron industry) in the 260 years after the Norman Conquest. Wood was so valuable when the lands of Hatfield House were marked out that individual trees were recorded. With firewood in short supply, straw was burnt for fuel. Since it was not ploughed back into the land, the organic content and thus the water retention and the fertility of the soil was significantly reduced. Farming on steep slopes led to soil erosion, and both of the factors combined to reduce yields of corn. The result was that the peasant farmer, dividing the same land between more and more members of his family, got less and less bread for his toil.

Rising prices meant that other methods of increasing food production, which had previously been thought unviable, became economic. The slopes of the chalk downs in Dorset were terraced to provide more level land. The Fens of England

and the lowlands of Holland were drained with the aid of windmills, providing highly fertile and thus valuable new lands. Another possibility was emigration: in the thirteenth century recruiting agents travelled throughout Europe to encourage the mass migration of landless peasants to the east, to develop grain production on the younger limestones of Poland.

The medieval ecological crisis

Across northern Europe, as population growth continued to outstrip production, the agricultural wealth that had built the towns was disappearing. The same sad process that is visible in the highlands of Ethiopia today was occurring. A shortage of firewood meant that peasant farmers burnt the straw and dung that should have been ploughed back in to the soil to retain moisture and restore fertility, and ground was being cultivated year after year rather than being left fallow, allowing it to recover its nutrients. The attempt to feed too great a population led to the destruction of the fertility of the land itself. Marginal lands on uplands and sandy soils were the first to become unproductive as they were least able to sustain this destructive mining of their reserves. As the crisis grew worse, dung was dried on the walls of Peterborough for fuel and firewood was in such short supply that even the town gates were burnt. Farmers, faced with the choice of starving today or surviving at the expense of destroying their prospects of growing food tomorrow, opted for the latter course, even to the extent of eating the seed corn. Villages on uplands with thin and acidic soil began to be abandoned, and hungry peasants fled in desperation to the towns. By 1270 King Henry III wrote an order to the city coroner of London demanding that the streets of the city should be cleared more quickly of the corpses of those who had dropped dead from starvation. Human society was paying the price of being out of balance with the natural productivity of the land. Then, as we also witnessed so tragically in Ethiopia, the weather forced a catastrophe.

The climate of the Middle Ages experienced great variation in temperature – both the warmest and the coldest periods since the last ice age occurred then. Now it began once more to change, cooling during the two decades after 1310. The shift from the warmth of the high Middle Ages to a climate only a degree or two colder than before had sudden and catastrophic consequences, because it changed the frequency of depressions and the consequent rainstorms crossing northern Europe. With devastating suddenness, a decade of appallingly wet years occurred.

It is rainfall that can have the most severe climatic effect on wheat harvests in northern Europe. Excessive rainfall can drown the seeds, wash away the natural nitrates, allow weeds to flourish, can flatten the stalks allowing the ears to touch the ground and 'lodge' or sprout, and (before it was possible to dry grain artificially) cause the sheaves of cut corn to blacken and rot.

The summer of 1314 was extremely wet, ruining the harvests and causing corn prices to rise sharply. In mid-April 1315 the rain began again in France, followed a month later in England. It poured in torrents throughout the summer and autumn, and flooding continued right through to the summer of 1316, when an already desperate food shortage became critical. At Winchester yields were a third down in 1315 and nearly halved in 1316. In a normal year a farmer could only expect to harvest 3.83 bushels for every bushel he sowed – fewer than four grains for each one sown. So when the yield dropped to 2.11 it meant that after seed had been set aside for the following year, the grain available for food was less than half (falling from 2.83 bushels to 1.11). At Bolton priory the yields were only one-fifth the normal amount – that meant they did not even have enough for seed-corn.

In about 1320 an anonymous poet caught the wretched feeling of the times:

Wynter wakeneth al my care;
Now thise leves waxen bare.
Ofte I sike and murne sare*
   Whan it cometh in my thogt
   Of this worldes joye, how it goth all to nought.

Al that greyn me graveth grene,*
Now it faleweth al bidene.*
Jhesu, help that it be sene,
   And shilde us from helle;
   For I not* whider I shall, ne how longe heer dwelle.

* *Sare* = sore
* *greyn me graveth grene* = the grain planted green (unripe)
* *faleweth al bidene* = withers quickly
* *not* = know not

(*One Hundred Middle English Lyrics*, R.D. Stevick, Bobbs Merrill Co, 1964)

The crisis hit pastoral farming, too, with widespread 'murrains' or epidemics among sheep, killing up to half of some flocks. In 1319 rinderpest struck the cattle, halving the number of plough-oxen in the Winchester herds – the essential energy-source for the fields. Adding to the difficulties, there was not enough sun to evaporate water to make the salt essential to preserve meat through the winter. As the famine lay right across Europe, no supplies could be bought from elsewhere. In France, Flanders, Germany and England, food ran out and prices soared. The price of grain rose tenfold, and eggs cost a penny each. Millions of peasants and poor died from starvation. Even gruesome cases of cannibalism were recorded in France.

> Parents killed their children and children killed their parents, and the bodies of executed criminals were eagerly snatched from the gallows.

(Fourteenth-century chronicle)

The weather then became very unstable; 1333 and 1336 had exceptionally hot summers, while 1335 was probably the coldest winter of the millennium. Thousands of the poor, weakened by famine, died of pneumonia, bronchitis and influenza. Some of the most appalling epidemics were caused by the ergot blight which grows on damp rye, and is the source of the hallucinogen LSD. Whole communities would suffer hallucinations, convulsions, and then gangrene, which rotted the extremities of the limbs, before death followed.

But worse was to come, to wreak a horrifying slaughter on the half-starved and weakened population of Europe. Along the trade route that had brought the riches of the East now came death in the form of the plague bacillus. The black rat had been introduced to Europe in the returning ships of the Crusaders in 1095, 1147 and 1191, and plague was carried by the rat flea. If that simple fact had been known, the history of Europe might have been different, but the insect vector of the disease was only discovered in 1903. (Pneumonic plague is also spread by sneezing, and the human flea which is a less efficient vector.) Yet the pandemic which followed was only the final act in what was really an ecological disaster, caused by the over-population and over-exploitation of the land – just as had occurred before in the Bronze Age.

The Black Death

The Black Death took its name from the dark spots on the skin caused by haemorrhages. The outbreak had begun in China, where it was endemic in gerbils, and was brought to Europe by the survivors of a settlement of Italian merchants besieged by Tartars at Caffa on the Crimean Straits in 1346. Plague had broken out among the besiegers and, turning this to their advantage, they catapulted the corpses of their dead over the walls into the fortified town. But the siege was relieved, and a shipful of Italians escaped to return to Genoa. Within days of their arrival the Black Death began, and by 1348 it had reached France, Germany, Spain and England.

> Death came driving after, and all to dust dashed Kings and Knights, Kaisers and Popes, learned and lewd, he let no man stand even, that ever stirred after. Many a lovely lady, and lemans of Knights, swooned and swelted for sorrow of Death's dints.
>
> (Fourteenth-century chronicle)

It is possible that between a third and a half of the entire population of western Europe died (some 40 million people). The numbers in England fell from about 3.7 million in 1350 to 2 million in 1377. At the height of the plague, in Paris 800 people died every day, in London, where the Black Death was again carried by trade, 50,000 died in 1349. In Provence and Languedoc at least half of the population died, while laden merchant ships swung to their anchors deserted in Marseilles harbour. Florence lost half its population, Sienna two-thirds, Venice a third, Montpellier and Zurich two-thirds.

The plague broke out as often as every ten years for four centuries. Then the black rat was largely displaced by the brown rat, which crossed the Volga into Europe in 1727, and which prefers the countryside to houses. (Because the brown rat is more dispersed, it may be a less efficient host for the disease.) The countryside was so hard hit that whole villages were deserted, such as Tusmore in Oxfordshire, where its lord was allowed to turn all the fields into parks because every villein was dead. In the Röhn Mountains of Germany, 70 per cent of the dwellings were abandoned. In Sardinia and Sicily 50 per cent of the villages disappeared. Plague was succeeded by conflict. By 1450 Normandy had lost three-quarters of its inhabitants and Paris two-thirds to famine, pestilence and war.

The depopulation of the countryside was so extensive that it set in motion huge social changes that were to reverberate around Europe for the next two centuries. The areas of marginal land that had been colonised in late medieval times were the first to be deserted, as the population decline led to falling prices for crops in the towns and an agricultural crisis. Initially farm labour was so short (in some villages only women and children were left) that the lords were unable to hold their labourers to past agreements, and had to make major concessions in wages, conditions and lengthened leases. The peasant began to acquire exclusive rights to his land and was a little better off. The surviving members of many families deserted the country for the towns where they would be better defended and have both a higher standard of living and more equitable social and legal conditions. Despite a real rise in wages, with a shrunken population, trade faltered, and with the feudal ties weakened, the poor and the landless began to foment another period of lawlessness and civil insurrection.

The end of the Age of Chivalry

The impregnability of the armoured and mounted knight had lain at the heart of the feudal system which had protected the open agricultural land of northern

A plague victim with rats and lice or fleas, Jan Snellinck 1627.

Castles could not withstand the impact of cannon fired at point-blank range.

Europe, but it had already been challenged by the development of new technology. The cross-bow could pierce chain mail at 200 metres, and halberds had been developed to attack horses. The first response was to form armour from sheet steel for both rider and mount, but in one of the first of many social conflicts that were to challenge the feudal order, at Courtrai in Flanders in 1302, the craftsmen of Bruges – on foot – took on King Phillip IV's army of 50,000 men, most of whom were mounted. When, by using their new weapons, the artisans won, the centuries of the supremacy of cavalry were effectively ended. This same knell for the knight tolled at the battle of Crécy in 1346 when the French cavalry were felled by the arrows of the English long-bows, which could fire five or six times as fast as the cross-bows that opposed them. Even greater changes came with the introduction of gunpowder and cannon early in the fourteenth century, which made the medieval fortifications of towns and castles obsolete.

The other bastion of society, the Church, was also under attack throughout Europe. With the price of crops falling, and the wages of workers rising, the agricultural income that had built the great cathedrals was destroyed. The immense cathedral at Sienna, which was begun in 1339, was never completed; the great age of cathedral-building had ended. Together with the loss of tithes, the Church had suffered grievous harm to its prestige. Even its spiritual power was questioned. If a merciful god ruled the world, how was it that he had permitted the agonies of famine and the plague?

The peasants had seen all too clearly how the Black Death had had no respect for rank, and watched as their rulers fled their palaces and abandoned their responsibilities leaving their people to die in misery – a recognition of human fallibility that was to survive and inform the social revolutions of later centuries.

Death lays his icy hand on kings:
Sceptre and crown
Must tumble down,
And in the dust be equal made
With the poor crooked scythe and spade.

(*The Contention of Ajax and Ulysses*, James Shirley, 1596-1666)

Now at Oxford John Wyclif furthered the cause of fundamental human rights by teaching that a man's salvation depended on his own conduct and faith, and translated the Bible for people to read the newly printed Word of God for themselves. The lordly gentle knight, no longer a landed vassal, reverted to war and plunder. From 1337, England's attempt to conquer France resulted in the interminable battles of the Hundred Years War. In Italy the city states fell into conflict; Bohemia suffered the Hussite wars, and in western Germany private warfare broke out between small armies. To the south the Turks were advancing. The protection of the countryside broke down, warfare as well as plague became endemic, and the development of Europe was set back three and a half centuries. The population of France in 1328 was about 17 million (England only had 2½ million) but not until 1700 did it reach 19 million.

Before the onset of the famines and plague the manorial society had already begun to crack with revolts among the urban artisans against their patrons. The next two centuries saw large-scale peasant uprisings as the old social contract of defence in exchange for service and rents broke down. The French *Jacquerie* of 1358, named after *Jacques*, the nickname of the peasant, was an uprising of serfs against their masters. Burnt manor houses led to brutal reprisals and 30,000 deaths. In England the Peasants' Revolt of 1381 led by Wat Tyler gained control of London when artisans sympathetic to their cause opened the gates. A mob freed prisoners and beheaded the Archbishop of Canterbury, in a protest not only against the Poll Tax, which demanded a shilling a head from those over the age of fifteen, but the power and wealth of the gentry and the Church. Their rallying cry became, When Adam delved and Eve span, who was then the gentleman?, Their specific demands for the abolition of serfdom and the change of services into rent showed how feudal values and submission were disintegrating in town and country alike to make way for the new concept of a nation state composed of free men. But meanwhile Europe sank into an economic depression and the forests crept back over the uplands and heaths to heal the wounds left by an unwise exploitation of the land.

CHAPTER EIGHT

FEEDING
THE CITIES

There is a further striking parallel between the agricultural collapse of medieval Europe and the tragedy that unfolded in the Ethiopian highlands in the 1970s to 1990s. There the land was reasonably fertile, and the downward ecological spiral which led to deforestation, erosion and famine was caused by an expanding population which had no alternative but to stay on the land. But famine was made inevitable by the poverty caused by a repressive feudal system. Under the Emperor Haile Selassie and his forebears, farmers had to give to their landlords as much as 75 per cent of their produce as rent, and this exploitation of the people led them in turn to over-exploit the land for centuries.

It was especially remarkable how the poverty of the people could be read on the face of the land. The only trees that survived on the highlands were in the churchyards. Unprotected from rain and run-off, the earth had been washed away to leave stony hillsides and gaping gullies. Rather than put manure back on the land to increase the yield, toddlers helped their mothers to pat cakes of cow-dung into shape to sell in the market as fuel for pennies, when a kilo of grain cost pounds. As the harvests failed with the final climatic trigger of the drought, even the wife's heirloom jewellery would be sold for a knock-down price to buy grain for bread, and the final stage of impoverishment was reached when the oxen that were essential to plough the land were sold too. From that point on there was no prospect other than for the family to starve and leave the land. This is how it must have been across Europe in the fourteenth century.

The comparison also extends to the political consequences of ecological collapse. The Ethiopian famine of 1972-4 led to the overthrow of the Emperor, and the substitution of a communist regime. It also led to warfare. The next drought, a decade later, brought a catastrophic death-toll. So, too, in fourteenth-century Europe, society was shaken to its foundations by famine which was closely followed by the Black Death.

The impoverished European agriculture took generations to recover. With the excessive human population removed, abandoned fields could lie fallow but still had to rebuild their humus; woods and hedgerows had to regrow to provide fuel. At first the surviving peasants were too poor to buy seed, let alone pigs, cows or oxen, so the countryside at first turned in on itself to exclude the towns, and it is of course on the surplus of agricultural production in the countryside that towns depend. In the lean years that followed, the Hundred Years War also severely affected trade. In Britain, cities like Lincoln and York, which had flourished on the wool trade, shrank in the fourteenth and fifteenth centuries as exports collapsed, following the loss of English possessions in France, and because the looms of Flanders and Florence were often cut off by warfare. By 1500 Lincoln had become so poor and depopulated that little more than a single street survived. Grass grew in the streets of Winchester, and York fell from its rank as the second wealthiest city of England to sixth.

The cost of armies demanded heavy taxes, and these were also raised on the export of English wool, making it too expensive for the weavers of Flanders, who turned their skills to making linen. This protected the English weavers of the hard-wearing and expensive woollen broadcloth from foreign competition. Plague was still endemic in most European towns, driving many citizens into the countryside, and in England it was there, away from the pestilence and restrictive gilds of the town, that the English cloth industry was to lead in a new era of sophisticated high-value trade. But the woollen cloth trade was also to have dire social consequences. The depopulation of the countryside had led to large areas of pasture and wasteland being given over to sheep, as the owners of manors, having lost their rents, looked for an alternative income. The price of corn fell too, because of over-supply, so that all but the richest land could provide a better return if used for grazing. In the second half of the fifteenth century, when cloth-making boomed and the price of wool rose by a third, a new crisis hit the surviving farming communities; yet more villages that had been self-sufficient became deserted, as peasant families were evicted from their land to make way for more sheep. Even when common land was enclosed, the serf had nowhere to graze his cattle and could not survive. In Warwickshire alone 75 villages were depopulated between 1450 and 1520.

In the fifteenth century cloth-making began to concentrate in the areas where sheep could be grazed and water-power was available to power the fulling-mills. (Fulling is a process of beating soaked woollen cloth to consolidate it.) Now the towns of the uplands – of Shropshire and Herefordshire, the Mendips and the Cotswolds – were to be transformed. Bristol reached a peak of prosperity in the early fifteenth century on its exports of woollen cloth to Gascony in exchange for wine. The value of the trade in wool and wine is enshrined in the grandeur of the parish church of St Mary Redcliffe, built with donations from merchant ship-owners, and the substantial churches of the west country wool towns such as Cirencester, Fairford, North Leach, Trowbridge and Steeple Ashton. The bulk of this expensive cloth was for local use, but the greatest export market was in the Low Countries, whence it was shipped from London and Yarmouth. Later Flemish weavers introduced to East Anglia the technique of making worsted cloth from combed fibres, with a fine even yarn and a glossy surface. This was cheaper, and captured the popular market in the early sixteenth century, raising Norwich to the point where it overtook Bristol as second city of the realm.

The landscape and the new social order

From the mid fifteenth century the population of Europe had begun to expand again and, with the reawakening of trade, the great geological diversity of the continent ensured many regional differences which could supply complimentary goods and markets. But geography had also already come to play an important part in influencing social development. France was by now divided into two separate societies by differing farming systems and degrees of agricultural development: while the broad sweep of the Paris Basin developed a highly organised open-field system for corn, more mountainous and less fertile southern France clung to a Mediterranean Gallo-Roman agriculture based on the vine, tree-crops and other non-cereal harvests. In southern France they even spoke a different dialect, the *langue d'oc* which was more closely related to Latin than the Frankish and Celtic *langue d'oil* of the north.

The Mesozoic plains of northern France had been fragmented by the feudal

A fifteenth century Flemish tapestry of a lady attending a hunt illustrates the sumptuous textiles and fashions of the court.

society into countless small manors. But their protection had failed with the demise of the supremacy of the knight. The new ascendancy of the footsoldier, using gunpowder and cannon, meant that the size of armies increased to be big enough to lay siege to castles and fortified towns. Large armies were of course expensive, and to furnish and control them needed larger taxes which could only be raised by larger political units. Thus it was the need to defend the open cereal lands and the introduction of gunpowder which became powerful factors leading to regional government and then to the nation-state. Much of the revenue to raise armies came from taxes on trade, and the nation-state was able, through its large armies and extensive territory, to protect long-distance trade in a way that the feudal lords could never do. It could also encourage and sustain trade in its own interest, by alliances, intrigues and treaties. Yet this was not always the case.

The degree to which the sovereigns of Europe were able to gain a monopoly on the powers of government, and thus influence trade, was to shape the future states. Paris, and the fertile Ile de France, became the germ from which the first

When wind and water power were employed it brought to the land the first new sources of energy since the harnessing of animals, freeing labour and increasing the productivity of the land. Dikes and windmills permitted the expansion and diversification of agriculture in the Netherlands.

nation-state was born, but in this case commerce suffered. As the French monarchy gained a firmer monopoly of power, and a distinct 'nobility' emerged, innovation and business activity were stifled, and agriculture was impoverished by imposing much higher taxes than in England. This tendency was even more marked in Spain. By contrast, in Holland, the importance of maritime trade had led to a legal and banking system that favoured a society effectively ruled by merchants.

During the warm period of early medieval times, the rising sea level caused by melting icecaps and the thermal expansion of the oceans had caused massive storm flooding in the northern Netherlands, which consist of the deltas of the rivers Rhine and Meuse. At least four floods in the thirteenth century had caused death-tolls of 100,000 or more, the worst killing three times that figure. Sixty parishes were lost in nearby Schleswig, and the great bays of Jade, Dollert, Biesbos and Braakman were claimed by the sea, as well as the immense Zuider

Zee (not to be controlled again until this century as the IJsselmeer). The coastal population had at first lived on artificial raised islands, separated by large areas of river and marshes from the feudal south. In the Middle Ages, to protect themselves and their lands, the communities progressed to building massive dikes and dams (thus Amsterdam, Rotterdam, Schiedam etc.). Even before 1300, West Friesland, a fertile area of marine clay, was encircled by a dike. By the mid-fifteenth century dikes protected all of northern Holland, and through its isolation the region had escaped the impact of manorial rule and institutions, and most of the land was owned by free peasants.

Thus geography gave these lowlands a very different society from the rest of Europe. The high water-table meant that the land was not well suited to grain growing and once trade allowed corn to be shipped from the Mesozoic cereal lands of Poland via the Vistula river and the Baltic, the farmers of the Netherlands began to grow valuable crops such as flax, hemp and rapeseed which they could sell. Freed from the need to be self-sufficient, horticultural diversity and specialisation were born. The peasants could invest in the crops needed for the textile industry: madder wool and dyers-weed, as well as barley and hops for brewing. By digging and manuring and more human labour, small quantities of land could be farmed much more intensively. Thus began the great economic upsurge of Holland that was to make it the centre of the European economy in the late sixteenth and early seventeenth centuries.

Meanwhile, to the east of the Elbe where an extensive river and lake system connected with the Baltic ports, the picture was very different because, despite the depopulation caused by the Black Death and thus reduced demand, the large-scale production of grain for export remained profitable. While in the west the manorial system was giving way to more freedom for peasants, in the east the landed nobility succeeded in excluding their tenants from a weak royal jurisdiction, and imposed their own labour contracts and harsh laws. In 1496, Polish peasants were formally bound to the soil. The towns were forced to surrender their rights of harbouring serfs, and the lords were even able to avoid using the towns and markets for selling their grain. By dealing directly with the merchants of the ports like Danzig (Gdansk), they increased their profit. This caused a decline of the country towns, a deepening servitude for their serfs, and a profound difference between eastern and western Europe which was to last well into the twentieth century.

Changing patterns of trade

Arable farming had never been easy in Norway, and had been abandoned in favour of pastureland as the climate worsened and the population collapsed. An indication of the poverty this caused can be illustrated by the fact that the price of land fell by half in the fourteenth century. Rye meal and malt were imported in exchange for butter and fish, and this sea trade in grain, as well as the products of the northern forests and mines, had been monopolised by the German cities along the southern Baltic coast, called the Hanseatic League. Centred on Lübeck, where trade was trans-shipped from the Baltic to the Elbe, and using high-sided, single-masted vessels called cogs which could dominate smaller pirate vessels, they continued the Viking connections with great trading posts at Bergen, Novgorod, London and Bruges.

Bruges had become the distribution centre for the Mediterranean trade that came overland along the ancient Rhône route via the great trade fair of Lyons. Thus in the first half of the fifteenth century, the Dukes of Burgundy derived

Hanseatic and
Venetian trade.

considerable power from their possession of the watersheds that led to the
Rhône, as they were able to tax this overland trade. From this base the Duchy was
able to absorb Flanders and neighbouring Brabant, then the richest land in
Europe, and appeared destined to carve out a powerful state between France and
Germany, until Charles the Bold was killed at the Battle of Nancy in 1477. His
inheritance was then partitioned among its neighbours, who were no doubt anx-
ious to stifle such a potentially powerful competitor.

Sea trade was of such importance that as the port of Bruges silted up, it lost its
pre-eminence, and the market for cloth, salt and goods from the east shifted to
Antwerp, together with the financial institutions that supported it. After 1400 the
Hanseatic League also declined as Dutch and English ships were built to more
advanced designs with sternpost rudders and several masts, and their sailors
became more daring, successfully challenging the monopoly in the Baltic, and
opening new routes to the Atlantic.

At the start of the sixteenth century the main axis of European trade was still
between northern Italy and Flanders, the two most densely urbanised and
industrialised areas. Both regions manufactured high-quality woollen cloth like
velvets. Italy also wove silks, while Flanders produced linens, tapestries and lace.
Spain displaced England as the principal exporter of the finest raw wool, as the
Merino sheep, which had been introduced into Spain by the Arabs, produced a

finer wool than any English breed and could not survive in the wetter northern climates. Instead England exported semi-finished cloths to be worked in Flanders and Brabant. As the population of Europe began to grow again, so did the demand for woollen cloth. The rising price of wool encouraged the landowners to convert more land to pasture and drew more enclosures across the uplands of England, depopulating yet more villages in order to make room for the flocks, and despite the terrible hardship caused to the dispossessed peasant farmers and their families.

As a more sophisticated trade in luxuries was born in the larger cities, their subsequent growth and wealth led to still more demand for goods. The declining power of the Church and lords restrained the building of huge cathedrals and castles, which in early medieval times had used so much labour and capital in an unproductive way (as the arms race did in the twentieth century). The grandest examples of Renaissance architecture, which began to replace Gothic in the fifteenth century, were not confined to cathedrals, but were commissioned by merchants who had aspirations to noble rank and sought the prestige of land and hewn stone about them. They were built in the Netherlands at the court of the Dukes of Burgundy, and in the two great commercial regions of Flanders and northern Italy. That they no longer felt the need for their homes to be castles is a reflection of the new strength of regional government.

By the end of the fifteenth century, with the exception of Paris, the largest cities were still in the Mediterranean region: Milan, Venice, Naples and Constantinople all had populations of over 100,000. The rise of the Seljuk Turks had weakened Constantinople, and the merchants of Genoa, and especially of Venice, had come to dominate Mediterranean maritime trade. Venice, secure on its islands within the lagoon, was well protected by its fleet. Moreover the steep barrier of the Dinaric Alps in Yugoslavia and the Pindus mountains of Greece not only protected the eastern shore of the Adriatic, and thus the expanding Venetian empire, from the incursions of the Muslims, but also supplied abundant timber for the Venetian galleys.

The Venetian maritime empire soon began to duplicate the trading patterns of classical Greece, and held a virtual monopoly of the pepper, spices and luxuries of the Orient. As their emblem of the Lion of St Mark spread on fortresses through the eastern Mediterranean islands, their galleys were frequently to be seen in the English Channel bearing cargoes from Beirut and Alexandria, or waiting at Rye or Sandwich for an easterly wind before sailing down channel at the start of their long journey home.

It was still cheaper, more comfortable and often quicker to travel by sea than by road, but as sea trade revived European society in the late Middle Ages, the bulk of that trade was shifting to the Atlantic seaboard. The improvements in ship design, and in sailing rigs (by marrying the Arab lateen sail to the square-sail of the Vikings) enabled faster voyages to be made. But in the 1430s there was a most unusual succession of severe winters. All the rivers in Germany froze, and in 1431 a ship from Flanders bound for Lisbon was blown off course far to the west and discovered the Azores. These islands, far out in the Atlantic, are still used as stepping-stones by yachts sailing to the Caribbean. Portuguese traders had discovered Madeira in 1422 and the Canaries in 1427 as they were blown down the north-east trade winds towards the coast of Guinea in search of slaves and gold. As the fifteenth century closed, with the knowledge that there were islands far beyond the ocean, sailors began to speculate about the possibility that the riches of the Orient could be reached by a sea route to the west. Two immensely important discoveries followed: of the Americas by Columbus (1492), and the sea route to India by Vasco da Gama (1499). These voyages opened undreamed-of opportunities to merchants. During the first half of the sixteenth century, no fewer than 200 ships a year sailed from Seville to the New World.

A flood of treasure from the New World tumbled into the coffers of the Spanish throne via the monopoly port of Cadiz. And it was not only the gold and silver of the Inca and Aztec mines that made Europe rich. Having cut out the taxes and countless middle-men on the overland route from the East, the profits to be made on the spice trade were enormous. The loss of the spice monopoly hit Venice hard, one merchant compared it with the loss of milk to an infant, and it was the ports facing the Atlantic that gained. The merchants of Portugal, France, Holland and England sailed to China to exchange the new gold for tea, to India for spices and the cottons and silks of Asia. All the benefits of trading with 'uncivilised' peoples were realised by the maritime trading nations that were already developed enough to make use of the apparently limitless opportunity offered by the new continents. The merchants and ports prospered: Liverpool and Nantes on the slave trade, London on sugar, Glasgow on tobacco. Amsterdam and Hamburg became gateways to trade with northern Europe. Over the next three centuries Europe would reap the benefit of new resources from all over the globe. But just as the ships bearing this new wealth began to sail in, the growing European population once more out-ran its food supplies.

The Little Ice Age

From about 1550 the climate again grew colder with the intensification of what is now known as 'The Little Ice Age' which had begun in the 1320s. In February 1565 Pieter Brueghel the Elder painted his famous picture *Hunters in the Snow*,

one of the first landscape paintings ever to be painted, which started a fashion for Dutch winter landscapes. It was the coldest winter in living memory, and a symptom of the sharp deterioration of winter temperatures that brought snowfalls to the Swiss Alps twice as often as in the previous twenty years. The cruelty of the cold apparently also inspired Brueghel to change the setting of his 1563 painting of the visit of the Magi to the Holy Family in an open stable. When he painted the scene again in 1567 the building was set beside a frozen river near a village with snow falling, relating it to the harshness of the rural life of his times.

The last half of the 1580s had cold snowy springs and wet mid-summers, seriously affecting the harvest, and in 1590 famine struck Italy, Spain and France. (In 1595 the sea froze at Marseilles.) Hundreds of thousands of hard-working peasant families died in abject poverty and misery. Well might Montaigne, who died in 1592, write: *Le continuel ouvrage de votre vie, c'est bâtir la mort* (The unending labour of your life is to build the house of Death). From this time on, the whole of the western Mediterranean would no longer be able to feed its inhabitants, especially in the great cities, and had to rely on imports. The Turks were now eating the grain from the plains of Thessaly, the Black Sea and the Nile delta, that had been so important in Classical times, and it was left to the post-glacial soils of Prussia and Poland, and the Baltic ports, to supply not just the northern seaboard but the Mediterranean cities as well. The Polish peasants, who were little more than slaves, were reduced to eating bread made from barley and oats, while so much wheat was exported that wheaten bread was only seen on the tables of the great lords. By 1610 almost 2500 ships a year were entering the newly constructed free port of Leghorn (Livorno) in Tuscany. The Dutch and English merchant ships dominated this new trade with fast heavily-gunned ships. Outgunned and outsailed, the Venetian and Italian traders lost their position as the leaders of European maritime trade, even in the Mediterranean.

The second agricultural revolution

Jonathan Swift had the king of Brobdingnag express one of the fundamental truths of human existence when

> He gave it for his opinion, that whoever could make two ears of corn, or two blades of grass, to grow upon a spot of ground where only one grew before, would deserve better of mankind, and do more essential service to his country, than the whole race of politicians put together.
>
> (Gulliver's Travels)

The breakthrough in feeding the growing cities of Europe indeed came when new methods of agriculture made the old lands more productive. The first 'agricultural revolution' had happened in Neolithic times when animal power had been harnessed to increase the energy applied to cultivating the land, but this time more food was to be won from the same amount of land by the introduction of new crops. The Arabs had introduced new plants to Spain, such as sugarcane, rice, cotton and citrus fruits, but it was the use of leguminous and root crops with new systems of rotation in the Netherlands that turned the tide away from starvation. There, in a densely populated and urbanised country, where some 10 square kilometres of land were wrested from the sea every year, good land management had a special value. Peat and lime came to be used to improve the soil, and the introduction of clover was particularly important (although it was not known at the time) because it fixes nitrogen from the atmosphere through bacteria living in nodules on its roots, thus fertilising the land. It could be mixed with grass-seed, and helped to overcome the old problem of how to establish fertile grazing or ley lands quickly. The other new field crop to be used in the mid-seventeenth century was the turnip. Weeds could still be hoed, and thus eliminated, while turnips were growing in the ground, and as well as human food they also provided a valuable fodder crop that could be used to feed cattle or sheep in the winter months.

Wheat cannot be grown on the same field two years running without severe problems of disease, pests and weeds, and successive crops of turnips-barley-clover-wheat, known in England as the 'Norfolk' rotation, not only broke the cycle of grain pests, but removed the need for an unproductive fallow period, so the production of food per hectare increased. But that was not all. Until the introduction of the turnip as winter fodder, many cattle had to be slaughtered at Michaelmas (29 September), and the survivors were so weak by the end of the winter that they were sometimes carried to the fields to eat the first growth of grass. Turnips allowed larger numbers of livestock to be fed through the winter, which not only increased the wealth of the farmer, but improved the land with their previously scarce manure, thus raising cereal yields. The productivity of the land had been dramatically increased, and on the basis of this extra food the population of Europe almost trebled between 1500 and 1800 – to about 188 million.

Bread and taxes

By 1600 Milan had 180,000 inhabitants, Paris 200,000, and London, Rome, Palermo, Marseilles and Amsterdam all about 100,000. Conditions in these cities were so unhygienic, and the mortality rate so high, that they could only be sustained by a constant influx of people from the countryside. In northern Europe the rural population was constantly retreating from the country into the towns to be fed on imported grain, and around 1650 an agricultural slump began which lasted for a century. The old trends surfaced again: uplands were depopulated as arable land was enclosed and turned over to pasture.

Peasant farmers produced only about 20 per cent more food than they needed for subsistence, so 80 per cent of the population still had to live on the land. But by this date there was more opportunity for rural families to turn to cottage textile industries such as spinning and weaving as an additional source of livelihood. In England the fertility of families had been controlled by late marriage – often a couple would not wed until land was inherited from one of the parents. As the average life expectancy of a woman was only some 36 years, a delay in starting to have children from teens to late twenties or thirties would make a substantial difference to the number of children born. (Infant mortality was about ten times as high as it is now.)

Not until a hundred years later, in the mid-eighteenth century, when the increasing use of child labour in industry and the coal-mines turned children into economic assets rather than mouths to feed, did earlier marriage return, and then the birth rate soared. What is remarkable is that by this time agricultural production, at least in England, had become so much more efficient that it was not only able to keep up with the expanding numbers, but also to yield a surplus. In 1750, 17 per cent of England's exports were foodstuffs. While the Netherlands had pioneered the improvements, in England it had become the fashion among the new class of 'gentry' to read books about new agricultural techniques. Reformers viewed improvements in agriculture as one of the greatest practical forms of enlightenment, and history has shown them to be right, though their harshly dispossessed tenants would not agree. Stock-breeding became a fashionable topic –

The port of London at the end of the eighteenth century, full of shipping which could supply the capital with food and fuel.

paintings of prize cattle and pigs adorned parlour walls, and Stubbs brought a nobility of style to his portraits of the horses of the gentry. There may have been a vast difference between these graceful beasts and the carthorse of the tenant, but as farms leased by yeomen – for three lifetimes or ninety-nine years – were extended out to take over peasant holdings, innovation changed the face of the field. In England, by 1750, more than ten grains of wheat were being harvested for every one sown, there were far fewer poor in the countryside and the fear of famine had been banished from the land.

Meanwhile, the sheer size of France, and the great distance between its larger cities, caused regions to develop in self-sufficient isolation. Grain was still the whole life of France, 'the manna of the poor'. Half of the peasant's income was spent on this basic food, for eggs cost six times as much as bread, meat eleven times and fresh sea fish sixty-five times. But despite being the largest industry, agriculture was always in trouble. In contrast to the rapid improvements in England, cereal yields were only sixfold. The previous century had seen the widespread adoption of the system of *métayage* where the *seigneur*, to whom the tenants still took an oath of subjection, owned not just the land but the farm implements, stock and seed, and took between a third and a half of the produce. In addition, taxes could take as much as a fifth of the harvest. A holding, even of as much as ten hectares, was barely adequate to feed the tenant's family on the most meagre diet of rye-bread and pease pottage, even in a good year. Many families lived lives of constant toil under the grim shadow of the knowledge that they might starve next year. It would be hard to invent a system more likely to encourage soil erosion and long-term degradation of the land. With such an emphasis on survival from day to day, no thought or coin could be spared for the future. Any natural accident of weather, or the passage of an army, or a new imposition of tax or debt, was enough to throw a family from their home on to the roads to

The quais of Paris below the Notre Dame bridge in the mid-eighteenth century are crowded with barges bringing sacks of wheat, sheep, hay and firewood into the city. The Seine was too long and winding for large vessels.

face destitution and death. In some villages around Versailles, 70 per cent of the family heads owned no land. Resentment simmered, and the shining splendour of the Court, and almost absolute power of Louis XIV, was built on shifting social sands. In the seventeenth century there were rebellions over taxation and bread prices in Normandy, Boulogne, Béarn, Bigorre, Guyenne and Brittany.

In most of the eastern Paris Basin the unimproved three-field system persisted, and increases in corn production could only be achieved by planting a greater area. So when urban demand began to raise grain prices in the mid-eighteenth century, there was once again a financial advantage in enclosing the common land used by the landless poor to feed their livestock for most of the year. But this reduced the manure available for the fallow fields. As one enlightened English eighteenth-century parish register recorded: 'Without wasteland there would be no sheep, without sheep there would be no manure on the farms, and without manure there would be no corn in the fields.' The new ploughing, the use of straw for fuel, and the subsequent loss of humus in the soil caused the usual crisis of erosion. Yields fell, prices rose, and anger followed hardship.

The problem of Paris

Paris was the political rather than the economic capital of France, and, partly in consequence, French roads – especially between Paris and the provinces – were notoriously bad. For example there was no road that travelled further west than Caen and Nantes, and it was not until the eighteenth century that a school of civil engineering for roads and bridges was created, while the grim forced labour of the *corvée* was used for highway maintenance. This made bulk transport for grain difficult and expensive. The cost of such carting doubled every 55 kilometres.

The best way of transporting grain was by water. During the second half of the eighteenth century, England developed an extensive and sophisticated system of canals, which also made it possible to transport heavy coal to replace firewood for fuel – with the important ecological consequence of saving woodlands. But in France the Seine had a meandering course, the Loire was shallow with meandering shifting channels, and the Rhône had a fierce current. Although navigation on these rivers had been improved, and indeed canals opened between the Seine and the Loire, and the Mediterranean and the Atlantic through the Languedoc, the sheer size of the rivers and the country hindered the movement of both food and fuel. Low river levels at the time of the harvest did not help.

By the 1780s the population of France had reached 27 million (compared with only 8 million in England), and Paris, with 650,000 citizens, was the third largest city of Europe. Only Constantinople and London were greater, but they were both ports, and could import food by sea. Eighty per cent of the food for Paris came from the Paris Basin, and around the city had grown concentric rings of specialised production. Closest, where the land values were highest, were market gardens, then there was forest to supply the huge demand for fuel-wood, then fields for wheat and rye. Furthest out was livestock pasture, as livestock were able to transport themselves along droving roads, though they lost weight and thus value in the process. A labouring family of four would eat about 12 quintals (1.2 tons) of grain a year; so over 2000 tons a day had to be brought by barge or carted into the city on bad roads. It was becoming increasingly difficult to feed Paris. In April and May of 1775 there were riots over bread prices in Paris and four northern provinces.

The price of privilege

France had the greatest population and power in Europe, and was the cultural and intellectual leader of a continent, but it had cost the country dear to maintain its prestige. The French economy had suffered grievous damage from almost continuous wars since the end of the Middle Ages; those under the rule of Louis XIV at the end of the seventeenth century being especially costly. In fact there had been a financial crash in 1720-21 when the government wrote off huge debts. Since then four other major wars, including the Seven Years War, had brought even heavier expenditure. There was no central government treasury to keep accounts, and it is possible that Louis XVI was unaware of the impending crisis when, in a gamble to destroy the British Empire, French forces were despatched to assist the Americans in their fight for independence.

In England a constitutional monarch now reigned with rights circumscribed by government, but as that government represented the people it was better able to raise taxes. In France, paradoxically, an all-powerful king was unable to infringe the rights laid down in medieval tradition, and could not raise taxes without the agreement of the nobles who formed his ministers. The French nobility, a class of some 200,000 males, who made up just 1.5 per cent of the population, owned perhaps a third of all the land and exercised seigneurial rights over most of the rest, enjoying about a quarter of the total income from agriculture. They dominated French affairs and even the armed forces, as nobles still did in most of the countries in Europe. Despising commerce, they were nevertheless deeply involved in finance and investment in industry. In France until 1695 they had been untaxed, but were now paying 15 per cent on the income of landed property.

Such was the power of the nobility that there was no way, short of using force, by which the King could further tax the wealth of the better off, and the burden fell heavily on the poor. To avoid the need for increased taxation, the American war was paid for by borrowing yet more money and in 1786 the crisis came. State expenditure was running at 25 per cent higher than income, but to make matters worse, the cost of servicing existing debt now consumed nearly half the annual revenue of the State, while more than half of the next year's income had already been anticipated. France was on the edge of a financial precipice, and the only recourse was to increase taxes.

With the American Declaration of Independence in 1776 French troops had helped to gain a glorious victory. They had been dazzled by the sight of a young nation building a constitution from first principles, and had seen the triumph of the concepts that men are born free, and should not be taxed without representation. Taxes in France varied greatly from district to district, and in Paris they were already the highest in Europe. Now the scent of revolution was in the air. Since conflict of some kind seemed inevitable, the nobles forced Louis XVI to summon a body which was the nearest thing that France had ever had to a forum representing the whole nation: the three estates of Nobility, the Church and the Common People. It was called the Estates General and it had not met since 1614.

Yet there was deep confusion in the Estates General about what changes to society were necessary. In August 1778, Louis took the extraordinary step of instructing communities to compile *Cahiers de doléances* (registers of grievances), to find out what the people wished. Though there was plenty to fill the registers, so conservative were the peasants and nobility that despite an outcry against taxation, dues and the price of bread, scarcely anyone complained about the feudal system itself. But the very fact of airing their grievances gave the peasants hope, and the prospect of some kind of change now made it impossible to maintain the *status quo*.

The extreme price of bread during the winter led to grain convoys being attacked in January 1779, and by the spring there was a nationwide revolt against paying taxes, tithes and feudal dues. Food riots, occurring everywhere at the same time, became the catalyst for a revolution that was neither expected nor wanted by the great majority of the people. Widespread rumours that the aristocrats were going to starve the rural population into submission by cutting down the green corn sent waves of panic across the nation.

The decade of 1780 brought unusual climatic variability: 1782 had a wet spring and summer, heavy thunderstorms spoilt the summer growing season of 1783 and were followed by an exceptionally severe winter and spring hailstorms. These caused severe erosion in northern France. Agricultural production was further crippled by a long drought in 1785 which was followed by a severe winter and another long drought in 1786. This caused a great mortality in cattle (in a drought cattle die from starvation not thirst). On 17 July 1788, a massive hailstorm not only did considerable damage in Paris but destroyed the crops over a huge area. Food prices jumped on average by 100 per cent, and by 200 per cent in some areas, reaching a maximum in the months before the next harvest, June and July. While imports could ease the crisis of supply, and thus lower prices in the French towns accessible from the Mediterranean, this was not possible for Paris, where a worker's daily bread now cost 97 per cent of his income. Suddenly, not only the food supply, but the purchasing power of the majority of the population had collapsed. Between 1787 and 1789, with no demand, industrial production fell by half. If the French Revolution was not born of climatic crisis, bad weather was at least the midwife.

The Paris uprising of July 1789 began when, despite frantic efforts to import grain, the price of bread rose to record levels. The movement of troops into Paris lent weight to rumours that the King was planning to dissolve the Estates General

The Hall of Mirrors, Versailles. This palace, the cultural focus of the continent, took over fifty years to build under the day to day supervision of Louis XIV. From 1682 one thousand great lords and 4000 servants lived in the palace itself, another 5000 servants in the service quarters.

and start a counter-revolution. During the night of 12 to 13 July all the gates in the wall around Paris, where customs enforced the tariffs on grain, were attacked and burnt by a crowd of wage-earners and shopkeepers. The next day was spent ransacking all possible sources of arms, culminating in the taking of the Bastille on the 14th – a symbolic rather than a practical victory for the people. With the likelihood of insurrection igniting the whole country, on the night of 4 August the Estates General, 'in a moment of patriotic drunkenness' as one deputy later called it, abolished feudalism, tithes, the privileges of nobility and the purchasing of offices. The *ancien régime* was dead. Two months later 6000 women marched the 20 kilometres from Paris to Versailles and captured Louis XVl and his Queen, Marie Antoinette. As they were carried back in triumph to Paris the women shouted to the crowd, 'You will not lack for bread in the future, we are bringing you the baker and the baker's wife.'

Despite all the horrors that followed, during what is sometimes called the second revolution – which claimed some 50,000 victims, the great majority of them commoners – the social order was fundamentally changed. One of its most enduring features was that once Napoleon Bonaparte had seized power in 1799, and the threat to the revolution was removed by his victory over Austria, it led to better stewardship of the land. With 'rational' boundaries now set at the Rhine,

the Alps and the Pyrenees, France was to be unified for the first time – in the name of equality and the rights of man. Yet despite Napoleon's famous dictum that an army marched on its stomach, food production in France stagnated for a whole generation. The cost of holding on for so long to a feudal system was dreadful. Two million French citizens died in the Revolution and the imperial and civil wars that racked France until, in 1815, the battle of Waterloo drove Napoleon into exile. Meanwhile, England gained an unchallengeable lead in agriculture, industry and world trade.

The third agricultural revolution

In contrast to France, in England and America science was being applied to agriculture. In 1701, Jethro Tull had published a description of a horse-drawn seed drill, which measured seeds into a furrow, and gradually superseded the age-old but wasteful method of scattering seed by hand. Robert Ransome patented a cast-iron plough-share in 1785, and John Deere made the first steel plough in America

Eighteenth century cartoon of a French villager, working all year to pay his taxes.

in the 1830s. The first factory for extracting sugar from sugar-beet was built in Silesia in 1802, and in the 1830s, in England, machinery was displacing manual labour to such an extent that farm workers rebelled against the introduction of threshing machines because they were taking away their winter employment. The celebrated chemist Sir Humphrey Davy published a book on agricultural chemistry in 1813; and in the 1830s Sir John Bennet Lawes had experimented with the effects of different manures and chemicals to increase the yield of crops.

When the first steam plough was invented in England in 1858 the third agricultural revolution really got under way. Animal traction was to be replaced by the energy trapped in fossil fuels (see Chapter 9). Fortunes were soon made from manufacturing steam traction engines which could pull ploughs or drive farm machinery with belts, and in 1892 the first successful petrol-driven tractor was made in the USA. Steam-ships and railways had already transformed communications, opening up the interiors of continents to international trade and ideas on an unprecedented scale. The speed with which new inventions could be taken up increased dramatically. By 1900 most of western America was settled, and huge quantities of grain were now imported into Europe from the vast new wheatfields of the Mid-West. Wool now came from Australia and New Zealand, and chilled beef and dairy products could travel thousands of kilometres from Argentina and the antipodes in the new refrigerated ships. The enormous acreages being brought under the plough in the Mid-West were beyond the capabilities of even the largest horse teams, and the shortage of food during World War I again stimulated the design of agricultural machinery, culminating in the Fordson tractor. But it was not until after the Second World War that European farming became fully industrialised.

Nevertheless, the urban population was expanding so fast that scientists were alarmed. In 1898, Sir William Crookes gave a Presidential Address to the British Association for the Advancement of Science, in which he claimed, 'England and all civilised nations stand in deadly peril of not having enough to eat.' He believed that since plough-land was finite in area, only another thirty years of population growth could be fed. The only solution was to increase agricultural yields yet again, and this was only possible by using artificial fertiliser. Natural chemical fertilisers were already being used, such as Chilean nitrate of soda, and guano from Peru (which consists of sea-bird droppings rich in phosphates). Mining them had become major industries, but the deposits would be exhausted in thirty years. Now it was only the chemist who could come to the rescue. Fortunately, the chemical revolution in agriculture had really begun fifty years before, when Lawes patented a process for treating phosphate rock to make superphosphate fertiliser, and in 1917 Haber discovered how to synthesise ammonia from the nitrogen in air – the key to manufacturing nitrates for fertiliser as well as explosives.

The geology of plenty

Already the geology and geography of the London and Paris basins had had a profound effect on the way human history had developed in these regions. But another consequence of the great Mesozoic seas which once covered them was to have an effect far more revolutionary on society than any government – and incidentally was to make Swift's observation come true. In the last hundred years one mineral – oil – has changed the shape of human civilisation. Present-day society, with its huge cities and long-distance transport of resources, would be inconceivable without it. Petroleum is also the raw material for the manufacture of plastics and synthetic fibres, and a huge number of man-made organic compounds like drugs, herbicides and pesticides. Indeed one of the most profound effects of petroleum on society has been on the productivity of agriculture.

Most of the petroleum and the associated natural gas which we use is still burnt for energy. In so doing we release the energy of the sun, stored over 150 million years ago by innumerable plants – microscopic algae and plankton – living in tropical seas. But it took a complex series of geological events to turn these tiny organisms into oil or gas, and it rarely happened. In the first place, when the organisms die and fall to the ocean floor the normal process of decay is caused by bacteria which consume oxygen. Only if oxygen is excluded and the sea floor becomes stagnant can the process which forms organic-rich mud begin. Then the sea-floor basin has to continue sinking slowly for millions of years, so that a considerable thickness of mud can be built up. Next it must be buried deep enough in the earth's crust by sediments to be compacted under their weight into mudstones and shales, and 'cooked' by the heat of the earth's core at a temperature of 100 degrees Celsius. When this happens, and hydrocarbons are formed, the oil or gas rises, because they are lighter than the rock, and if there is a porous sandstone above, they will permeate into it. The hydrocarbons will then usually flow to the surface and be lost at seeps. It was from such seeps that oil and tar were first discovered and mined (even Noah caulked his ark with pitch). Before a reservoir can be formed underground the permeable rock must first be capped with an impermeable layer and then curved upwards in a hump. If the oil-bearing strata are tilted and the rising oil blocked with a geological fault or an intruded salt-dome this can also form a pocket where oil or gas can collect. So the petroleum minerals are seldom found in the rocks where they were actually created, and only found where this remarkably complex series of geological events has taken place. To make petroleum even more scarce, normally only 30 per cent of a deposit can be extracted.

Limits to the granary

In the last decade of this millennium there is a new crisis on the great Mesozoic grain lands of northern Europe. The political will to make Europe self-sufficient in food, which lies at the heart of the European Community agricultural programme, came from the experience of the Second World War; when food supplies ran out and the Allies depended for their daily bread on convoys across the Atlantic (see Chapter 11). This policy has resulted in huge quantities of grain being grown, often on unsuitable uplands, as well as in traditional stock-fattening areas like the English Midlands. Even marshes like the Isle of Sheppey (which takes its name from grazing sheep) have been ploughed up for grain and fertilised with large amounts of artificial fertiliser subsidised by the Community, to be sold at unrealistically high Community-subsidised prices. Yields are astonishingly high by medieval standards, reaching 13 tons per hectare, and averaging 7 tons in England, compared with 0.85 tons in the thirteenth century. In less developed countries yields are still at the medieval levels, and it is the use of artificial nitrate fertilisers that has made most of the difference. Nitrate fertiliser is made from natural gas and petroleum, non-renewable resources, which should give us cause to wonder how long our cities can be fed by this means.

There is concern that the run-off of fertilisers into the rivers that feed the Baltic and North Seas is causing toxic blooms of algae that use up oxygen and kill fish; about 100,000 square kilometres of the Baltic Sea are already deficient in oxygen. The amount of nitrogen and phosphorus in the German Bight and Kattegat has

doubled since 1950, during which period world consumption of nitrogen fertilisers has increased by a factor of nine. In 1987 the neighbouring countries agreed to halve the quantity of nutrients reaching the North Sea by 1995 by installing more sewage treatment plants. Paradoxically the dead algae sinking to the bottom of the Baltic, which are threatening to 'kill' the sea, are causing the same conditions that led to the formation of petroleum in the first place.

There is, however, a more immediate problem in that artificial nitrate applied to crops, as well as the natural nitrate released in large quantities when grassland is ploughed, are leaching into drinking-water supplies, arousing concern as a possible cause of stomach cancer and 'blue baby' deaths. In 1986, the European Community set a legal limit of a maximum of 50 milligrams of nitrate per litre of drinking water, yet almost all EC countries fail to reach this standard in some agricultural areas. In 1989, 1.6 million British people in the main farming areas of the Midlands and East Anglia were affected, as was 10 per cent of West Germany's drinking water. The same year the EC published a directive that if nitrogen in drinking water exceeded 50 parts per million, compulsory restrictions on using fertiliser would come into effect. If the rule were to be applied this could have a devastating effect on grain production in England; more than half the arable area of the country, including all of East Anglia and most of the Severn-Trent and Thames valleys, might have to be converted to unfertilised pasture or woodland. The Paris Basin would be similarly affected. The Netherlands has already had to take severe restrictive measures on manure and fertiliser use. However, much of the excess nitrogen may have been caused by the ploughing up of grasslands during the Second World War which released huge quantities of natural nitrate that took a further 40 years to get into the water supply.

Another more fundamental, and much more worrying, problem is related to our use of oil. In agriculture, the amount of food produced can be measured in

A country meeting of the Royal Agricultural Society of England at Bristol in 1842. The new-fangled machines were already fashionable.

relation to land area, labour employed and energy consumed. In Europe, the amount of grain produced has increased enormously in the last century, especially when measured against the area of land sown and the number of people employed on the land. The more fossil energy is substituted for human labour, the more people each labourer can feed. But the amount of grain harvested per unit of energy has actually gone down.

When Neolithic man had to feed himself from a smaller area because of pressure from his neighbours, his only recourse was to intensify food production from the same area of land. By using as draught animals ruminants which extracted energy from the cellulose in the grasses they eat, he acquired an energy source to apply in ploughing (and to eat), which did not compete with him for food. Some 10,000 years of the evolution of agricultural methods reached its culmination in Europe in seventeenth-century agricultural techniques, and these were only improved upon in China, where the amount of land needed to support a human being was reduced to 100 square metres. The amount of energy extracted as food remained throughout that long period about forty to fifty times greater than the quantity used to produce it.

Since the industrialisation of agriculture, the productivity of each agricultural labourer has increased fifty-fold, so that over 80 per cent of the population now lives away from the land. But the ratio of energy extracted as food to that used in growing it has declined dramatically. The energy used includes direct items such as fuel oil for tractors, or electricity to heat greenhouses, and indirect uses such as the amount needed to make bag fertiliser and pesticides, and the energy used to manufacture machinery and packaging. Wheat is now one of the better crops, but it yields only 3.3 times the amount of energy used to grow it. Carrots only yield 1.5 times, but intensive beef farming requires two units of energy to be expended for every unit of food energy received in return. Frozen broiler chickens need ten times as much energy to be spent as is got back as food. Most of the energy spent comes from oil and natural gas which means that food prices are tightly linked to oil prices. They are of course non-renewable resources and the price can only go up in the long term.

Food on the table looks even worse in this light. Packaged sliced white bread returns half the energy used to make it, and even to catch and deliver fish from the sea – our modern equivalent of hunter-gathering – uses up five times the energy that we get back as food. With our recent understanding of the atmospheric limits to energy use (see Chapter 13) it is a worrying trend. Intensive production with high energy use and high cost also means that farmers, faced with a small drop in prices, will strive to increase output to keep up profits in order to pay for bank loans on machinery, etc. This is often achieved at the cost of damaging the soil by inadequate provision against erosion and soil degradation. All these trends must have a destabilising effect on future food production, and, history would suggest, on politics and society.

There is an alternative. A standard urban allotment garden (0.025 hectare) planted with vegetables and fruit can yield 2 tons of food per year for 350 hours of work (less than eight hours a week) at an energy ratio greater than 1.3. The allotment can yield 50 per cent more weight of food per unit area than a farmer growing heavily-fertilised and sprayed potatoes. If even half the residents of cities with back gardens used a quarter of their land in this way, the cities would become self-sufficient in temperate fruit, potatoes and vegetables, and have a massive surplus for export! The inhabitants would probably be healthier too, provided the land is kept unpolluted.

CHAPTER NINE

KING COAL

In the middle of the eighteenth century, France was not only richer and culturally more advanced than her neighbours, but appeared to have a more promising future. Already by 1681 when Louis XlV's architects constructed a vast pumping-machine to lift water from the Seine at Marly-la-Machine to supply the fountains of the formal gardens at Versailles, they were applying the most advanced technology of the day. The new palace's great gallery of mirrors reflected the solid agricultural wealth of the Paris Basin, and the nobles that strolled there were taking advantage of a long period of increased prosperity for the great estates by selling food to the towns at a profit. Some of this wealth was employed in trade and manufacture, and feudalism was beginning to blend into capitalism – at the expense of the peasant and family farm. But there was more than one revolution in the eighteenth century that would destroy the *ancien régime*. Beside that for the rights of man strode another with a promise of undreamed-of prosperity that would derive from deep in the history of the earth. It was to benefit some parts of Europe which were least well endowed for agriculture, and in place of the Sun King, Louis XIV, it would install as ruler the fossil energy of the sun – the power saved in vegetation from previous aeons. The new king was called Coal, and his dominion began in Great Britain.

In 1760, the population of France was 23 million, and that of Great Britain only 4 million, yet by 1880 the British population had overtaken that of France, almost entirely as a result of industry and coal. There were many indirect reasons for this dramatic population explosion, but the new energy source was crucial to its sustainability. In the past the energy used to support human activities had been only available from renewable sources such as animal power, wind, water and firewood. If too much of the earth's natural productivity was burnt as fuel (especially dung and straw) it upset the ecological balance between man and the land, which in turn caused the human population to collapse until stability could return with less demand for food and fuel. Once fossil fuel was burnt this negative feed-back no longer applied and the human population could expand. Indeed greater numbers could be fed by exploiting more fossil energy to increase crop yields from the land.

Coal had been known as a fuel for millennia, but a substance only becomes an important resource when society possesses the knowledge and techniques to make use of it; and far from there being a sudden coal-fired 'Industrial Revolution', coal made its way most hesitantly onto the European stage. The cliffs of the Northumberland coast of the north of England are banded with seams of coal, and as storms erode the cliff face it drops to the shore where, because it is lighter than the stone, the sea washes it into beds. When weathered it looks very similar to charcoal, and came to be known as sea-coal. Even in the thirteenth century coal had been substituted for wood in domestic hearths, and it was unpopular from the start. The sea-coal was soft, with a high sulphur content, and it produced clouds of choking smoke. Queen Eleanor was driven out of her castle in Nottingham by the smoke in 1257, and in 1307 Edward I issued a royal proclamation prohibiting the use of sea-coal in kilns. When 'grievous ransomes' proved an insufficient deterrent to air pollution, one offender was tortured, hanged and decapitated. But supplying the expanding cities with firewood had long been a problem, it was bulky to transport and in great demand. Wood was also needed for timber-framed houses and farm carts, but that was not all. By the 1680s Britain was the biggest naval power in Europe, and it took 2000 oak trees – some 20 hectares of forest – to build a man o' war. Oak trees had become so important strategically that the Spanish Armada sailed with orders to destroy the Forest of Dean. Trees were also vital to the growing economy; to smelt a ton of iron ore took 20 tons of wood turned to charcoal. So despite the careful husbandry of plantations, as the population grew and cities expanded, wood became scarce and expensive. Price alone began to make coal more attractive to burn as fuel.

The fuel problem

By the sixteenth century, the population of towns had recovered sufficiently from the ravages of the Black Death to make the demand for fuel-wood exceed the supply. Smoke from coal the only practical alternative once again became a problem, and Queen Elizabeth commanded brewers to stop using sea-coal to make ale. But by 1632 firewood was again so scarce that Londoners were 'constrained to make fires of sea-coal . . . even in chambers of honorable personages'. A generation later the diarist John Evelyn observed

> 'A Hellish and dismal cloud of Sea-Coale' was so thick in the Palace of Whitehall that 'Men could hardly discern one another for the Clowd, and none could support, without manifest inconveniency' an 'impure and thick Mist, accompanied by a fuliginous and filthy vapour, which renders them obnoxious to a thousand inconveniences, corrupting the *lungs*, and disordering the entire habit of their Bodies,' from which cause '*Catharrs, Phthisicks, Coughs and consumptions* rage more in this one city, than in the whole Earth besides.'
>
> (John Evelyn *Diary*)

Coal had already taken the place of charcoal for making glass, brick and lime because wood was too dear. Then social attitudes caught up with expediency. Horace Walpole, who claimed that the best way to ensure summer in England was to have it 'framed and glazed in a comfortable room', by 1768 had come to the opinion that 'the best sun we have is made of Newcastle coal'. By then the output of coal from the mines exceeded a million tons a year. Coal had already begun to make the fortunes of a whole new entrepreneurial class. It was to release the energy, both human and fossil, that would cause the greatest change in human lifestyle since the beginning of agriculture, and create the first industrial world power. But before Great Britain could take her position as the workshop of the world a marriage had to take place – a bond between coal and iron.

OVERLEAF An early pithead steam engine is used to raise coal from two shafts in the Midlands.

Ever since iron transformed the bronze-age societies of Europe it had been indispensable to human survival. As iron forms about 5 per cent of the Earth's crust (the second most abundant metallic element after aluminium), it is in plentiful supply, though some ores are more easily smelted than others because of their chemistry. The problem for early iron-makers was not so much to find iron as to find the huge quantities of charcoal needed to smelt it from its ores. Already by the fifth century BC wood had to be brought to Attica by ship to smelt the silver and iron ores of Laurion.

The first European iron, such as the Greeks made on Elba, was extracted by the bloomery process, where iron ore is heated with carbon in the form of charcoal in a small furnace blown with bellows for many hours. Although such a furnace is not hot enough to melt the iron itself, it does melt the other components of the iron ore such as silica, which form a liquid slag with the ash at the bottom of the furnace. Once the furnace has cooled, a sponge-like lump of iron called a bloom can be lifted out of the open top. This bloom is heated repeatedly in a forge and hammered to expel most of the slag, welding the particles of iron together, first into a billet, and then into a bar of wrought iron. This very laborious process took a whole day to convert a bloom 20 centimetres in diameter to a small piece of usable metal, and 90 per cent of the iron was lost in the process.

Unlike copper and bronze, iron forms alloys with carbon, and the great secret of iron- and later steel-making was to control the amount of carbon allowed to mix with the iron. The major disadvantage of the first iron-making process was that it only made a few kilogrammes at a time. But as furnaces grew bigger, with taller chimneys 6 to 8 metres high, the charge of iron ore and charcoal could be deeper, and the ore was pre-heated by the hot gases rising through it. The carbon monoxide chemically reduced the iron oxides, and the iron absorbed more carbon. This had the unexpected consequence of reducing its melting point by as much as 400 degrees Celsius, and it trickled down to the bottom of the hearth. The major difference from the bloomery furnace was that the iron melted, and as the droplets of iron settled at the base of the furnace, limestone, which was used as a flux, also melted to form a slag. As limestone is lighter than the molten iron it floated on top, absorbing many of the impurities from the ore and fuel. When, twice a day, the furnace was tapped at its base, the slag would first be run off and then the metal. The molten iron flowed into a channel shaped in sand with secondary troughs leading off it, likened to a sow feeding its piglets, and, from a very early time, cast iron ingots came to be known as pig-iron.

Still blown by large bellows, these 'blast furnaces', as they came to be known, were apparently introduced to Europe from the Orient sometime in the thirteenth century. By the sixteenth century, equipped with water-driven bellows, they were in use in Britain, expanding from the Sussex Weald to the Midlands in 1561, and to the Lake District in 1711. Running continuously for six to eight months at a time they could produce as much as a ton of iron a day, and once lit and 'blown' they were usually only halted by a shortage of water to power the bellows in the summer months. Their introduction increased the consumption of charcoal enormously. (Such furnaces are still being used in the Carajas area of the Amazon in Brazil, and are having a catastrophic effect on the rainforest. European companies import the pig-iron they produce.)

Large items could now be cast in iron, but its use was limited because cast iron is crystalline as it solidifies or crystallises from a liquid form. It contains up to 5 per cent carbon, and is very brittle. Early cast iron also contained impurities such as sulphur, silicon, manganese and phosphorus, making it useless for tools.

Although adequate for fire-backs, cannon and cannon-balls, for most purposes it still had to be converted to wrought iron, which is both tougher and more resistant to corrosion. This could be done by reheating the cast iron in a hearth called a finery where it was blown with a jet of air. This oxidised some of the carbon and, as the melting point rose, reduced the molten metal to a pasty mass which could be removed in a lump and then smithed like a bloom.

As early as the thirteenth century, as the demand for nails, horse-shoes, wagon-wheel tyres and ploughshares increased, the strong-arm power of the blacksmith had been replaced by heavy trip-hammers driven by water-power. The blast furnaces were built near the sources of the heavy iron ore, but in England these forges clustered round supplies of water and charcoal such as the Worcestershire Stour, the south slopes of the Clee Hills in Shropshire, and the Weald. Hammer-ponds, which stored water for use in the summer, became a feature of the forest landscapes, especially in Sussex. Most forges have long since gone from the charcoal-burning areas, but a water-powered forge is still in working order at Finch's Foundry at Sticklepath, Devon. Here the River Taw provides the power to lift two tilt-hammers to shape agricultural implements on the anvils beneath. With simple water-powered machinery, eight men could make 400 hoes in a working day. Similar forges spread throughout Europe where there were adequate streams in hilly forested areas.

So greedy were the new blast furnaces for charcoal, that despite managing forests by coppicing – where the stump of a mature tree is allowed to grow saplings for some ten to fifteen years for the quick production of charcoal – much of Europe as far north as Scotland was deforested. In 1702, iron smelting even moved to Ireland following available timber, despite a relative lack of ore, and by the eighteenth century much of the pig-iron for Great Britain came from Sweden, Russia and even her American colonies, where trees and thus charcoal were more plentiful. The obvious solution was to use coal instead of charcoal for iron-making, but there was a major problem. When coal is formed, the action of bacteria also creates sulphur; with other impurities like phosphorus this makes iron too brittle.

A nation of shopkeepers

The Industrial Revolution can be described as the change from an economy that was mainly agricultural, to one based on large-scale manufacturing by labour-saving machines, and at first it was water-power that turned Britain into an industrial nation. In Britain it was also much more of an evolution than a revolution, and the agricultural worker, whose seasonal work left him unpaid free time, was at first essential to the process. By 1750, subsistence farming by peasants had almost disappeared, and the rural poor were paid farm labourers. One of the industries which could not have begun without them was cotton weaving, and the manufacture of this fibre, imported from the Middle East, the southern States of America and the West Indies, began the industrial age.

Cottage industry had started centuries before with the wool trade, and to reduce costs, merchant-manufacturers 'put-out' the raw material to cottage workers who were paid less than those in towns because they had a lower standard of living, and also had the free time to eke out that living with other employment. They were unencumbered by the restrictive practices of gilds and the whole family could assist in the work. Four women spinsters using the traditional spinning-wheels (which had reached Europe from China in the thirteenth century) were required to supply each weaver with yarn. So after the invention of the flying shuttle, which doubled the output of weavers, there was a bottle-neck in yarn supply. At the same time foreign markets were expanding and the increased demand could not be met, especially during harvest time when the women could earn more in the fields. The evolution of spinning machines (the spinning jenny in 1765 and water-powered spinning machines in 1771) and then the power loom followed. The later machines were too large and expensive for use in anything other than a specially constructed and equipped building with its own source of animal or water-power. The factory was born and cotton became the pace-maker of industrial change. As the industry expanded, prices fell, and more people could afford to buy cotton clothes – so the market increased, and more factories were built.

Another feature of industry was the increasing specialisation of work: the division of labour. As Adam Smith showed with the example of the pin-maker, one man on his own could not make twenty in a day, but with the aid of machines in a small manufactory he saw ten men make about twelve pounds weight, 'upwards of forty-eight thousand pins in a day'. When machines were used to make more machines, industrialisation began to spread like a disease. Light industries were widely dispersed; because the cotton industry required access to a major port, a damp climate, soft water and water-power, it developed in the Lancashire valleys. But the heavy industries based on iron and energy grew up on coal, and the map of the British Industrial Revolution is superimposed on the map of the coalfields, except for the north-east which exported much of its coal, and London which was still the biggest manufacturing city and which shipped in sea-coal.

In response to the rising road traffic in Britain, forty new roads a year were being built by private 'turnpike trusts'; not only to distribute agricultural produce, but the products of the mines and industry to towns, and via ports to the increasingly important overseas markets. Since Tudor times the key to English foreign policy had been to retain mastery of the waters that surround the British Isles. At first this had been solely for defence against invasion, which had meant building a strong navy. But, by the eighteenth century, that navy could also defend what had become the largest fleet of merchant ships in the world. Together they could exclude rival trading nations like the Dutch from foreign

Mule spinning.

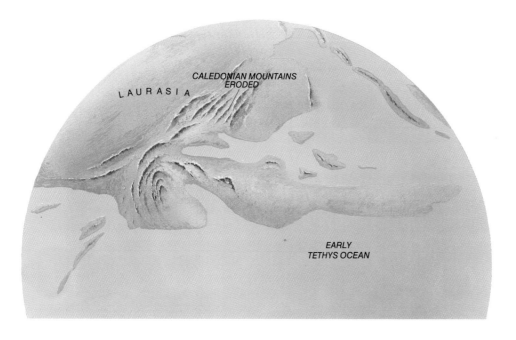

CALEDONIAN MOUNTAINS ERODED

LAURASIA

EARLY TETHYS OCEAN

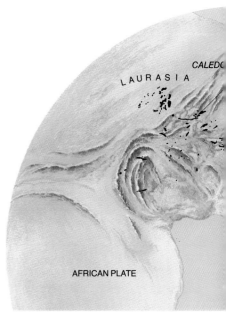

CALEDO

LAURASIA

AFRICAN PLATE

markets, and London thrived while Antwerp declined. British foreign trade developed during that century from being largely directed towards Europe to encompassing the whole world. Large fortunes were made by merchants from a commerce so conspicuously successful as to earn Napoleon's famous but ill-judged comment that England was but a nation of shopkeepers.

By their transactions those shopkeepers or merchants not only made London the financial capital of the world, but were to find the markets and raise the capital that led Great Britain to industrialise almost a century before France. By the mid-eighteenth century, London, which was a major industrial centre, had a population of three-quarters of a million – twice the size of Paris its nearest rival – and export industries had increased their output by three-quarters. They were to increase by another 80 per cent in the next twenty years, largely because of coal. The future development of Europe would no longer be ruled by the great Mesozoic resources of the agricultural basins, but by the coalfields that had formed in an earlier epoch.

The origins of coal

The coalfields of the northern hemisphere stretch in a great belt from beneath the valley of the Don in the Soviet Union through Silesia, the Ruhr, Lorraine, the Pas de Calais, Kent, the north of England and south Wales, to re-emerge on the other side of the Atlantic rift in Pennsylvania and West Virginia. This is because the Atlantic Ocean opened long after the coalfields were laid down. At the beginning of the coal-forming Carboniferous period, some 310 million years ago, England lay on the Equator and a warm shallow sea deposited limestone between France and southern Scotland. Slowly this sea filled up with sediments eroded off the mountains, until much of Europe and eastern North America were covered by vast tropical swamps and mudflats crossed by meandering streams almost at sea level, much like the Achafalaya swamps of Louisiana today.

It is known from the fossils found in coal that the vegetation was very different from that of today. The swampy river deltas were covered with large trees, 50 metres high, which were not trees as we know them but club-mosses. Despite their size they had a short life-span and when they fell they formed thick peat

The formation of Europe's coalfields (shown in black) in the swamps at the foot of the Hercynian mountains.

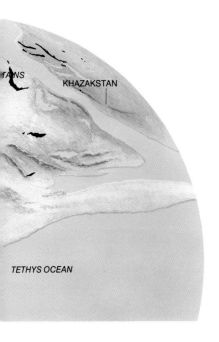

deposits. Around open water grew giant horse-tails, while the banks of the rivers supported both tree-ferns and smaller herbaceous ferns. Seed-bearing trees related to conifers lived on the higher ground, while the swamps themselves were the home for amphibians and the first reptiles. There too, insects were evolving rapidly, with giant dragonflies, and a multitude of scorpions.

In those steaming forests, plants were storing the energy of the tropical sun by the process of photosynthesis, converting carbon dioxide from the atmosphere into living plant matter and oxygen. When the trees and plants died their carbon remained in the peat. It takes 100 metres of peat to form a 10-metre coal seam, so not only does the peat have to form faster than it rots (this is helped by the acidity of the water which slows bacterial action), but to build up a thick layer, the swamp itself has to be slowly sinking over a long period because of the subsidence of the earth's crust beneath. This slow subsidence, which allowed the layers of peat to build up, began as one of the three great mountain ranges that give Europe its great geological diversity was formed, thrust up by the collision of continents. Some 280 million years ago, Africa crunched into a united Europe and America to form a range known as the Hercynian or Variscan mountains (named by geologists after localities in Germany). These were once as high as the Himalayas.

The subsidence happened in two different ways. At first the continental plate stretched, allowing land to drop down between parallel faults to form grabens (like the Rhine graben of today); as the land sank, very thick seams of coal were deposited. Then other swamps formed on the sinking continental edge. The rocks of these later coal measures show a cyclical process; from time to time the sea invaded the swamps, drowning the coal forest and forming shales, before river deltas, carrying sand eroded from mountains to the south, again silted up the sea to form sandstones and a base for the next layer of delta mudstones and then more swamp and thus coal. Each cycle of strata may be about 15 metres thick, but the total thickness of what are known as the coal measures can reach 2000 metres, as it does in north Staffordshire.

It is when the peat is buried and compressed, and the water is driven out, that coal is formed. The deeper the burial, the higher the quality or calorific value of the coal. It varies from the comparatively young soft brown lignite, found in Germany and recently in Northern Ireland, which is 70 per cent water, and in which the tree-trunks of Sequoias have still not been fossilised, to rock-hard black anthracite from the deep mines of South Wales which is 98 per cent carbon. The folding and faulting, caused by the continental collision between Africa and Europe which raised the Alps, then buried and split the coal formations, pushing some of them deep underground and raising others to be eroded away completely, so that the minable coalfields were scattered over a wide area, at greatly differing depths. Some were later re-buried by the sediments of the Jurassic seas, like those of Kent, and some have only recently been discovered, like the vast coalfield which lies beneath Oxford.

The other resource on which the Industrial Revolution was founded was iron, and a curious combination of chemistry and geology led to the happy coincidence of ironstone being found in all the major British coalfields. Siderite (iron carbonate) is the principal constituent of ironstone, and it is found as nodules in the mudstones, and especially in what is known as the seat-earth immediately underneath coal seams, on which the swamp forest originally grew. No one is quite sure how the ironstones got there. Iron is a major component of the Earth's core, and it is assumed that iron from mountains was eroded into the rivers which saturated the coal basins and precipitated out within the sediments. It could then rise and be concentrated as the sediments were compacted and the water driven out. Possibly the coal lying underneath released carbon dioxide to produce the carbonate. Normally only a few centimetres in diameter, the nodules can at times weigh as much as several hundred kilogrammes. Siderite also forms bands and tabular masses in the mudstones up to 2 metres thick. These nodules and tabular ironstones were mined from the Carboniferous layers as early as the twelfth century.

The industrial landscape

As another part of the process building the Hercynian mountains, huge plumes of magma pushed upwards through the European continental crust to solidify as dome-like granite 'batholiths' in the core of the mountain range, causing metals like gold, silver, lead, tin and copper to distil upwards into veins where they could later be mined. Now all that remains of the massive Hercynian range are outcrops of these hard granitic rocks, some of which were already well known in the Bronze Age as the source of tin, stretching from Brittany to the Caucasus.

These uplands with their hard rock and acidic soils had an influence not just on their vegetation but even their human culture. Isolated from the mainstream of life on the corn-growing lowlands they became islands of independent thought and religious fundamentalism. Lacking the warmth for vines or the soil for plentiful cereals for brewing, their pastoral inhabitants distilled strong liquors and regaled their distant neighbours with bagpipes made from the skins of the sheep they bred. These regions had always had an importance for mining but now entrepreneurial investment was moving away from agriculture into industry and the Hercynian uplands were to come to a new importance as new resources came to be used.

In Britain at least, the lack of war made defensible sites for towns unnecessary, so valleys in the marginal, infertile regions had begun to attract industry and settlement in the seventeenth and eighteenth centuries. From the 1750s, coal, above all, was the magnet, and the reason for using coal was, of course, that it was cheaper than charcoal. But coal was so heavy and expensive to transport overland that it doubled in price 15 kilometres from the pithead. So it either had to be burnt near the mine, or be carried by water.

Using coal to smelt iron was not a straightforward process. In 1621 Lord Dudley discovered that many of the impurities, including the sulphur which made iron brittle, could be driven off by heating coal first in a reducing atmosphere to form coke, but almost a century passed before the technique was applied to smelt ironstone. However, coke was used in maltings, where the sulphur in coal spoilt the flavour of the brew. Early in the eighteenth century a malter's apprentice, Abraham Darby, learned that trade before setting up his own brass-wire business in Bristol. He was an enterprising young man and travelled to the Netherlands to investigate Dutch methods of brass working. In 1707 he took out a patent for casting iron pots in sand. Seeking to expand his casting business, he chose Coalbrookdale in Shropshire as the site for his foundry. It was on the Severn river, which was by then perhaps the busiest river in Europe after the Meuse. It was linked by coastal shipping and overland transport to a large area from South Wales through Cheshire and Lancashire to the Lake District, which had made the East Shropshire coalfield one of the most productive in Britain.

Coalbrookdale was already a centre of iron-making, and in 1709 Darby bought the ruins of an earlier blast furnace which had been wrecked by a flood. By now the scarcity of charcoal was seriously holding back iron production. The crucial

difference at Coalbrookdale was that Darby began to fire his furnace with 'coal coak'd into Cynder, as is done for drying malt' rather than charcoal. By good fortune, Coalbrookdale had a variety of coal particularly suited to coke-making. It was very similar to charcoal, and had the added benefit that it was much stronger, so a greater weight of ironstone could be charged into the furnace without the fire collapsing. This meant that a greater quantity of iron could be smelted at a time and larger objects could be made. Other natural advantages were local good-quality ironstones, and limestone which was required as a flux. Darby's business boomed, making cast-iron pots, kitchen utensils and grates for the local market, but the coke-smelted iron still had contaminants like phosphorus which made it too brittle to be of use to make wrought iron. This problem had to be overcome, as the major demand was for wrought iron not cast, but Darby never solved it.

He died in 1717 when his son, also called Abraham, was only six. The younger Darby was almost excluded from his share of the business but by the age of

The Coalbrookdale works, with coke-making by the River Severn and a team of six horses hauling away a newly cast cylinder for a Newcomen engine.

twenty-one he had become assistant to the manager. There is a story, but there is no evidence, that after six days and nights without sleep beside the furnace, he finally discovered the secret of casting coke-blast iron fit for forging. He then secretly sent a quantity to one of the many forges in the area without revealing its origin. When it was accepted as being good quality the whole industry began a slow but momentous change. It was nothing less than the start of a new iron age. The effect on the location of the blast furnaces and thus the iron industry was slow but dramatic. Major centres, like the Weald, the Forest of Dean and Furness, began to decline rapidly until today scarcely any evidence of their industrial past remains. Instead other regions with coalfields, which had been wild countryside, like the valleys of South Wales, became booming industrial centres as English businessmen began to exploit the local coal to smelt iron; building new towns like Merthyr Tydfil and Blaenavon.

The power of steam

Each new discovery hastened the development of further industrial processes, and although by modern standards the pace of innovation was leisurely, an ever-faster chain reaction of invention and application began to shape a new industrial society. This whole new world of machines depended on coal and iron, and both depended on mining; so it was hardly surprising that many important innovations were first made in the mines to make them more efficient, and most important of all, deeper. The greatest difficulty with deep mines was to keep them pumped dry. Water had always been a problem, and since at least Roman times, elaborate systems such as cascades of water-wheels driven by slaves and chains of buckets worked by windlasses were used to pump them out. The deeper the mine the harder the work to lift the water, and coal-mines, because of the size of the excavations, were particularly prone to flooding. In one colliery 500 horses were said to be used for pumping alone. Necessity again became the mother of invention, and gave birth to the machine that more than any other was to transform industry and human lives – the steam engine.

It was a Devon blacksmith, Thomas Newcomen, who developed a practicable machine, first put to work in 1712, to replace horsepower for pumping out mines. In this first atmospheric engine, a cylinder contained a piston coupled by chains to one end of a massive beam, pivoted in the centre, with the other end chained to rods which worked the pumps. Water was boiled in a copper boiler to make steam at little more than atmospheric pressure and was allowed to pass through a pipe and valve system into the cylinder as the weight of the pump-rods lifted the piston. A spray of cold water was then injected into the cylinder to condense the steam, and the partial vacuum this caused allowed atmospheric pressure to force the piston down again, raising the pump-rods. (It was thus atmospheric pressure not steam pressure which did the work.) This ponderous, simple and extremely reliable monster was an outstanding commercial success, but its true significance was that it had converted the energy of coal into mechanical work. For the first time since the water-mill and windmill were invented, mankind had a new source of mechanical energy.

Soon the Coalbrookdale Company was making most of the parts for Newcomen engines out of cast-iron, even the large cylinders, which were up to 3 metres long and nearly 2 metres in diameter. Miners were able to dig deeper to satisfy the rapidly increasing demand for coal and iron, and by 1769 there were 57 such pumping engines in use in the Newcastle coalfield alone. They were so successful that they were still in use in the nineteenth century.

KING COAL · 191

The ENGINE for Raising Water (with a power made) by Fire

Nevertheless these primitive atmospheric pumps were barely able to control the dangers of flooding and the consequences could be horrific. This was vividly shown in 1815 at the Heaton Colliery when water broke in from a neighbouring disused pit trapping seventy-five men and boys underground. The pumps available were so inadequate that it took nine months to clear the water, and when the miners were finally reached it was found that they had eaten their horses, their candles and even the bark from the fir pit-props before dying. One man had only been dead a short time.

There was one major problem. Even improved Newcomen engines had a thermal efficiency of only one per cent – in other words only one per cent of the energy stored in the coal was converted into mechanical energy. It is not surprising that the engines were mostly confined to coal-mines where there was an abundant supply of unsaleable small coal so that the quantity used was unimportant. And it is also not surprising that Abraham Darby II's blast furnaces were still powered by water-wheels, and in 1812 water-wheels were still being installed to drain Blaenavon colliery.

In 1763, James Watt, who was employed as an instrument maker at Glasgow University, was given a model Newcomen engine to repair, and he realised that the main reason for its inefficiency was that the cylinder had to be heated by the incoming steam and then cooled by the water spray, for every stroke of the piston. He saw that, ideally, the cylinder should be kept as hot as the steam all the time. He also realised that if the steam could be connected at the right moment to a cold chamber where it could condense, this could be achieved. His invention of a separate condenser cut coal consumption by 75 per cent. In Cornwall, where coal was expensive, the pumping engines were rapidly replaced by his new design, manufactured by a Birmingham industrialist, Matthew Boulton.

Early steam engines had an output of about 20 horsepower, well within the range of the power available from water-wheels, but their advantages were that they did not have to be used near a water-supply and were unaffected by both frost and drought which frequently brought mining and blast furnaces to a halt. At first the adoption of steam-power was slow but when the up-and-down motion of the Newcomen piston was successfully converted into rotary motion, again by Watt, steam was able to drive the wheels of industry. So the Boulton and Watt 'rotative' engine enabled industry to move away from the streams of the hills into the towns. This began another huge geographical shift of population, because when steam moved industry into the towns it took much of the rural population with it. It is hard to over-estimate the importance of the application of steam to the growth of European society. Even nuclear power-stations use steam-power to drive the turbines that generate the electricity for the European grid, and it was the harnessing of coal energy through steam which was to transform manufacturing and the world.

At the start of the eighteenth century, towns reflected their origins as markets for agricultural produce and were still scattered over the lowlands of England, but in the next fifty years new towns based on water power grew rapidly in Lancashire, Yorkshire and the West Midlands, with St Helens, Burnley and Bradford growing at over 10 per cent a year. In the second half of the century it was the turn of the towns based on coal and heavy industry, in south Wales, north-east England and the west of Scotland, such as Cardiff, Mountain Ash, Middlesbrough, Jarrow and Clydebank. By the end of the eighteenth century, over a third of the rotative engines were in use in the textile industry and most of these were involved in the cotton mills. The sites where Boulton and Watt engines were installed reflect very accurately the location of centres of industrial development, and are still recognisable as the industrial areas of today. The effect of mechanisation on production was startling; in the 1760s English cotton exports were worth an average of £200,000 a year, by 1829 they were worth over £37 million, and Manchester had increased in size ten-fold, with 'hundreds of five and six storied factories, each with a towering chimney at its side which exhales black coal vapour' . . . William Blake's 'dark satanic mills'.

One of the characteristics of the British Industrial Revolution was that it was a regional phenomenon, which developed on a small scale, with limited amounts of capital, in widely separated parts of Britain. Heavy minerals were usually exploited locally because they were too expensive to move, and the local wealth they created encouraged regional independence of a kind that was impossible with the centralised bureaucracy of the other great European power, post-revolutionary France. This was reflected in the rapid rise of Manchester – which looked for its interests not to London and Europe but across the Atlantic. This self-sufficiency and internationalism gave the region an exposure to independent thought and ideas, which were able to take root in a new increasingly wealthy middle class. It was to have a powerful effect on a developing English north-south cultural divide between the conservatism of the traditional ruling class, born from a hierarchical agricultural order and unwilling to abandon the social and religious values of the past, and a new pragmatism based on the individualism and wealth of the cotton mill-owners, and ultimately on coal. This was to bring a robust liberal influence to bear on British politics.

The transport revolution

It was one thing to move the steam engines to the towns but it was another to keep them supplied with heavy coal. Because Britain is an island with a greatly indented coastline, no mine could be further than 112 kilometres from the sea and water carriage cost only half as much as road transport. So there was a strong motive to build canals. Already by 1750 river improvement schemes had given Britain some 2200 kilometres of navigable rivers. A decade later coal brought the canal age to England when the 3rd Duke of Bridgewater had a canal constructed from his coalmines at Worsley to Manchester. By 1830, after a halt caused by the collapse of trade during the American War of Independence, a further 4000 miles of water routes had been provided by canals. They were privately financed and were dug by shovel and wheel-barrow with the assistance of only the most basic machines. Considering that many canals took ten years to complete (the Leeds & Liverpool took 46 years) it is remarkable that local businessmen and landowners were able to raise the very large sums of capital required. But the colliery or pottery owner had much to gain, and by 1830, £20 million had been invested in waterways, at a time when the average labourer in the Midlands earned less than £20 a year.

At first they were short cuts between mines and rivers, then they were built to overcome local needs like that for coal to evaporate water in the Mersey salt-refineries. Others completed links between extensive river systems. Their importance was enormous, as, for the first time, with locks and aqueducts, water transport could defy topography and penetrate to the mineral riches of the hills. By 1790, the Mersey, Trent, Humber, Thames and Severn were linked in a great network across the centre of England, thus distributing the raw materials of industry and unifying the market that was so essential to industrial growth. But there was still a great divide – the northern canals from the Mersey to the Humber were broad, while those linking this system to the south through the great industrial hub of Birmingham were narrow. To send goods south meant reloading into narrow barges, and in practice this was less attractive than shipping overseas – a further encouragement to develop exports.

The promotion of new canal companies became a national mania and some were spectacularly successful; the Loughborough Navigation returned an average dividend of 154 per cent in the late 1820s, the Oxford canal paid 30 per cent for 30 years. The ones that prospered were always those that carried coal to supply the insatiable demand of the growing towns. A packhorse in the eighteenth century carried a load of about one-eighth of a ton, a horse on a surfaced road could pull two tons and by canal barge 50 tons. The investment in canals had increased the return of both horsepower and manpower enormously, and for the first time heavy industries could develop away from natural waterways. But goods haulage still moved at walking-pace.

Heavily laden mineral wagons did so much damage to roads that wooden railways had been used in the coalfields of Newcastle and Staffordshire from the early eighteenth century to link mines to waterways. In 1794, the Glamorgan Canal was opened to carry pig-iron from Merthyr to Cardiff. But a shortage of water and disputes led to the construction of a cast-iron tramroad 15 kilometres long from the foundries to Abercynon. Along it a single horse could pull a load of ten tons of iron, five times as much as by road, and bypass the contentious stretch

The opening of the Stockton and Darlington Railway.

of the canal. In 1728 the first iron railway wheels were cast at Coalbrookdale, but it was the combination of iron, steam and a wager that brought the first steam locomotive to the Merthyr line, and a Cornish genius was behind it.

Richard Trevithick had grown up around the mines of Camborne, where his father was a manager or 'captain'. These mines were winning metals formed around the granite masses of the heart of the ancient Hercynian mountains. They were far from the coalfields, and coal had first to be shipped and then carried overland to the pumping engines. The efficiency of the engines, in terms of the amount of water pumped per ton of coal, could make the difference between a mine paying and being closed. Having a great aptitude for practical engineering, Trevithick was soon busy trying to invent ways of making Watt's engines more efficient. The other greatest use for energy in the mines was in winding spoil and ore up the shaft – from ever greater depths. And while a well-designed mine could be pumped dry from one shaft, winding was frequently moved from one shaft to another. The immensely heavy Newcomen and Watt engines, with their huge beams of wood or cast-iron, were quite unsuited to being moved, so winding was often still done by horses. In his search for more power from a lighter engine, Trevithick designed an engine which operated at the unheard-of steam pressure of 1.7 atmospheres.

At that time, the steam for beam engines was raised at little more than the pressure at which it comes out of the spout of a kettle, and some boilers in Cornwall were even built as chambers made out of blocks of granite. When Trevithick directed the exhaust steam (which puffed from the piston at the end of the stroke) up the chimney, he discovered that it improved the draught through the furnace. This made the fire hotter and thus increased the amount of steam raised. These were two of the most important modifications ever made to the steam engine, and revolutionised its design, making the idea of an engine which propelled itself a practical possibility. It was believed at the time that there was not sufficient friction between a wheel and the ground or a rail to move a vehicle by driving the wheels, but Trevithick, who was an exceptionally strong man, experimented with a one-horse chaise, propelling it up hills by turning the wheels.

Railways *circa* 1840
Coalfields

On Christmas Eve 1801 he put this knowledge to the test. His first locomotive, the 'Puffing Devil', as the locals called it, made a number of successful journeys carrying seven or eight people uphill in the Camborne area, before burning itself up in a fire four days later. The very first steam-powered road carriage was actually built in Paris by Nicolas Joseph Cugnot in 1769, but it was of unstable design with a boiler overhanging the front wheel, and it ran into a wall. His second larger one, built soon afterwards, overturned on a street corner, and both vehicle and inventor were imprisoned as a potential danger to the public.

After unsuccessful attempts to raise interest and finance for his invention in London, with a steam carriage which he drove up and down Oxford Street – terrifying the horses pulling other vehicles, Trevithick decided to take advantage of the booming iron industry of South Wales. Joining forces with the ironmaster of Penydarren, he built a new engine, and in 1804 his Penydarren locomotive successfully pulled ten tons of iron and seventy men the 15 kilometres from the foundry to Abercynon on the Glamorgan canal. This won a wager of 500 guineas (then an immense sum) from the canal-owner who had claimed it to be an

British coalfields and railways *circa* 1840.

impossible feat. But the engine weighed 5 tons, and its unsprung weight fractured the short cast-iron 'plates' used as rails which were only designed to carry 2 tons. So the locomotive, despite its success, was put to work driving a tilt-hammer. Although he exhibited an improved engine running on rails in London, the 'Catch me who can' in 1808, Trevithick failed to arouse public interest in his idea of displacing horsepower.

The same need to move heavy materials, on this occasion coal for export, from mines at Bishop Auckland via Darlington to the mouth of the Tees at Stockton, gave birth to the first commercially viable railway, 50 kilometres long, in 1825, and indirectly to the new town of Middlesbrough. Wrought-iron rails had overcome the problems of the Penydarren plate-way and it was soon able to turn in a dividend of 15 per cent. The locomotives, designed by George Stephenson, were aided by stationary winding-engines on the hills, and still shared the same railway line with horse-drawn traffic. In fact it was open to all who would pay a toll like a turnpike or a canal. But the fact that a railway could be profitable soon led to the building of the Liverpool and Manchester Railway, opened five years later. This was to link the cotton factories to the sea and to break the monopoly tolls of the canal, built earlier for the same reason. With the young Robert Stephenson's 'Rocket' engine incorporating the new invention of a fire-tube boiler (which raised steam more quickly because the hot gases from the furnace passed through the water down many tubes) it became a completely unexpected success, carrying passengers as well as the expected freight at the inconceivable speed of 48 kilometres an hour.

Large sums of capital had been accumulated through the success of British trade and industry, which were in need of profitable investment, and two 'manias' of railway and building followed, from 1835 to 1837 and from 1845 to 1847. This explosion of interest was generated not so much by demand, as by the enthusiasm of the stock exchange. Nevertheless, by 1850, nearly 10,000 kilometres of track had been laid. This gigantic web, stretching across the nation, was to link even the remotest regions to the capital and to the products of industry. Britain was transformed, and the public perception of what was possible was changed more than at any time since the invention of the wheel.

One small flavour of this change is that before the need for a common time-table for trains on the Great Western Railway, the clocks in Bristol had been set to the correct solar time – fifteen minutes later than those in London. Now time was not only unified, it was transformed by the speed and comfort of railway travel. Technical innovation rapidly followed and by 1850 the railways had reached a standard of speed and performance not seriously challenged for another century.

It was not only on land that coal and steam revolutionised transport. In 1838 the famous contest to cross the Atlantic under steam-power resulted in the little *Sirius* from the port of London arriving in New York only hours ahead of Brunel's *Great Western*. And the union of steamship and railway produced a further acceleration in trade (British exports expanded at 7.3 per cent a year between 1845 and 1855, faster than they ever have since). By the time of the Great Exhibition in 1851, held in the Crystal Palace – itself a magnificent example of innovative architecture in cast iron and glass – Britain was producing over 40 per cent of the entire world output of traded manufactured goods.

This astonishing domination of world trade, never to be achieved by any other country before or since, was promoted by an outward spiral of supply and demand based on coal, iron and steam. At its peak the construction of the railways themselves used up about 40 per cent of the country's production of iron,

and enormous quantities of coal. By consuming this the railways made it possible to move iron and coal and manufactured products into ever greater markets at ever cheaper prices with ever greater speed.

While new industrial areas grew alongside the railway-lines, London, now easily and rapidly accessible, was able to suck trade and finance out of the provinces, and once more reasserted its political and financial supremacy. Perishable food items no longer had to be produced within the radius of a few kilometres that horse-drawn vehicles could manage in a day, and the city could begin a rapid encroachment on the countryside. Its population swelled to 4.7 million by the end of the century. Thriving on the commanding supremacy of British, and mostly English trade, the British Empire expanded until London was capital to a third of the world.

Machinery displayed in the Great Exhibition in Hyde Park, London, in 1851.

The material advance of the eighteenth century had been bought at dreadful cost: of enclosures of common land, the destitution of skilled craftsmen whose jobs had been mechanised, the institutionalised labour of children in mines and mills from the age of five, the desperate poverty which followed unemployment when the factories could not sell their products and the appalling conditions in the huge slums of Manchester and London. However, conditions had already been harsh in the countryside, and on balance, by the end of the century, the greatly increased population was better clothed, better fed and longer-lived than their forebears, and coal had been the cause. But instead of living lives tied to the soil and the rhythm of the seasons, with their fate at the mercy of weather and harvest, the majority of the population now took the rhythm of their lives from the crankshaft and the iron wheel.

CHAPTER TEN

POWER
AND FRONTIERS

Resources alone have never been sufficient to transform a society, but there is no doubt that coal set in motion the astonishing change that swept across Britain in just a few generations from the mid-eighteenth century to make England the most powerful country in Europe. Why then did the same revolution not occur in France and Germany, where the same resource was available? The answer, of course, is that it did but it began almost fifty years later. Manufacturing spread across Europe like a flame, igniting the coalfields one after another, and from them drew both physical and economic power. But no other coalfields set industry in motion spontaneously on the scale that had occurred in England. The sparks had first to cross the Channel. Britain now had an unchallengeable lead in the manufacture of heavy machinery and manufactured goods, and continued to press its commercial and technical advantage, not only with exports, but through its expatriate ironmasters and engineers.

Just as the progress of art and science depends on the extraordinary talent of individual human beings, so the story of the development of the coal resources of Europe is, to a remarkable extent, the story of individual British entrepreneurs. Skilled in the ways of coal and iron and steam, they exploited the opportunities that local communities either did not recognise, did not know how to develop or could not afford to. The Greeks had transported their civilisation around the shores of the Mediterranean through trade and settlement, bestowing their accomplishments in pottery, architecture and bronze, as well as their language and religion; so now the British were to carry the gospel of steam from Gibraltar to the Urals. It is an extraordinary fact that there was not one major industry in any of the greater European powers that was not set in motion by British pioneers, engineers, iron and steel masters, machine builders, skilled craftsmen or providers of capital. They promoted what was to become a world system of industry based on the British model.

In 1800 Britain mined five times as much coal as the rest of Europe put together, and by mid-century Britain still smelted ten times as much iron as Germany, and five times as much as America. While British exhibits at the Great Exhibition in 1851 were the products of machines and factories to be sold to the masses, the French exhibited high-quality luxury goods: silks from Lyons, Sèvres porcelain, Gobelins tapestries and Aubusson carpets. The English merchants scoffed that 'the Frenchmen work for the few, but we for the millions'. While the famous French banker Rothschild said, 'There are three ways of losing your money . . . women, gambling and engineers. The first two are pleasanter, but the last is much the most certain.'

Britain's old rival, France, had a larger labour force, a bigger potential market, and flourishing overseas trade, but both France and Germany had been exhausted by long wars in the eighteenth century. Well before the French Revolution, skilled English workers were being recruited by agents to work in France, for example in the watch-making industry where accurate chronometers were needed for navigation. English expertise flowed across the Channel in such quantities that it led to a ban on recruiting 'artificers or manufacturers' to work abroad, for fear of the loss of secret processes. But young men cared little for such laws. One prominent example was John Holker, a Catholic and a Jacobite, who had served as a lieutenant in the Young Pretender's army. He was captured but escaped to France, cheating the gallows to become the architect of the modernisation of the French cotton industry. He even returned secretly to England for three months and smuggled out both English machinery and craftsmen to work at the royal textile factory at Saint Sever, Rouen.

The French State was in favour of increasing industry, but the conservatism of the *ancien régime* stifled initiative. There were also practical impediments to change. In France the abundance and thus cheapness of timber and labour meant that there was less pressure to replace charcoal with coal for iron-making. Although the internal tariffs which had hampered trade had at last been abolished in 1790, cotton import tariffs were still high in 1835, and most important of all was the high price of coal. Paris was still suffering from its poor access to heavy goods, and coal, which came from Mons, cost ten times as much as it did in Manchester and London.

Although scornful, the French nevertheless viewed Britain's increasing industrial supremacy with dismay. In particular by the mid-1770s the French military were becoming concerned at the superior quality of British iron-making. Many of the early ironmasters, including Abraham Darby, were Quakers or dissenters who refused to be involved in the manufacture of arms. But William Wilkinson, an iron-founder, already sold cannon to the French under the guise of drainpipes (an interesting parallel with the attempted export in 1990 of components for Iraq's 'super-gun' under the same disguise). Following a tour of inspection of English ironworks by a French ironmaster, he was invited to set up a naval cannon foundry on the island of Indret in the River Loire. By 1779 the first cannon were cast and bored in his new water-powered works but there was an acute shortage of pig-iron. Wilkinson was offered the immense salary of 60,000 livres to set up blast furnaces, which he built at Le Creusot, on the proposed Canal du Centre between the Loire and the Saône, where coal and iron occurred together, just as they had at Coalbrookdale. There the first coke-fired furnace on the continent was successfully blown in 1785, a good 40 years after Darby's. France was by then supporting the Americans in their War of Independence and the fire-power of their navy was in no small part due to British ironmasters.

The last round of a century of rivalry between Britain and France commenced with the coup d'état of 1799 which began the dictatorship of Napoleon Bonaparte. Bringing warfare and upheaval to every corner of continental Europe, he won for France a huge territory stretching from the Pyrenees to Denmark, and from Catalonia to Rome. Only Nelson's great victories at the sea battles of

Aboukir, the Nile and Trafalgar confined him to the mainland of Europe. In an attempt to vanquish British power by destroying her trade, Napoleon forbade all commerce with Britain, stifling Hamburg, Bremen and the other North Sea ports, while Britain in turn blockaded the French coast from Brest to the Baltic. But despite the recession this caused, the effect was to stimulate Britain to develop other trade outlets, such as Brazil and Argentina, while the protection offered to French goods at home discouraged competition and development in her own industries. After Napoleon's disastrous march on Moscow ended with his greatest army being destroyed in the snow, the Anglo-Belgian and Prussian forces ended 20 years of war at Waterloo in 1815. A flood of cheap British imports could now enter Europe.

Even the convulsions of the Napoleonic Wars had been unable to stop the spread of industrialisation. As in Britain, it was the marginal, infertile areas away from the rich agricultural basins which industrialised first, and there is an interesting contrast between the experience of what is now Belgium and the Netherlands. The Dutch failed to industrialise, despite their long tradition of textiles, trade and wealth from their rich agriculture, born on the delta soils of the Rhine, while their neighbour, poorer in both soils and incomes, did make the change. It was along the valleys of the Sambre and the Meuse, where coal and iron occurred close together, that Belgian industry developed and the British were behind it. In fact as the countries of the continent first followed and finally transcended Britain's example, they followed an extraordinarily similar sequence of events. Identical machines were imported from Britain, or built to British designs, often from stolen plans: the same spinning mules, furnaces and steam engines set the wheels of industry turning. Local businessmen were quick to seize the new

Le Creusot ironworks in 1865.

opportunities and with the advantages of coming later to the field, costly mistakes and delays could be avoided; inventions could be applied in a more logical order and with the precedent of British profits, investment could be more easily secured. Because the system was imported complete by entrepreneurs and financiers rather than inventors of new technology, it could proceed so rapidly that it could indeed be called a revolution, but it always required precisely the same natural resources of water-power, coal and iron.

Coal and the Cockerills

Napoleon had set his frontier at the logical limit of the Rhine, but frontiers, mere accidents of history, were to be largely irrelevant to this rapid encroachment of a new industrial society on the old. Its distribution depended on the geological past of Europe and its progress owed nothing to the social imperatives of the past. As the new way of life approached it was viewed by conservative landed interests as dangerous and revolutionary. But they were powerless against the energy released from coal. Tariff barriers on trade and traffic might delay it, but nothing could halt the spread of the conflagration.

The long, narrow coalfield of the Sambre-Meuse valley runs roughly east-west, and it was there, to the banks of a busy river, that the whole grimy panoply of British industrialisation was most easily and quickly transported. There the same key industries of wool and cotton again fostered the growth of ironworks, coalmines and factories to make machines that made machines. As mines were driven deeper, the first Newcomen pumping engine had been installed there as early as 1720, before most British mines had acquired one.

One family, perhaps more than any other, was to propel the eastern, shallower end of this coalfield, in what is now Belgium, into being the centre of an ever-widening region of industrialisation, the first and most influential of continental Europe. The fact that they were English, working in an area ruled by France, when the two countries were at war, shows how little nationalism had to do with industrial commerce. William Cockerill had been recruited to modernise the biggest woollen factory in Verviers which had been badly affected by two French invasions. His son, James, was smuggled back to England in 1802 to buy machinery and recruit skilled workers, but he was arrested at Hull as a spy, and imprisoned in York Castle. He managed to escape, and helped his father to mechanise and develop the industry of Verviers with such success that by 1810 it possessed 86 manufacturers employing 25,000 workers.

Nearby at Liège there had been a tradition of iron-making by the bloomery process, which had made it the centre of an armaments industry, and there the Cockerills began to manufacture their cloth-making machinery. They also expanded westwards to the centre of the French textile industry, setting up another factory at Rheims; while the younger son, John, built a woollen textile factory in Berlin, as well as a large works for making steam-driven textile machinery. But the collapse of Napoleon's empire meant that what is now Belgium and Holland ceased to be a part of France, and were joined to form the United Netherlands, ruled by King William of Orange. The post-war decline of the woollen industry encouraged the younger brothers, John and James, to diversify. They concentrated on manufacturing steam engines (importing a Boulton and Watt engine to copy), pumps and hydraulic presses in their factory at Liège.

William I had returned to Belgium from exile in England burning with zeal to emulate English industry in his new kingdom, and when John Cockerill went to have an audience with him in 1816, the King sold him his castle and estate at

Seraing – for a tenth of its true value. It was an ideal location, near Cockerill's existing factory at Liège, right on top of a coalfield, close to supplies of limestone, and by the River Meuse which offered transport. There the Cockerill family built the finest ironworks in the Low Countries, with five furnaces and machine-building shops. They also began to build steamships, and in the same year found time to advise the Tsar on the modernisation of Warsaw's woollen mills.

By 1823 Britain had 250 coke-fired blast furnaces but Belgium none, so John Cockerill was able to persuade the Belgian government to give him a large loan to fund a coke furnace with rolling and slitting mills driven by three steam engines. It was a sign of the priorities of the day that the loan was to be repaid, not in gold or silver, but in bars of iron. Next, John Cockerill purchased the neighbouring coalfields, which meant that new shafts could be sunk in the grounds of the ironworks themselves. The company soon formed the largest and most modern integrated iron-making and manufacturing enterprise in Europe. Industrialisation was now sweeping Belgium so fast that despite its success the company still could not supply machinery fast enough to keep up with orders. John Cockerill went back to the King, who promptly lent him a million florins and became a partner in the business. 'Carry on with all your great enterprises,' he said, 'and remember that the King of the Netherlands always has funds to spare in the service of Industry.' By 1830, 2500 men were employed in the Seraing works, and the weekly wages bill was almost twice the figure Cockerill had originally paid for the castle.

The family exploited many new British inventions, rapidly copying them, and as they travelled abroad they took with them an almost missionary faith in the new industrial order, with plans 'to fill the whole world with machinery'. Meanwhile their personal empire in the world of machines grew to an astonishing size. Besides the wool factories at Verviers and flax spinning at Liège, they made printed calicoes at Andenne, and manufactured textile cards and spindles at Spa. James and William had their woollen mills in Berlin, and family businesses in Guben and Grünberg, a cotton factory at Cottbus, and a zinc mine near Aachen. In Poland the Cockerills had a cloth factory, in Spain a cotton mill, and in Surinam a sugar-plantation and steam-driven sugar factory, besides owning shares in a Rotterdam steamboat company, French blast furnaces and coalmines.

Above all, it was John who drove the company forward. In 1835, a visitor to Seraing caught both the mood and the significance of this remarkable man's enterprise:

> John Cockerill travels on the great highways in his coach. Here he builds furnaces and there chimney stacks. He covers fields with his tents, and then when all his preparations have been made he erects the steam-engines which breathe life into the great piles of bricks. And the next day the peasants hear a loud rhythmical noise coming from the factory – like the breathing of some enormous monster who, once he has begun to work, will never stop. And John Cockerill climbs back into his coach and government officials unsuspectingly sign his passport as if it referred to a consignment of wine and they do not realise that this silent man who seldom puts pen to paper is far more likely to turn their old world upside down than many a revolutionary who has his pockets stuffed with political programmes and manifestoes.

> (Nisard, 'Souvenirs de Voyages: Le Pays de Liège',
> *Revue de Paris*, December 1835. Trans. W. O. Henderson)

Nevertheless, revolutionary politics could overturn the best laid plans of the industrialists. In 1830, a revolt separated Belgium from the Netherlands and cut off the factories from their markets in the Netherlands and Dutch colonies. Massive industrial bankruptcies and unemployment followed, and for several years the Seraing works, too, was in trouble. But the new state, and its King, Leopold I, had the foresight to realise that Belgium's economic future could be built on the opportunities newly offered by steam locomotives for moving goods inland across frontiers by railway; and that Belgium had the great advantage of lying between the growing industry of Westphalia, the Ruhr and the port of Antwerp. Unlike Britain, where industrialisation and railway construction had been carried out with private capital under a *laisser-faire* policy, in Belgium the state continued to take a direct role in promoting and financing the industrial transformation. A commission soon recommended the construction of a railway to Cologne, and another to the south-west towards the French border and coalfields via Mons.

The iron road

In France, another region of the ancient Hercynian mountains, the upper Loire Valley, had also begun to develop on the combination of its coal, its proximity to the great trade-route of the Rhône, and access to Lyons, which dominated the world markets in silk textiles. Coal had been used for iron-making, following British methods, and crucible steel-making followed, introduced by workers from Sheffield and Birmingham. There, in 1827, the first major railway line in continental Europe was built, when Marc Séguin constructed a horse-drawn track, 18 kilometres long, from Saint-Etienne to the Loire at Andrézieux. This was followed five years later by the first European line to use locomotives, which ran

Railways and coalfields in Europe.

— Railways in Europe 1850

— Railways in Europe 1850-1870

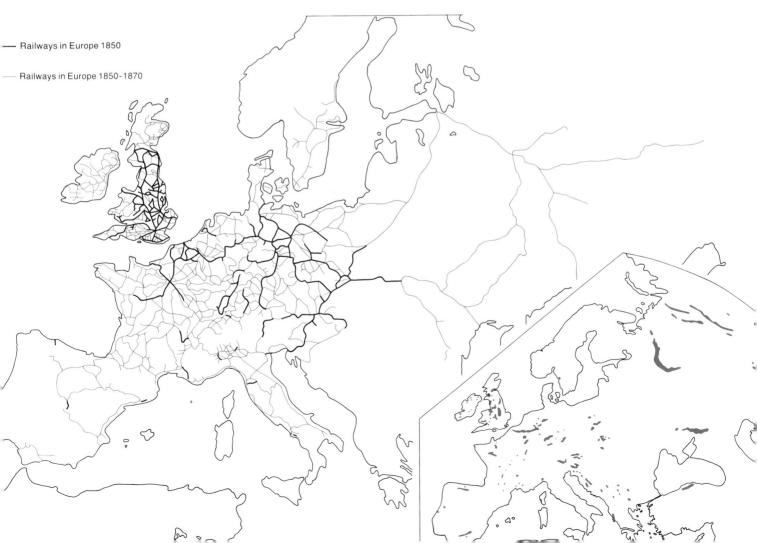

for 58 kilometres from Saint-Etienne to Lyons, across the heart of the coal and iron region.

In Belgium one of the first tracks was laid in 1830 from the Grand-Hornu colliery at Saint-Ghislain to the Mons-Condé canal. It was not popular with the carters who were put out of business, and they took their revenge by sacking the home of the managing director of the colliery. Nevertheless, the first 20-kilometre track was opened in 1835 from Brussels to Malines. Cockerill supplied rails, and Robert Stephenson the first five locomotives, but within six months of the Stephenson locomotives arriving, one of them had been taken to Seraing, to be dismantled, copied, and reproduced by Cockerill as 'La Belge'. The railways, with their huge requirements for wrought-iron rails and rolling-stock, rejuvenated the continental coal and iron industries, and by 1839 the Seraing works was able to manufacture locomotives at the rate of one every ten days. They were soon working on an order for a hundred locomotives for the Austrian railways, as well as constructing the first Belgian passenger steamer to ply the route from Ostend to Dover.

The transformation that all this industrial development wrought on the valley of the Meuse, where the Cockerill family had first started, was graphically described by Victor Hugo after a visit in 1839.

> At this moment a singular sight suddenly presented itself. At the foot of the hills, which were scarcely perceptible, two round balls of fire glared like the eyes of tigers. By the roadside was a frightful dark chimney-stack, surmounted by a huge flame, which cast a sombre hue upon the adjoining rocks, forests and ravines. Nearer the entry to the valley, hidden in the shade, was a mouth of live coal, which suddenly opened and shut, and, in the midst of the frightful noises, spurted forth a tongue of fire. It was the lighting of the furnaces . . .
>
> After passing the place called La Petite Fémalle, the sight was inexpressible – was truly magnificent. All the valley seemed to be in a state of conflagration – smoke issuing from this place, and flames arising from that; in fact we could imagine that a hostile army had ransacked the country, and that twenty districts presented, in that night of darkness, all the aspects and phases of a conflagration – some catching fire, some enveloped in smoke, and others surrounded with flames . . .
>
> This aspect of war is caused by peace – this frightful symbol of devastation is the effect of industry. The furnaces of the ironworks of Mr Cockerill, where cannon is cast of the largest calibre, and steam-engines of the highest power are made, alone meet the eye . . .
>
> (Victor Hugo, *The Rhine*, Trans. D.M. Aird 1853)

It would be nearly forty years before that peace would be destroyed by the cannon of France and Germany turned against one another, and till then the spreading web of iron rails would draw the cities and the countries of Europe into an ever tighter union forged by the entrepreneurs.

The industrialisation of France and Germany

The industrial zone of the Meuse followed the coalfield westwards across the French border into the departments of Nord and Pas-de-Calais, and there the greatest expansion of French industry began. The Anzin company had been mining coal since 1757, and had become one of the largest businesses in France. But the coal seams were much deeper than at the Belgian end of the field, and thus the coal was more expensive. So it could only be sold by raising tariffs on Belgian coal and by obstructing the waterways to Belgium. The French textile industry had grown up in the hills of Champagne but mechanisation there was

TOP The first railway train in Saxony.
BOTTOM Leipzig railway station.

slow; the first power-loom was installed in Rheims in 1844. But as cheap British machine-made textiles were imported, the competition was felt most by the cotton industry of Nord, centred on Lille, Roubaix and Tourcoing. To survive, the mills were forced to mechanise, deriving their source of energy from the local coal, and, just as had happened in Lancashire, the cotton industry led the process of industrialisation, transforming the region into the industrial heart of France.

Only in the second half of the eighteenth century, when steam winding engines displaced the horse-powered winding-gins to raise coal up in the shafts, could production expand in deep coalmines. The first deep pit was dug in the Pas-de-Calais at Courrières, in the western part of the coalfield, in 1851, and it became a new focus for industry. The grim conditions in the mines have been immortalised in Emile Zola's *Germinal*, but, at appalling social cost, they nevertheless fuelled the growth of France's industrialisation. By 1913 the mines of the Pas-de-Calais produced half the French output of coal.

No less a man than Voltaire had been of the opinion that Germany would be condemned to everlasting poverty – her natural assets seemed so poor. In the north the retreating ice sheets had left sandy moraines which made poor agricultural soil and were covered with forest. They also blocked the drainage of the land, causing large areas of peat bog. The commerce of the Baltic ports was hampered as Denmark controlled the exit to the North Sea. The main artery of trade, the Rhine, flowed through the Netherlands before reaching the sea, and the two great ports of Hamburg and Bremen were not well sited for the Atlantic trade. To the east, autocratic landowners, called Junkers, preserved a near-feudal economy based on growing rye, a crop that was rapidly becoming unmarketable when

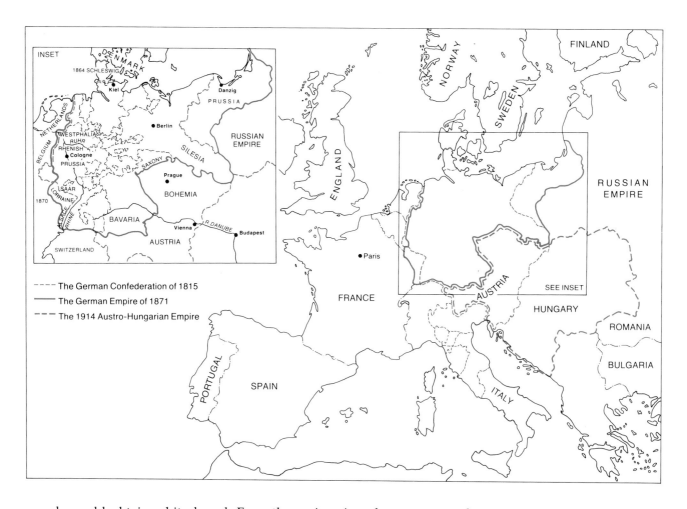

The German Confederation of 1815

The German Empire of 1871

The 1914 Austro-Hungarian Empire

people could obtain white bread. Even the main mineral resource, coal, was scattered round the edges of the states in the Ruhr, Saar, Silesia and Saxony, and Germany was also chronically short of iron. By the 1840s half of her iron was coming from abroad, mostly from England. When a succession of poor harvests raised the spectre of famine, several million Germans, seeking a more prosperous future, emigrated to the United States.

At the end of the Napoleonic wars, Germany consisted of no fewer than 39 separate states, and when the left bank of the Rhine was recovered from France, including major coalfields, industrialisation had scarcely begun. Saxony was the first to industrialise. Though lacking good soil, the kingdom benefited from a long mountainous frontier with Austria for water-power, plentiful forests for timber, and most important of all, coal and iron. A thriving textile industry grew up, first on wool and linen, and later, using British machines, on cotton spinning and weaving mills. The next step, inevitably following the English model, was for Saxony to exploit her coalfields to become a major exporter of both textiles and machinery to the other principalities of Germany.

The silver mines of Silesia had already helped to found the wealth of Austrian banking and territorial power. The region had also advanced on textiles, but now failed to mechanise, and it was only in coalmining and iron-making that its industry flourished. In 1796 the first blast furnace using coke was installed by a Scotsman, John Baildon, but coal production was insignificant compared with that of English mines. There were also two areas on the right bank of the Rhine where hilly country made a poor base for agriculture but provided streams for water-

The unification and expansion of Germany.

The giant steam hammer 'Fritz' in the Krupp works at Essen, 1911.

power and timber for charcoal; the iron-making region of Siegerland, where ore from Nassau was smelted and forged with charcoal to produce the same basic domestic, agricultural and military goods that had begun the iron industry elsewhere, while spinning and textile finishing grew up in the valley of the River Wupper, centred on Elberfeld and Barmen. Each of these industries was helped by the easy access to the Rhine and thus its cities, which provided both markets and capital.

However, it was further to the north in the valley of the River Ruhr that coal wrought the greatest transformation of Germany's unpromising condition. It began when the Cologne to Minden railway reached the Ruhr in 1848. In Westphalia the coal and iron-ore lay nearly 80 kilometres apart but now the railway could bring them together. As iron-making boosted industry, the population began to expand rapidly, swelled by large numbers of immigrants from the poverty-stricken eastern provinces, providing both labour and a market for finished goods. In 1848 the first coke-fired blast furnace began production at Mülheim, and deep shafts were sunk in the coalfield to the north of the Ruhr at Essen and Bochum. Once again, the technology that wrought the industrial revolution in the Ruhr came from England. Even Alfred Krupp 'the cannon king', whose works at Essen were to become the industrial heart of Europe, seldom made original discoveries. But few people played a more important role in introducing British designs to Germany than the Prussian, Peter Beuth. As a volunteer soldier in the campaign that defeated Napoleon, he had been quartered on the Cockerill family at Liège. He was so impressed with what he saw there that it was he who invited

John Cockerill to set up works in Berlin. In 1816, he established an Industrial Institute there, buying new machines in England; he made models of them for the Institute, to train German engineers, and then passed on the originals to German manufacturers to copy.

When the Stockton to Darlington railway was constructed it, too, had been inspected with enthusiasm by German engineers, and when the first railway in Germany was opened in 1835 (a track of only 6.5 kilometres between the Bavarian towns of Nuremberg and Fürth) it employed two locomotives built by Robert Stephenson. But a much more significant track linked Dresden with Leipzig four years later, and by 1845 England had supplied 237 locomotives and a large proportion of the iron and steel used in the building of the German railway system.

Coal had been mined in the Ruhr since the thirteenth century but its modernisation owed much to an Irishman, William Mulvaney, who set up the Hibernia mine in 1856 near Gelsenkirchen and the Shamrock mine at Herne. Starting later than Britain and Belgium, the Ruhr was able to equip with the latest machinery, and from the beginning its mines and ironworks were also developed on a much larger scale than in Britain. Although the German railways had been built piecemeal in the separate states, with no over-all plan or policy, they were able to draw in the raw materials and industry of distant coal-bearing regions such as the Saar and Silesia. From its late start, thanks to the railways being able to move coal and iron, German industry developed with astonishing rapidity, actively aided by state investment. By mid-century the arteries of industrialisation, the railway networks, of Britain, Belgium and Germany were mostly complete but many of the French lines were still only on paper.

Blood and iron

The first Industrial Revolution was founded on coal and iron, but coal and iron could make another material which was to have an even greater impact on Europe, and that was steel. A new British invention was to transform the process of making steel, and with it the history of Europe. In the 1850s steel (iron alloyed with a precise proportion of carbon) could only be made by the crucible process, where wrought iron was heated with flux in an air-tight crucible in which the metal could be melted without oxidising. When poured into a mould it had a much better structure than forged wrought iron, but only 45 kilogrammes could be made at a time. Consequently it cost ten to twenty times as much as pig-iron. But in 1856 Henry Bessemer patented a process where air was blown up through the mass of molten cast iron to burn off impurities and some of the carbon content. Because the air burnt the carbon it generated heat, and Bessemer could boast that he had discovered the way to make steel without fuel. This not only reduced coal consumption and thus cost, but opened the possibility of casting large amounts of steel in one melt, with obvious advantages including dramatically reduced cost. Coal, of course, was still needed in immense quantities to smelt the iron prior to steel-making.

The railway industry was a great consumer of steel, but so was the expanding arms industry – Bessemer was looking for a way to make better cannon. Naval cannon were at that time mostly made from crude cast iron, while armies, where weight was crucial to manoeuvrability, used expensive but still heavy bronze, which could only be fired a limited number of times. Further refinements in steel-making were made by two German engineers, William and Friedrich

Siemens, who were also working in England when they developed a method of pre-heating the air blown into the molten iron. This saved still more fuel.

It is ironic that Friedrich Krupp, the founder of the famous steelworks at Essen, had squandered a substantial family fortune in a vain search for 'the secret of cast steel' (the very discovery that Bessemer had now made) when at the same time he was manufacturing coin-dies to stamp money for the Prussian mint. But over-ambition and lack of water for power bankrupted him and he died at the age of thirty-nine. When his son, Alfred, inherited the company in 1826 at the age of fourteen, it only employed seven men and a single horse. By the age of twenty-three he had invested in his first steam engine, running it on water brought in buckets from a nearby pond, and by 1838 the fortunes of the family had improved enough for this tall, gaunt young man to be able to visit England, 'properly booted and spurred', where he found that the factory proprietors were flattered to have such a well-dressed continental visitor, and unwittingly let him adopt their latest processes. His works were now making railway springs, axles and cast steel tyres for the rapidly expanding railways. Although Prussia had long been an expansionist state, at this stage the Prussian army took no interest at all in Krupp's greatest enthusiasm – steel cannon.

There were other great European engineers and industrialists; Gustave Eiffel was to revolutionise the construction of iron and steel structures like railway bridges, but no single family dynasty was to do more to challenge Britain's supremacy as an industrial power than that of Alfred Krupp and his son Friedrich. Alfred was more than a little eccentric. Believing that he gained inspiration from the odour of horse-dung, he had his study built over his stable, with ducts to carry the scent up to him as he worked. Tyrannical and unscrupulous he was interested only in his steel, having 'no time for reading, politics and that sort of thing'. A single-mindedness which came in handy when he was later selling guns to both sides of opposing forces. By 1851 he could send a six-pounder cannon to the Great Exhibition in London where fashionable ladies found it 'quite bewitching' and a two-ton steel block, cast from no fewer than 98 crucibles, which stole the show from a British one half the size. It would prove to be all too true when Krupp claimed, 'we will make the English open their eyes'.

By the mid-century, the drive to unify a Germany now drawn together by a rapid means of transport, had become a struggle between Prussia and the Austrians. The growing economic power of Prussia, led by the political skill of Otto von Bismarck as chief minister, now allowed Prussia to challenge Austria's political leadership. It was a good place and time to be an armaments manufacturer, and already in 1859 Krupp had won a contract from the Prussians for 300 steel gun-barrels. Another large Russian order followed. He was now able to install a Bessemer steel converter and buy the Sayn ironworks from the state. The size of his works expanded rapidly, until in 1864 he was employing 6000 men. That year his works were visited by Bismarck who wanted to acquaint himself with the growing industrial power of the Ruhr. Bismarck recognised that a united industrialised Germany was to play a new role on the centre of the European stage. 'Place in the hands of the King of Prussia the strongest possible military power,' he exhorted, 'then he will be able to carry out the policy you wish; this policy cannot succeed through speeches, and shooting matches, and songs; it can only be carried out through blood and iron.'

In 1864, the German confederation, led by both Prussia and Austria, had gone to war against Denmark, and annexed the two Duchies of Holstein and Schleswig. (This was later to allow Germany to build the strategically important

The Prussian bombardment of Strasbourg, August 1870.

Kiel Canal to the Baltic.) By provoking a quarrel over their administration Bismarck gained an excuse to declare war and invade Austria. The decisive engagement took place at Königgrätz, where 20,000 Austrians were killed, and at the battle of Sadowa in Bohemia (1866) Austria was defeated after only seven weeks of war. The North German Confederation was established under Prussian control and the Austrian Empire was confined to the basin of the Danube.

France now no longer faced a 'cluster of insignificant states under insignificant princelings' but the foremost industrial and military power in continental Europe, and Bismarck provoked the weak monarch Napoleon III into the folly of declaring war. In the guise of retaliating against French aggression, his army crushed Napoleon's troops at Sedan (1870). The Prussians were able to occupy Paris the next year, and Germany was able to annex Alsace and Lorraine. The Prussian victory owed much to Krupp's cast-steel field guns which were both more accurate and had a longer range than those of the French. And for Germany they won a most important prize. With the new territory Krupp gained the largest iron-ore deposits in western Europe. These were high-phosphorus ores, and phosphorus makes steel brittle, so at the time they were useless. But they also have a rich iron content, and only six years later, in England, S. G. Thomas and Percy Gilchrist discovered a way of using high-phosphorus iron ore by lining the furnace with lime or magnesia. With the speed of travel transformed by the railway, ideas and knowledge spread fast, and the pace of industrial development had quickened dramatically: within five years of its invention, the Gilchrist-Thomas process had been adopted in eighty-four converters, including those of Krupp. Germany's possession of the Alsace-Lorraine iron was now to be of profound importance to the Ruhr, and to the industrial might of the new nation.

The German Reich was formally and dramatically founded when the King of Prussia accepted the crown of a fully united Germany in the Palace of Louis XIV at Versailles in 1871. Symbolically and practically, Germany had superseded France as the dominant land-power in Europe. Germany was now the second largest coal-producing country in the world after Britain, and steel-making boomed as never before, rising from 0.9 million tons in 1886 to 17.6 million tons in 1914, more than was produced by Britain, France and Russia combined. Powered by ever-increasing quantities of coal, the industrial capacities of Britain and Germany were now set to compete, not just for world markets but in a technical arms race that became a contest for military supremacy and national precedence. A contest to dominate a planet where already only a fifth of the land-surface was not under a European flag, or settled by Europeans.

The second Industrial Revolution

While Germany was growing rich on coal and steel, another revolution had been taking place in industry. For centuries chemicals had been made from natural products – alkalis from potash, kelp and the barilla plant, dyes from madder-root and indigo – and farmers used natural manures. But now, in the manufacture of chemicals, Germany rapidly overtook Britain. A superior education system for scientists, together with banks that were ready to make massive loans, and large-scale investment in long-term research, paid off in the production, not just of the principal acids and alkalis, but of artificial fertilisers, pharmaceuticals, coal-tar products and artificial dyes. By 1914 companies like Bayer and Hoechst produced 90 per cent of the industrial dyes used in the world. At the turn of the century the six largest German dye firms employed 500 chemists, in Britain there were less than forty, of lower qualifications, in the whole industry.

Now new chemical techniques were to provide other riches from the same coalfields that had fired the first Industrial Revolution. Carbon chemistry produced plastics, and even artificial textiles, in the form of artificial silk (rayon), were to follow. But the greatest innovation which was first to extend the use of coal enormously and finally to usurp it was, once again, made in England. In 1831, Michael Faraday demonstrated at The Royal Institution that a magnet thrust into the centre of a coil of wire produces a momentary electric current and a spark. Prophetically he claimed, 'although the spark is very small, so that you can hardly perceive it, others will follow who will make this power available for important purposes'.

The pioneering industrialists were now the Germans, and another family in particular, the Siemens, were to do for electricity what the Krupps had done for guns. As a young army officer Werner von Siemens had been imprisoned for duelling, but he managed to set up a laboratory in his cell and developed a silver- and gold-plating technique which he sold, after his release, to a leading Birmingham factory. With his brother Wilhelm, who took British nationality as William, he made important inventions, such as the regenerative furnace (which heated the incoming air, making the furnace far more efficient). They now succeeded in producing a machine to generate an electric current using permanent magnets. This could strike a powerful arc between carbon points – which in 1862 illuminated Dungeness lighthouse. Then, four years later, Werner invented the dynamo-electric machine. This relied on coils to create the powerful magnets which in turn generated electricity – the dynamo.

The dynamo made the large-scale generation of electricity a practical proposition, and opened the door on a whole new era, not just of instant power and light, but of long-distance communication by electric telegraph, telephone, radio and finally computer. But the greatest significance of the dynamo was that the energy stored in coal could now be used in many different ways. The heat produced by burning it could be converted into mechanical energy by using a steam engine, and then into electrical energy. This could be used in a variety of forms – not just for power to turn machines but as light, heat, sound and so on.

In 1879 Werner von Siemens made the first successful electric train, while William invented the electric furnace for steel-making. The world's first public electric street lighting was installed by William in Godalming in Surrey in 1881. It displaced gas-light because it was 20 per cent cheaper. Supported enthusiastically by the German banks which sensed huge profits, the electricity industry boomed in the 1890s. Electricity brought tramways to the cities and safer light into homes. German electric motors soon drove factory machines, doing away with the inefficient, dangerous and noisy shaft-and-belt systems required to transmit steam-power. Ever more ingenious and bizarre inventions were constructed to use surplus electricity in the day-time (from the ticker-tape for stock-market prices to the electric mouse-trap).

There were two other aspects to electrical power which we now take for granted but which would be crucial to the future development of Europe and the world. The street lighting at Godalming had another distinction – the dynamo was driven by a water-wheel, and when William Siemens visited the Niagara Falls in 1876, he saw a prodigious amount of energy running to waste. He already knew that you did not always have to use coal to drive dynamos but the falls also inspired him with the idea of transmitting large amounts of electric power to a distance by cables – as there was no industry to use it near the falls. Transmitting electricity down power lines could remove all the problems of transporting

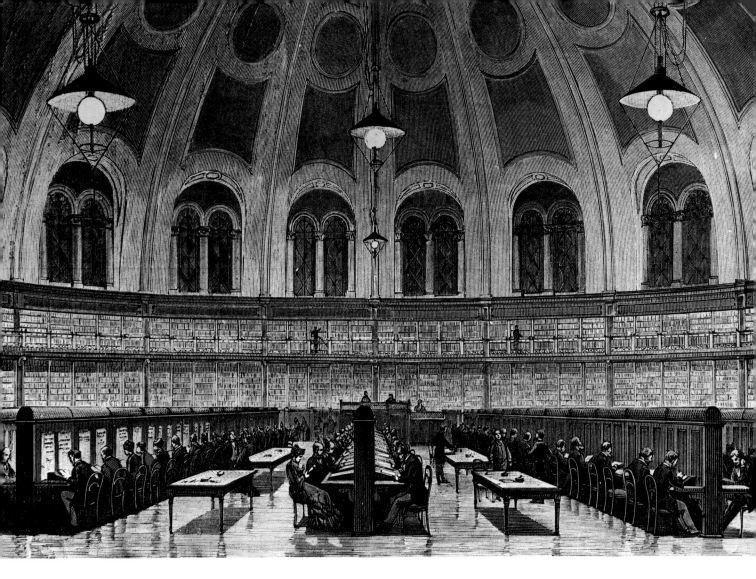

heavy tonnages of coal in order to have power. Factories would no longer need steam engines in their back yards. The usefulness of long-distance electrical transmission had already been dramatically proved in another way when, in 1871, William Siemens was able to complete the electric telegraph to send messages overland by morse code from London to India. Successful submarine cables were then laid across oceans.

Even when the new century dawned and too much competition lowered prices and profits, the industry still flourished. The German banks and companies organised into two great cartels, AEG (the German Edison Company, which had 10,000 employees) and Siemens and Halske. These soon dominated the world market and contributed substantially to making Germany the second largest trading nation by 1914.

By the mid-nineteenth century some economists were already alarmed by the dependence of European civilisation and British Imperial power on the energy from coal, and were wondering what would happen when it was all used up. But once industry was powered by electricity, the other lesson of Niagara Falls was that the prime energy source could be changed. This great flexibility would become more and more important in the next century until in the present day oil, gas and nuclear power-stations compete with coal to give us energy. Electricity also gives us the life-saving opportunity to return to renewable energy sources such as sun, wind, tide and biomass. The very energy sources from which our civilisation first sprang.

Electric arc-lamps illuminate the reading room of the British Museum.

Russia awakens

The greatest reserves of metals and mineral fuels in Europe are in Russia but in comparison with western Europe Russia has the major geographical disadvantage of being a massive land-locked continental country penetrated by few navigable rivers. This has made internal and external communication and trade very difficult even to the present day. What is worse, the congress of continents around the North Pole reduces circulation of warm water, so the seas to the north of Russia and even her ports and rivers freeze in the winter, cutting her off from the outside world, except through the Black Sea. In the first half of the nineteenth century, most of those valuable warm-water shores were still part of the collapsing Ottoman Empire, ruled by Turkey.

Despite these formidable handicaps, Tsarist expansionism, beginning with Peter the Great, demanded industrial development of the massive resources that lay within Russia's frontiers. This had been encouraged by excluding imports and by the state setting up joint enterprises with merchants. Until 1762 these factories were able to purchase whole villages which meant they could force their serf inhabitants to work at the machines; while nobles compelled their own serfs to work in factories to use the raw materials from their great estates. Not surprisingly, the standard of workmanship was very low. The lack of competition from abroad, and between state factories which were isolated from outside influence and had virtual monopolies, resulted in the enterprises being very inefficient, with very low productivity. Even at the end of the nineteenth century, the Urals coal and steel industry employed ten times as many people per ton of output as were then used in Belgium.

Such was the size of Russia that despite this backwardness, the nation was the strongest military power in Europe following the defeat of Napoleon, and the Tsar's attention turned to the Balkans and the straits at the Bosporus linking his only warm-water ports to the Mediterranean. These were vital for the export of Russian grain which paid for imports. But in 1841, fearing Russian power, an international Straits Convention closed the Bosporus to the Russian fleet. Russia then sank the Turkish fleet and invaded what are now Rumania and Bulgaria. In 1854 Britain and France declared war to prevent Russia taking control of further Turkish territory, and this 'Crimean war' turned into a year-long siege of the naval base of Sevastopol.

Russia's humiliating defeat, forbidding her to keep a fleet in the Black Sea, fired the determination of Tsar Alexander II to industrialise as quickly as possible in order to equal the military might of his western neighbours. The Tsar's first step was to liberate the serfs in 1861, but they still had to buy their freedom in the form of an onerous annual tax and this did much to maintain the rural and agricultural poverty and backwardness of Russia. In place of medieval serfdom the peasants and poor now faced an aggressive capitalism as the floodgates were opened to an onrush of entrepreneurship, knowledge and capital from abroad. (As is happening in Eastern Germany today.)

To protect Russian factories prohibitive taxes were imposed on imports, and the state spent huge sums on loans, subsidies and land grants to encourage manufacture. The autocratic state already controlled the primitive banking system, the railways, other major industries and even the sale of vodka, and thus could dictate where investment should take place. Realising that huge profits could be made from the same resources that had built the industries of western Europe, but which in Russia still lay unexploited, foreign capital poured in, followed by British machines and entrepreneurs. A century before, two Englishmen

Manhandling a Bessemer converter in a Russian steelworks.

had obtained a monopoly of cotton-weaving, and now Luwig Knoop (who though born in Bremen had worked in Manchester) imported from Lancashire enough cotton machinery, steam engines and electrical equipment to enable him to build 122 factories before he died in 1894. So many English workmen were employed in the Russian cotton industry that in 1912 an English football team was playing in the Moscow league.

Russia's coalfields lay near Moscow, in the basin of the River Donets near the Sea of Azov (now known as the Donbass), to the west of the Urals, in Poland and in Siberia (the modern Kuzbass, where the coal seams are 15 metres thick). But in 1870 Russia produced a meagre 350,000 tons of pig-iron, still smelted with charcoal, because previous attempts to modernise had all failed. A new iron industry was now set up in the Ukraine by a Welshman, John Hughes, who chose an excellent site to build the works of his New Russia Company, on the Kalmius river close to the rich coal seams of the Donets basin. The state gave him free land, a loan, an inflated price for his pig-iron, an order for rails and permission to build a railway to the Sea of Azov, giving access to the Black Sea and the world beyond. The town of Hughesovka (Yusovka then Stalinsk) quickly sprang up to house 8000 employees and the company several times yielded dividends of 100 per cent. Such rich pickings attracted other investors, and Belgian and French investors developed the coalfields.

In 1837 an enormous deposit of rich iron ore had been discovered at Krivoy

Rog, 350 kilometres to the west of the Donets coalmines, but it was too remote to be profitably exploited until, in 1884, they were linked to the coking coal of the Donets by the Catherine Railway. Thirteen great ironworks could now be set up in ten years, almost totally dominated by foreign investment. Of them, the South Russian Dnieper Metallurgical Company was an offshoot of none other than the original pioneer John Cockerill Company of Seraing. It became the most famous, profitable and successful of all the steel companies in Russia. Krivoy Rog is now the biggest open-cast mine in Europe, producing 100 million tons of iron ore a year, and it still has reserves of 17 billion tons.

There was much lost ground to be made up, but by starting so late, and by employing enormous loans, Russian industry developed on a giant scale, with giant strides. By 1901 Russia was making more pig-iron than France and most of it was being used to build railways, which were laid across the country at the rate of 2000 kilometres a year until they formed the largest network in Europe. Yet even then the country was so undeveloped that only one Russian in ten lived in a town and only one in every fifteen worked in industry.

Iron and tears

A substantial proportion of the investment in the Donbass had come from German banks and industry, particularly since Germany was still short of iron ore herself. In fact, the narrow basis of German resources was beginning to worry her new leaders. By 1914, half her ore supplies came from French Lorraine and Sweden, while Krupp imported from the iron-mines of Spanish Biscay. At the same time Germany found herself at the railway crossroads of Europe, with an industry that ignored national boundaries: indeed, German industrialists began to talk of their economic domination of Europe. Both Italy and Germany had only recently achieved national unity, and were intent on improving their standing among the imperial nations of the world. With the memories of the easy victories in Austria and France, and a peace that had lasted 25 years, the old Prussian militarism revived under the Emperor Wilhelm II. It was not unnatural that some of the industrialists, who like Krupp dealt in armaments, might begin to think that the way to sustain their supra-national economy was by force. Since power derived from the barrels of their guns, war would be good for business. Just as the Teutonic tribes before them had set off down the Rhône towards the fertile shores of the Mediterranean, so, now, the nation's leaders began to dream of 'a place in the sun'.

France had never forgiven Germany the annexation of Alsace-Lorraine. By now hopelessly outclassed both militarily and economically by Germany, she made a protective alliance with Russia. The Germans, however, were alarmed at the speed with which Russian industrialisation was increasing her military might, and began to think of a two-front pre-emptive war: a lightning strike against France through the Belgian coalfields, followed by a slower mobilisation against Russia to seize the resources of the Ukraine. Great Britain had been preoccupied with the affairs of Empire, but she was now outclassed by German industry in both quantity and technology.

Then Germany increased the tension by starting to construct a huge navy. There was only one possible need or use for such a fleet – to challenge Britannia's rule of the waves, and indeed Kaiser Wilhelm demanded 'Neptune's trident must be in our fist'. At the Kaiser's suggestion, Alfred Krupp's son, Fritz, had bought the Germania shipyards at Kiel in 1896, and within fifteen years had built nine battleships, five light cruisers, thirty-three destroyers and ten submarines. The

The Battleship *Bismarck* under construction at Kiel, 1900.

massive industrial power of Britain and Germany was turned to the most costly arms-race in history, and even the Liberal British Government was forced to adopt a 'two keels for one' policy, doubling the German rate of ship construction. Britain was forced to make clear her intention to contain German ambition by guaranteeing the independence of Belgium.

Europe, having forged itself with its coal into a civilisation unified by a common scientific and technological culture, could not agree to share the fruits of that success among its peoples. Instead it was to destroy its world supremacy in politics, economics and military power in the first of two wars to contain the nationalist ambitions of one of its members. The glory of the European nation states was destroyed, as the glory of Greece was destroyed, by the greed and ambition of rulers, their nationalistic peoples and their self-seeking politicians.

The coalfields had been formed before the Atlantic ocean opened, and beyond that ocean they had allowed the same industrial progress to take place. But in 1914 America mined twice as much coal as Germany and Britain together. Borne up by a flood of cheap and motivated immigrant European labour, financed by massive European loans, her power would grow to sweep Europe from the world stage for the rest of the century.

The factor of a million

The release of the stored energy of the sun had converted Europe from a continent of farmers into a continent of city-dwellers reliant on machines, but it had not changed the nature of its land nor its quarrelsome peoples. The pursuit of riches had set the iron wheels turning, and the greed for power would break whole peoples on those wheels. Yet there was another gift from the Hercynian mountains that was to yield three million times more energy, kilogram for kilogram, than the coal of the Carboniferous swamps. Here was a source of power beyond men's wildest dreams.

As the continents collided and the earth's crust remelted deep beneath the new mountains, metals distilled and condensed in cracks to form veins. Gold, silver, copper, arsenic, iron, all had contributed in their individual ways to the progress of civilisation, but now a metal was discovered which could threaten the very existence of that civilisation on the planet. In 1789 Martin Klaproth, a Berlin pharmacist, announced a discovery which was possibly to have more profound consequences for mankind than the revolution of that same year which began a supposedly rational age of liberty, equality and fraternity. As Albert Einstein observed, it was to give birth to the most revolutionary force since prehistoric man discovered fire. The metal which Klaproth proudly introduced to the Prussian academy of science had been extracted from ores mined in the Erz and Bohemian mountains, and he called it uranium after the recently discovered planet Uranus, then believed to be the last in the solar system.

Perhaps more than any other material, uranium exemplifies the fact that a resource is only a resource when the technology exists to make use of it. Even a century after Klaproth's discovery, when J. J. Thomson took the first step towards the realisation of nuclear power by discovering the first component of the atom, the electron, the toast at the annual dinner of the Cavendish laboratory was: 'to the electron, may it never be of any use to anybody'. It was only under the extreme pressure to innovate weapons, caused by global war, that that power was first realised. It was December 1942 and in great secrecy, in a squash court heated by charcoal braziers beneath the University stadium under the crowded suburbs of Chicago, that Enrico Fermi added the final layer to a pile of 50 tons of uranium oxide and 6 tons of refined metal set in a pile of moderating graphite bricks. As the last cadmium control rod was eased out, and students sat on top with buckets of cadmium nitrate in case it got too hot, the geiger counters began to roar in response to the first man-made chain reaction. The calculations were right, a possibly catastrophic accident in one of the most densely populated areas of the nation was averted and the reaction subsided when the cadmium control rod was replaced. But the genie of atomic power was out of the bottle, and Fermi's team celebrated with Chianti out of paper cups. It was in Russia, at Obninsk, southwest of Moscow, only twelve years but two bombs later, that the first electricity was generated by nuclear power.

It is too soon to write the chapter on how the use of the energy of the atomic nucleus changed the history of Europe but, had the atom bomb been completed earlier, Franklin Roosevelt might have done as he planned and used it on German cities as well as Japanese. That Europe at least was spared. But it can be argued that the awesome power of the atomic nucleus wielded the balance of terror which froze the frontiers of central Europe for forty-five years. Scientists still do not fully understand the power of the atomic nucleus; many of us fear it, and human society has certainly not learned how to live with it, yet many have had their lives saved by it. The one thing that is certain is that all our lives will be touched by it. Whether our insecure grasp of this almost mythical source of power be for good or ill is one of the greatest challenges facing our scientists and our politicians and indeed ourselves today.

CHAPTER ELEVEN

THE TRIUMPH
OF OIL

U ntil one hundred and fifty years ago, European civilisation was, for the most part, the product of the continent's own resources. There were notable exceptions: the gold and silver of the Americas, crops like cotton and tobacco, plants like the potato; all of which had had an important effect on both economy and society. Trade with the rest of the world had helped to fund the agricultural and industrial revolutions, but the relative wealth of countries in the 1890s was still closely related to the mineral resources within their own frontiers and especially to the availability of coal as the prime source of energy. Just as in the dawn of the age of metals the copper of Ai Bunar had allowed the chieftains of the Varna burials to grow powerful and rich, so had coal and industry built the empires of the arms barons like the Krupps.

It was no accident that to celebrate the centenary of the French Revolution in 1889 it was decided to build an iron tower 300 metres tall, by far the highest building in the world, as a proud symbol of French arts, science and industry. It was, after all, no more than an eloquent expression of the way industry was dominated by iron and industry was the most revolutionary force in Europe. At the Universal Exhibition which the Eiffel Tower adorned, the most wonderful exhibit celebrated the same spirit of industrial enterprise. It was the huge Hall of Machines, and among the European countries whose pavilions flanked the Quai d'Orsay and the Champ de Mars, it was those that had successfully industrialised by exploiting their own coal that were economically and politically dominant. Through them Europe ruled the world, but their pre-eminence rested on the geological story of the continent itself.

A unique continent

Europe is unique in its geological complexity. The plates of the earth's crust that form other continents like Asia, Australia and the centre of North America remained relatively unchanged as the continents jostled against each other, but for more than 3000 million years Europe was a malleable buffer zone between them. The repeated upheaval of mountain ranges, crumpled up when plates collided, left it a unique legacy of resources. While volcanoes still erupt in Italy, and may do so again in France, Germany and Greece, as Africa presses the Alps still

The Eiffel Tower under construction in 1888 for the international exhibition to celebrate the centenary of the French Revolution.

higher, they are the symptoms of only the latest collision. Similar events had taken place to form the granite heart of the Hercynian mountains, the older chain which gave us coal and uranium, which stretches through central Europe and emerges with another flourish of coal and metals as the Urals at the continent's eastern limit.

The Caledonian mountains, more ancient still, which were once as great a range as the Himalayas, still dominate the Atlantic coasts of Scotland and Norway, etched now by the work of the ice ages into fjords and U-shaped valleys. These were formed when an ocean (called Iapetus by geologists) was squeezed out by the approach of two continents 450 million years ago. One of these continents (Laurentia) consisted of what is now Greenland, North America and northern Scotland, the other (Baltica) was the rest of Europe. But the oldest rocks, crystalline banded gneisses, are found on the edge of the island of Lewis in the Outer Hebrides. Eroded by the pounding of Atlantic storms today, their contorted patterns reveal the effects of some unknowable geological paroxysm which rained down ash and sand about 3000 million years ago. Not long afterwards the first traces of life began to appear on Earth.

The story, which only the rocks themselves can tell, is that these fresh layers were buried up to 20 kilometres deep in the earth's crust and partially melted, then they were uplifted, squeezed and reheated, then injected with volcanic veins of dark basalt. They were buried deep again and reheated once more, injected this time with granite and lifted up again. The massive continental convulsions that caused all this can only be guessed at in the most general way as three mountain-building episodes, but they give an impressive idea of Europe's complex past. These Precambrian rocks form the stable heartland of the continent, 50 kilometres thick. Flat plains ground down by aeons of wind and water and ice, they lie beneath the surface from the Cotswolds to the Urals. In some regions they are buried deep beneath younger rocks, like the chalks laid down by the Jurassic seas, but they form the bedrock of Europe and emerge in Finland as a monotonously flat but beautiful patchwork of forest and lakes. Scraped clear by the ice, the acid rocks grow little but birch, fir and peat in bogs which are 10,000 years old. Across eastern Europe lie the rich beds of loess soil left by the ice ages, which had seen the first introduction of agriculture, and are now major corn-growing regions, while far to the south the rocks outcrop again as the Ukrainian shield. These ancient rocks are often mineralised, and here and there they are spectacularly rich in iron.

On the eve of the First World War – or the Great War as it was more accurately known at the time – the state of development of European countries reflected their endowment of resources and geographical advantages which ultimately derived from their tectonic past. In Britain, thanks to coal, as early as 1820, more people were employed in industry than in agriculture. Belgium and Germany had soon caught up, but France, with bigger areas for agriculture, poor communications and less coal, buried deeper, would not reach that stage until after the Second World War. In Sweden, Italy and Austria, where energy sources were scarce, twice as many people still tilled the fields as worked in factories. Despite pockets of highly developed industry, Russia, Hungary, the Czech lands and Spain were still for the most part pre-industrial economies, while Greece and the Balkans had still not left the agricultural age. The great advantage now held by the industrialised countries with strong economies was that by paying with manufactured exports they could draw on the many resources that could be imported from the rest of the world.

Black gold

Yet within the single lifetime of some of its oldest inhabitants today, Europe has undergone another astonishing transformation, a transformation largely wrought by a different resource – oil. The vagaries of supply of that resource from inside and outside Europe have literally changed the history of the world. As the new century began, the dominance of coal was to be challenged by oil, and at the same time the need for a nation to control its own resources within its frontiers became less important. The railway had allowed coal to be brought to landlocked cities, and electricity allowed power to be used away from its source. The increasing size of steamships, steam-powered cranes and mechanical systems for loading meant that raw materials could be brought from all over the globe to wherever industry might be sited, provided costs were competitive and that a country could pay for them. The problems were not so much practical as political. To be sure of overseas supplies of strategic raw materials, merchant ships must be guaranteed a clear passage. As the Romans had seen the need to clear the Mediterranean of pirates to ensure grain could flow to Rome, so Britain had to have mastery of the sea to guarantee an unimpeded exchange of trade with its empire. That was one reason why the Kaiser's decision to build a huge fleet was seen in Britain as such a threat.

As Europe industrialised, the population had increased dramatically, from 140 million in 1750 to 423 million in 1900. With this expansion came a huge consumption of resources from overseas and one which was increasingly in demand was oil. Coal-gas was used for lighting in London from 1812, but until the 1860s, houses or factories remote from a supply of coal-gas had to rely on tallow candles and oil for light, which was made from vegetable or animal sources. New kinds of cheap oil lamps were readily affordable in Britain by the 1850s and a shortage of oil promoted a boom in whaling. Even the most distant corners of the Antarctic seas were hunted by five to six hundred whaling ships at a time. The price rose as demand outstripped supply, until turtles in Brazil and even penguins from the islands of the Southern Ocean were thrown into 'digesters' to be pressure-cooked into lamp oil.

The rising price also encouraged the use of another kind of oil found in the ground – petroleum. Natural seepages of oil and escapes of natural gas (which occurs in association with petroleum) had been known and used for thousands of years. In 1272, Marco Polo had described the sacred and eternal flame of gas burning in the Zoroastrian fire-temple at Baku in the Caucasus near the Caspian Sea, and some hillsides bore a crop of flames even in the 1900s. In the seventeenth century there was a 'burning fountain' near Grenoble, and even a burning spring of coal-gas at Wigan. Noah caulked his ark of gopher wood with pitch (made by burning crude oil), and the town of Hit provided pitch to caulk the canoes and coracles of the Marsh Arabs of the Mesopotamian estuary, a tradition which may go back 5000 years, when the same town had supplied the Babylonians with bitumen to consolidate their streets with a kind of asphalt.

Oil had been a natural pollutant of wells in Poland, and since medieval times peasants had used oil from seeps on the surface to grease the axles of their carts. In the 1840s, the story goes, Ignacego Kukasiewicza, who had graduated in pharmacy from Vienna University, was brought some of this oil by a peasant who had the bright idea of distilling it to make vodka. Kukasiewicza was looking for a replacement for expensive vegetable oil to use in lamps and, on 1 March 1853, the light of a kerosene (paraffin) lamp was publicly exhibited, illuminating his shop in Lvov. The next year he began what is claimed to be the world's first commercial extraction of mineral oil, at Bobrka – from a hand-dug well – five years before the first well was drilled in America.

In 1859 Edwin Drake struck the first major oilfield with his first well drilled to a depth of 21 metres near Titusville in Pennsylvania. Two years later the brig *Elizabeth Watts* set sail from Philadelphia bound for London with a cargo of kero-

Daimler and Benz motorcars.

sene, and the world's richest export trade began. Kukasiewicza gave a deputation from Rockefeller the secret of how to distil kerosene, free of charge; and by 1865 Britain, France and Germany were importing American kerosene. Since the lubricant oils and paraffin wax previously supplied from whale oil were now mostly of mineral origin, the whaling industry collapsed, but not before it had done devastating damage to many species.

The challenge to steam

By 1902, 11 million lamps were lit every night in England and Wales alone. Germany had begun to lead European oil production with the discovery of an oilfield at Ölheim in the 1880s, but as coal-gas and then electric lighting rapidly spread in popularity, demand for oil seemed set to decline. Yet just at that moment another invention appeared which was to stimulate oil production all over the world to unprecedented levels – the internal combustion engine. The concept of burning fuel to expand gases to move a piston was older than the steam engine. In the seventeenth century Christiaan Huygens, a Dutchman, had devised a machine that used gunpowder to raise a piston. But it was not until 1859 that a Frenchman, Etienne Lenoir, made an engine that would work continuously. A mixture of coal-gas and air was drawn into a cylinder and ignited alternately on either side of a piston. But it was very inefficient and three years later the more effective four-stroke cycle was invented by another Frenchman, Alphonse Beau de Rochas. This separated the actions of induction and exhaust. Gas was drawn into the piston and compressed before being ignited in one rotation of the crankshaft, while the power stroke following the explosion and the exit of the burnt gases took place in the next rotation. A patent was taken out but it was a German, Dr N. A. Otto, who got it to work. In 1876 it was the 'Otto Silent Engine' which was offered for sale. This gas engine was a success because it was far more efficient (and thus cheaper to run) than steam. The long-held supremacy of the steam engine was at last to be challenged.

The early engines were ignited by a flame inside the cylinder which had to be relit after every explosion from another outside by means of a sliding valve. Rudolf Diesel, however, developed an engine which compressed air so highly that it became hot enough to ignite fuel oil injected by a pump into the cylinder. Although the diesel engine was the most efficient, it was at first too heavy to be used in vehicles, and it was left to Gottlieb Daimler of Württemberg to patent the first small high-speed lightweight engine which ran on petroleum spirit (petrol) in 1885. At the same time Karl Benz's stationary gas and oil engines were selling well from his factory in Mannheim. Like many a visionary who has changed the world he had a dream, which he doggedly sought to attain. His was to produce a 'horseless carriage'. Finding no encouragement from his partners, he nevertheless persevered on his own, and in 1885 began to test the first vehicle powered by internal combustion. It was a three-wheeler using the Otto cycle, with a slow-speed (250 rpm), single-cylinder, four-stroke petrol engine like a gas-engine. Already it was quite a sophisticated engine, with electrical ignition and water cooling. Mounted horizontally at the back, it drove the vehicle at about 12 kilometres per hour.

Karl Benz was an extremely cautious man, and made numerous timed trial runs to try out various improvements, always after ten o'clock at night so that he could keep his invention secret, before he applied for a patent in January 1886. But there were few buyers, and in August the following year, his two young sons and their mother decided that a cross-country expedition would attract the favourable publicity that the vehicle needed. Taking a new 'Patent-Motorwagen' from the factory at five o'clock in the morning, without telling Karl Benz, they set off to drive some 50 kilometres to Pforzheim to visit the boys' grandmother. Stopping only to replenish cooling water and fuel, they successfully completed their journey by a deliberately difficult hilly route, a feat which stood the company in good stead at the Power and Machine Tools exhibition in Munich a month later. They also set the pattern for a century of cross-country car rallies.

Daimler's engine (which ran at 900 rpm, still only a quarter of the speed of a modern car engine) was fitted to a carriage in 1886, and he was successful in licensing his design to the French company of Panhard and Levassor, who soon built their own motor vehicles. In 1889 Daimler built a vehicle with a four-speed gear-box that founded the fortunes of the firm, which finally merged with Benz in 1926. Curiously, the two pioneering inventors never met.

Russian oil

As demand for oil rose, more and more was imported. Not until 1872, when the Tsarist regime started to auction off sections of the oilfield in the Aspheron peninsula near Baku on the Caspian Sea, did three Swedish brothers – Ludwig, Robert and Alfred Nobel – begin the process that turned Baku into one of the first large commercial oilfields in Europe. Alfred Nobel had gone to Baku in search of walnut trees to make into rifle stocks in the family arms business in St Petersburg, instead he bought oil-bearing land. After scrutinising American methods, the Nobels imported six Pennsylvanian drillers to Baku and transformed Russian oil-production techniques.

There were still formidable problems in transporting the oil and refined kerosene to the markets. The whole system of transporting wooden barrels had to be transformed, but so great were the Nobels' profits that, by 1880, the first oil pipeline in Europe took the crude to Baku, they had launched the world's first oil-tanker, the *Zoroaster*, and had built the first continuous-process refinery. The following year the Nobels acquired an oil-tank train to carry their products to St

Petersburg. Then in 1880 Baron Alphonse de Rothschild agreed to finance a railway to compete with them by carrying oil from Baku to Batum on the Black Sea, from where it could be shipped to Trieste for the whole European market. The output of the Aspheron oilfield, which covered only about 15 square kilometres, increased spectacularly. One of the Nobels' wells could, for a while, produce 4.5 million litres a day, far in excess of any well in the United States, and by 1888 production had soared to 2.5 million tons a year.

Some of the Russian oil producers at Baku became rich beyond their wildest dreams and began to behave accordingly. One built a palace out of gold plate, another a house like a house of cards and another used platinum to construct storage tanks. While they imported droves of beautiful Asiatic women and employed private armies for their defence, they housed their workers in wooden barracks and at times paid them only in bread and water. Nowhere, even in Tsarist Russia, could the extremes of wealth and poverty have been so grotesquely obvious.

By the turn of the century, John D. Rockefeller's Standard Oil company had come to dominate the refining and retailing business in the United States by ruthlessly undercutting prices in areas where there was competition, while raising them where he had a monopoly. This all-powerful 'Trust' protected the producers at the expense of the public and was similar in its effect to the cartels of the German coal and electrical industries. The expansion of the oil industry had been so rapid that Standard Oil was already the largest industrial enterprise in the United States, and, as America was the only substantial exporter of petroleum products, there was good reason for European businessmen to seek other sources of supply. Only the flood of oil from Baku prevented Standard Oil gaining a similar monopoly in Europe.

The refineries had been producing lamp-oil by distilling crude oil into its main components: heavy fuel oil, petroleum spirit and kerosene (paraffin). Petroleum spirit (petrol or gasoline) was a waste product, used in small quantities as a thinner for paints and for cleaning clocks, watches and printing type, and for removing stains from clothes. The crude oil from Baku only yielded 30 per cent kerosene, so up to 70 per cent of the crude production was burnt off as waste – including the petrol. Thus the invention of the Daimler and Benz engines was a windfall for the oil companies, as it gave them a market for what had been useless.

The mass-produced car

The first twenty years of motoring saw slow progress in the design of motor cars. Petrol vaporisation, ignition, valves, clutch, transmission, steering, brakes, pneumatic tyres, all had to be developed and at first cars were constantly breaking down. They were also highly dangerous, not just in making horses shy and in their propensity to roll over but in knocking down pedestrians. They were so lethal that from 1904 in Britain they had to be registered like fire-arms. (By the early 1920s, in America one motorist in seven was involved in an accident causing injury or death every year.) It was France that stole the lead in manufacturing lightweight high-speed engines in Europe, and one of the most popular cars was the eight-horsepower de Dion-Bouton.

Motor cars in the early 1900s were strictly luxury toys for the rich but the internal combustion engine was soon to be adopted for public transport. Horse-buses had appeared in cities in the 1820s and 1830s; suburban railways had followed, allowing cities to expand further outwards, with the first underground railway in the world opened in London in 1863. Electric trams began in the late 1880s, but it was not until 1909 that motor buses begin to replace horse-buses in London. This was the same year in which Henry Ford began to sell his Model 'T' for $950. This first people's car, whose price was to drop dramatically as mass-production and the first assembly line were introduced, became the pace-setter in the popularisation of the automobile. In Europe cars remained a luxury, but by 1914 they were so popular that 400,000 were registered in Britain alone. Yet transport in general was still overwhelmingly dependent on coal and horsepower.

Oil and the Dreadnoughts

The Russians had pioneered the use of fuel-oil as a substitute for coal or wood for heating boilers because in Baku it was so much cheaper than the alternatives. By the end of the nineteenth century it was used widely in Russian trains and factories. Yet it was in warfare that the influence of oil as a source of energy would affect the development of Europe most profoundly, and it was the British Royal Navy that recognised its advantages for warships first. The advent of steam-power and the explosive shell had totally changed naval construction. A warship powered by a steam engine rather than sails could operate in a flat calm, and it could also steam into a head-wind. Reluctantly the Admirals had to admit that the age of wooden walls and hand-to-hand fighting was past. The need for armour to resist shells fired from rifled barrels led to the first warships made wholly of iron, while the gun-turret mounted on the centre-line allowed long-range guns to fire to either side.

Though Great Britain may have lagged behind Germany in iron and steel production, the nation had a huge capacity and experience in ship-building, which responded to the German threat by building the *Dreadnought*, launched in 1906. This revolutionary battleship, which was to give her name to a whole philosophy of naval warfare, was bigger, faster and heavier-gunned than any other ship in history. With a length of 161 metres the *Dreadnought* had Parsons steam turbines

The romantic ideal, power and elegance.

in place of unreliable reciprocating steam engines, and could steam at 21 knots, 3 knots faster than her fastest rival. She had five twin 12-inch (30.5-centimetre) guns in turrets but, most remarkable of all, she was completed in just 14 months from laying down the keel.

By 1900 much of Britain's food and most of her raw materials came from abroad. British naval policy had always been that the enemy's coasts were the frontier of Britain, and made sure that her fleet was stronger than that of any combination of European powers that might challenge her. Only a decade earlier Britain had been provoked by the combined power of the French and Russian fleet into building seven new Majestic class battleships. Appalled at the cost of what some English Liberals called 'this wanton and profligate ostentation', France and Russia dropped out of the battleship-building race.

Coaling large ships was a time-consuming, exhausting and filthy business, and HMS *Dreadnought* burnt 17.5 tons of coal an hour. The weight and volume of coal severely limited the range of battleships, and coal-dumps had to be set up and guarded right around the world. At any one time a quarter of the fleet had to leave its station at sea to return to port to coal, wasting fuel on the journey. Stoking the furnaces and raking out the ash and clinker was done by hand, an arduous physical task made almost impossible in the heat of the tropics.

The technical breakthrough was made in 1902 when a means of atomising fuel-oil under pressure was developed so that it would burn at a jet, and within three years the British Navy led the world in the new marine oil-burning technology. Winston Churchill, as First Lord of the Admiralty, was easily persuaded of its technical superiority. He saw that oil-burning ships could get under way more quickly, were faster, had 40 per cent longer range and could be refuelled simply by connecting hoses – a process which could even be done at sea in calm weather. But most important of all, the decrease in weight of the fuel meant that ships could carry more gun-power for less size and cost. Churchill was also one of the first to appreciate the strategic importance of oil and that there was one overriding problem – security of supply. To adopt oil as the fuel of the fleet was in Churchill's borrowed words, 'to take arms against a sea of troubles'. European oil supplies, apart from Baku, were restricted to a little from Germany and Galicia, and smaller quantities from Hungary and Romania, but Britain had only the Scottish oil-shales. The Royal Navy needed a substantial source under British government control.

In 1901 William Knox D'Arcy, an English solicitor, was offered an oil concession by the debt-ridden Shah of Persia, Muzaffar ed-Din. For £20,000 in cash and £20,000 in shares, plus a 16 per cent share in any future profits, D'Arcy was given rights for sixty years over one and a quarter million square kilometres of territory and complete exemption from all taxes. But after three years of exploration, hampered by extreme temperatures, plagues of locusts, smallpox and rebellious tribes, and the expenditure of £225,000 of his own money, he had only succeeded in drilling dry wells. It began to look like a bad bargain. In 1905 he got financial help by forming the Anglo-Persian Oil Company, together with the Glasgow-based Burmah Oil Company, but their joint efforts were equally unsuccessful. In May 1908 they gave up hope, a cable was sent to the director of drilling operations in the Zagros mountains at Masjid-i-Salaman (Solomon's Mosque) telling him to stop drilling and come home. After six years of dry wells, the engineer decided doggedly to persevere at least for the six weeks until the confirmatory letter arrived. Two weeks later the well struck a huge reservoir of oil and began the Middle East oil industry.

Churchill was not prepared to leave the lifeblood of the Royal Navy in the hands of international oil companies which might put commercial advantage above the needs of Britain. Six days before the outbreak of war, feeling sufficiently sure that Britain could dominate events in Persia, Churchill persuaded Parliament to pass an Act authorising the purchase of two million pounds' worth of shares in Anglo-Persian Oil. The Government in return obtained a long-term contract to supply fuel-oil to the Royal Navy. The keel of the first huge battleship designed to be oil-fired, HMS *Queen Elizabeth*, had already been laid. Because of the saving in fuel weight she could be armed with 15-inch (38.1-centimetre) guns, which fired a shell weighing a ton, double the weight of that of a 12-inch gun. Her displacement was 27,500 tons, 10,000 more than the original *Dreadnought*, and twenty-four oil-fired boilers could drive her at 25 knots. Nine other 15-inch gunned battleships were under construction, including three sister-ships. Besides their superior speed, range and armaments these warships had another great advantage – the oil burners, when properly tuned, did not produce the huge tell-tale plume of black smoke which (in the days before radar) betrayed the presence of a coal-fired ship long before the hull appeared over the horizon.

In less than ten years, with a quite extraordinary expenditure of money and human effort, the Royal Navy had been totally transformed. By 1914, including the Dreadnoughts, Britain had undertaken to build thirty-one battleships or battle-cruisers in little more than nine years, while Germany built seventeen battleships and four battle-cruisers. But the British supremacy of the seas had become entirely dependent on overseas oil.

On the outbreak of war in August 1914, the British Grand Fleet steamed to a secret anchorage at Scapa Flow in the Orkney Islands. The strategy of a close blockade of the German coastline, as used in the Napoleonic Wars, was no longer necessary and also too risky to the Dreadnoughts on account of the newly developed mines and torpedoes. The Channel Fleet stood by in Portland harbour to deny Germany supplies from merchantmen steaming up the Channel. It was enough to bottle up the German High Seas Fleet in their home ports. Admiral Tirpitz wanted to engage the British fleet to shoot it out after the manner of earlier naval battles but the Kaiser was too proud of his new fleet and did not fancy losing it. He ordered Tirpitz to wait, hoping to reduce the superior numbers of the British fleet through attrition by mines and submarines.

The confrontation between the two great fleets finally came in May 1916 off the Jutland peninsula. But it took place in poor visibility and failing light and the two fleets lost contact in the dark. Although the Germans, helped by the vagaries of visibility, sank three British battle-cruisers and three armoured cruisers, against their own losses of one obsolescent battleship, one battle-cruiser and four armoured cruisers, they had not won a victory despite their claims at the time. Their fleet had turned away from battle and fled back to the safety of Wilhelmshaven, leaving the Royal Navy in possession of the North Sea. Both sides felt a sense of anti-climax and British public opinion was incensed at the lack of a decisive victory. But there was not to be another opportunity. Only in October 1918, just before the armistice, was the High Seas Fleet ordered to sail to engage the British. The naval ratings, suspecting the motives of their officers might be to die a glorious death in battle to retrieve the honour of the fleet, mutinied and refused to weigh anchor.

Since the days of the Trojan War the control of access to the Black Sea via the straits of the Dardanelles had had enormous strategic importance, and in 1914 they were the only supply route to Russia's warm-water ports. The Ottoman

Empire had formed an alliance with the Central Powers (Germany and Austria-Hungary) against Britain, France and Russia, and the straits were dominated by the forts of the Ottoman Empire on the peninsula of Gallipoli which defended the approaches to Constantinople and cut off Russian supplies. Churchill conceived the strategically imaginative plan of forcing the straits with an Anglo-French fleet of seventeen battleships, supported by destroyers and mine-sweepers, to open up the warm-water route to the Russian front. But the attack failed in February 1915 with a third of the battleships sunk or put out of action before they reached the narrows. Instead an attack was launched on the peninsula by French, British and Australasian troops to seize the forts. This also failed and cost Churchill his position on the War Council. He rejoined the army and commanded an infantry battalion on the Western Front – an experience which was later to have a profound influence on the conduct of land warfare.

The sea surrounding the British Isles had long spared them the grim grey tides of warfare that had flowed and ebbed across Europe, but now it became a supply route fraught with danger. Fuel as well as food, raw materials and munitions came from overseas, and the Germans began a new kind of warfare to attack those supplies. After Jutland it was the U-boat (*Unterseeboot*) which effectively ruled the North Sea and stalked the Western Approaches, seeking to strangle Britain's war effort by closing off the sea lanes. Again dependent on oil, diesel engines powered the U-boats on the surface by night while they charged batteries which drove electric motors while they were submerged during the day. They sank eleven million tons of shipping in what soon became an unlimited policy of attacking all ships without warning: passenger or cargo, armed or defenceless, enemy or neutral. They sent 875,000 tons to the bottom in the month

The might of the Royal Navy, massed for the Spithead review in 1911.

of April 1917 alone, and brought the British to the brink of starvation. Then the convoy system was introduced, where freighters travelled in packs defended by warships and many more got through. Even the huge industrial might of the British Empire was exhausted by the war; Britain was not only running out of supplies it was running short of the ability to get more loans from America to pay for them. In desperation Lord Northcliffe, the proprietor of *The Times* and the *Daily Mail*, cabled Washington 'If loan stops war stops'. That same month the U-boat menace to American vessels provoked the United States into entering the war. The Great War became a World War and the balance of shipping and shipbuilding swung decisively in Britain's favour. She could now continue to pit the resources of the world against those of a blockaded Germany.

War takes to the air

The war in the air had begun with balloons being used to direct artillery fire by telephone. However, the Wright brothers had failed to arouse any interest in their flying machine, which had made its maiden flight barely ten years before. The attitude of the military was summed up by General Foch, 'that's good sport but for the Army the aeroplane is worthless'. As a consequence, at the outbreak of war there were only 63 aircraft on the British front. Yet aircraft were to change the face of warfare beyond all recognition.

At first, they too were used for spotting troop movements and the fall of artillery shells, having to communicate by dropping messages attached to streamers, signalling with coloured lights and even releasing carrier-pigeons. Twice in the early months of the war such reconnaissance revealed invaluable information: of the German attempt to outflank the British Army at Mons and their swerve

No. 1 Squadron of the Royal Air Force in 1918.

towards the Marne. By 1915 aeroplanes were also used for aerial photography and this led to an urgent need to shoot them down. A deadly development of the aeroplane into a pure fighting machine was the building of the Fokker Eindekker monoplane with a machine-gun which fired straight ahead, synchronised to fire through the propeller. This was far more effective than pivot-mounted machine guns. At the same time Zeppelins, also powered by petrol engines, which had originally been intended as the aerial eyes of the German fleet, began to strike across the barrier of the Channel to bomb military installations. At least that was the intention but the difficulty of distinguishing military and civilian targets was soon an excuse to develop a policy of indiscriminate bombing of towns and cities. Zeppelins flew higher than the underpowered aircraft of the time and were relatively immune from attack until the explosive anti-aircraft shell and incendiary bullet were developed.

The urgency to develop a high-speed rate of climb and increased manoeuvrability had led to rapid improvements in engine and airframe design, and by 1917 fighters were climbing to 20,000 feet (6000 metres), and flying twice as fast, at 250 kilometres an hour. The Allies strove to maintain an offensive with special squadrons of 'fighter' aircraft over the enemy lines to destroy their opponents and allow reconnaissance to continue unmolested. The French successfully did this at Verdun early in 1916 and the British at the Somme but, because air battles took place in three dimensions, command of the air could never be achieved with the same success as command of the sea, and the quest for air superiority, by throwing ill-trained pilots into the fray, cost Britain dear. In 1916 the average life expectancy of a British pilot at the front was three weeks. By 1917 it was only two. In the end it was sheer numbers that told. In 1918 the United States began to supply huge quantities of planes and pilots to the front. A total of 4500 DH4 planes were built, and 10,000 pilots trained. Enormous dog-fights sprawled across the sky above the German trenches, and when Armistice came the Royal Air Force had 22,500 aircraft in service and nearly 300,000 men.

When the armies left their trenches they became much more vulnerable from the air. When the British front was broken by the Germans in March 1918, French and British fighter squadrons were used to good effect in slowing and containing the advance. But bombing was never developed (except by the British Navy) into an economic assault on the production of war material. Just as the Allies could have crippled the munitions factories of the Ruhr and Rhine, so Germany never struck at the three railway lines from Calais and Boulogne along which seventy-one trains a day supplied food and ammunition to the British Army. There were only six days' supplies held in forward positions. The day of the bombers would come but in the Great War the obsession with fighter combat meant that the overall impact of aircraft was far less than that of another weapon.

The launch of the landships

The original German advance through Belgium had been checked by the French at the River Marne, then, thanks to steamships and the railways, the British brought their troops to the front with remarkable speed. Meanwhile the Russians mobilised so quickly, again using trains, that two German army corps had to be moved from the French battlefields to reinforce the Russian front. By the end of September 1914 both sides had begun to dig in on the Western Front, constructing a multiple line of deep trenches that would reach in an unbroken ribbon of earthworks and barbed-wire from the Channel to the Swiss frontier. The German hopes for another swift victory over France were ended.

Mark IV tanks in action. Allied commanders were unprepared for their spectacular success in breaking through the German lines at Cambrai.

The principal reason for this stalemate was that the initiative in war had swung in favour of defence because of the machine-gun. In combination with barbed wire, which made rapid advance across open ground impossible, it was a formidable opponent not just to infantry but especially to cavalry, on which rapid advances and mobility had formerly depended. A soldier could lie flat to make use of cover, a man on horseback could not. With their huge industrial power turned to making armaments, both sides attempted to pulverise the enemy defences with massive artillery barrages that could last for weeks before the infantry were sent 'over the top'. (During ten days at the battle of Passchendaele in July 1917, British artillery fired four and a quarter million shells, 4.25 tons for every metre of the front.) But troops sheltering in well-constructed dug-outs were only destroyed by a direct hit, and the exploding shells created a quagmire of mud which was almost impossible to cross. For two years, dreadful casualties were suffered by both sides for minute gains of ground. The British army lost 57,000 men on the first day of the battle of the Somme, on 1 July 1916.

The British Army 'Landships Committee' began to investigate vehicles which could bring the advantages of the warship to the land – fire-power, protection from the machine-gun, and the ability to cross trenches, wire and mud. Under the young Winston Churchill's chairmanship, this committee finally persuaded the traditionalist generals that the stalemate could only be broken with the aid of a mechanised army. To keep the project secret, the early track-laying vehicles were referred to as 'tanks' and the name stuck.

It is hard now to appreciate the psychological impact that the first tanks had on the battlefield, but the surprise and shock of a totally new kind of attack was of immense tactical importance. The first tanks had such a devastating effect on the morale of the infantry that British troops sometimes fled at the approach of their own tanks, fearing they were those of the enemy, and on one occasion 3000 men ran at the sight of three steam ploughs being used to evacuate agricultural machinery. To us the early tanks look bizarre, but although primitive, they were

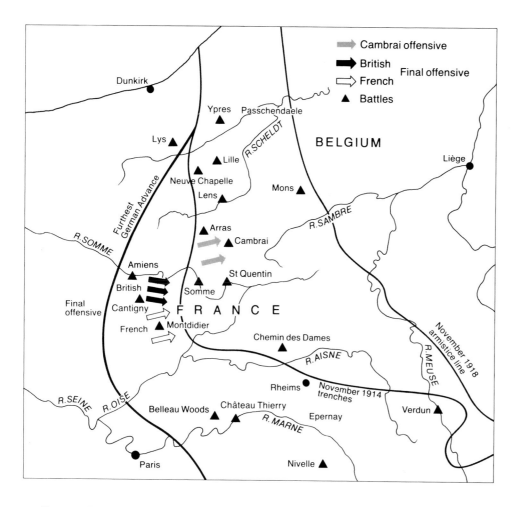

The Western Front.

well suited to their role. However, at first they were used with insufficient planning, either in ground that was too soft to cross, or in too small numbers, and were relatively ineffective.

The French developed their own Schneider Char d'Assaut and the light Renault FT 17, the first to have a turret, and the British General staff were fearful that the tactical advantage of using tanks would soon be lost as the Germans developed their own. However, the first cumbersome German tank, the A7V, was not used until March 1918.

The first decisive tank battle was one that had been properly planned, using a mass of tanks together. It also took place on firmer Jurassic soils that gave better going. On 20 November 1917, at Cambrai, a force of 474 British tanks, carrying huge rolls of brushwood to drop as bridges into the newly dug German anti-tank trenches, crossed one of the strongest sections of the German Hindenburg Line in a surprise attack that was preceded by only a brief artillery bombardment. Three slowly rolling waves of tanks crushed their way through deep banks of barbed-wire and crossed the trenches, destroying the machine-gun posts so that infantry could follow in their wake. They overran the German artillery line behind the trenches and gained an unprecedented 11 kilometres of ground. But there was no follow-through by cavalry, which could not survive in a fire-swept battle-zone, and the opportunity was lost. Muscle had been proved to be no match for machinery, but the church bells rang across England to celebrate a hollow victory.

The following year saw a major blow for the Allies. The war had destroyed the

Russian Tsarist state, and in March the Bolsheviks signed the Treaty of Brest-Litovsk, allowing the Germans to make huge territorial gains. The Germans could now concentrate on the Western Front, and made large gains in a spring offensive. Only in August 1918 did the counter-offensive begin. Then over 400 tanks smashed through the German defences at Amiens in another carefully planned surprise attack. This time it was effectively followed by armoured cars which caused panic among the retreating German troops. The shock of surprise was so total that the resolve of the enemy command and government gave way. The Kaiser said that the war must be ended and soon abdicated, fearful of the revolutionary socialist tide that was sweeping in from the east. The new German government requested an armistice on 'honourable terms'. Afterwards General von Zwehl declared 'it was not the genius of Marshal Foch [the Allied commander in chief] that beat us but "General Tank"'. Had General Tank been used effectively two years earlier, countless numbers of the ten million lives lost to direct military action would have been saved.

As Lord Curzon, the British Foreign Secretary, claimed, the Allies had 'floated to victory on a tide of oil'. The Bolshevik Russian revolution of October 1917 had cut off oil supplies from Baku but Britain had been fuelled from around the globe: from Persia, from the East Indies, from Mexico and most of all from the United States. Germany, lacking control of the seas, had struggled for supplies as she was to struggle again in the Second World War. Under the Treaty of San Remo in 1919, in recognition of oil as a strategic resource, Great Britain and France carved up the oil-bearing lands of the Middle East. Britain gained control of Mesopotamia (Iraq) as well as Persia, while France was awarded Syria.

Reparations, revolution and revenge

In the glittering pomp of Versailles, where the German empire had been founded, it was now, in Germany's view, humiliated by punitive peace terms imposed without negotiation by France and the Allies. Since Germany's industrial might was still the greatest in Europe, the Treaty of Versailles was intended to make her powerless. Germany had to surrender all her colonies and return the important industrial areas of Alsace-Lorraine to France, Upper Silesia to Poland, and Eupen-Malmédy to Belgium. Germany's possession of the new machines of war – tanks, heavy artillery, aircraft, airships, submarines and large naval vessels – was prohibited. But most damaging of all, Germany had to make financial reparations of £6600 million, plus interest, for damage to Belgium and France. The resentment which this Treaty caused the German people was later exploited by Hitler. It became his justification for recommencing what was essentially the same conflict – as the Second World War.

Europe was transformed; a belt of new independent states stretched from Finland across the heart of the continent to Yugoslavia, including an independent Ukraine. Russia was consumed by civil war between the Bolsheviks and White Russians, her economy was shattered, reduced to only one-seventh of its pre-war capacity. Germany was divided by a corridor which gave Poland access to the Baltic Sea in the gulf of Danzig, a sore on the Prussian ego. The European economy was severely unbalanced. There had been an enormous increase in industrial capacity but, because it had been used to make weapons, there was no corresponding increase in markets or consumer demand. Industrial power had grown at the expense of the countryside, which had lacked investment for a generation, limiting food production. In 1921 there was a severe drought in southern Russia, and two million people died in the subsequent famine.

When the Great Depression began in October 1929 the shaky edifice of European prosperity collapsed. Industrial production fell by 47 per cent in Germany, and in many industrial countries a quarter of the labour force lost their jobs, causing widespread civil unrest. In Spain the Generals began nearly three years of civil war by attacking the Popular Front government. Germany, the most industrialised country of central Europe, was doubly hit; first by the hyperinflation and financial collapse of 1922–3 which had destroyed the savings of the middle class, and wiped out the private wealth earned by the country's huge industrial progress, then by the Depression which threw seven million men out of work, including many in the salaried class. The romantic appeal of a return to strong leadership proved irresistible. The Nazis became the largest elected party, and Hitler was made Chancellor in January 1933. Throughout central and eastern Europe right-wing or royal dictatorships took power. Only Czechoslovakia succeeded in retaining a democratic government. Between 1928 and 1933 in the Soviet Union, Stalin's programme of forced collectivisation of peasant farms cost more than seven million lives.

The end of the armistice

The industrialised countries which had expansionist aims in the 1930s were those that had been left out of the first imperial division of the world's resources. Japan, with few resources of its own, invaded China in 1937 for coal, agriculture and markets; and threatened the European trading centres of Shanghai, Hong Kong and the oil of the Dutch East Indies. When Britain and America applied economic pressure it drove the Japanese into the German camp. In Italy, Mussolini sought nationalist prestige by invading Ethiopia in 1935 and by intervening on the side of the Fascists in Spain. Later, partly in a quest for mineral resources and 'autarchia', the concept of a self-sustaining economy, he invaded Croatia, Dalmatia and Albania.

Hitler's declared aims were to redress the 'injustice' of the German losses of 1918, but deeply embedded in Nazi philosophy was the idea of a right to break through the narrow boundaries of the Bismarckian era to seize a share of the world's rich resources for the 'master race' and the need for *Lebensraum* (living space) in which to expand. Geopoliticians like Karl Haushofer argued that Germany could not be self-sufficient, nor could she rely on overseas trade, so she must expand her control over more territory and to the east Germany had no natural frontiers. Hitler and the Nazis adopted as one of their aims an expansion into the fertile agricultural soils of Poland, Byelorussia and especially the Ukraine, inhabited by people he deemed to be 'sub-human' Slavs and Jews, whom he intended to enslave or exterminate. (Despite their persecution as scapegoats, in Germany Jews played only a minor role in banking.) Hitler also coveted the industrial heartlands based on the coalfields of Silesia and the Donbass, and planned to seek a colonial empire elsewhere at a later stage. In his own words he sought an 'empire limited in space only by the *Herrenvolk*'s ability to rule the lesser breeds'. Rearmament was also a way for Hitler to expand the German economy and fulfil his election pledge of 'bread and work'. One by one, he began to break the terms of the Versailles Treaty.

When Hitler began to rearm in 1935, Hermann Goering persuaded him to give precedence to the new air arm, the *Luftwaffe*. But there were young officers who had taken to heart the crushing lessons of the last war, and in particular the importance of the tank as the key to mobile warfare. One of them was Heinz Guderian who realised that tanks would never be used to their full effect until the

Hitler reviewing a parade of police at Nuremberg.

other weapons on whose support they relied were brought to the same standard of speed and cross-country performance. What was really needed were whole mobile armoured divisions. While tank development in England was held up by regimental reluctance to subordinate the role of traditional cavalry and infantry, Guderian was busy studying British tank training manuals and the results of British exercises.

Meanwhile France had spent six billion francs on an 'impregnable' fortified defence, to bolster the age-old natural frontier of the Rhine. The Maginot Line was in effect a modernised version of First World War trench defences on an enormous scale. The Line was strongest along the Alsace-Lorraine frontier, where the Prussians had attacked before, but it could not be built facing Belgium for diplomatic reasons – even if France could have afforded it.

In 1934 Guderian demonstrated to Hitler a secretly developed motorised force comprising motor-cycle platoons armed with machine-guns, towed anti-tank guns, armoured-car platoons and high-speed tanks. 'That's what I need! That's what I want,' Hitler exclaimed, and the idea of the armoured Panzer-divisions was born. The prospect of rapid invasion which they offered gave Hitler several advantages. The German rearmament was ingeniously augmented by a considerable element of bluff. Despite the propaganda, the German economy was not geared for, and could not sustain, a long-drawn-out war. Nor did Hitler think he could survive one politically. He hoped to complete his invasion of Eastern Europe before France and Britain had time to respond. A surprise strike deep into a country's territory was expected to paralyse the opposing leadership's will to continue fighting, while a war fought and won quickly also meant that huge supplies of strategic resources from abroad would not be required.

The 'Blitzkrieg' or lightning-war tactics proposed by Guderian were for reconnaissance troops in light tanks, or on motor-cycles with machine-guns mounted in side-cars, to seek out enemy weakness. Then tanks were to advance rapidly *avoiding* strong-points to seize vital objectives and hold them until motorised infantry and anti-tank guns could secure them against counter-attacks. The commander, riding in the forefront, could also call up dive-bombers by radio to provide the equivalent of an artillery barrage. But there were two important weaknesses in the blitzkrieg strategy. One was that although Germany had plenty of coal, the iron for three tanks out of four had to come from Sweden, from the Kiruna mine on the Arctic Circle which exploited an enormous high-quality iron source in some of the oldest Precambrian rocks in Europe. When the Baltic froze in winter, this ore was carried by rail to the port of Narvik on the Norwegian coast which could be blockaded by Britain. The other and more dangerous weak link was that Germany had little oil, the very substance on which the whole of modern warfare and the blitzkrieg concept depended. So in 1933 a contract was given to I. G. Farben to build plants (like the huge Leuna plant near Merseberg) to synthesise petroleum fuels from coal by the hydrogenation process. Germany also hurriedly secured trade agreements for oil from Romania and the Soviet Union. The 1936 4-year war plan also had measures to lessen Germany's reliance on imports of iron-ore and rubber.

Blitzkrieg

The Nazi propaganda machine was so successful in vaunting German military superiority that after an 'Axis' pact was signed between Berlin and Mussolini, German troops were 'invited' into Austria to restore order in March 1938. Czech-oslovakia was now almost surrounded by German-held territory, and 3 million Germans lived in the fortified and highly industrialised eastern border lands of the Sudetenland. At Munich on 30 September 1938, Chamberlain and Daladier (the British and French Prime Ministers) gave Hitler the Sudetenland in the vain hope of retaining peace in central Europe. In return Hitler averred that he had 'no

German Panzer III tanks advancing in Flanders.

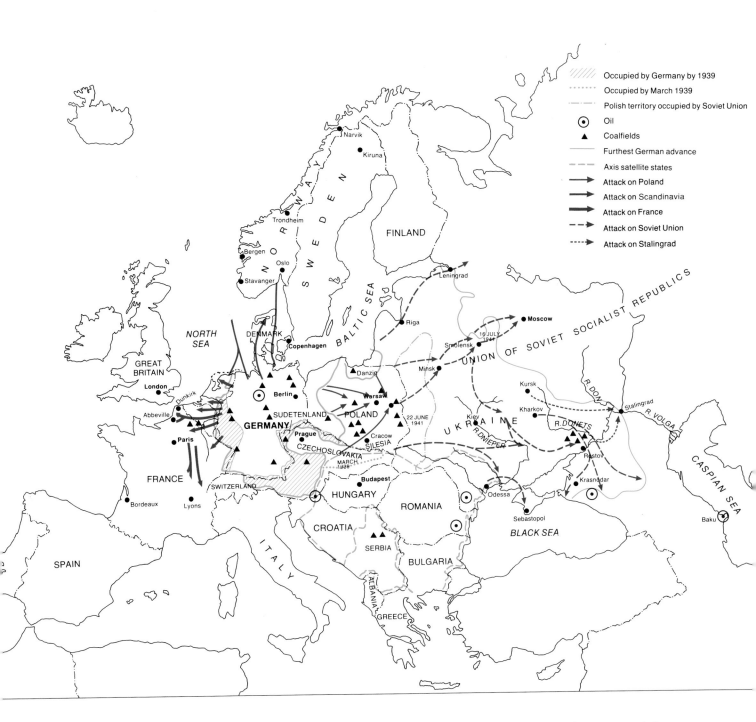

Hitler's resource aims and the Blitzkrieg.

further territorial ambitions in Europe'. Six months later Hitler occupied the rest of Czechoslovakia, including Silesia, the largest industrial area between the Ruhr and the Urals. He gained the huge Skoda armaments factory and enough military equipment to supply four armoured divisions and fifteen infantry divisions. So far despite Western protests, not a shot had been fired.

Believing that France and Britain were too democratic and degenerate to go to war, Hitler turned his attention to the recovery of the Polish corridor to Danzig, which still divided Germany. But now, realising that appeasement had failed, Britain and France guaranteed to come to the aid of Poland if German troops invaded. However, Hitler had a trump card. Realising that he might be drawn into a war with France, he changed his priorities and, in order to gain time to complete the manufacture of his war-making machine for the assault on the Ukraine, he signed a non-aggression pact with Stalin, an astonishing alliance between the extremes of Fascism and Communism. To avoid a second eastern front, Hitler was prepared to allow Stalin to occupy the eastern half of Poland, Finland, Estonia and Latvia.

When Germany invaded Poland on 1 September 1939, the Polish army had 11 cavalry brigades, but only 313 tanks, a force totally inadequate to repel the 3200 tanks that attacked. The six German Panzer divisions, supported by Junkers 87 'Stuka' dive-bombers, thrust deep into Poland in a great pincer movement, until, within a week, the armoured divisions from the north and south met at the gates of Warsaw. Most of the Polish airforce had been destroyed on the ground and the Polish Infantry surrounded. Cities were terror-bombed into submission by the Stuka dive-bombers. A second pincer movement by Guderian drove far to the east through Brest-Litovsk to join another attack from the south headed by General Kleist; this encircled more Polish forces on a massive scale. Although only six out of Hitler's sixty divisions were motorised the blitzkrieg had been a dramatic success. The dominance in land warfare of mechanised forces and aircraft and thus of oil and industrial capacity shocked the world.

The British considered a pre-emptive occupation of Norway to control the vital supplies of iron ore from Kiruna and to deny the ports of Trondheim and Narvik to the Germans as submarine bases. But the Germans got there first, landing troops from warships to take Narvik, Trondheim and Bergen. The British had thought that the command of the sea would decide the issue but they lacked air support and, though many German warships were sunk, it was command of the air that decided the outcome. Yet another new form of warfare reliant on aircraft – assault by paratroops – was used to take Oslo and Stavanger. This capture of the eastern shores of the North Sea prevented Britain mounting an effective blockade of Germany, as she had done so successfully in the First World War.

Assault to the west

Blitzkrieg tactics again triumphed in May 1940 with the attack by ten Panzer divisions, including 3000 armoured vehicles, on Holland, Belgium and France. Avoiding the Maginot Line, the main German attack was forced through the Ardennes hills, which the Allies had thought too difficult for armoured warfare, between the French front and the British defending the Franco-Belgian border. Crossing the River Meuse in rubber dinghies, the Germans floated bridges across to allow the panzers to advance. Heinkel 111s bombed railway junctions and airbases in France, while gliders were used to land troops to take Rotterdam and The Hague. Within ten days Guderian had reached the Channel at Abbeville (disobeying orders to halt to allow the infantry to catch up), successfully splitting the Allied armies and surrounding the British Expeditionary Force at Dunkirk. The success of the campaign had been such as tank commanders might dream of. The Belgian Eastern front was broken too and their army surrendered.

The Germans then turned their 140 divisions against France's 65. The French had few aircraft and were almost powerless against the rapid advance of the German armour. As the Panzer divisions rumbled across France, French morale collapsed, the French Government fled from Paris and on 22 June Marshal Pétain signed a humiliating armistice. The Germans then held the coastline from the Pyrenees to the Arctic Circle and could plunder all the resources of the continent. Hitler thought the war was won and so did many others. The international oil companies, especially Texaco, began to court the Germans as the potential victors. But Britain had found a determined leader in Winston Churchill and, standing alone against the victorious Nazis, Britain would not make peace.

A German Heinkel 111 during a daylight bombing raid on the London docks.

To invade England, which was a war he did not want, Hitler had to have command of the air, or the Royal Navy and Royal Air Force would sink his invasion fleet. So the first great battle of the air, the Battle of Britain, began on 10 July 1940. During the rearmament before the war, German aircraft production had concentrated on bombers, the British on defence by manufacturing Spitfire and Hurricane fighters. They were directed by the new invention of radar and concentrated on attacking the bombers, rather than engaging the Messerschmitt fighters which only carried enough fuel for half an hour's flying over southern England. By August nearly 2000 German aircraft were flying to the attack, and 75 were shot down on just one day of that month. From 7 September, eight days of bombing were to precede the invasion (Operation Sealion) and German bombers attacked Royal Air Force aerodromes, harbours, naval targets and finally towns and cities. So much damage was done to British airfields that it seemed that the Royal Air Force might not be able to keep up the defence, but following a British reprisal bombing raid on Berlin, Hitler switched his bombing to British cities. By 14 September the Nazis had lost 146 aircraft in 8 days, and the next day when 230 German bombers attacked, escorted by 700 fighters, the RAF downed a further 56 planes. Hitler realised that he could not control the skies and his invasion plans were abandoned in favour of bombing cities by night, when it was harder to shoot down the intruders.

With the immediate risk of invasion past, it was now the battle of the Atlantic which would be decisive for the outcome of the war – the struggle against U-boat attacks to keep Britain supplied with food, oil and munitions from her Dominions and America. The scenario of the First World War was being replayed, with Britain reinforced with resources from abroad – especially through American lend-lease aid. Then Mussolini invaded Egypt from Libya to gain control of the Suez Canal and Britain's oil from the Persian Gulf. His troops suffered humiliating defeat from the British tanks but it opened a new theatre of the war. Following another Italian failure to capture Greece, Hitler occupied the strategically essential Romanian oilfields and pressured the Balkan countries to join the Axis powers, invading Yugoslavia in ten days and mainland Greece in a week. Britain had already destroyed oil storage and pumping plant in northern Iraq and the oil pipeline from Iraq to the Mediterranean to deny them to the Nazis.

The eastern front

In his book *Mein Kampf* Hitler had described Russia as 'the deadly enemy of Germany's future'. Stalin would have done well to distrust him, for Hitler was now able to return to his original aim, the conquest of the Ukraine. In flagrant violation of his non-aggression pact, he attacked his ally the Soviet Union. 'Operation Barbarossa' was launched with seventy-nine divisions, on a 3200-kilometre front in June 1941. There were three main thrusts to the attack, the northern army group was to make for Leningrad, the centre two-pronged attack was towards Moscow, and the southern attack was to take Kiev, the Ukraine, the Donbass industrial area and then press on to the Black Sea coast and the vital oil supplies of Baku. It was the biggest military operation in history but it began seven weeks later than planned because of the Nazi invasion of the Balkans. Yet it still caught Stalin completely by surprise. However, Hitler was over-confident and the seven lost weeks before the onset of winter were to be crucial.

At first the success of this greatest blitzkrieg was spectacular. Having first gained control of the air, the Germans soon surrounded Leningrad. The central attack by two Panzer groups under Hoth and Guderian also made huge gains, sweeping 300 kilometres north and south of the main Russian troop concentration to meet at Minsk. Within five days they had surrounded thirty Russian divisions which could then be destroyed by German infantry and artillery. Hoth and Guderian pushed on to Smolensk to close their attack behind the Russian reserve armies, encircling another 300,000 troops, and moved on towards Moscow. The brilliant advances had been too fast for the infantry to be able to keep up, supplied as they were by horse-drawn carts. But even when surrounded the Russians continued to fight, and the Germans were dismayed by the tenacity of their fighting and also by the size of the Russian reserves. They were also surprised by the quality of the Russian T34 tanks with sloping armour from which the German shells bounced off. The secret manufacture and trials of German tanks, which had been carried out in Russia to elude the Versailles Treaty, had allowed the Russians to learn vital lessons about tank construction and deployment.

Hitler now took the fateful decision to intervene in the campaign, and directed Guderian away from Moscow, southwards to join Kleist who had already made an immense advance to the Dnieper river. Kiev was surrounded, in the biggest encirclement of all, but Stalin ordered his five trapped armies to hold their ground. After five days of slaughter, 600,000 Russian prisoners were taken and the whole Ukraine was occupied. In October the attack on Moscow was resumed with a huge force of Panzer divisions. But where Napoleon had failed, Hitler failed too. The attack on Kiev had consumed valuable supplies and time, and had allowed the Russians to build up their defences. The German advance reached the outskirts of Moscow but it was beyond their grasp and now they had a second enemy, the winter. Equipped only for a summer offensive, the German troops and their machines were unprepared and had now to face the rigours of temperatures as low as minus 50 degrees Celsius. In Leningrad, which endured a siege and bombardment lasting 900 days, about a million Russians died of starvation.

The blitzkrieg had ground to a halt and a war of attrition between Communists and Nazis had begun. Russia had lost roughly half of its industrial capacity but Stalin's brutal policy of forcing the population to resite Soviet industry near the resources of the Urals, forcibly moving ten million people in the process, now paid off. The Russian counter-offensive under General Zhukov began but the Germans, by now desperate for supplies of petroleum fuels, made another advance towards the oilfields of the Caucasus and Baku in the summer of 1942. Again Hitler made a disastrous error by ordering an attack on Stalingrad (Volgograd). His tanks were quite unsuited to fighting in a city, and the besiegers found themselves surrounded by a counter-offensive under General Zhukov. After grim fighting through the winter which reduced 99 per cent of the city to ruins, the Russians took half a million prisoners. Hitler's armies never reached the oil of Baku and the tide of the war turned. The Germans attempted to renew the attack five months later but it was to be Hitler's Waterloo. Near Kursk 2500 German tanks and assault guns were concentrated, supported by over 1000 air-craft. But the Russians brought up even greater forces and, after the greatest tank battle in history, which lasted for ten days, the German losses were so great that they had to retreat on the whole eastern front. Now there was no hope of the Germans competing with the combined manufacturing capacity of Britain and America who together made 30,000 tanks in 1943.

After the surprise Japanese attack at Pearl Harbor, instead of leaving Japan and America to fight it out in the Pacific, Hitler had made another fateful step by declaring war on the United States in December 1941, making the war global. It was an act which began the end of the era of western European global supremacy. After the D-day landings, despite the fact that at first the British forces equalled the American, it was an American General who took command. From now on the United States and the Soviet Union were to be the two super-powers. The German forces fell back, their vital synthetic petrol plants were bombed and, lacking fuel to keep her fighters in the air, Germany's industries, ports and cities were laid open to the terrible vengeance of the Allied bombers.

After the surrender of the German 6th army at Stalingrad, Soviet soldiers escort prisoners. Of some half million German, Italian, Romanian and Hungarian prisoners taken, 80 per cent died before the end of the winter.

CHAPTER TWELVE

HOSTAGES
TO OIL

Russia and the United States insisted that only unconditional surrender by Germany could end the war against Hitler. They wanted no repeat of the argument about the 'unfair' terms of the Versailles armistice that had provided Hitler's excuse for territorial seizures. It was a fight to the bitter end, and when Germany finally capitulated at Rheims on 7 May 1945, it was not only German ambition and industrial might that lay in ruins; cities and factories had been laid waste from Derby to the Donbass. In 1946 European steel production was only one-third of the pre-war figure, while coal-mines managed only 60 per cent of the 1939 output. The railway system was in ruins and agriculture was in a worse state than industry.

Following the destruction of Europe's industrial power came the traumatic loss of the Dutch and French colonies in the East Indies and the dismantling of the British Empire. While, by 1948, eastern Europe had become a buffer zone of Stalinist puppet states, armed to protect the Soviet Union from a perceived threat from the West. The grim division of Europe into Christian and Communist camps began and would last for over 40 years. It was the end of European political domination of the globe but the nature of Europe had not changed. It would retain the unique inherent advantages born of geography and geology that political division had caused to be squandered. The massive resources and advantages of Europe could still be of great account, were it possible once again for political cooperation to allow Adam Smith's necessary requirements of peace, easy taxes and justice to reign.

The war had changed society and, with it, governments. In the West the old autocratic moulds were broken and a hope of rebuilding the ruins in a spirit of social justice and equality inspired the servicemen and women returning to civilian life. The lesson of the Depression had been learned too, and the need for massive investment in reconstruction to provide employment was obvious. Ironically, it was the fact that the American economy had boomed throughout the second half of the war through supplying resources and equipment to the Allies, which now enabled the United States to mount the Marshall Plan for massive financial aid to rebuild the Western European economy. George Marshall had been the Chief of Staff of the US Army, and became Secretary of State in 1947. He proposed that the United Sates should grant aid to rebuild European industry on condition that the European governments should collaborate in restructuring their economies. This they agreed to do, with the notable exception of the whole of Eastern Europe, and the immense sum of $17 billion was spent in Western Europe between 1948 and 1952.

At first conditions were grim. Millions of starving refugees trekked westwards, from Russia into the formerly German-occupied territories, from Eastern Europe back into Germany, and from Germany to France, Britain and the United States. Europe was still in turmoil when an unusually severe winter began in November 1946. Even in Kent German prisoners-of-war were put to work clearing snowdrifts 3 metres deep which cut off villages, and bombers were put to a new use air-dropping containers of bread to marooned villages. The homeless suffered terribly in central Europe's shattered cities, while the shortage of coal caused blackouts in electricity supplies across the continent. These privations focused the minds of politicians as never before on the fact that after food, energy supplies were the crucial resource for national security and that Europe was self-sufficient in neither.

On the outbreak of war, 90 per cent of Europe's energy had still come from burning coal and it was now recognised that there was a severe 'Energy gap'. In 1948 no less than 58 million tons of coal had to be imported, and the United States was by far the largest supplier. At the same time the shortage of dollars in Europe led to an emphasis on rebuilding the mining industry to make the continent self-sufficient in coal. Coal and steel were not only by far the biggest industries, they were still the basis for military might. So, in 1947, the British coal industry, which still had 1500 pits employing three-quarters of a million men, was nationalised. France followed, while the German industry remained under the control of the Allied occupation. A massive investment in modernisation was begun in both old and new pits to produce as much coal as possible. Coal-mining was viewed more as a public service than as a business and the return on the money invested was not even counted.

As production recovered, it was France's old fear of the industrial supremacy of the Ruhr that became the inspiration for her Foreign Minister, Robert Schuman, to propose a union between the French and German coal and steel industries – a coal and steel community – to be ruled by a supranational 'High Authority' that would make 'war between France and Germany . . . not merely unthinkable but materially impossible'. Such a union, which might be joined by other nations, was also to eliminate tariffs, to improve competition and specialisation and to control potential cartels in the Ruhr (50 per cent of western Europe's output) and in the Nord and Pas-de-Calais coalfields.

The European Coal and Steel Community was created by the Treaty of Paris in 1951 and, under the presidency of the visionary Jean Monnet, began the long economic and political progress that finally led to the European Community. Under it the six members (Belgium, France, Italy, Luxembourg, the Netherlands and West Germany) surrendered control of prices, quotas, subsidies, restriction on movements etc. to the High Authority. France also saw it as a means of guaranteeing supplies of German coal to its own steel industry, but Britain would have nothing to do with a body that was 'utterly undemocratic and responsible to nobody' and would not join. Before they would sign, the Italians, for geological reasons less well-endowed with both iron and coal than their neighbours north of the Alps, obtained a deal for access to Algerian iron ore for twenty years. But the Coal and Steel Community did not solve the energy gap, and the immense importance of petroleum was missed. No one guessed that it would be the

availability and price of this single resource, imported from abroad, which would determine the future development of Europe. In the meantime, the demand for steel was rising steadily, coal prices and thus miners' wages were high, and King Coal seemed firmly seated on his grimy throne.

Oil and politics

The new mood of egalitarianism was not confined to Europe. At the end of the war Venezuela was the biggest exporter of oil, and it became the first country to demand a fairer share of the vast revenue being earned by the international oil

A new skyline for European industry, an oil refinery at Antwerp.

companies. The Venezuelan government wanted 50 per cent of the profits made on their oil, and despite competition from new discoveries such as the enormous Saudi Arabian fields, which began production in 1950, they got it. Persia (which was officially renamed Iran in 1935) had been occupied by British and Russian troops in 1941 to safeguard oil supplies to the Allies and to secure a supply route to the Russians fighting in the Caucasus. Now a militantly nationalistic Prime Minister, Mohammed Mussadeq, argued that the Anglo-Iranian Oil Company was plundering the country of its oil and must pay for it so that the wealth of the country could be spent on its own inhabitants. Refusing all deals offered by the company, he gambled on Britain's need for oil, maintaining huge popular support by claiming that if the company were nationalised all poverty would disappear from Iran. Finally, in 1951, he expropriated all the company's assets and gave the workers at the Abadan refinery a choice: either work for his nationalised company or leave.

By threatening Anglo-Iranian, in what was the first great confrontation between a state and the increasingly powerful international oil business, Mussadeq had made a major mistake. The British knew that the Iranians alone would be unable to keep production going, as well as not having the expertise to market the oil without a tanker fleet and distribution system. All the expatriate workers left, Britain blockaded the Persian Gulf and Iran's oil production stopped for three years, throwing 70,000 Iranian employees out of work, and strangling the economy of the country. In the two years following nationalisation, only the equivalent of one day's output was sold. For a while, Britain had to spend dollars to get her oil but the longer-term effect on Anglo-Iranian was to stimulate its production and exploration elsewhere. The company already had a half share in the Kuwait Oil Company and a substantial interest in Qatar, and soon the output from these two countries alone made up for the loss of the Iranian supplies. Kuwait (a British protectorate until 1961) was to reap the greatest benefit from the blockade of Iran, becoming for several years the leading Middle East producer of oil.

As new sources of oil were found, the international companies began to build huge refineries on the politically more dependable shores of western Europe. Not surprisingly these were built at the great ports – gateways of the traditional trade-routes to the heart of Europe – at the mouth of the Rhône at L'Etang de Berre, at Rotterdam on the Rhine, Marghera near Venice and at Fawley on Southampton Water.

Far more petroleum was being found than the experts had predicted. Vast reserves were found in Libya in 1959, while France, which already had a stake in Iraq, sought oil in her African colonies for the same strategic reasons that Churchill had wanted an oil supply under British control in 1914. She had been forced to give Morocco and Tunisia full independence soon after the war, but Algeria was still a colony with over a million settlers of European origin. Oil was discovered in the Algerian Sahara in 1955 by BRP, wholly owned by the French Government; but a national insurrection against French rule had begun just before. The following year another Algerian oilfield and a huge natural-gas field were found. However, a brutal and bitter war of liberation began, fought by the French colonists supported by the army and paratroops, against the FLN (Front de la Libération Nationale), with atrocities against civilians committed by both sides. As the French generals gained a military advantage in this Algerian War, they united Arab opposition, but still insisted on keeping Algeria French. An important factor in their obstinate resistance to Algerian independence was the strategic value to France of the oil and gas reserves. The war so divided public opinion in France that it led to a revolt by right-wing extremists and, when the generals and settlers turned against the government, it caused the fall of the Fourth Republic in May 1958. For a while there was a real danger of civil war, until the formation, by Charles de Gaulle, of a 'government of national safety'.

Western Europe's petroleum consumption more than doubled between 1954 and 1960, but available supplies rose even faster, so the price fell, especially when demand fell during the recession of 1958. This troubled the United States Government because production costs were now higher there and, as foreign oil began to flow into the nation in larger and larger quantities, there was a fear that small producers with no overseas business would collapse. The Government also wanted to protect home production for strategic reasons, as the cold war with Russia intensified. So, in 1959, President Eisenhower imposed compulsory controls on imports of petroleum. The many independent oil companies which had invested huge sums for exploration in the Middle East had to sell their oil elsewhere and turned to the expanding European market, cutting their prices. The price of heavy fuel oil fell by 58 per cent, and this was bad news for coal.

The coal crisis

Coal powered not only the post-war recovery but an economic boom in the mid-1950s, with the West German 'economic miracle' fuelled once again by the Ruhr. But the European economy could only expand as fast as the fuel supply and the demand for energy had grown faster than coal could be mined. So the share from burning imported oil increased. Even in 1872 the Russian chemist Mendeleyev had argued, 'This material is far too precious to be burnt. When burning oil we burn money; it should be used as a chemical base material'. Now some of the fastest-growing industries were those using the by-products of oil refining, ethylene and propylene, to make plastics and artificial fibres – which again stimulated oil production.

There had also been a significant change in the way energy was being used both in the home and the factory. The infamous London fogs were caused by having coal fires in every room of every house – even the bedrooms. As late as 1952 the Great London Smog caused 6000 deaths. But in the post-war years there was an alternative to coal – electricity. Coal was increasingly being viewed as a 'dirty' fuel and, especially in the foggy climate of Britain, the cleanliness and convenience of coal-gas or electric fires soon made them more attractive. This removed the smoke pollution from the city centres to the power-stations whose tall chimneys were designed to put it higher into the atmosphere. More and more electricity was being used to power industry. Many European railways had been electrified during the post-war reconstruction, and the disappearance of steam locomotives from the European countryside, replaced by electric or diesel-electric engines, was just one symptom of the declining use of coal. As 'clean', easy-to-handle oil became used more, it was also found to be far cheaper in maintenance and servicing costs.

Two mild winters and a recession in the late 1950s were enough to drive down fuel prices, sharpening competition between the energy sources. Coal was now beginning to look expensive and demand fell while oil imports continued to grow. Electricity had the virtue that it could be generated equally well from oil or coal without affecting the consumer and this again resulted in a replacement of coal by cheaper oil. To protect jobs in the mines, the British government asked the Central Electricity Generating Board to continue to burn coal and imposed a fuel-oil tax, but agreed that new oil-fired power stations could be built. Every time a new one was opened it cost 5 million tons of coal sales a year. Old power-stations were converted, too – when Tilbury power-station was switched to oil, it stopped burning 26,000 tons of coal a week and effectively closed down a mining village. In 1954 oil had provided only a fifth of Europe's energy needs but by 1960 it supplied over a third, and for the first time since the Industrial Revolution the amount of coal burnt was actually falling.

In the 1950s coal declined from providing 70 per cent of West Germany's energy needs to little more than a third, despite massive investment in the mines

to increase productivity and thus lower the pithead price. By the 1960s the con-
traction of the European coal industry was even more severe, and because so
many people were employed in the mines, it began to have dramatic social consequences. These were comparable in scale to those experienced when man-power
was first replaced in the factories by coal, thousands of miners lost their jobs,
throwing whole communities into crisis and provoking a severe challenge to
social services, at great expense to governments. In the Ruhr the labour force had
already been cut by more than half, but two months' output still stood unsold at
the pitheads, although this was partly because of the reduction in steel-making. A
huge political crisis developed with the miners throwing lignite briquettes (made
with the product of the competing open-cast lignite mines) at the Bundestag. By
1968 all the private mining companies had been rationalised into the Ruhrkohle

The gigantic opencast
lignite (brown coal) mines
between Cologne and
Aachen provide a quarter
of western Germany's
electricity. The excavator
in the foreground has a
bucket wheel 21 metres in
diameter which can dig
350,000 tons a day. This
Fortuna mine has now
been exhausted.

The end of an era of deep coal mining. The miners' locker room at the Marine mine, South Wales after the last shift had gone home.

AG which was soon in serious financial difficulties, requiring hundreds of millions of Deutschmarks in subsidies.

In Britain demand was a third less than predicted a decade before, and 400 pits were closed, mostly in South Wales and Durham; while the chairman of the National Coal Board, Lord Robens, caused a sensation when he forecast that the number of miners would be 80 per cent less by 1980, predicting a loss of 300,000 jobs. In France, where the deep coal seams made mining even more expensive, a decision was made to switch electricity generation from coal to oil in 1962, with a 'planned crisis' shutting down one pit a year. Although this was intended to avoid redundancies, it sparked off a series of ugly confrontations, with sympathy strikes by public employees, shopkeepers and even doctors. But despite heavy government subsidies, demand for coal fell twice as fast as planned.

Holland imported increasing quantities of cheap open-cast coal from the United States, and the sudden discovery of the huge Groningen natural-gas fields (which had been formed naturally from a coal deposit), with a stake owned by the state mining industry, provided further competition for the Limburg mines. In Belgium there was severe rioting in 1959 when uneconomic mines were closed in the southern coalfield of the Borinage; but rationalisation in an area like Liège, where 60 per cent of workers depended on the mines, was helped by the fact that most of the miners were, by now, migrant workers from Italy, with an annual turnover of 35 per cent. This statistic reflected the great internal migration happening within Europe as people from the Mediterranean, including Turkey, moved north to the old industrial heartlands and the great Rhine-Rhône trade axis, where even low-paid jobs gave them better opportunities than at home.

By 1967 Belgian coal consumption had declined to such an extent that the government began to shut down even the highly productive modern state-owned coal-mines of Limbourg, provoking riots which lasted for three days. Paratroops were called in and two miners were killed. The social impact was felt most in the industrial regions of the coalfields, which had once been the heavy manufacturing heartland of Europe, but now began to decay. While recognising the desperate social need to try to preserve jobs in mining communities, governments were powerless to act against the commercial reality of steadily falling energy prices and a contracting industry. Once again the accidents of geology determined the success or failure of the mines. When coal could be shipped relatively cheaply around the world it was not the quality of European coal that was in question but the depth and thickness of the seams and thus the cost of winning it.

Because Europe had been a zone where the edges of continents had collided and deformed, much of its coal was buried deep, while on undeformed continental landmasses, like Queensland or New South Wales in Australia, erosion had removed the overburden and left the coal near the surface where it could be mined open-cast. Russia has 60 per cent of the world's coal reserves and the Russian and Polish seams on the rigid continental heartland of Europe were not as deep as those of France, and were thus cheaper to mine. Regions like South Wales, where the seams of coal are confused by folding and faults, caused by the raising of the Alps, were the most expensive. As Lord Robens was later to admit in 1984, 'Every coalfield in Britain, with the exception of the East Midlands and Yorkshire, was a dead loser, and I don't believe that South Wales or Scotland have ever made a penny profit for the National Coal Board.' The British mines had been run as a national service, rather than for profit, and the cost of this policy was reflected in all the countries in the Coal and Steel Community, which now shared the same dilemma of what to do about it.

Another massive blow to the old industrial areas came with the closure of obsolete steel-mills. The technology of steel-making had also undergone a revolutionary change with the invention of a method of using oxygen rather than air to refine molten iron into steel. Once oxygen was cheap enough, a process was developed in the 1950s in Austria – the Linz Donauwitz or basic oxygen steel process – which could be used to make steel continuously, and thus in larger quantities and more economically than in the old converters. This process is used in steel plants like Redcar in Yorkshire, where the biggest steel plant in Western Europe now produces 10,000 tons of metal a day. But the new technology required high-quality iron ore – 65 per cent iron with a low phosphorus content – and few European ironstones met these new requirements. Enormous new iron

deposits had been found: in Western Australia at Hamersley and Mount New-
man, and at Carajas in Brazil, as well as in other countries. As a consequence
more iron ore now travels the oceans than any other commodity except oil. The
200,000-ton bulk carriers which discharge at Redcar and Port Talbot in South
Wales (a port originally founded on local coal and iron) now bring their loads
from Labrador or Australia, and even the massive underground mine at Kiruna in
Sweden finds it hard to compete. The Soviet Union has enough high-grade ore at
Kursk to supply the present rate of world consumption for 3000 years. It does
supply East Germany and Poland, but the problem, of course, is that overland
transport is far more expensive than shipping costs. Railways compete with giant
bulk-carrier ships no better than pack animals did with sailing ships in Roman
times, making this Russian source a less attractive one.

The life-blood of a new Europe

In 1956 British troops were finally withdrawn from Egypt. Six weeks later President Nasser nationalised the Suez Canal Company, which was largely owned by
British and French investors. In 1955 the Canal had carried 69 million tons of oil,
and the British Prime Minister, Anthony Eden, pronounced that Nasser 'must not
have his thumb on our windpipe'. British and French troops invaded the Canal
Zone, while a simultaneous attack by Israel occupied much of the Sinai peninsula. But the Anglo-French attack was opposed by the United States, which
feared that Nasser would be driven into the Communist camp. The Anglo-
French invasion force had to withdraw, signalling as never before the supremacy
of the United States over Europe in world affairs. The Suez Canal was blocked
and it provoked the sudden realisation in European nations of the vulnerability
of their oil supplies from the Gulf – and not only to governments. Although shipping was stopped for only four months the Suez crisis caused petrol rationing in
several countries. British motorists discovered, to their horror, that they were
permitted to drive only 320 kilometres a month.

The global balance of economic power was changing in other ways, as Japan
industrialised rapidly, and the oil-exporting countries suddenly found that they
had enormous purchasing power. But against all precedent, and almost without
its peoples knowing, Europe was about to take a revolutionary step in the progress of pooling its resources; achieving progress towards a political unity not
seen since the Empire of Charlemagne. Germany had been divided up between
the four Allied powers (Britain, France, America and the Soviet Union) at
Potsdam in 1945, thus ending the 'German Problem' and the old fears of France.
But by 1950 Stalin had moved the threat to European security from the natural
frontier of the Rhine to that of the Elbe (where communist control began). The
western countries were now given common cause in the defensive alliance of
NATO. The increasing prosperity of France and Italy made Communism less
attractive to their voters, and the leaders of both left and right began to adopt
common political aims of economic growth, social welfare and full employment.
Discovering that they had interests in common, West European governments
also found themselves willing to surrender narrow nationalistic aims for the
greater collective good.

The Treaties of Rome, signed by Belgium, France, West Germany, Italy,
Luxembourg and the Netherlands – the 'Six' – brought the European Economic
Community into being on 1 January 1958. The 'Common Market', as it came to
be known, was to be an association founded on free trade, the free movement of
capital and labour, and with joint social and financial policies. It was the most

fundamental political change in Europe since the birth of the nation-states, and its aim was no less than to substitute cooperation for European civil war.

It seems odd now, but one of the first priorities of the Treaties was to put the infant atomic industry in common control under Euratom, for the purpose of promoting nuclear research and to speed the large-scale use of nuclear energy for peaceful purposes. It was an era when there was an enormous and rather innocent expectation that science would be able to solve most of the problems of society, including that of energy supply. An atomic future was embraced with such enthusiasm that there were even plans to build atomic-powered aircraft. The purpose of Euratom was 'to ensure the exclusively peaceful development of atomic energy'. It was also to ensure that the signatories shared their atomic know-how and industry, to produce abundant cheap electricity that would drive a new renaissance of European industrial power. In both aims Euratom was a signal failure. The Soviet Union had already exploded its first atomic bomb in 1949, the British in 1952 and France in 1960. Neither Britain nor France had any intention of surrendering the secrets of their ultimate weapon into the hands of others, nor would the Americans provide theirs, and Jean Monnet's dream of a United States of Europe being the continent of the future, 'a federal power linked to the exploitation of atomic energy', so dazzled the bureaucrats that they failed to notice the rising tide of cheap oil which would wash their vision away.

As in the case of the Mussadeq embargo, the blocked Suez Canal had a dramatic effect in diversifying the supply of oil, especially from Africa. France already had its agreement with Algeria, but Libya, which produced only 20,000 barrels of oil a day in 1961, was pumping 3.3 million barrels by 1970, and by then Nigeria was producing almost half that amount. The conflict also encouraged a change to larger refining units, bigger tankers and bigger oil-terminals. In 1960 two-thirds of the world's tanker fleet were under 30,000 tons deadweight (and none bigger than 90,000 tons). Ten years later less than a fifth were as small as that and the super-tanker had been born, a third being over 100,000 tons. This huge increase of scale was partly to economise on freight costs on the long sea-route from the Gulf around the Cape of Good Hope to Europe, which avoided the uncertainties and high tolls of the Canal.

In the 1950s Stalin wanted to continue his pre-war policy of catching up with the industrial power of the West (born Joseph Djugashvili, it was doubly significant that he had adopted the name of Stalin, meaning steel). The very harshness of the climate in the USSR and the physical difficulties of permafrost and desert had inspired the great Stalinist schemes 'for the transformation of Nature'. While the Soviet electrification and energy programmes of the 1920s and 1930s had been hailed as an outstanding success, industrialisation had been achieved at the cost of the lives of millions of the more prosperous peasant farmers whose land was forcibly collectivised and who were sent to work in labour camps to build the new industrial centres. Collective farms were supposed to feed the cities and the countryside better, but in practice there was at first a catastrophic collapse of agricultural productivity, and millions died in the subsequent famines. Once challenged by Churchill about the dreadful human cost of his industrial policy Stalin had replied, 'what is one generation?' The Soviet Union, in Stalin's view, had to be almost self-sufficient in resources to maintain its strategic independence from the West, and the development of the Volga-Baikal industrial zone, far from any ocean and independent of overseas trade, but also at a safe distance from foreign frontiers, was unique. Russia's thousand-year struggle to get an easy outlet to the sea had never succeeded and the Soviet Union had far more large cities over 1000 kilometres from the sea than any other nation. But Marxist contempt for geographical realities such as climate and distance did not alter their fundamental economic consequences, and it was more than one generation that would suffer.

Stalin also wanted to keep Germany divided and to retain the frontiers of the formerly Tsarist empire. To do so he tied the economies of Eastern Europe to the Soviet Union by establishing the Council for Mutual Economic Assistance, COMECON. This body coordinated the planned economies and for example proposed that Romania and Bulgaria should be agricultural lands while Czechoslovakia and East Germany were to be predominantly industrial. While there was some geographical and resource logic in this, the centralisation in Moscow of national economic planning infuriated the countries concerned. In practice the Soviet Union maintained its control on virtually a barter basis between ministries, by exporting energy, armaments and raw materials to the socialist countries, while importing manufactures such as locomotives, machine tools and machinery in return. The immense wealth of minerals in the Soviet Union, particularly its 'unlimited' hydro-electric and hydrocarbon energy reserves, allowed this odd reversal of the role normally played by a developed country with its client states. While the communist aim was for the economic invulnerability of the East in food and energy, the view of the recipient satellite countries like Hungary was that they were being forced into inefficient energy-intensive manufacture of

The major oil and natural gas fields of Europe and western Siberia, with their pipelines linking them to cities.

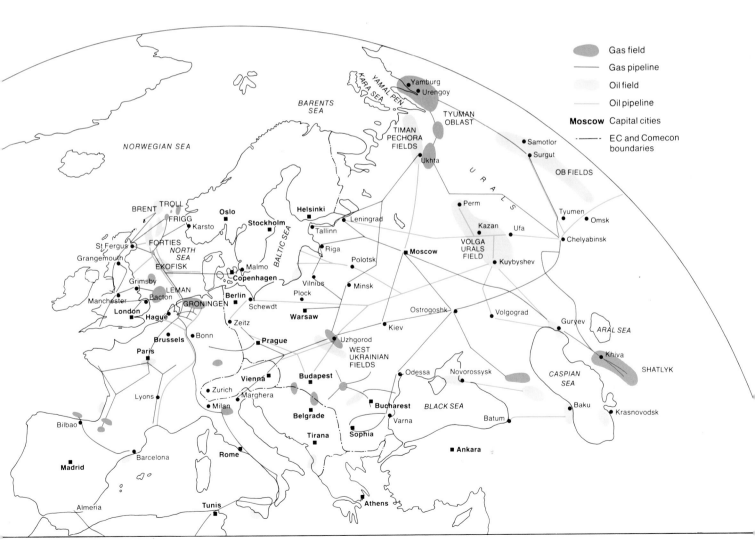

low-priced articles. The location of factories and plants followed ideological and strategic needs rather than practical economic factors such as the availability of raw materials, transport costs, labour and markets.

Many steel plants were deliberately located in backward areas to disperse industry. Eisenhüttenstadt (Stalinstadt) in East Germany, Košice in Czechoslovakia, Galaţi in Romania and Nowa Huta in Poland were all built to use Soviet iron ore from Krivoy Rog and Kursk. Nowa Huta was deliberately built near Cracow to proletarianise the ancient capital of the Poles, one of Europe's finest Renaissance cities, which it is now destroying with its pollution.

Popular resentment came to a head in 1956 when Khrushchev denounced the excesses of Stalin, and the Hungarian people seized the chance to demand democracy, leaving the Warsaw Pact (the Communist defensive alliance equivalent to NATO) which had been set up the year before. While the West was distracted by the Suez Crisis, the Russian Army, supported by others from the Warsaw Pact, brutally suppressed the Hungarian National Uprising. The following year the appearance of the first artificial satellite – the Russian Sputnik – circling the earth confirmed Russia's entry into the forefront of military rocket technology. From then on the space race and the arms race went hand in hand. Russia became more distrustful of the intentions of the countries of Eastern Europe, and strengthened East Germany against Western influence by suddenly building the Berlin Wall in August 1961, to cut off the annual exodus of 200,000 refugees. Churchill's metaphor of an Iron Curtain across Europe had become a fact. In 1964 the 'Druzhba' (Friendship) oil pipeline from the Volga-Urals oilfield was completed to pump Soviet oil to Hungary, Czechoslovakia, Poland and East Germany. It further tightened the bonds of COMECON by making the Soviet satellite countries dependent on Russian oil. It is arguable that only the fear of atomic holocaust restrained the East and West from going to war.

Western affluence: fifteen maids in a mini, 1966.

The swinging consumer

In 1958 only about 15 per cent of industrial production in Western Europe was for consumer goods, but then began a revolution in spending power. Prolonged peace and full employment, with a rising number of two-income families, had spawned not just unparalleled prosperity but an impatience with paternalistic government and tradition. Mass production and the extensive use of plastics, plus the availability of credit, had lowered the price of the larger consumer goods such as televisions, washing machines and most especially cars, until they were within the purchasing power of ordinary working-class families. The 'swinging sixties' rocked to the rhythm of the new scientific advances, the transistor radio and the contraceptive pill – which was soon to stabilise west-European population growth.

It became the age of the car. The *autobahns* had begun in the 1930s in Germany but the first motorway did not open in Britain until 1958 (there would be 1600 kilometres by the early seventies). Prophetically, it was also the year when the first curb was put on the motorist's freedom of movement, with parking meters being installed in London. The Volkswagen, the Fiat 500 and the Mini began the personal transport revolution that swept away an era of flat caps and bicycles and increased the number of cars sixfold between 1950 and 1980. As car manufacturing became a leading industry, comparable in its effects to the railway or cotton industries of the mid-nineteenth century, it affected whole economies.

Each car assembly plant created a long chain of demand reaching back to steel-mills, glass-works and rubber trees. Cotton for upholstery, linseed oil for paints,

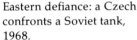
Eastern defiance: a Czech confronts a Soviet tank, 1968.

molasses for solvents and anti-freeze, soya bean for enamel, were all in demand for manufacture, but that was only the beginning of the story. Roads needed concrete, iron reinforcing bars, steel bridges, bitumen surfaces and armies of construction workers with their complex machines. The whole structure of towns and society came to be built around the car, while new industries clustered round motorway intersections. And all depended on oil. Petrol consumption in Britain quadrupled between 1957 and 1975.

New patterns of power

The population of Europe in the 1960s was not only better off and better educated, it was also better informed of world affairs, because of the ubiquitous eye of television. And in the world beyond Carnaby Street and Tin Pan Alley the power blocs were realigning. The decade had begun with the Sino-Soviet split, which broke the simple cold war division of the planet between communism and capitalism. By 1968 Czechoslovakia was making overtures of trade with the West and, for a brief spring of hope, welcomed 'socialism with a human face' before the government was crushed beneath the tracks of Warsaw Pact tanks. In the same year half a million US servicemen were fighting in Vietnam. That year they dropped a greater tonnage of bombs on North Vietnam than had fallen on Germany and Japan in the entire period of the Second World War. American resources and industrial strength had proved decisive in two world wars, but the bitter disgust felt by many Americans as well as Europeans at the conduct of the Vietnam War, and the division it produced between the right wing and the liberals, brought home to the United States the true cost of their belief that America standing alone was invincible world-wide. The Vietnam disaster, which cost 56,000 American dead, marked a waning of this dangerous illusion that American military might was omnipotent, and started a new era of negotiation rather than confrontation; of 'jaw not war'. President Nixon visited both Moscow and Peking in 1972, becoming the first American President to set foot on the Asian continent. The kaleidoscope of economic power was also shifting to new, more complex patterns. In 1970 Japan had the second largest economy in the non-communist world.

The oil shock

Of far more importance to Europe, however, were developments in the Middle East. By 1973 the continent was dangerously dependent on energy sources from overseas, with two-thirds deriving from imported oil and coal. Two-thirds of that petroleum was coming from the Arab countries, and their continued striving for better terms from the oil companies had resulted in the formation of the Organisation of Petroleum-Exporting Countries (OPEC). The oil producers had suddenly realised that when oil was scarce they could control the industry, rather than submit to the cartel of the international oil companies. It was to be Israel that provided the excuse. In June 1967 Israel had responded to the closure of the Gulf of Aqaba by the Egyptians with a remarkable six-day campaign against Egypt, Iraq, Jordan and Syria, in which they occupied the West Bank of the Jordan, the Golan heights and the Sinai peninsula. The conflict was rejoined in October 1973 when the Egyptians and Syrians launched a surprise attack on Israel on the holiest day of the Jewish Calendar, Yom Kippur. This time the Israelis suffered heavy casualties from their Russian-armed opponents, and Nixon, alarmed by reports that Soviet nuclear weapons had been flown to Egypt, began an airlift of arms to Israel. There was a real fear that America and Russia, by supporting opposing sides, might be drawn into a new world war. In the outcome it was not Israel's probable possession of her own nuclear weapons which had the lasting effect, but Arab use of the 'oil weapon'.

Two events had made the oil market unstable already: the first was that in 1971, the United States, where gasoline (petrol) consumption was increasing by 7 per cent a year, had become a net importer of oil for the first time; the second was that in the following year both Libya and Kuwait cut back supply in the interests of conservation. Despite the opening of new fields in western Siberia, world oil supply now barely exceeded demand. Then, also in 1973, Colonel Muammar Qadhafi had announced that he would nationalise all five oil companies operating in Libya, and put the price of Libyan oil up to $6 a barrel, almost twice the price of oil from the Persian Gulf.

Now the OPEC countries, led by the Shah of Iran, stunned the world by declaring that they would henceforth set the figure at $11.65. The price of oil had quadrupled in only two months. In addition OPEC announced that production would be cut back by 5 per cent a month until Israel withdrew to its pre-Six Day War frontiers. Saudi Arabia, which was now the world's largest producer, demonstrated convincingly that OPEC had suddenly become the most important financial power in the history of the world by announcing a 10 per cent cutback in production and an embargo on oil to the United States and the Netherlands as a sanction for supporting Israel. Petroleum now provided 64 per cent of Western Europe's energy, and matters were made worse by Rotterdam being the oil port for the whole of central Europe. By the time the clamour on the international markets had died down, OPEC's output had been cut back by 17 per cent. It was left to the oil companies to share out the supplies by reallocating oil from non-Arab sources on the basis of 'equal misery', and an embarrassing free-for-all ensued as countries scrambled for deals direct with Arab states. France and Britain behaved particularly badly, while Americans were furious at their impotence at the hands of 'a bunch of Sheiks and a Shah'.

Almost every importing country was faced with a serious balance of payments deficit and rapid inflation. Speed limits and bans on Sunday driving reduced petrol consumption, while the shortages at the pumps revealed some of the most disagreeable facets of human behaviour. The vital role played by petroleum in

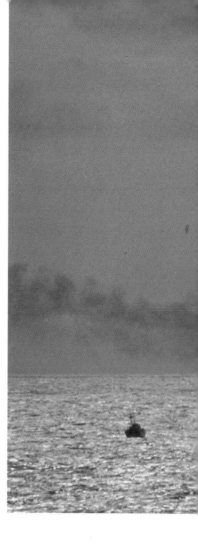

North Sea oil rigs on the Brent field burn off natural gas. The amount they can flare is now controlled by law.

modern society was revealed all too clearly when in California drivers actually shot each other to get fuel.

West European oil

In 1755, at Charmouth in Dorset, the seaside cliff had caught fire, much to the wonder of the local people. A section of blackish rock about 6 metres below the summit smouldered for about ten years. In 1970 it caught fire again. The rock was oil-shale, rich enough in mineral oil to burn, and by then it was known by geologists as the Kimmeridge shale. Beneath the North Sea the Kimmeridge shale forms the source-rock for one of the world's major deposits of fossil hydrocarbon fuels, the Brent Province.

The British oil industry began in 1851 when a chemist, James Young, began to distil oil from oil-shale at Broxburn in central Scotland. Three years later Kimmeridge shale was being distilled for export to as far away as Australia. A ton of shale gave up a barrel of oil, and 1000 tons of oil a year were exported. But of more commercial value to Western Europe at the time of the OPEC crisis were Germany's oil resources; by 1959 there were 97 oil fields and 23 gas fields in West Germany. With a peak production of 54 million barrels of oil in 1972, it was by far the biggest production in Western Europe, but tiny by Arabian standards. However, in 1956, the Ten Boer well in the Groningen area of the Netherlands yielded gas, and this one new gas-field contained so much gas that it would alter the whole fuel economy of north-west Europe.

Until the late 1960s most geologists had dismissed the idea of there being any oil beneath the North Sea but, as a result of the Groningen discovery, seismic surveys of the underlying rocks were carried out. These revealed 'highs' that were potential oil traps. The governments neighbouring the North Sea had agreed on the subdivision of the sea bed and jointly auctioned off blocks for exploration. Drilling pushed northwards from the shallow depths of the southern North Sea where jack-up drilling rigs could be used. Exploration was encouraged by the discovery of several gas-fields, but the search for oil proved fruitless for several years until, in 1969, the billion-barrel Ekofisk, Montrose and Forties oilfields were found, followed in 1971 by the huge Brent field and the Frigg gas-field. After the fourth round of licensing in 1972, improved oil-rig technology and the huge increase in oil prices allowed the oil giants to move out into the deep water between Norway and the Shetlands. There eight major oilfields were found in four years, in what is known as the Brent Province. As a direct result of the rise in oil price, in little more than a decade, the economies of the European countries bordering the North Sea had been completely transformed by the new discoveries. Their presence was another fortunate consequence of the Jurassic seas which had first brought agricultural wealth to northern Europe.

The biggest oil reservoirs were found in Jurassic rocks, formed as the Atlantic Ocean was opening and to the south the limestones which now form the Cotswold hills were being deposited. Muddy seaways then stretched across what is now the Midlands and there, 150 million years ago, dense seasonal 'blooms' of plankton and algae sank to the bottom to die in the stagnant oxygen-depleted mud. As the seas slowly retreated, Britain was tilting down at the south-east, and the North Sea basin continued to stretch and subside, allowing a thickness of the muds to build up which provided the source of the oilfields. One sea stretched from Lincoln to Moscow but there was dry land over the area of the Thames Estuary, and another limy sea to the south of it produced the Portland limestones. Oil has been found there, too.

The somewhat haphazard way in which oil has been discovered within the Jurassic basins has been repeated in the Paris Basin. Oil men refer to drilling strategies as 'plays' – they are such a gamble – and in 1958 the first play won oilfields to the east and south of Paris at Coulommes and Chailly-Chartrettes. Another field at Châteaurenard was found the next year. Not until 1975, after more accurate seismic surveying, was a second phase of drilling begun and this led to the discovery of the largest field at Villeperdue, and in 1983 the Chaunoy field, south-east of Paris in a deeper reservoir. As underground mapping improves, wells are in production in Paris suburbs, and the oil men are optimistic.

A new perspective

On 21 July 1969 an event took place as dramatic as any that had occurred in human history. Neil Armstrong stepped out from *Apollo 11* on to the surface of the moon. The Americans had overtaken the Russians in the conquest of space, though their aims were, and still are, very different. But the lasting effect of this triumph of engineering, courage and technical skill was not so much the footprint in the dust of the moon's surface, but the startling recognition of the finite nature of the pale blue sphere that the astronauts had left behind as they hurtled into space. The shock that the continents really did look like the maps in the atlas was succeeded by the recognition of the beauty of the unique planet that is our home and of the interdependency of all mankind and all life on its surface. The old human urge to explore and conquer new frontiers had drawn us into space to reveal to all peoples just how puny, dangerous and foolish both human and national ambitions are when weighed on the scale of creation.

The early 1970s saw increasing concern at the multiplying human population, at the finite nature of natural resources and of approaching 'limits to growth', as ever-expanding economies caused the consumption of most key raw materials to increase in a geometric progression. It reached its peak at the United Nations Conference on the Human Environment in Stockholm in 1972. Governments responded to pressure from their voters by setting up agencies and ministries supposed to take account of the environmental consequences of their policies but, faced with an energy crisis, such concerns were low on the political agenda.

Instead, the world recession which followed the OPEC crisis caused a sharp change in economic trends and the graphs of consumption levelled off. It was a classic example of the effects of adjustments in a market economy. The boom of the 1950s and 1960s had led to an increase in demand for resources which could only be met with difficulty, projections of future needs were made on the basis of past trends and the future looked bleak so resource prices went up. But in terms of world resources as a whole, supply dictates demand, rather than the reverse. When a commodity becomes scarce and the price goes up, more expensive sources of supply become economic so the quantity available increases; if the price goes higher, alternative resources or patterns of industrial behaviour may be cheaper, when they are used these cut back consumption of the original resource and its price falls.

To the oil industry, the dramatic increase in prices meant that exploration and production became economic where it had not been before, particularly in off-shore fields. The British Government took a leaf out of OPEC's book by announcing that it would take a 51 per cent stake in all its North Sea Oil concessions. But in the meantime the European countries relying on oil for their electricity were literally caught over an oil barrel. Italy, which had little coal of its own, generated 59 per cent of its electricity from oil in 1973, and was now on the point of economic collapse; France was caught out by its switch from coal, and was reliant on oil for 39 per cent of electricity generation. In England and Wales where coal still provided 69 per cent of electrical power, the oil share was none the less serious enough to provoke a crisis over pay to coal-miners. Industry was put on to a three-day week, and the Conservative Government fell, causing the leadership of the party to pass from Edward Heath to Margaret Thatcher.

The public panic at the petrol pumps changed people's long-term behaviour remarkably little, but high energy costs did change political priorities, and allowed projects of questionable environmental impact to go ahead, which were to have long-term consequences. President Nixon got permission to build the Alaska pipeline to bring south the oil production of the arctic North Slope. There was a sudden scramble, not just for alternative supplies, but for alternative sources of energy.

The most obvious was nuclear power. The Suez Crisis had been enough for the United Kingdom to treble its atomic energy targets; now the EEC called for a fourteen-fold increase in nuclear electricity supply, and the price of Uranium (found in the Hercynian mountains of France and Czechoslovakia) trebled in months. In 1974 the British Central Electricity Generating Board wanted to build 39 reactors by 1980, the German industry had comparable plans, and France began to build 34. But these plans were laid on the basis of the historical growth in electricity demand, and just as the expansion plans of the coal industry had been caught out by changing energy use in the late 1950s, so, too, the predictions of electricity consumption made in the early 1970s would prove to be disastrously wrong.

At that time the future for Western Europe's energy supplies certainly looked insecure. The imbalance between consumption and supply was far worse than in any other continent, and the Romanian and Volga-Urals oilfields were already running dry. But the combination of world recession and a mild winter had dramatically changed the short-term global energy picture even by 1975. OPEC had cut back pumping to 35 per cent below capacity, with Saudi Arabia reducing production not for political ends but to maintain the price of oil and thus OPEC's income. The slump in demand had caused fleets of tankers to be laid up and a collapse in freight rates. The long-distance pipeline across the Arabian peninsula had been shut down because it was too expensive to run, and Burmah Oil, the original British oil company, had collapsed. The United States and Britain were now actually fearful that the oil price would fall; the USA because a return to cheaper energy would inhibit conservation, expensive domestic production and the development of alternative domestic energy sources such as oil-shales; the UK because Britain was about to become a major oil exporter herself.

Once again the response of the European nations depended on their geophysical attributes. At one extreme, Norway, which had once been poverty-stricken because she had so little level cultivable land, was now benefiting from the presence of the Caledonian mountains. These provided her with a higher proportion of cheap hydro-electric power than in any other nation, and thus a very high standard of living. Norway also had the good fortune to have opened the first North Sea oilfield (the giant Ekofisk field) in 1969. The quadrupling of oil prices had made offshore oil and gas exploration viable to far greater depths, and it now expanded rapidly. Offshore oil production more than doubled in the 1980s.

In France, by contrast, oil was still scarce, and another dramatic shift in national energy policy was made. With their massive switch to oil now seen to be a mistake, they embarked on the world's biggest nuclear-power programme. The resignation of De Gaulle in 1969 marked the end of his insistence on using French designs, and allowed the adoption of American pressurised water reactor technology. By using existing technology, construction proceeded far more rapidly than in the United Kingdom, where the development of new gas-cooled designs caused long delays and massive overspends. But the colossal plan to build 66 billion watts of capacity by 1990 absorbed about 25 per cent of France's entire national industrial output. It resulted in France having the capacity to generate over 80 per cent of her electricity from nuclear power, but at a very high cost. The company Electricité de France in 1990 had a colossal burden of debt of 226 billion francs, the equivalent of the cost of twenty reactors, and a foreign debt greater than that of many developing nations. In 1990, with a turnover of 156 billion francs, it made a profit of only 100 million francs. By the end of 1989 there were 416 nuclear power plant reactors in operation in the world, of which 215 were in Europe. Western Europe, with 147, was the most heavily nuclear-powered region in the world.

In the North Sea the emphasis on oil distracted the industry from natural gas exploration, but Britain had already started to pipe gas ashore from the West Sole field in 1967, and a huge investment in converting every gas-burning house in Britain from coal-gas to natural gas caused a marked shift in British behaviour, as people bought gas-fired central heating. By 1990 three-quarters of the energy used in British houses came from natural gas, further reducing demand for coal. By 1974 eighteen oilfields had been found in the UK sector of the North Sea, and the following year the first oil was landed from the Argyll field. More and more fields were discovered in the basins of the central and northern North Sea, and

During the Iran–Iraq Gulf war, offshore oil production platforms were attacked by both sides. This one, which had been used as a base for Iranian attacks on neutral shipping in the Persian Gulf, was shelled and set ablaze by US Navy gunfire.

east of the Shetland Isles, and by 1983 the North Sea had replaced the Middle East as the largest supplier of Europe's oil.

More oil shocks

The instability of the Middle East again rocked the world's economies in the eighties. Iraq's military dictator, Saddam Hussein, saw the political chaos and civil insurrection which followed the departure of the Shah of Iran in January 1979 as an opportunity to take control of the Shatt-al-Arab, where the combined waters of the Tigris and Euphrates rivers enter the Persian Gulf. This waterway had had great strategic importance ever since the Anglo-Persian Oil Company built its refinery there at Abadan. Despite huge sums spent on modern equipment the Iraqis had learned few of the lessons of motorised warfare, and instead of striking deeply into Iran they besieged Abadan and Khorramshahr. The Gulf War, as it was then known, became a confrontation of attrition for eight long years between poorly trained young soldiers. It caused huge numbers of casualties reminiscent of the worst excesses of the First World War; even to the extent of the Iraqis using poison gas. Many oil installations in both countries were destroyed, and despite escorts of American and British warships, tankers had difficulty running the gauntlet of minefields and fighter-planes to the other oil sources in the Gulf. The price of oil rose a further 250 per cent (a tenfold rise in a decade) driving the world into the worst economic recession since the Great Depression of 1929.

Western governments took fright at the new attack on their balance of payments, and promoted energy-saving campaigns, while raging inflation and soaring interest rates removed the purchasing power of the consumer. Oil consumption dropped; the EEC countries reduced their energy consumption per unit of production by 20 per cent between 1973 and 1983, and the combination of reduced demand, and increasing production in the North Sea, proved to be the undoing of the OPEC cartel. EEC countries halved their imports of OPEC oil by 1985, and despite the loss of production because of the Gulf War, in 1986 the oil price collapsed from $30 a barrel to around $10. In complete contrast to the pessimistic forecasts of the early 1970s, the reserves of oil, natural gas, coal and uranium once more appeared to be adequate for world needs, at least for the foreseeable future.

While the West could boom again on cheap energy, the story was very different in Eastern Europe. By 1979 both Romania and Poland had become net energy importers, drawing on the Soviet Union for oil, but being impoverished in the process. No less than 90 per cent of Soviet exports in 1984 were minerals, and 67 per cent were oil. By now the biggest oil producer in the world, the Soviet Union, was supplying a third of Western Europe's needs. But the Volga-Urals oilfields in Russia had been exhausted, with much oil lost through trying to extract it too quickly. While huge new fields had been found in western Siberia, they were proving difficult and very costly to develop, given the constraints of climate and the immense distances that the oil had to be piped overland. Soviet oil production actually declined in 1985 and this reduction, coupled with the fall in price, halved Soviet foreign exchange revenues in 1986. These were vitally necessary to import industrial equipment, and especially grain, which was needed to make up for the serious failure of Soviet agricultural production. This has remained virtually static since the mid-seventies, despite a massive investment in Khruschev's Virgin Lands project, huge new irrigation schemes and the use of twice as much fertiliser per ton of grain as other major producers. The Marxist belief that man could dominate the environment had failed, too.

As all the world now knows, despite the vast natural resources of the Soviet Union and the huge size of its economy, the Soviet system failed to deliver goods to the consumer and that consumer began to realise that he, too, had a right to a decent standard of living. The miners of the Donbass struck for lack of soap. Following the collapse of the oil price, Soviet hard currency earnings were halved. This was a final blow to the ailing Soviet economy and the prestige of the old Soviet hierarchy. Mikhail Gorbachev became General Secretary of the Communist Party, and first announced the need for *perestroika*, the restructuring of the Soviet economic system, in February 1986. By 1989 the Soviet trade deficit was 4 billion roubles (then 4 billion pounds). Two important consequences followed the collapse of Soviet earnings, the need to reduce expenditure on Soviet arms, and the rapid adoption of nuclear power to free more petroleum for export.

It was ironic that a glut of oil should be dictating a fall in energy prices and thus having a major impact on the political future of Europe, when, despite the size of the immense Brent and Forties fields, North Sea oil production was already showing signs of running out. For tax and accounting reasons oil companies tend to understate their reserves but they were now saying that all the big reservoirs had been found. Predictions were being made that Britain would no longer be self-sufficient after 1992. But fall the prices did, and the result was further pressure on the British coal industry. In 1984 a billion pounds had been spent developing the thick seams of Selby in Yorkshire to produce coal at a quarter of the cost. But the claim by the President of the National Union of Miners, Arthur

Scargill, that Britain produced the cheapest deep-mined coal in the world was of no avail. When the coal price fell by two-thirds the deep pits could not compete with world prices, and only 25–30 per cent of the coal burnt by British Steel now came from the United Kingdom. Arthur Scargill's 1985 strike over the closure of six pits failed after more than a year's agony, and by December 1990, no fewer than a hundred and one of the less productive pits had been closed. Although the number of miners was cut by 62 per cent, production fell only 17 per cent. The British coal industry was now almost competitive, yet half its remaining 68 pits were under threat. Belgian and German coal was still heavily subsidised and French coal was planned to be phased out completely by 1991. Once again cheap oil had decimated the European coal industry, but in terms of total energy consumption the European Community – now twelve countries formally joined by the Single European Act of 1986 – was less dependent on imported energy than it had been since the early 1970s.

Cheap oil brought a false sense of security, energy saving campaigns lost their financial incentive and, as economies expanded, world consumption rose again. It had fallen from 62 million barrels of oil a day in 1980 to 58 in 1983, but rose again to 65 million in 1989. Of that figure, 16.6 million barrels a day came from the Middle East, and Iraq and Kuwait supplied 4 million. The same figure was pumped by Western Europe, while the Soviet Union and Eastern Europe produced 12.9 million barrels a day. Cheap oil had already had massive political and social consequences, but it was to be a brief interlude. On 2 August 1990 Saddam Hussein's Iraqi tanks rolled into Kuwait in the expectation that his enormous tank force, bought from the Soviet Union with profits from the sale of oil, would meet little resistance. But he totally misjudged the change in global politics wrought by the oil-price effects of his own previous campaign against Iran. In an unprecedented illustration of the new unification of purpose within Europe, the Soviet Union voted with the EC and the USA in the United Nations Security Council, first to impose an embargo on trade with Iraq until Saddam Hussein should withdraw and, later, on the resolution that permitted the devastating counter-attack on Iraq and its forces by the coalition of 37 nations in January 1991.

The price of the 'benchmark' Brent crude oil, which stood at $16 in July, more than doubled to peak briefly at $42 in October. The Soviet Union was an unexpected beneficiary, as every dollar increase in the price of oil improved their export earnings by $500 million, giving a small but welcome relief from the harsh economic realities which were prising the Union apart. It was not the world's fear of the loss of the production of Iraq and Kuwait that sent the price soaring, but the fact that Saudi Arabia, next door, held, and still does hold, 25 per cent of the world's known oil reserves, and these had been threatened. Ironically, in October 1990, the state-owned Saudi oil company announced the discovery of massive new reserves of high-quality, low-sulphur oil and natural gas in the central and south-eastern desert, hundreds of miles west of their existing fields. They are large enough to allow the Saudis to pump oil at the present rate of production beyond the end of the twenty-first century.

Saddam Hussein missed his chance of moving straight on to the Saudi oilfields before the international coalition, led by the USA and Britain, invited by Saudi Arabia, airlifted in the forces that would defeat him. But the invasion of Kuwait invalidated every prediction of economic performance and energy consumption for Europe till the end of the millennium. Once again, as had already happened four times in the last forty years, the political instability of Arabia had put the economy and the prosperity of Europe and the world in jeopardy.

CHAPTER THIRTEEN

THE RECKONING

In the 1980s public concern shifted from the fear of fossil fuels running out to the consequences of continuing to burn them. During the sixties Western European cities had been successful in cleaning their air by following London's example of a ban on coal fires in the Clean Air Act of 1968. Buildings like St Paul's Cathedral, which had been blackened by centuries of soot, emerged transformed to their original beauty. But these were local solutions to local problems and they were nothing new – the first ban on coal-burning was in 1273. The first evidence that all was not well with the atmosphere at a regional level came in the late sixties. Scientists began to link declining fish stocks in Scandinavian lakes to an increase in acidity in rain. This acid rain was caused by sulphur dioxide drifting from the power-stations and industrialised areas of Britain and Germany which were upwind. The very success of removing sulphurous smoke from the cities meant that it was being put higher into the atmosphere by power-station chimneys, where it could be carried long distances before it was rained out. Extensive study showed that lakes and streams in the oldest geological regions, which are short of alkaline rocks like limestone and thus have a low acid-neutralising capacity, were becoming sufficiently acid to kill all fish and aquatic organisms. By 1988, 14,000 lakes in Sweden were unable to sustain sensitive aquatic life, and 2200 were virtually lifeless. In Norway, fish in waters covering 13,000 square kilometres had been exterminated and acid lakes had been found in many other countries.

It is easy to forget how bad the smog from coal fires in cities used to be. Europe still burns 4.3 million tons of coal *a day*.

In the early eighties it was found that acid rain was also causing trees to die in the forests of West Germany. The first survey, in 1982, revealed that 8 per cent were damaged but by 1986 the die-back was so extensive that 54 per cent of trees were affected. A survey two years later showed that 35 per cent of Europe's total forested area was damaged, and this was before the dreadful extent of forest destruction in Eastern Europe became known. The problem had begun there a decade earlier. By 1989 only 17 per cent of Poland's once vast expanse of forest was undamaged, and only 29 per cent was unaffected in Czechoslovakia.

West Germany was by now the richest country in Europe and the government had been congratulating itself that industrial production had gone up 30 per cent without any increased energy use, but now it was pressurised by the newly

formed 'Green' political party into taking action to save the trees. A total of 22 billion Deutschmarks was spent on fitting 'scrubbers' to power-stations which removed 86 per cent of sulphur and 73 per cent of nitrogen oxides from flue gases. Only then was it discovered that the problem was more complex than had been thought and that ozone smog from traffic was a further serious cause of forest die-back. Being a regional problem, it was particularly suited to action by the European Community, and Germany once again took a dominant role; this time having the EC set standards for car exhausts which will require catalytic converters to be fitted to all new cars in Europe by the end of 1992. Having resisted such moves for years because they would add about £300 to the price of a car, the manufacturers suddenly began to flash advertisements to proclaim how 'green' they were.

The Community now requires reductions of an average of 30 per cent in sulphur emissions at power-stations by 1998. Britain has agreed to a 20 per cent cutback by 1993, and 40 per cent by 1998. As three-quarters of her electricity is still generated from coal, and only three flue-gas desulphurisation scrubbers are being fitted at Drax in North Yorkshire (at 4000 megawatts, Drax is Europe's largest coal-fired power-station) it appears as though the newly privatised electricity industry plans to import large quantities of low-sulphur coal, rather than burn British coal, which has a higher sulphur content. This would cut remaining British coal production by more than half and raise once again the question of the security of the European energy supply. British underground coal-mining is now by far the most efficient in the world, and was subsidised by the government at the rate of only 15 pence a ton, compared with £40 in West Germany in 1989 and £60 in Belgium. With large untapped coalfields, Britain has more than half Europe's energy reserves, but once a coal-mine is closed following a drop in energy prices it cannot be opened again. The doubling of the price of oil in August and September 1990, even without the Saudi Arabian oilfields being involved in the Iraqi conflict, dramatically changed energy cost comparisons but was too brief to help the price of coal. With North Sea oil production at a peak and oil crises in the Middle East (which, even before the new Saudi finds were announced, had 66 per cent of the world's proven oil reserves) occurring roughly every ten years, it appears prudent to question the wisdom of relying only on market forces to determine how energy is used. Yet previous attempts to predict energy supply and demand have always gone seriously wrong, as they did over the introduction of oil-fired power stations in France.

Ecological disaster in the East

In Poland, the inability of the communist system to provide the population with such basic needs as food and clothing resulted in the first free elections for forty-five years restoring democracy in September 1989 and – just two centuries after the French Revolution – began the extraordinary and relatively bloodless overthrow of the communist empire which had so signally failed to produce a workers' paradise in Eastern Europe and which ended with the dramatic reunification of East and West Germany on 3 October 1990. Yet, amid the rejoicings, as scientists and the public at last began to be free to speak, the dreadful cost to both people and planet of the tyranny of the COMECON system of production was revealed. Ever-increasing production quotas had been demanded from factories, based on pre-war and even Victorian designs, with no economic or political mechanism to check or even measure the human and environmental cost. In Poland the legacy is a foreign debt of $40 billion and a bankrupt industry, consuming up to three times as much energy as Western processes, while generating ten to twenty times as much pollution.

A dense plume of air-borne pollution begins above the factories and lignite-powered generating stations of eastern Germany. Blown by the westerly wind across the industrialised north-east of Czechoslovakia it thickens above Upper Silesia; there, some twenty industrial towns contribute 40 per cent of Poland's pollution. With no filters on chimneys to remove sulphur dioxide or smoke particles from power stations, steel-works and so on, air-borne dust rises to forty times the levels permitted by the World Health Organisation. Lead contamination exceeds them by sixty times. In 1985, the Polish Government declared four regions of the country to be 'Ecological Disaster Areas' (Upper Silesia, Cracow, Gdansk bay and Leignitz/Glogow). Officially declared unfit for habitation, these areas were nevertheless home for 11 million Poles – a third of the population.

For years, collecting statistics on children's health was forbidden, and, having at last gained the freedom to compile and analyse information, scientists and doctors woke up to the full horror of their environmental catastrophe – their land and people were actually dying. Poland's soil, air, water and people are the sickest in Europe, perhaps in the world. Production of sulphur dioxide pollution is six times as high *per capita* as in the West. The Vistula, for centuries Poland's artery for trade, carries the untreated sewage of 400 communities and some 10,000 factories along its banks into the Baltic Sea, which is itself rapidly becoming poisoned and has been described as the most endangered waterway in the world. Half the country's rivers and lakes are officially classed as unfit even for industrial use. Seventy per cent of the country's drinking water is polluted, a fifth of the commercially grown food is so polluted that it is unfit to eat (three-fifths in Cracow), but is sold just the same.

To its inhabitants Cracow is known as 'The city of Death', and some areas in the Katowice region have the highest infant mortality in Europe – as many as 44 babies in every 1000 die in their first year. Of the survivors, half of all children aged 4 have chronic illnesses, and by the time they are 10, three-quarters are so sick that they need regular medical treatment. A horrifying trend is that increasing numbers of children are being born with the genetic consequences of pollution – mental and physical handicaps. Four hundred children a year are now being born with congenital malformations in towns near Zarbze in Upper Silesia. Cases of leukaemia in children have doubled in the last decade, and average life-expectancy is reducing.

The other industrial regions of Eastern Europe have suffered almost as badly as Poland. In Espenhain in eastern Germany four out of five children develop chronic bronchitis or heart disease by the age of 7 on account of the sulphur from the lignite-fuelled power-stations. At the notorious 'black town' of Copsa Mica in Romania, where everything is covered in a layer of carbon soot, horses can be used for only two years. The Danube and the Volga rivers are dying. In Czechoslovakia half of the drinking water is unfit for infants, in Hungary every seventeenth death is caused by air-pollution.

This seemingly criminal contempt for the consequences of communist industry to the land, and thus the very people it was supposed to enrich, was common to all COMECON countries. One of the last acts of Nikolai Ceausescu's brutal Romanian Government was to veto a thirty-five-nation pan-European agreement on the protection of the environment, because he objected that it would give citizens the right to voice their concerns to governments.

Even where steps have recently been taken to protect the environment, as in the Soviet Union, they are powerless against the inbuilt profligacy of the planned production quota system which encourages production at all costs. In January 1988 the State Committee for the protection of the Environment GOSCOMPRIRODA was instituted. The greatest sanction it can apply to a polluter is a fine of 100 roubles – just $16 at the new tourist rate of exchange. In contrast the Kuznetsky Metallurgical Combinat steelworks, which was built in the 1930s and made half the Soviet tanks that defeated Hitler, needs an investment of 400 million roubles.

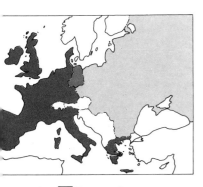

■ European Community

□ Comecon (Council for mutual economic assistance)

■ Left Comecon to join European Community in 1990

West and East European trade associations in 1990.

Eastern Europe is faced with having to change not just the whole basis of its economy but its entire system of industrial production. In Poland it is believed that this would cost $200 billion. Even then the frightful legacy of poisoned people and soil will last for generations. In the meantime the eighty most polluting factories in Poland have been told by their new democratic government that they must be made both profitable and environmentally safe or they will be closed – with the loss of tens of thousands of jobs. It is a grim irony that it was Solidarity, the union of the shipbuilding and steel workers, that destabilised the communist regime in Poland, starting the domino-like collapse of the communist governments of the Soviet bloc. Yet it is their members who will now lose their jobs for the sake of the health of their own children. No such need for self-sacrifice had been expected, as the environmental catastrophe had been hidden by the régime.

The decision may not even be theirs. Faced with real competition in an unprotected hard currency market many of the most inefficient factories of Eastern Europe will close simply because they cannot compete – as has already happened in eastern Germany.

The scale of the remedial work needed to improve the East European environment is daunting. When West Germany cleaned up its power plants it added 25 to 30 per cent to the capital cost of each plant, and increased the cost of generating electricity by 3 pfennigs a kilowatt to 17.4 pfennigs. It is estimated that it would cost 20 million Deutschmarks to clean up Poland's power plants, but the price of electricity to the Polish consumer in December 1990 was only 1.5 pfennigs. Similarly, natural gas was being sold in Poland at a ninth of the world price. Western Germans have six times the income *per capita* of those in Eastern Europe, they could better afford to clean up their country.

In the West, the 1986 Single European Act gave environmental policy in the Community a legal basis for the first time, and allowed the European Environment Agency to be set up in 1990. In a deeply symbolic first-ever meeting at ministerial level between the twelve nations of the European Community and six of the seven countries of Eastern Europe (the Soviet Union was represented but Romania was not), which took place in Dublin in June 1990, the six pledged to base their development policies on environmental principles established by the EC. These included the 'precautionary principle' of acting on the basis of risk rather than proven damage, the requirement that environmental damage should be rectified at source and the key principle that the polluter should pay. The European Community has begun to offer aid, originally £35 million for a three-year scheme to help Hungary and Poland but now expanded to include the rest of democratic Eastern Europe. Hundreds of billions of pounds are needed, and nothing on this immense scale has been attempted since the reconstruction of Europe after the Second World War but compared with the need the sums volunteered so far are tiny.

While the world recession, intensified by the Gulf War, makes it harder for the EC to find the funds, the sudden rise in the price of oil, which the countries of Eastern Europe had to pay for in hard currency from 1991, caused them a further economic burden. This is likely to force the new governments to concentrate on economic survival at the expense of industrial and environmental reforms. Even in Germany, where the Green party had been the first to gain representation in a European parliament, it was wiped out in the first elections of the reunited nation. Fortunately Helmut Kohl has already been obliged to adopt many of its policies. By December 1990, as the energy crisis in the East worsened, Bulgaria

Copsa Mica, Romania, perhaps the most conspicuous but not necessarily the most dangerous pollution in Europe.

had already imposed petrol rationing and, despite having five nuclear reactors, had been forced to impose electricity blackouts for one hour in every four.

Despite its economic strength, the West still has severe pollution problems of its own. The Rhine is poisoned and the North Sea is steadily deteriorating. Cars and planes are now used for 80 per cent of the journeys made in western Europe, and urban air-pollution from traffic is the most obvious form to its citizens. This is the result of ever-increasing urban populations and cities structured around the ownership of cars. Both Madrid and Milan regularly exceed the levels of SO_2 at which it is recommended in the United States that those with respiratory or heart problems should stay indoors and rest. Thousands of people are admitted to hospital every year in Athens and Naples on account of smog from traffic, and many cities as different as Athens, Oslo and Rome are beginning to exclude private cars from their centres. Yet in the UK trucks and cars are forecast to increase 40 per cent by 2005, and roads are being planned to make room for them because the British Government will not subsidise public transport.

Nuclear catastrophe

On 28 March 1979, the Unit 2 reactor at Three Mile Island in Pennsylvania narrowly escaped a total meltdown. After human errors in operation had shut off the cooling water, the core heated to over 5000 degrees Celsius, and a third of it melted; the nuclear nightmare had begun. Local residents claim that there was a substantial release of radiation. Twenty-four dentist's films were fogged in their drawer several kilometres away, and hundreds of examples of plants with mutations, like two-headed sunflowers and dandelion leaves a metre long, consistent with radiation damage, have been found. But it was not the possible grim effect on human health that mortally wounded the American nuclear industry (it claimed that nobody died as a result but two thousand lawsuits were begun for compensation for cancers, miscarriages, birth defects, leukaemias and thyroid problems). The decisive blow was the cost of the clean-up, which in the first 10 years after the accident already amounted to a billion dollars.

On 26 April 1986, human error was again responsible for the explosion and fire in the number 4 reactor at Chernobyl, 130 kilometres north of Kiev in the Ukraine. Unlike most western reactors this RBMK design had no containment vessel and a huge quantity of radiation was released as three-quarters of the intensely radioactive fuel was scattered. This soon caused the deaths of 31 people and the evacuation of 115,000 people from the towns within a 30-kilometre radius. Five years later the full effects of the environmental catastrophe which followed were still not known, but in April 1990 the Supreme Soviet funded a further emergency programme costing 16 billion roubles, recommending that another 200,000 people be evacuated as a matter of urgency.

A year later, the scientist in charge of the evacuated zone, himself dying from cancer from radiation exposure, claimed that towns like Pripyat were evacuated too late and that the disaster had already killed 7–10,000 people. He maintained that the 3.5 million inhabitants of Kiev itself should have been evacuated. Rainfall caused an uneven distribution of the radiation that was released, 70 per cent of which fell on Byelorussia, where as many as 2 million people, a fifth of the population, could be affected, and a fifth of agricultural land is now unusable. Soviet doctors have claimed that 160,000 children living in contaminated areas in the Ukraine, Byelorussia and Russia were exposed to enough radiation in the first few days to give them cancer of the thyroid, and 800,000 may be at risk from leukaemia. In one village 30 deformed children had been born within four years of

●	Site of nuclear power reactors
○	Site with at least one reactor closed down
▲	Uranium mine

Nuclear energy in Europe.

the accident (foetuses are extra-sensitive to radiation). In solely economic terms the cost of the accident may rise to over 200 billion roubles by the end of the century, said to be four times the estimated total net benefit of Soviet nuclear electricity generation. Lenin once defined communism as Soviet power plus the electrification of the entire country, now the Soviet people were learning the consequences of the pursuit of that goal regardless of cost.

As the plume spread across Europe, rainfall caused concentrations of radioactive isotopes like caesium-137, strontium and plutonium in Poland, Finland and Sweden. Reindeer had to be slaughtered in Lapland, sheep in Britain, and the radioactive cloud travelled round the world. Radiation from caesium-137 twenty to thirty times higher than background-level, has even been found in Antarctica.

The Soviet Union has a massive economy with the greatest iron and steel production in the world, and the ministry in charge of this greatest of all European manufacturing industries sets five-year plans, giving targets for production without regard for demand or realistic pricing. It was the need to finance this kind of profligacy which led the Soviet Union to rely heavily on the use of petroleum and gas for export. Despite huge reserves of oil and gas, the need to save oil consumption at home in turn led to the rapid expansion of nuclear power. (There was also the factor that the great new oil and gas reserves were in western Siberia, thousands of kilometres from the centres of population.) Nuclear power now provides 12 per cent of Soviet electricity, despite the fact that it costs twice as much as that generated from coal, and three times as much as using gas. Following the Chernobyl disaster there was a severe winter in 1986–7 and widespread power cuts occurred because of a lack of generating capacity. But environmental protest movements have gained a voice within the Soviet Union since Chernobyl. Their increasing political power has led to the abandonment of the target of producing 20 per cent of Soviet electricity from nuclear reactors by the end of the decade. This has added to the government's export earning crisis, while economic collapse has put further stress on the cohesion of the entire Soviet state. Yet the electrical energy wasted through inefficient and outdated steel production alone is equal to the entire nuclear output.

Against a background of falling energy prices, and rising environmental awareness, the Three Mile Island and Chernobyl accidents were enough to halt the nuclear industry in most of the world. In the United States no new nuclear power plants have been ordered since 1975, and 53 have been cancelled. In Sweden a referendum in 1980 called for all 12 nuclear power-plants to be shut down by 1996. In Austria reactor construction was stopped after a referendum, and a plant at Zwetendorf, completed in 1978, is being dismantled. In early 1991 Britain was building one new plant with pressurised water reactors – Sizewell B – and with the need to take into account real costs for the first time, the newly privatised electricity companies had been absolved of the responsibility of running all the existing reactors. Sizewell B was under threat of cancellation as costs wildly exceeded the estimates. Controversy surrounded the decommissioning of Berkeley power-station, Britain's first nuclear power-station, which only started up in 1962. It was proposed that the reactor be entombed in a huge mound of earth rather than removing the intensely radioactive core. Belgium, Germany, Italy, Spain and Switzerland have all halted their nuclear construction programmes, while Denmark, Ireland, Greece, Luxembourg, Norway, Portugal, Poland and Romania still have no nuclear power. By 1995, 40 per cent of the electrical energy consumed by the European Community will be generated by reactors, but if no new ones are built, they will all reach the end of their useful life by about 2030. However, as energy prices have risen during the Gulf War, it has immediately given hope to the nuclear lobby who are now demanding that fifty nuclear power-plants will have to be built every year to supply world energy demand.

As the twentieth century ends, the immediate threat to the survival of mankind from the massive use of nuclear weapons is receding but is being replaced by the fear of environmental catastrophe from accidents at nuclear power reactors. A fire in cables at Greifswald reactor in East Germany in 1975 almost led to a major disaster, but after reunification experts who saw these plants were horrified at the management of them and shut all four reactors down. There have been numerous accidents and fires at reactors in the West, such as the Windscale fire in 1957, but most suspicion must hang over the 17 Soviet-built nuclear reactors in Bulgaria, Czechoslovakia and Hungary; although not of the RBMK design, they are operating with questionable technology and staff, and lack basic safety features. To stand beside these unquantifiable environmental risks have come the very real figures of the immense costs of disposing of spent fuel and obsolete reactors. The Soviet Union will no longer accept radioactive waste from Eastern Europe. This may prove to be the biggest economic and political obstacle to the continuation of the nuclear industry, as well as a colossal burden to impose on future inhabitants of this planet. In the long term, despite the instability of Middle East petroleum supplies, public awareness of the dangers of ionising radiation has now reached a point where the nuclear industry is unlikely to have much success in an informed democracy.

People have come to distrust an industry which has hidden the truth so often in the past not just about its costs but also its safety. The exception is Hungary which

Tax incentives have encouraged wind farms to be built in California, like this one at San Gorgonia Pass near Palm Springs.

in 1989 cancelled, for environmental reasons, the huge Nagymaros hydro-electric project on the Danube. As compensation for the lost construction project Hungary must pay back Austria 259 million dollars worth of electricity over 20 years and is proposing a joint venture with Electricité de France to build two reactors – a nice irony considering the Austrian public's rejection of reactors on Austrian soil. Yet at the end of 1990 the arguments against nuclear power still look compelling. It may even prove to be the first time that a new source of energy has ever been discovered by mankind and then rejected.

Human beings began like any other animals, their basic source of energy was from the sun, captured by plants (by photosynthesis) and turned into food. The progress of our entire civilisation has come about through our harnessing increasingly powerful additional sources of energy. First animal-power, then the natural power of water, wind and the energy from fuel-woods, followed by the fossil solar-energy released by burning coal, petroleum and natural gas, and finally the energy of the atomic nucleus. But having already begun a retreat from the last and most complex technology, the whole beautiful and intricate balance of life on the planet has been called into question by the consequence of burning hydrocarbon fuels.

Après nous le déluge?

The fate of Europe and the world may now hang, not on the politicians whose names get into the history books, but on a relatively simple matter of physics. The energy of the sun warms the Earth's surface and much of the heat is prevented from radiating back into space by the blanket of the atmosphere. If the amount of carbon dioxide in the atmosphere doubles, it conserves more heat, causing the average temperature of the surface to rise by between 1.5 and 4.5 degrees Celsius. This is the so-called 'greenhouse effect'. The temperature change does not sound much, but a change of 4 degrees in the other direction is enough to cause an ice age. Not for some 10 million years has the Earth been so warm as it may now become within fifty years. Such a warming would not only have dramatic effects on vegetation, including of course food-crops and forest (which absorbs carbon dioxide), but would also raise the sea level. This is not because it would melt the polar ice caps – in fact the northward extension of strong winds will carry great blizzards into the presently rather arid poles to build up the ice. But ice is less dense than water, and this, coupled with the expansion of the oceans in warmer latitudes as they become hotter, will cause the volume of the oceans to increase enough to threaten whole countries like Bangladesh and the Netherlands. If we continue to increase the greenhouse gases, not only will the planet warm but it will go on warming. Our climate will never be the same again and what we now consider to be normal will be gone for ever.

There is argument about the scale of the warming (believed to be 0.5 degrees Celsius in the last hundred years) and about the role of biological systems such as marine plankton as a triggering factor, but there is no argument about the physics. At the height of the last ice age there was a third less carbon dioxide in the atmosphere than a hundred years ago. It is known from Antarctic and Greenland ice-cores that the quantity of CO_2 in the atmosphere has increased by a third since pre-industrial times, and measurements in the pollution-free air of Hawaii have shown that global output of CO_2 has trebled in the last forty years and is now increasing at the rate of half a per cent a year. A fifth of the CO_2 problem has been caused by burning tropical forests but four-fifths has been caused by the industrialisation of society, mostly in the northern hemisphere countries. 'Business as usual' would mean a further 25 per cent increase in CO_2 by the year 2005, and 70 per cent by 2025. It has been suggested that the European climate has already returned to the temperatures of the medieval optimum. It may only be a coincidence, but the eighties had the five hottest years of the century, and in 1988 a severe drought hit the North American corn belt, 'the breadbasket of the world'. Europe has seen unusual extremes of heat and drought, with hurricane force winds due to the increasing depth of the depressions crossing the Atlantic.

It is an insidious crisis on a planetary scale, as is the related problem of damage to the ozone layer. Other environmental problems have been local or regional in their effects but this one will affect us all, from the stockbroker in the city to the still 'uncivilised' Indian tribesman living in balance with nature in the Brazilian jungle. It has come about precisely because of the way that the tribesman has become the stockbroker – by using more and more energy; with a market economy encouraging the basic human driving forces of curiosity, ambition, greed and fear, which first drew our ancestors out of the forest on to the plains and began the ever-quickening progress of technology and civilisation. Humankind is now facing the devastating consequences of its success in dominating the planet and has yet to come to terms with the restrictions dictated by the Earth's own natural systems. It requires a whole change in our perception of our place as just one part of an inter-acting living system, and thus of how resources can be used – the very resources which have made possible the growth and dominance of the European way of life world-wide. It is nothing less than the greatest challenge that human society has ever faced.

Already politicians are beginning to respond to the change in public mood. The Montreal Protocol of 1987, which called for 50 per cent cuts in the use of CFC (Chlorofluorocarbon) gases by 1999, because their release is causing damage to the protective ozone layer, not only over Antarctica but now over Europe, was the first step in the right direction, controversial and imperfectly upheld as it is, because it is the *first* global legal constraint binding on all countries.

In the eighties, about half of the greenhouse effect was caused by carbon dioxide, whose life in the atmosphere is about seven years. Another quarter was caused by methane, the product of organic breakdown in swamps and paddy-fields, leakages of natural gas and produced by the digestive processes and flatulence of cattle and termites. This gas is thirty times worse than CO_2 in reflecting heat and lasts in the atmosphere for ten years. CFCs as well as causing ozone damage, already contribute 14 per cent of the greenhouse effect. These gases are 10,000 to 20,000 times as effective as CO_2 in trapping the sun's heat and the quantity released is increasing at present by one per cent per year. But by international agreement, CFCs are already being controlled. To reduce methane emissions we must seriously consider whether we need so many cows, and the idea of the Beefeater as an English national symbol begins to lose its attraction. But what can be done about CO_2? Further international agreement and control is certainly necessary if irreversible damage to the planet is to be halted.

Slowly the concept that the bottom line is not the dollar but Nature is beginning to penetrate political consciousness. But to reverse the destruction of the Earth as a living system requires more than a political will, it needs enormous amounts of cash. The twelve countries of the EC are major players on the world stage, manufacturing a fifth of the global production of goods. To do so they contribute 15 per cent of the world's CO_2, while Eastern Europe contributes 24 per cent for a smaller production. Some of the greatest and cheapest savings in CO_2 production can be made by closing or modernising the most wasteful industries

Tyumen, Western Siberia. A natural gas pipeline on the Urengoy Surgut Chelyabinsk route is coated with bitumen before it is laid in a trench.

of Eastern Europe. This will undoubtedly happen but the West cannot propose its standards to the East and the rest of the world without setting its own house in order. The *per capita* production of carbon from fossil fuels is still by far the highest in the United States and what was West Germany. This is because of the amount of energy used by wealthy industrialised societies.

For a hundred years the emphasis has been on the need to supply the demand for energy rather than to control it, and nowhere more than in the Soviet Union. Siberia means 'sleeping land', its resources have only recently begun to be extracted and it has a huge store of hydrocarbon fuels. With exploitation begun by Stalin's *gulag* forced-labour camps, Siberia already produces about half of the Soviet Union's hard currency earnings from gold, diamonds, and especially petroleum and natural gas. Beneath the permafrost of the Yamal peninsula and under the Kara Sea lies the biggest gas-field in the world – in a zone that is an extension of Europe, propelled northward by the thrust that raised the Ural mountains. The Novy Urengoy gas-field now has 1400 wells, the product of a crash campaign of exploration when European Soviet oil reserves were declining in the 1980s. It already produces 1.4 trillion cubic metres a year, two-thirds of all Soviet production, and the Yamburg field will soon add half as much again. The Samotlor oilfield in the Tyumen Oblast of western Siberia was begun in 1969; now it has the highest production in the world – 780 million barrels per year.

In 1989 minerals still made up 90 per cent of Soviet exports to the West, oil 40 per cent and natural gas 10 per cent. But a striking indication of the appalling difficulty and cost of the extraction of these energy resources and the poor quality of the management, is that only half of the gas that enters the pipelines in Siberia arrives at the other end. The rest is either burned in pumping it some 3500 kilometres or is lost on the way, a serious addition to the greenhouse effect. There are four accidents for every 1000 kilometres of pipeline every year, and a major break every two weeks. This was horribly demonstrated by the petroleum pipeline explosion which wrecked two trains full of school-children on the Trans-Siberian Railway at Ufa near the Urals in June 1989.

The International Energy Agency in Paris predicts an increase of 50 per cent in the energy consumption of the Soviet Union and the countries of Eastern Europe as they climb out of the economic abyss into which they have sunk. Their populations *want* our western way of life, but still have much catching up to do to equal our lifestyle. Yet at present many aspects of their lives are less wasteful of energy than those in the West. Soviet flats are only a third the size of those in western Germany. They use a fifth as much electricity in their homes as western Germans, and a thirteenth as much as the Swedes. Soviet citizens have only a tenth of the number of cars as western Germans and have to wait ten years for a new one. As we have seen, the moment there was monetary union between East and West Germany, the East Germans poured across the border to buy second-hand cars. There is a huge unsatisfied demand for energy-consuming devices. With *glasnost* the opportunities for travel will increase, and air travel, already high, could double in the next fifteen years.

Choices

Even if remedial action on greenhouse gases is taken *now*, it is probably unrealistic to expect less than a 2 degree Celsius increase in global temperatures before they stabilise (the Maldive Islands would still be submerged). Yet, to achieve this figure would require a 50–80 per cent reduction in CO_2 production. How on earth can it be achieved?

December 1989 Years of reserves remaining at present rate of production

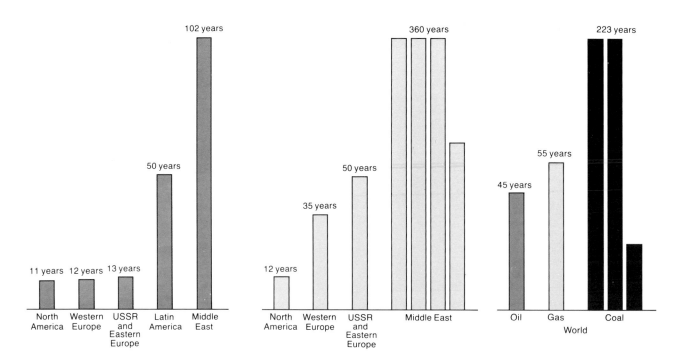

In 1900 it took 1.2 kilogrammes of coal to generate a kilowatt of electricity, now it only takes a third of a kilogramme – but still only about a third of the energy in a lump of coal is turned into electrical energy in a conventional power-station. The rest is lost, more than half of it as warm water (the purpose of cooling towers is to get rid of this heat) and power-stations are responsible for creating 11 per cent of the world's CO_2. With the most modern combustion techniques, and by using the waste heat for domestic central heating and hot water, as much as 90 per cent of the energy in a lump of coal can be used, but such systems cannot be added on to large power stations sited away from towns. It requires a start from scratch, as has already been done in towns like Stuttgart in Germany and Västerås in Sweden.

The nuclear industry has seized on the greenhouse effect as its potential saviour, claiming that it is a 'non-polluting' industry that does not contribute to global warming. Its spokesmen point out that to replace the output of Sizewell B power-station with wind-powered generators would need a wind-park 500 square kilometres in area. But they neglect the fact that a pound spent on increasing energy efficiency is five times more effective in reducing CO_2 than a pound spent on nuclear power. This immediate benefit also represents a more profound truth, that simply to substitute less polluting sources of energy will not work. If demand keeps on going up we will quite quickly get back to where we were before. This applies as much to burning natural gas (which releases 40 per cent less carbon for the same energy as coal) in power-stations as it does to improving the number of kilometres that a car will run on a litre of fuel (which is pointless if there are more cars and they are stuck in traffic jams). On the other hand, even a 2 per cent annual improvement in energy efficiency will flatten out the graphs of

World oil and gas resources known in 1989.

CO_2 production and then cause them to decrease. Most important of all, it is only when consumption has been reduced that renewable sources of energy such as wind, waves, tide, biomass and sun can make up a significant part of the total.

Electricity generation is the largest single source of CO_2 in the EC, and yet the technology already exists to reduce electricity consumption by at least 70 per cent. For example, a third of all electricity is used for lighting, and every time a compact fluorescent lamp (consuming 18 watts and lasting thirteen times as long) is used to replace a 75-watt lamp, it saves a ton of carbon dioxide in the atmosphere. In some American States and Denmark the power companies themselves are waking up to the fact that it is far cheaper to get people to save electricity by handing out these lamps free and subsidising insulation than it is to operate existing generating plant, let alone to build new plant. By reducing demand they can become more profitable by using their most efficient power-stations and closing down the worst. Everybody gains; electricity bills are lower, profits are greater and the atmospheric load of carbon is reduced. Yet it requires such a reversal of normal thinking that countries and individuals are slow to adopt them. (Have you bought a compact fluorescent bulb yet? It will save you money in the long run and help to save the planet.) Already in the United States, where it is now compulsory to state on the sale ticket the consumption of electricity of a new appliance and the cost of running it, companies are springing up which will contract to achieve reductions in electricity consumption – 'negawatts' – for power suppliers, and are competing for the privilege of 'megawatt mining'. Even the UK Department of Energy admitted in an unguarded moment that up to half of Britain's £40 billion bill for energy could be saved. But the signals to the consumer, especially when confused by cheap energy prices, have to be set by government, and too often they are wrong. In Britain, VAT is presently charged on insulation and compact fluorescent light bulbs but not on domestic electricity. Taxes in the EC encourage the use of coal and oil rather than natural gas which produces less carbon dioxide.

Carbon taxes will no doubt appear in the 1990s, which will penalise carbon-producing fuels such as coal and petrol, and make a frozen chicken more expensive than a fresh one because of the energy it has consumed. Denmark has had a heavy tax on electricity which has helped to promote savings and in Sweden, where quadruple glazing is normal, they are switching taxation away from income to energy. A carbon tax, from 1991, will make coal very expensive to use, raising the cost of district heating by up to 75 per cent. Power-stations are already negotiating with the Soviet Union to burn fuel wood instead. This should be on a renewable crop basis. Such methods have to be used with intelligence; transport produces a quarter of the CO_2 emitted by the EC, but doubling the price of petrol with such a tax makes far less difference to the use of cars than banning them from cities and improving public transport, as has already happened in towns like Schiedam in Holland. Such a ban cuts down pollution too. Within the EC the countries which are the most environmentally responsible can act as examples for general EC action. In 1988, Holland adopted a twenty-year National Environmental Plan, concentrating on energy-efficiency, which aims to cut carbon dioxide emissions by more than 40 per cent by the year 2000. In response, the EC states set targets to stabilise their emissions but mostly these lacked the force of law.

But what of Europe as a whole? The removal of the EC barriers to trade in 1992 is likely to be damaging in ecological terms with a 30–50 per cent increase in cross-border traffic, and massive structural funds being spent on improving

OVERLEAF There are over 120 million cars in use in the European Community, their average life is under 12 years.

roads. Yet it also brings opportunities for the richer countries within the twelve to subsidise the cleaning-up of the power-stations and industries of the poorer. In the East, beyond the appalling immediate problems of reversing forty years of environmental destruction, the way ahead lies in financing joint ventures which are ecologically sound. Already there are 900 joint ventures in the Soviet Union, from making Pepsi Cola and Fiat cars to marketing Soviet gas. Let us hope that the memorial to the democratisation of the East, and our concern for the planet, will be more than a discarded Pepsi Cola can.

The 1990s will be a decade of coming to terms with the consequences to the global environment of our addiction to energy consumption and our ever more complex technology. It began with a most significant accord, signed by 137 countries in November 1990, at the World Climate Conference in Geneva. It was agreed to establish a convention by 1992 to draw up international laws to reduce carbon dioxide emissions, while aiding the Third World to industrialise with minimum environmental impact. But just as the socialist economies were blind to the needs of the individual and the environment, so is the unrestricted market economy blind to effects on values which are not costed in conventional terms: stability, equality, justice and environmental impact. Even if the polluter must pay, how do you value the air you breathe, or the creatures of the forest that die when it dies, or the life of a child dying of leukaemia, or the lack of the clear blue sky behind the Parthenon?

What is needed is nothing less than a new global social contract that binds the costs to the environment to our individual and social behaviour. The time has come to chose between our individual freedoms and the health of the planet and the future for our children. Future generations will be astonished by our wastefulness, as the whole concept of what constitutes acceptable social behaviour will have to change. Turbo-charged fast cars may yet be seen to be as anti-social as fur coats. In the medium term the shock of yet another oil crisis, despite its horrific human cost, may have done the planet and humanity a favour, by raising energy prices, cutting consumption, and putting the emphasis back on to saving in a savage way. But at this time of profound social readjustment within Europe there is also a unique opportunity, as it struggles to unify after the dramatic events that began in November 1989.

As the short-range nuclear missiles are wheeled out of Germany, the Warsaw Pact is dissolved, and the 'Declaration of London' concludes a non-aggression pact between East and West, it even becomes possible to think that part of the huge cost of financing a green future might come from a saving on the massive arms budgets of East and West, the so-called 'peace dividend'. On 20 November 1990 the Conventional Forces in Europe Treaty was signed by the twenty-two nations of NATO and the Warsaw Pact which will scrap 25,000 tanks and 13,000 artillery pieces. The Treaty covers the whole geological continent from the Atlantic to the Urals, and it declared that the signatories 'were no longer adversaries and would extend to each other the hand of friendship'; at last a formal end to a century of hostility. As NATO begins to be shadowed by the 35-nation 'Conference on Security and Co-operation in Europe' there is talk of a European security organisation.

While the end of the great East–West schism allowed unprecedented co-operation between nations to drive Iraq from Kuwait, television again made us witnesses to history. We saw not just the astonishing and horrifying spectacle of Baghdad's communications and energy infrastructure destroyed by a new generation of weapons guided by microchips, but Saddam Hussein's unique

ecological vandalism in setting fire to over 500 Kuwaiti oil wells. Yet the real lesson of that unforgettable conflagration – burning 6 million barrels of oil a day – was that it did not affect the world oil price. It was, in the eyes of conventional economics, unimportant – only a tenth of the oil we burn daily in the world's machines. We are still hostages to burning oil, and never has our civilisation been so fragile.

The West was shocked that Moscow should cynically take advantage of the Gulf War to send tanks to crush the freely elected governments of Lithuania and Latvia, but the overwhelming dominance of the Soviet Union has already passed. It is not beyond the bounds of possibility that it may dissolve peacefully into a stable federation of sovereign states. Meanwhile the financial supremacy of the United States is fast fading. The need for the resources and energy of Germany and its reunited people to be part of a federal Europe has never been plainer, and, despite EC disunity over the Gulf War financial unity within the EC beckons as the next great step along that path. But Europe is only one player on the world stage, and taking a long glance back at the history of the continent the threat to a reunited Christian Europe could come from an increasingly fundamentalist Islam, and the Middle East holds 62 per cent of the world's known oil reserves. With this in mind, and without the need for East and West to buy and arm allies, should we not also learn from the evil wrought by the arms merchants before two world wars, and restrict these sales – this misapplication of the wealth of the land and the ingenuity of our peoples?

With the birth of a unified Europe, whose rich natural endowments first permitted the growth of our world civilisation, we have the opportunity and can yet find the wisdom to work with, rather than against, the fundamental laws of nature for the betterment of all her inhabitants. We already have the means. Perhaps the threat to our very survival as a planet will provide the incentive to bury our national, racial and religious differences for a brighter and more equitable future.

FURTHER READING

General

BARRACLOUGH, G. and STONE, N. eds. *The Times Atlas of world history* Times Bks., 3rd edn., 1989.

BRAUDEL, F. *On history* Weidenfeld, 1981.

JONES, E. L. *The European miracle: environments, economies, and geopolitics in the history of Europe and Asia* Cambridge U.P., rev. edn., 1988.

ROBERTS, J. M. *The Pelican History of the world* Penguin, 1980. op.

SHERRATT, A. ed. *The Cambridge Encyclopedia of archaeology* Cambridge U.P., 1980. op.

Chapter One

CHAMPION, T. et al. *Prehistoric Europe* Academic, 1984. op.

DARWIN, C. *Voyage of the Beagle* various edns.

FOLEY, R. *Another unique species: patterns in human evolutionary ecology* Longman, 1987.

FOLEY, R. and DUNBAR, R. 'Beyond the bones of contention' *New Scientist* 14 Oct. 1989, (1686), 37–41.

GOUDIE, A. *Environmental change* Oxford U.P., 2nd edn., pbk., 1983.

JOHANSON, D. C. and EDEY, M. *Lucy, the beginning of humankind* N.Y.: Simon & Schuster, pbk., 1988.

SCARRE, C. *Past worlds: the Times Atlas of archaeology* Times Bks., 1988.

Chapter Two

ANDERSEN, S. H. 'Tybrind Vig: preliminary report on a submerged Ertebølle settlement on the west coast of Fyn' *J. Danish archaeology* 1985, 4, 52–69.

BOCQUET, A. 'Lake-bottom archaeology' *Scientific American* Feb. 1979, 240 (2), 48–56.

BURL, A. *Megalithic Brittany: a guide* Thames & Hudson, 1985; pbk., 1987.

COLES, J. M. and LAWSON, J. eds. *European wetlands in prehistory* Oxford U.P., 1987.

JACOBSEN, T. W. '17,000 years of Greek prehistory' *Scientific American* June 1976, 234 (6), 76–87.

JOUSSAUME, R. *Dolmens for the dead* Batsford, 1988.

LEGGE, A. J. and ROWLEY-CONWY, P. A. 'Gazelle killing in stone-age Syria' *Scientific American* Aug. 1987, 257 (2), 76–83.

PETREQUIN, A. M. and P. *Le néolithique des lacs: préhistoire des lacs de Chalains et de Clairvaux* Paris: Errance, 1988.

SREJOVIČ, D. *Lepenski Vir, guide* Beograd: National Museum, 1983.

WILLIAMS, D. et al. *S236. Science, a second level course. Geology Block 4: Surface processes* Open U.P., 1983.

Chapter Three

DURMAN, A. *Vučedol – three thousand years B.C.* Zagreb: Musejski prostor, 1988.

ELUÈRE, C. *Le premier or de l'humanité en Bulgare 5e Millénaire* Paris: edns. réunion des musées nationaux, 1989.

KOVÁCS, T. *The bronze age in Hungary* Budapest: Hereditas Corvina, 1977.

PENHALLURICK, R. D. *Tin in antiquity* (Book 323) Inst. Metals, 1986.

TÁLAS, L. *The late neolithic of the Tisza region* Budapest: Szolnok, 1987.

TYLECOTE, R. F. *Early history of metallurgy in Europe* Longman, 1987.

Chapter Four

BASS, G. F. 'Oldest known shipwreck reveals splendours of the bronze age' *The Scientific American*, 1987, 172 (6).

COTTRELL, L. *The bull of Minos* Bell & Hyman, rev. edn., 1984. op.

HÄGG, R. and MARINATOS, N. 'The function of Minoan palaces' *Skrifter Utgivna av svenska Institutet i Athen* 1987. XXXV, 4.

ROSSITER, S. ed. *Crete* P. Cameron (Blue Guide) A. & C. Black, 5th edn., 1988.

SAKELLERAKIS, J. A. *Herakleion Museum* Athens: Ekdotiki Athinon S.A., 1985.

WARREN, P. 'Minoan palaces' *Scientific American* July 1985, 253 (1), 74–81.

Chapter Five

ANDREWES, A. *Greek society* Penguin, new edn., 1971.

BOARDMAN, J. *The Greeks overseas: their early colonies and trade* Thames & Hudson, 2nd edn., 1981.

DEISS, J. J. *Herculaneum* N.Y.: Harper & Row, pbk., 1985; Malibu: J. P. Getty Trust, pbk., 1989.

FINLEY, M. I. *The ancient Greeks* (Peregrine) Penguin, 1986.

GORE, R. 'The dead do tell tales at Vesuvius' *National Geographic* May 1984, 165 (5), 557–613.

GRANT, M. *The Etruscans* Weidenfeld, 1980. op.

JOHNSTON, A. *The emergence of Greece* (Making of the past) Elsevier-Phaidon, 1976. op.

LEVI, P. *Atlas of the Greek world* Phaidon, 1984.

MOSCATI, S. *World of the Phoenicians* Weidenfeld, 1968. op.

RIDGWAY, D. *The Etruscans* (Occasional paper, 6) Edinburgh U. Dept.

Archaeology, 1981.

J. PAUL GETTY MUSEUM *Guide to the villa and its gardens* Malibu: J.P. Getty Mus., 1988.

Chapter Six

COLLIS, J. *The European iron age* Batsford, 1984.

CUNLIFFE, B. *Greeks, Romans and Barbarians: spheres of influence* Batsford, new edn., pbk., 1989.

CUNLIFFE, B. *Rome and her empire* Bodley Head, 1978. op.

WISEMAN, P. A. transl. *Julius Caesar, The battle for Gaul* Chatto, 1980. op.

Chapter Seven

BARBER, R. *The Penguin Guide to medieval Europe* Penguin, 1984.

FREMANTLE, A. *The age of faith* (Great ages of man) Amsterdam: Time-Life, 1965.

GIMPEL, J. *The medieval machine: the industrial revolution of the middle ages.* Wildwood House, 1988.

HOLMES, G. ed. *The Oxford Illustrated history of medieval Europe* Oxford U.P., 1990.

KEEN, M. *The Pelican History of medieval Europe* Penguin, new edn., 1969.

LE ROY LADURIE, E. *Times of feast, times of famine: a history of climate since the year 1000* Allen & Unwin, 1972. op.

SMITH, C. T. *An historical geography of western Europe before 1800* Longman, 1978. op.

Chapter Eight

BRAUDEL, F. *Civilisation and capitalism, 15th–18th century. Vol. 1. The structures of everyday life* Collins, 1981, Fontana, pbk., 1985.

BRAUDEL, F. *The Mediterranean and the Mediterranean world in the age of Philip II. Vol. 1.* Trans. by Siân Reynolds. Fontana, new edn., pbk., 1986.

DOGSHON, R. A. and BUTLIN, R. A. eds. *An historical geography of England and Wales* Academic, 1978.

DOYLE, W. *The origins of the French Revolution* Oxford U.P., 2nd ed., 1988.

GROVE, J. *The little ice age* Methuen, 1988.

BATH, B. H. SLICHER VAN *The agrarian history of western Europe A.D. 500–1850* Arnold, 1963. op.

Chapter Nine

CLAYRE, A. *Nature and industrialisation, an anthology* Oxford U.P., 1977.

DEAN, P. *The first industrial revolution* Cambridge U.P., 2nd edn., 1900.

HOBSBAWM, E. J. *The Pelican Economic history of Britain. Vol. 3. Industry and empire, from 1750 to the present day* Penguin, 1969.

HOBSBAWM, E. J. *The age of revolution, Europe 1789–1848* Abacus.

LANGTON, J. and MORRIS, R. J. *Atlas of industrialising Britain 1780–1914* Methuen, pbk., 1986.

TINDER, B. *The Darbys of Coalbrookdale* Phillimore, 2nd edn., 1978.

Chapter Ten

BATTY, P. *The house of Krupp* Secker, 1966. op.

BICKEL, L. *The deadly element; the story of uranium* Macmillan, 1979. op.

HENDERSON, W. O. *Britain and industrial Europe 1750–1870: studies in British influence on the industrial revolution in western Europe* Leicester U.P., 3rd edn., pbk., 1973. op.

HENDERSON, W. O. *The industrial revolution on the continent: Germany, France, Russia, 1800–1914* F. Cass, 1961.

POLLARD, S. *Peaceful conquest, the industrialisation of Europe 1760–1970* Oxford U.P., 1981.

Chapter Eleven

JONES, G. *The state and the emergence of the British oil industry* Macmillan, 1981.

HOWARTH, D. *The Dreadnoughts* (Seafarers) Amsterdam: Time-life, 1979.

LIDDELL HART, B. H. *History of the first world war* Pan, rev. edn., pbk., 1972.

MACKSEY, K. *The tank pioneers* Jane's, 1981. op.

MILWARD, A. S. *The German economy at war* Athlone, 1965. op.

OVERY, R. and WHEATCROFT, A. *The road to war* Macmillan, 1989.

PADFIELD, P. *The battleship era* Hart-Davis, 1972. op.

TUGENDHAT, C. and HAMILTON, A. *Oil, the biggest business* Eyre Methuen, rev. edn., 1975. op.

Chapter Twelve

LUCAS, N. J. D. *Energy and the European communities* Europa, 1977.

PALMER, A. ed. *The Penguin Dictionary of twentieth century history, 1900–1989* Penguin, 3rd edn., 1990.

WORLD COMMISSION ON ENVIRONMENT AND DEVELOPMENT *Our common future* Oxford U.P., pbk., 1987.

WORLDWATCH INSTITUTE *State of the world 1990, report on progress towards a sustainable society* ed. L. Brown. Norton, pbk., 1990.

Chapter Thirteen

BRITISH PETROLEUM (BP) *Statistical Review of World energy, 1990.*

BELGRAVE, R. *et al.* eds. *Energy Security to 2000. Energy paper no. 23* PSI/RITA, Gower, 1987.

GRUBB, M. *Energy policies and the greenhouse effect*, Vol. I: Policy appraisal. Royal Institute of International Affairs/Dartmouth, 1990.

INDEX